SCOTT KELBY

The Travel Photography Book

Step-by-step techniques to capture
breathtaking travel photos like the pros

The Travel Photography Book

The Travel Photography Book Team

MANAGING EDITOR
Kim Doty

TECHNICAL EDITOR
Cindy Snyder

ART DIRECTOR
Jessica Maldonado

PHOTOGRAPHY
Scott Kelby

PUBLISHED BY

Rocky Nook
1010 B Street, Suite 350
San Rafael, CA 94901

©2022 Scott Kelby

Composed in Myriad Pro, Univers LT, and Input Serif (Adobe Systems Incorporated) by Kelby Media Group Inc.

Trademarks
All terms mentioned in this book that are known to be trademarks or service marks have been appropriately capitalized. Rocky Nook cannot attest to the accuracy of this information. Use of a term in the book should not be regarded as affecting the validity of any trademark or service mark.

Photoshop and Lightroom are registered trademarks of Adobe Systems, Inc. Nikon is a registered trademark of Nikon Corporation. Canon is a registered trademark of Canon Inc. Sony is a registered trademark of Sony Corporation. Olympus is a registered trademark of OM Digital Solutions.

Warning and Disclaimer
This book is designed to provide information about travel photography. Every effort has been made to make this book as complete and as accurate as possible, but no warranty of fitness is implied.

The information is provided on an as-is basis. The author and Rocky Nook shall have neither the liability nor responsibility to any person or entity with respect to any loss or damages arising from the information contained in this book or from the use of the discs, websites, videos, or programs that may accompany it.

ISBN 13: 978-1-68198-783-5

10 9 8 7 6 5 4 3 2

Distributed in the UK and Europe by Publishers Group UK

Distributed in the U.S. and all other territories by Ingram Publisher Services

Library of Congress Control Number: 2021935019

Printed and bound in Korea

www.rockynook.com
www.kelbyone.com

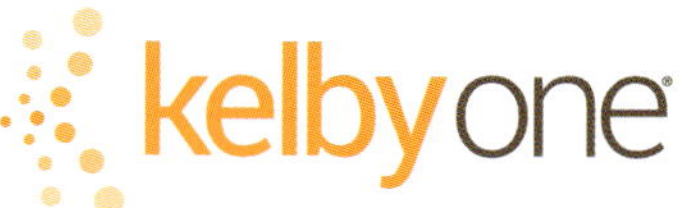

*This book is dedicated to my dear friend
and beloved member of our family,
Maxx Hammond.*

*Thanks for being such a great friend to my son,
and for being such an important part of our lives.*

*Also, thanks for always covering me while I get my loadout,
and for making me laugh every single game
(he's walkin' with his dawg!).
You rock!*

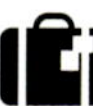
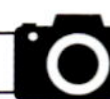

Acknowledgments

Although only one name appears on the spine of this book, it takes a team of dedicated and talented people to pull a project like this together. I'm not only delighted to be working with them, but I also get the honor and privilege of thanking them here.

To my amazing wife Kalebra: This year we celebrated our 32nd anniversary and you continue to reinforce what everybody always tells me—I'm the luckiest guy in the world.

To my son Jordan: I just can't believe my "little boy" has already graduated from college. It all happened so fast, but I'm so thrilled for you and for the many adventures, and for the fun, love, and laughter your future holds. If there's a dad more proud of his son than I am, I've yet to meet him. #rolltide!

To my beautiful daughter Kira: You are a little clone of your mom, and that's the best compliment I could ever give you. I love your sense of humor, your constant dancing, the hilarious faces you make, and your heart. I love the young woman you are becoming, and I particularly love when you and I go grab lunch or dinner together. Those times are so precious to me. I super-love you!

To my big brother Jeff: Your boundless generosity, kindness, positive attitude, and humility have been an inspiration to me my entire life, and I'm just so honored to be your brother.

To my editor Kim Doty: If there's a Book Editor Hall of Fame, you should truly be in it. You are so talented, organized, and awesome, and your amazing attitude, support, and ideas are what keep me going when I'm deep in the weeds, and I'll be forever grateful to have you on my team. You rock!

To my book designer Jessica Maldonado: I love the way you design, and all the clever little things you add to everything you do. Our book team struck gold when we found you!

To my dear friend and business partner Jean A. Kendra: Thanks for putting up with me all these years, and for your support for all my crazy ideas. It really means a lot.

To Erik Kuna: Your suggestions, ideas, and good counsel have made this book, and the ones before it, that much better. I value your friendship so much, and feel very blessed to have you in my life.

To Cindy Snyder: Thank you so much for working on my books and catching tons of little things others would have missed.

To Ted Waitt, my fantastic "Editor for life" at Rocky Nook: Thanks for being such a great friend, a world-class sounding board, and for helping these ideas become a reality.

To my publisher Scott Cowlin: I'm so delighted I still get to work with you, and grateful for your open mind and vision.

To my mentors, John Graden, Jack Lee, Dave Gales, Judy Farmer, and Douglas Poole: Thank you for your wisdom and whip-cracking—they have helped me immeasurably.

Most importantly, I want to thank God, and His Son Jesus Christ, for leading me to the woman of my dreams, for blessing us with such amazing children, for allowing me to make a living doing something I truly love, for always being there when I need Him, for blessing me with a wonderful, fulfilling, and happy life, and such a warm, loving family to share it with.

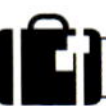
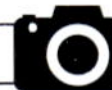

About the Author

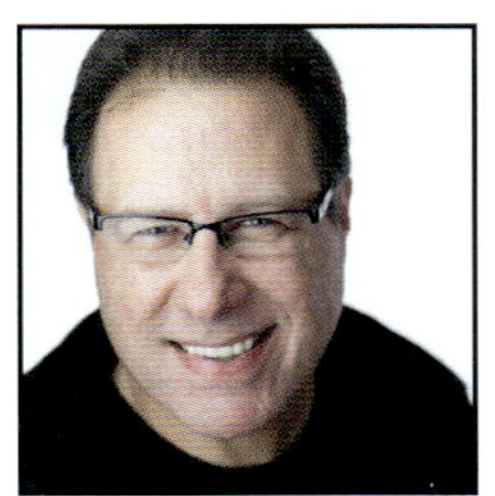

Scott Kelby

Scott is President and CEO of KelbyOne, an online educational community for photographers. He is Editor, Publisher, and co-founder of *Photoshop User magazine*; host of *The Grid*, the influential, live, weekly talk show for photographers; and is founder of the annual Scott Kelby's Worldwide Photo Walk.®

Scott is an award-winning photographer, designer, and author of more than 100 books, including *The Landscape Photography Book*; *Light It, Shoot It, Retouch It*; *The Adobe Photoshop Book for Digital Photographers*; *Photoshop for Lightroom Users*; *The Natural Light Portrait Book*; *The Flash Book*; and his landmark *The Digital Photography Book* series. The first book in this series, *The Digital Photography Book*, part 1, has become the #1 top-selling book ever on digital photography.

His books have been translated into dozens of different languages, including Chinese, Russian, Spanish, Korean, Polish, Taiwanese, French, German, Italian, Japanese, Hebrew, Dutch, Swedish, Turkish, and Portuguese, among many others. He is a recipient of the prestigious ASP International Award, presented annually by the American Society of Photographers for "…contributions in a special or significant way to the ideals of Professional Photography as an art and a science," and the HIPA award, presented for his contributions to photography education worldwide.

Scott is Conference Technical Chair for the annual Photoshop World Conference and a frequent speaker at conferences and trade shows around the world. He is featured in a series of online learning courses at KelbyOne.com and has been training Photoshop users and photographers since 1993.

For more information on Scott, visit him at:

His daily Lightroom blog: **lightroomkillertips.com**

His personal blog: **scottkelby.com**

Twitter: **@scottkelby**

Facebook: **facebook.com/skelby**

Instagram: **@scottkelby**

Contents

Chapter 03

Gear & Settings 43

What to Take (What to Leave Behind) and Which Settings to Use

Chapter 04

Travel Photography Accessories 57

Those Extra Little Gadgets That Can Really Make a Difference

Chapter 05

Capturing Images of People 75

Coming Home with More Than Just Images of Buildings and Monuments

Contents

Chapter 06

Composition 93

How to Arrange Things for More Compelling Photos

Chapter 07

Other Cool Stuff to Shoot 113

Well, That Headline Kind of Kills the Need for Me to Write a Subhead. Still Did, Though

Chapter 08

When to Shoot with Your Phone Instead 127

Sometimes It's Just Faster and Easier

Chapter 09

What to Shoot 145

And What You Can Skip

Contents

Chapter 10

Sharing Images from Your Trip   169

Let's Get Those Awesome Images Out There!

Chapter 11

Travel Photography Tips & Tricks   181

Tips for Working Smarter, Faster, and Better, and Keeping Your Gear Safe

Chapter 12

Editing Your Images   203

How to Post-Process Your Travel Images Using Lightroom and/or Photoshop

Chapter 13

Photo Recipes to Help You Get the Shot   231

The Simple Ingredients That Make It All Come Together

Seven Things You'll Wish You Had Known…

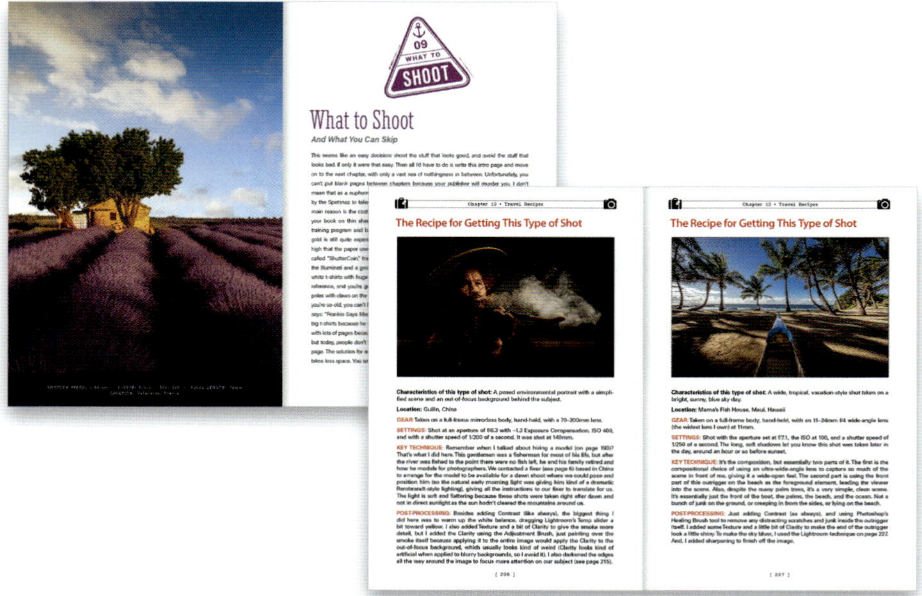

(1) Here's how this book works: Basically, I treat this like it's you and me together somewhere awesome (Paris? Santorini? Tokyo?), and I'm sharing with you the same tips, advice, and techniques I've learned over the years. When I'm out shooting with a friend, I skip all the technical stuff. So, for example, if you turned to me and said, "Hey Scott, I want those beer mugs on the bar in focus, but I want the bar and everything behind it out of focus," I wouldn't give you a lecture about the relationship between the focal plane and distance to subject in relation to aperture. In real life, I'd just turn to you and say, "Use the lowest-numbered f-stop you can and zoom in tight on the beer mug." I'd tell you short and right to the point like that, so that's pretty much what I do throughout this book.

(2) I include all the locations: When I see a beautiful image in a magazine, or when a photographer posts a travel image online, it drives me crazy when they don't tell you where that location is. That's why I included the location for every shot in the book.

(3) Warning: The chapter intros are whacked. In a normal book, the intros at the beginning of each chapter give you some important insight into the coming chapter. But, mine…um…well…kinda don't. These quirky, rambling intros have little to do with what's actually in the chapter. They're designed to simply be a "mental break" between chapters, and they've become a tradition in my books. A lot of folks really enjoy them (so much so, that we published an entire book of nothing but chapter intros—I am not making this up), however some "serious type" folks hate them with the passion of a thousand burning suns. I'm warning you now just in case you're one of those folks who would hate stuff like that. If that sounds like you, I'm begging you, please just skip the chapter intros altogether, because the rest of the book is pretty straightforward.

…Before Reading This Book!

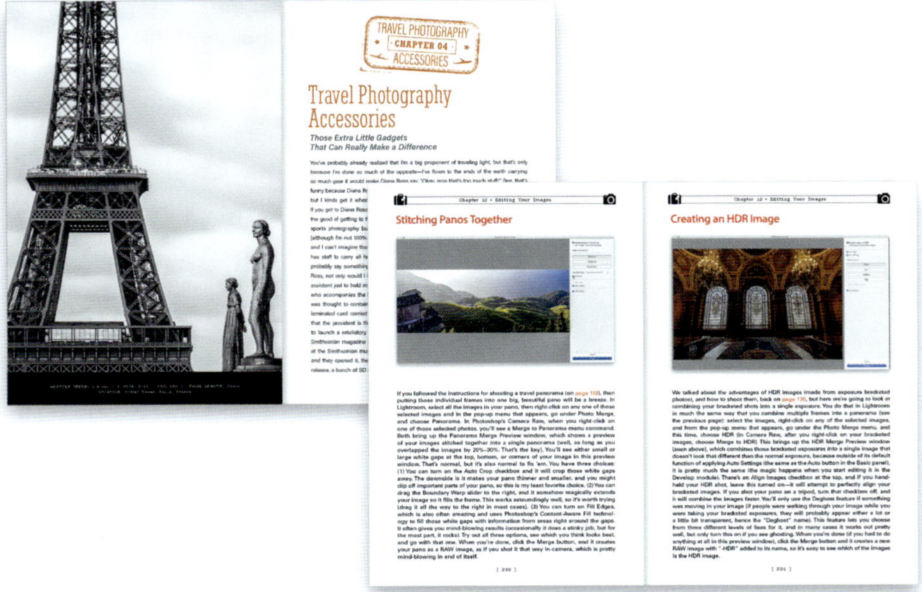

(4) You don't have to read this book in order. This is a "jump in anywhere" book, so if there's a particular area of travel photography you want to read first, you can just jump to that chapter and dive right in, no sweat. If you're brand new to all of this, then it would probably be helpful to start up front and work your way through, because later chapters build on earlier chapters.

(5) Sometimes you have to buy stuff. This is not a book to sell you stuff, but sometimes to get pro-level results, you have to use some accessories that the pros use. I don't get an affiliate fee from any companies whose products I recommend (rats!). I'm just giving you the same advice I'd give a friend.

(6) I wound up making some video tutorials on the post-production stuff. Some of the post-processing stuff is easier if you watch a video, so I made some short little videos just for you that support what I wrote here in the book if you find that easier. Here's the link: **kelbyone.com/books/travelbook.**

(7) Keep this in mind: This is a "show me how to do it" book. Like I said earlier, I'm telling you these tips just like I'd tell a shooting buddy, and that means, oftentimes, it's the bigger picture of photography (the creative and vision stuff that really makes a difference), but sometimes, it is just which button to push, which setting to change, what lens to use in a particular situation, without all the nerdy technical explanations. I figure that once you start making great travel photos, you might want to buy one of those "tell me all about it" books that goes into all that technical stuff and you'll learn concepts like "lens diffraction" and "chromatic aberration" and "hyper focal distance." But for now, it's time to pack up your gear, grab some snacks for the road, and let's head out for our first shoot.

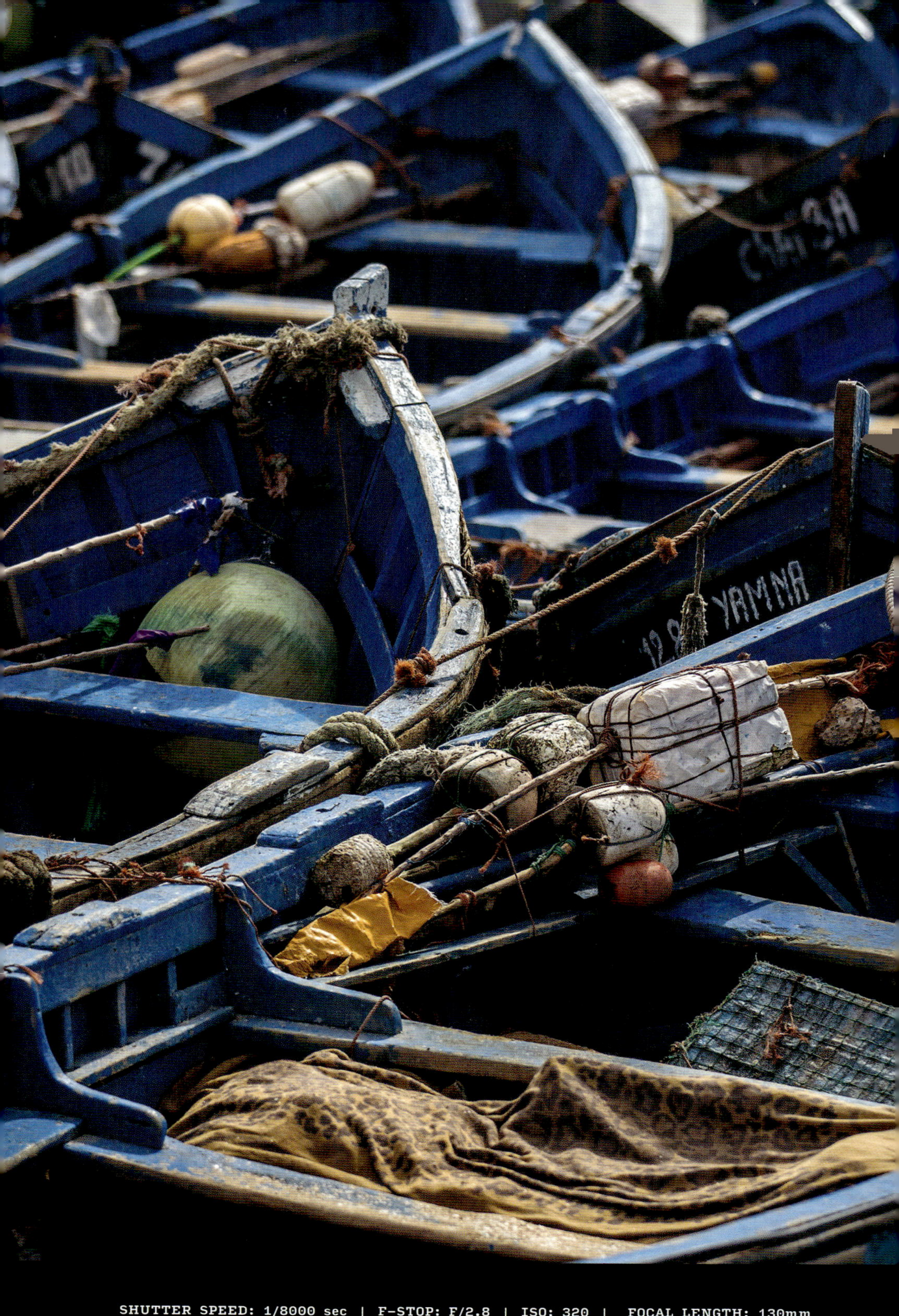

SHUTTER SPEED: 1/8000 sec | F-STOP: F/2.8 | ISO: 320 | FOCAL LENGTH: 130mm

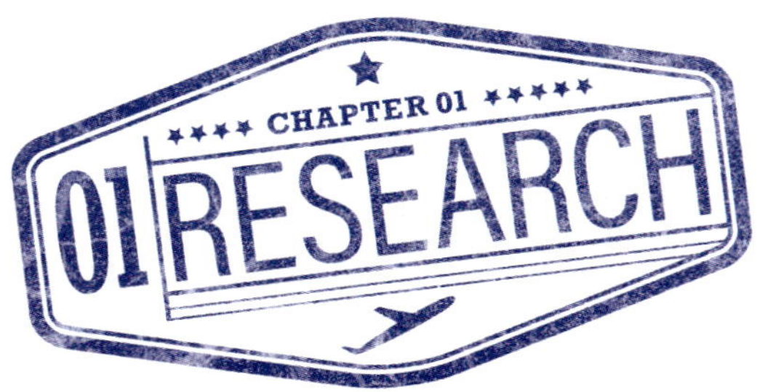

Doing the Research Before Your Trip

Doing a Little Work Up Front Can Set You Up for Some Amazing Shots!

A few years ago, I had to go to Phoenix for work, so I thought I'd leave a day early and go shooting in Sedona. I'd always wanted to shoot there, so after we landed, my photo assistant and I made the two-hour drive. During the drive, my assistant asked me, "So, what's the plan once we get there? Where's our shooting location?" and I said, "We'll figure it out once we get there." Huge mistake. You can imagine how badly things turned out. We drove around for hours, aimlessly searching for a decent sunset shoot location without any luck. We barely had a cell signal, so the internet was spotty, and we wound up settling for some stupid location (that explains why we were the only photographers there), and I was really upset with myself. One thing that helped a lot, as we looked out over a small canyon, was that while we were gazing at the vast nothingness of our sunset location, I casually reached over and gave my assistant a little shove and he went careening down the mountain. Well, it was more like a rocky hill than a mountain, but still, watching him bounce off the rocks on his way down into the steep crevasse was a hoot and got me out of that bad mood fast. Oh, now, don't freak out—he was fine, and within six weeks, he was up and walking with a leg brace, no problem. He still walks with a limp, but we still laugh about what we call the "Sedona Sunset Shoot Calamity" and how the whole thing could have been avoided if we had just spent 20 minutes doing some simple research before we got on our flight. It reminds me of the time we planned a big fashion shoot downtown, right by a busy freeway, but I forgot to apply for a shooting permit from the city. Anyway, we had a whole crew and had hired a model, and now we'd blown the whole shoot, and as my assistant and I were standing there looking onto the busy freeway, with cars whizzing by, I casually reached over and....

My First Stop? 500px.com

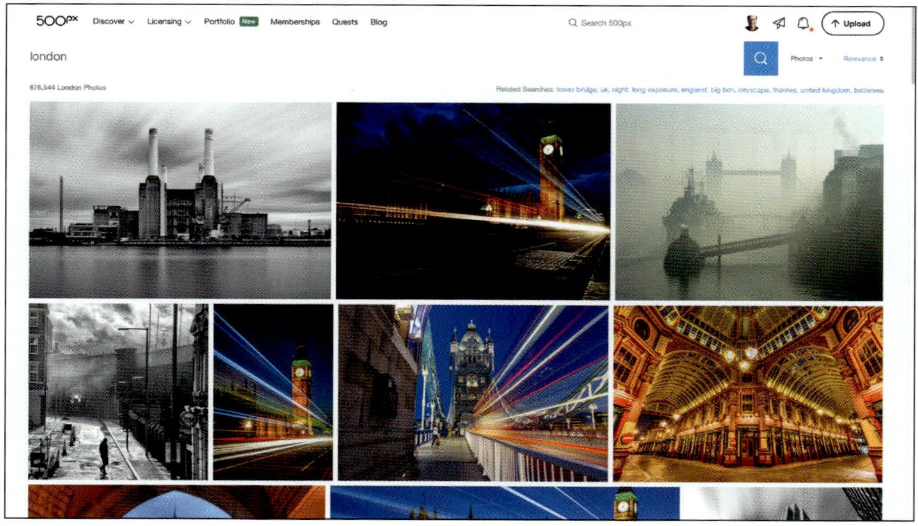

When we're doing research for a trip, we're looking for great locations, ideas for places to shoot, and inspiration, so my first stop for this type of research is a site called 500px.com. It's a worldwide community of serious photographers and all you have to do is type in a city or location, like Cairo, Egypt, or the Dalmatian Coast, and hundreds, if not thousands, of photos from that area, often taken by top-notch photographers, will fill your screen. I have used this site many times and have uncovered places I surely would have missed, lots of places I hadn't heard of, and viewpoints I might not have considered. Better yet, when you see an image that captures your attention, click on it to find out more info about that photo, which often will include the exact location (if not in the written description, in the keywords [search terms] they apply to the photo), and sometimes the photographer even gives you the exact GPS coordinates where their shot was taken. Make sure you read the comments people post below the photos because there's often great info there as well, like other places nearby, or someone just asking the photographer where that shot was taken (if they didn't mention it in their description). *Note:* This is a membership site, but you do *not* have to be a member to search the site, look at images, and do your research. You just need to be a member to post your own images or comment on others. That being said, I've been a member for years and it's totally worth it. Either way, 500px.com is always my first stop when I'm researching a town or country to visit.

Next, Head to Pinterest

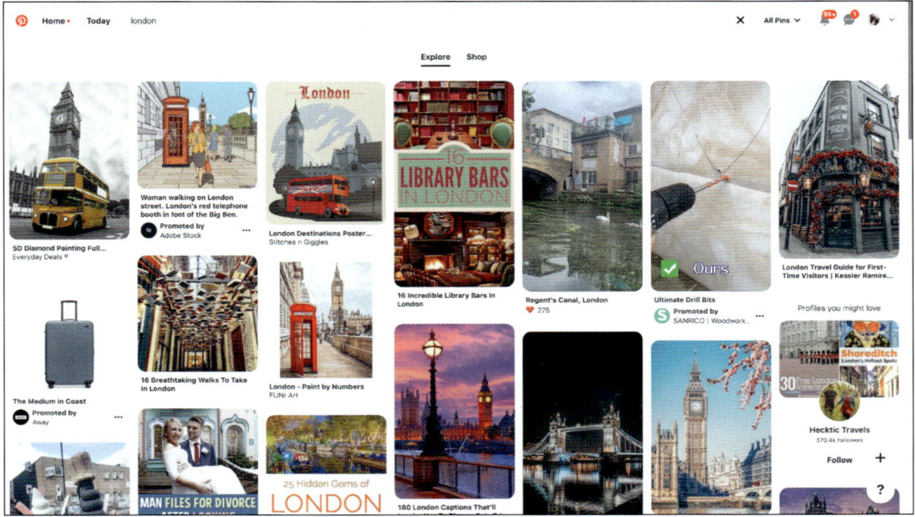

My next stop in researching travel locations is Pinterest.com. It's much different than 500px.com (it's not made up of serious photographers), but it has its own distinct advantage. Where 500px.com is a bunch of individual photographers showing you their shot from a particular location, Pinterest is regular folks who have curated their own collections of great images from a location, but from all different photographers. You use it in a similar way to 500px.com in that you just type in a search term and loads of photos appear. Okay, what's the downside? Well, a lot of those photos that appear on your screen are actually ads for products. They work hard to make it look like they're not ads, but when you click on them, they take you to a page about tour services, or luggage deals, or travel insurance, or whatever. You'll also see regular ads from all the big names, from auto manufacturers to big box stores, which is kind of a drag (simply because there are just so many ads), but visiting Pinterest still has value, and you'll uncover some shooting locations or ideas you might not get from 500px.com, so it's still my second stop on my research journey.

Make a Shot List

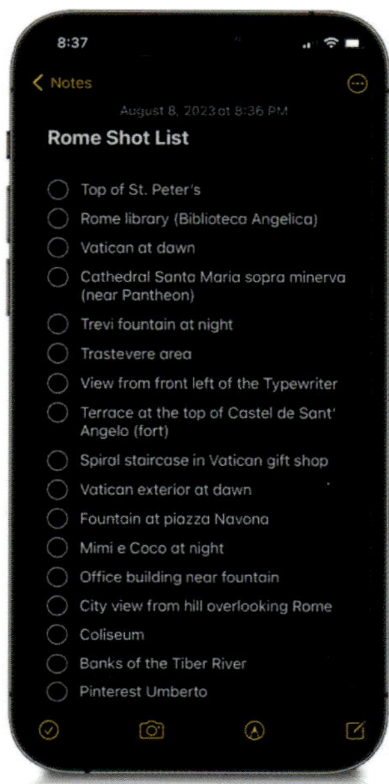

I do this on my phone, well before I arrive in a town, and I make: (1) a list of all the places and locations I want to shoot while I'm in that town, and (2) a list of the type of things I want to capture. So, this second list might include: classic architecture, interesting subway stops, cathedral spires, sidewalk cafes, photos of waiters, any fountains, and so on. Having these lists will not only keep you on track, but they'll have you coming home with more photos than you otherwise would have. These lists are great for when you're standing there thinking, "I'm not sure what to shoot" (which happens more often than you'd think). I like to review these lists on my phone when I'm having a cup of coffee, waiting in line, waiting for a tour bus, etc. Try this once, and you'll be making lists like this every time because they help you make the most of a location.

Make Your Own Pinterest Board

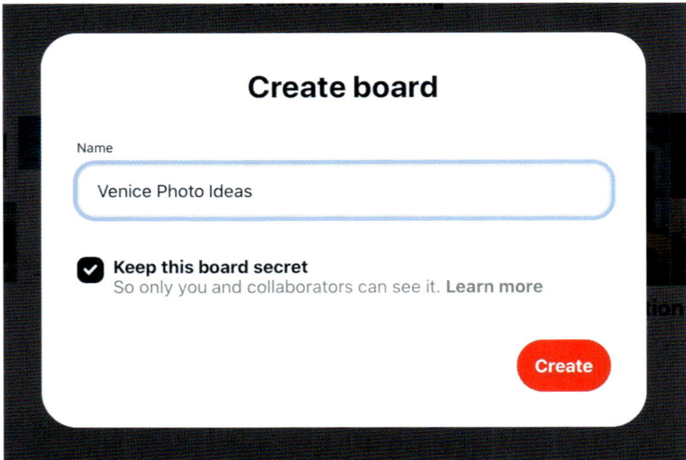

One thing I love to do when I'm researching on Pinterest is to create a custom "board" (a collection of photos) of my favorites of other people's shots from a particular location. Let's take Venice, for example: I search for the topic of "Venice" and when I see a shot I particularly like in the results, I create a Pinterest board (as seen above) and now I can add that shot to my Venice Photo Ideas board. That way, when I'm actually in Venice and I need some inspiration or ideas, I can just go directly to that board where I know (a) I'll see only shots and locations in Venice I already like, and (b) I won't see any ads because it's my own custom board. It's a big time saver and inspiration-maker. Also, you'll have the option of keeping this board private (just turn on the Keep This Board Secret checkbox when you first create your new board and then only you can see this board). You can create as many of these private or custom boards as you like (if you don't make a board private, anyone on Pinterest can see your board and the images you added, which may not be a bad thing, but just so you know).

Find a Fixer

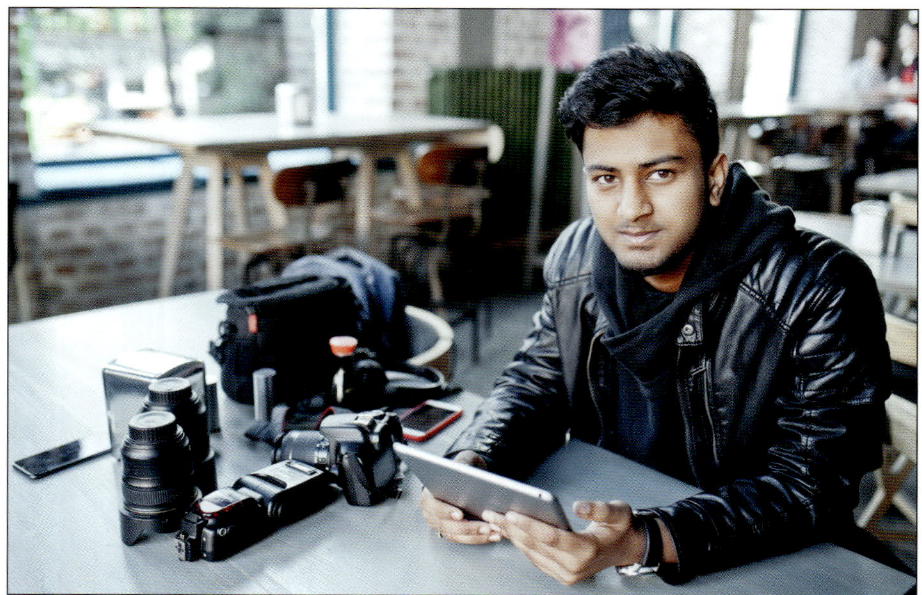

There is a "trick of the trade" that many top travel photographers and journalists use to make unique or really fascinating shots, especially in a foreign country, and that is to hire a "fixer." They are more than tourist photo guides. They are people with serious connections, who can get you access to people and places you could rarely get to on your own. They know the language (and can act as your translator), they know the local customs, they can help get permits, and they know the local laws to keep you (and them) out of trouble. They know which guards to bribe to get you access to the top of a building for sweeping cityscape shots at dawn, or they know the maintenance guy at a local market, who can get you access to a second-story window overlooking the scene. They can get you backstage at the opera house when it's empty, and maybe behind the scenes at a restaurant or old factory. They may also get you into the homes of locals to make incredible natural light portraits or they might arrange a professional model, in full local costume, to pose in the perfect spot. They seem to have the keys to the kingdom and can open doors and make things happen that nobody else can. They're usually not too expensive, but can be a little hard to find because they don't hang a sign out that says "photo fixer here." The best way to find one is to reach out (on social media) to other photographers who have traveled to a specific area and ask for a recommendation. It's a bit like an underground network—you'll have to do a little digging, a little asking, a little bit of checking or posting questions in photography forums—but remember, the person you're looking for is a photography "fixer." Not a guide. Whatever you spend on one, and however much digging you do to find one, I promise you, you'll look at your images and know right then, it was all worth it.

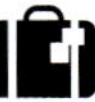
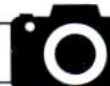

Try Google Earth

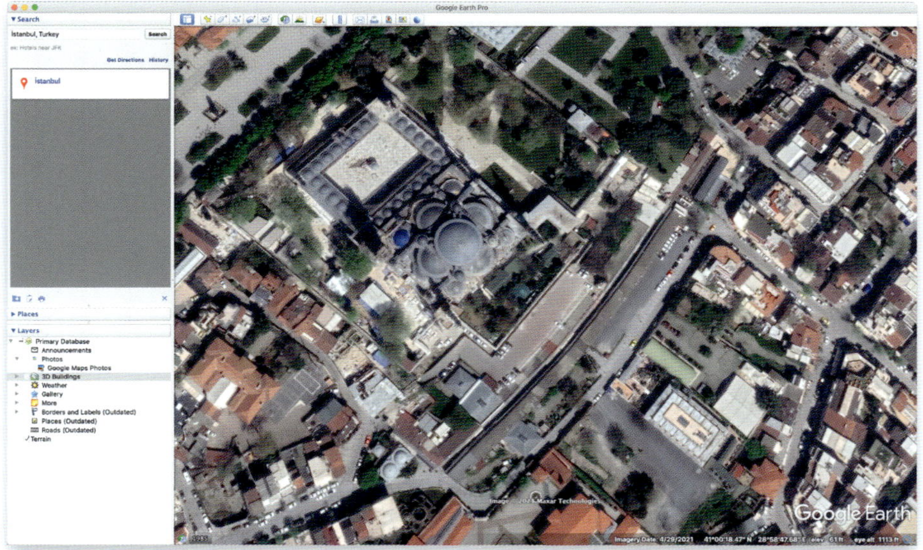

I look to Google Earth (it's on the web, but I prefer using the free Google Earth app), once I've found someone else's photo online and I want to narrow down exactly where it was taken from. For example, there was a particular view of Sacré-Cœur Basilica in Paris that I had never seen before and I wanted to shoot from that same area, but put my own spin and angle on the scene. So, I used Google Earth to not only figure out which street it was taken from (the name of the street and cross street), but also to find other places nearby where I'd still have a view of the cathedral. One thing that really helped was searching for the name of one of the businesses I saw in the photo. That helped me quickly narrow down the location, and before I knew it, I was standing in that same spot (well, digitally), thanks to Google Earth, and then when I got to Paris, I was right there in person. It's also great for seeing if there is easy access to a shooting location or if I will have to park the car and then do a lot of hiking to get out to that location. (And, what does that hike look like? Is it all uphill? Does it cross a stream? Does it look dangerous up there?) Just another great research tool that works as an extension of what you're doing with the other sources you've already learned in this chapter.

The Hidden Power of the Concierge

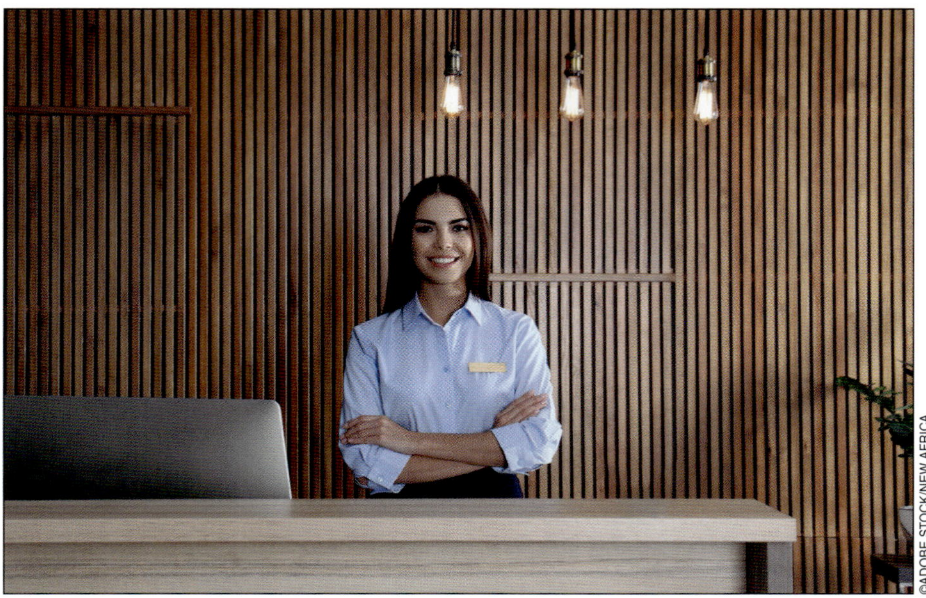

There's a big advantage to staying at a hotel with a concierge. For example, let's say you want to take a shot at dawn from the hotel's rooftop restaurant. Do not, I repeat, *do not* ask the hotel manager. It's very unlikely they'll let you up there because there's nothing in it for them (only hassles). Instead, go to the concierge because they work for tips, and letting you do things that get them a tip is their jam. It's what they do. They're about making your wishes come true (which, in turn, earns them a tip). Just tell them you're a photographer and how you'd love the opportunity to take a cityscape shot from the rooftop bar, but at 5:30 a.m. They'll coordinate with the security guard who will be on that shift (and who they'll prob-ably have to give a little tip to, as well) to make sure they unlock the door for you. I have had situations where the concierge couldn't get me rooftop access, so they asked if it would be okay if they got me out on the balcony of the Presidential Suite on the top floor (the guests had checked out) so I could shoot from there. Of course, I made sure to leave them a nice tip. The concierge has incredible power in their hotel (and sometimes with other concierges at other hotels or venues), and they have access, connections, and they're motivated. It's like a fixer right in your hotel, so don't overlook what they can do to help you achieve your photographic vision while on their property.

Hire a Photo Guide

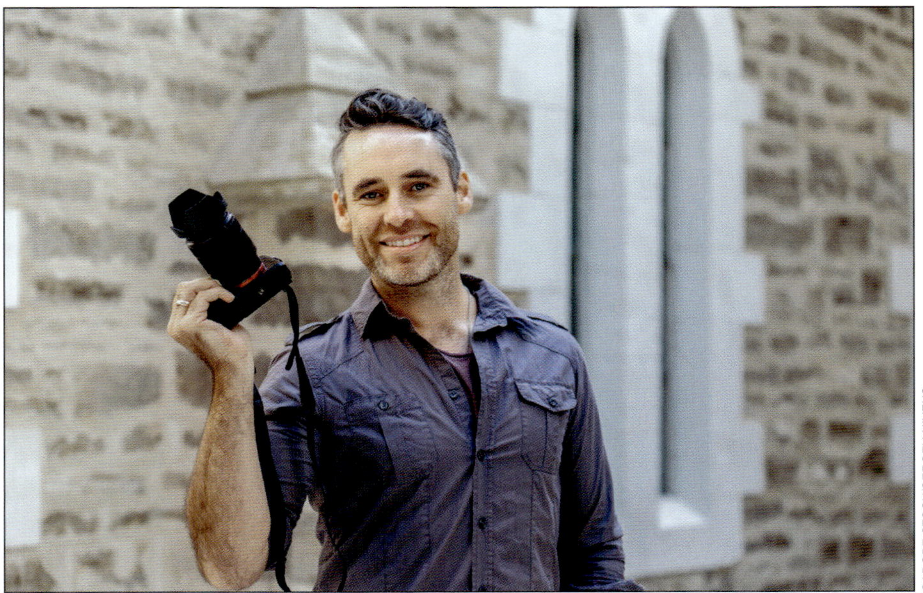

I hire a photo guide when I haven't had the time to really research the area I'm traveling to—maybe it was a last minute trip, which happens surprisingly often, or I'm just swamped with work right before a trip. If I don't get a chance to do the research like I want to before I leave on my trip, I pay the price, which is whatever the local photo guide charges. However, while I've done this a few times, I've had pretty mixed results with photo guides. Some have been pretty helpful and took me to places I probably wouldn't have found on my own, and others took me to the most obvious places imaginable (like they'll take you to the Colosseum in Rome or the Leaning Tower of Pisa. You would have wound up there on your own anyway). I've also had photo guides that obviously have arrangements with local vendors where they get kickbacks or commissions, so during the day you wind up at stores and restaurants you didn't really want to visit. One way to find a good photo guide is to look at their personal photography—find their Instagram account and see what kind of photos they're taking when they're not with their clients. If the photos are pretty average, you can imagine they're going to take you to pretty average places (after all, if they knew better places, they'd be shooting there, right?). If they've got some great shots, your chances of a good experience (and making your own great shots) go way up. One more thing: there is probably zero chance of your actual photo guide looking anything like the handsome gentleman you see here. Just so you know.

Location Scouting

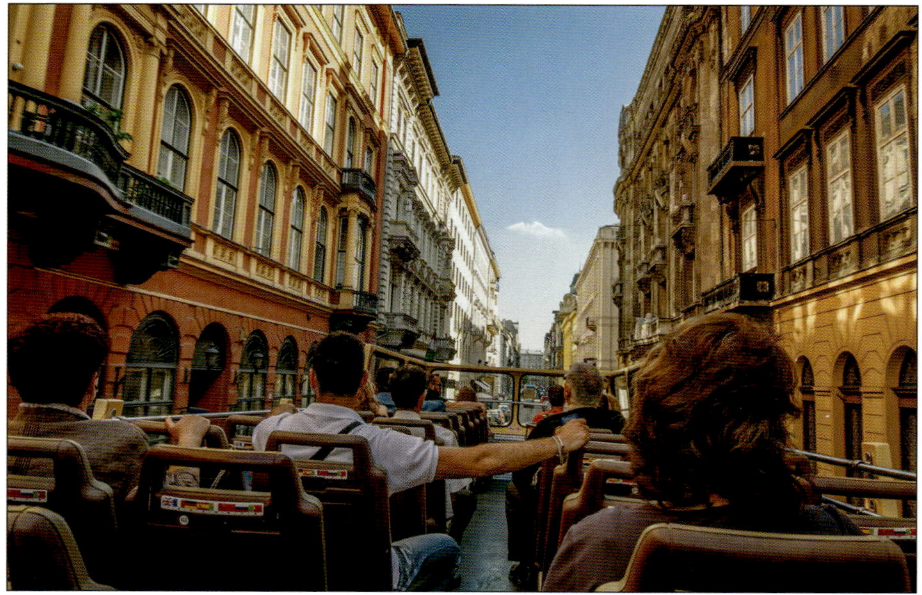

I'm going to share with you one of my best time-tested tips for getting great shots in a city you've never been to before. It's going to sound very touristy, and at first you might dismiss this idea, but I promise you, if you do it, it will pay dividends (well, photographically anyway). The tip is this: when you first get to a city, book a two-hour bus tour of the city and (this is the hard part) leave your camera behind. That's right, leave your mirrorless or DSLR back in your room and just take your phone because what you're doing is location scouting. If you take your regular camera, you'll spend the time shooting, instead of finding great places to return to with all your gear to get great shots. You'll get a great overview of the city, and you'll see places on your list that you'll realize aren't going to work. This happened to me in Paris. I was planning to get up at dawn to shoot the exterior of the Opera House, until on that bus tour, when I saw a big part of it was covered in scaffolding, so I did a dawn shoot at a different location that worked out great. Not only will you find places being restored, or that are just closed, or that have stuff in the way that kills the shot, you'll also find some places that you wouldn't have found, like a charming little fountain on a side street, or a courtyard that doesn't show up in any guide, or a charming restaurant you want to try for lunch. Be sure to take pictures with your phone of places you want to return to because it will automatically embed the GPS data into each shot, so you'll know exactly how to get back to those spots (enter the GPS data into Google Maps, or open the image in Lightroom, and in the Metadata panel, next to GPS, click the right arrow to take you to a map showing a satellite image of your exact position when you took the shot). If nothing else, the bus tour will give you two full hours to relax and really see the city without having a camera pressed up to your eye.

Make Local Connections on Social

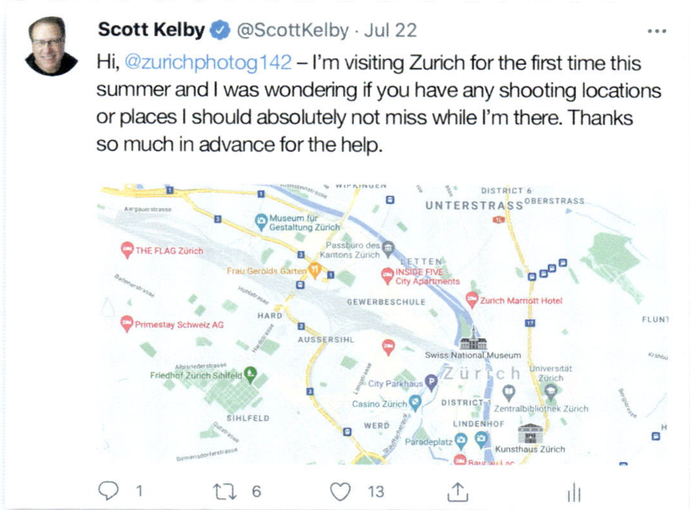

When heading someplace, especially a foreign country, before you go, do a little research on social media and contact some of the local photographers in that area. Let's say, for example, you searched on Facebook for photographers based in Zurich, Switzerland, and you found a few that are posting in English (or your native language). Just drop them a comment on a recent post saying that you're a photographer, too, and that you're coming to Zurich for the first time, and ask if they have any photo locations you definitely should not miss on your trip. Photographers are often really happy to help point you in the right direction, and they might even share some of their own favorite spots. Just this minute, I went to Instagram and typed in "French Photographers" and it brought up lots of France-based photographers (and lots of good ones, too!). Just drop them a comment—connecting with local photographers is a great way to find unique shooting spots and opportunities. Don't overlook this one—it can really make a difference.

Follow Local Instagram Accounts

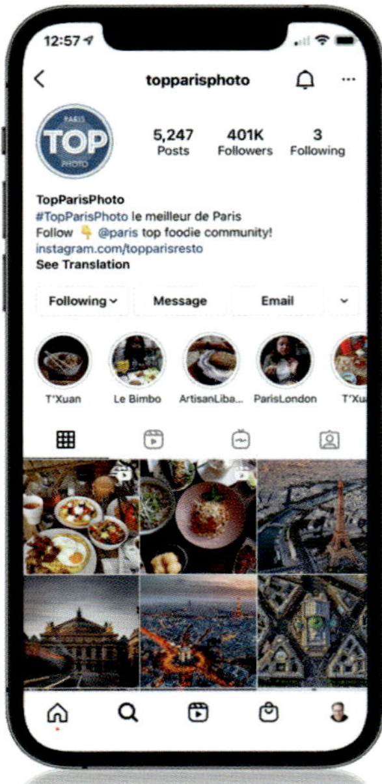

This will help you like you cannot believe: go to Instagram and find the official accounts for local tourist boards, or local travel agencies, or just some of the really popular accounts from an area you're visiting. For example, I follow two accounts called "TopParisPhoto" and "TopFrancePhoto" (they have lots of affiliated accounts, like "TopLondonPhoto," and so on), and they share wonderful shots of Paris and France. You'll see tons of great ideas, great locations, great photos, and lots of inspiration. Of course, there are many more accounts that aggregate wonderful photos from a particular area on Instagram—all shots of the place you're traveling to—and all it takes is a little searching, then following those accounts that inspire you, and you'll find all sorts of gems on their pages. I love the Instagram account of the Namibia Tourism Board (even though I've never been, but it sure makes me want to go). I cannot tell you how much this has helped me when I'm visiting a new area (or even ones I've been to before). Start following them now and you'll have lots of great ideas when you land.

Access Might Be an Issue

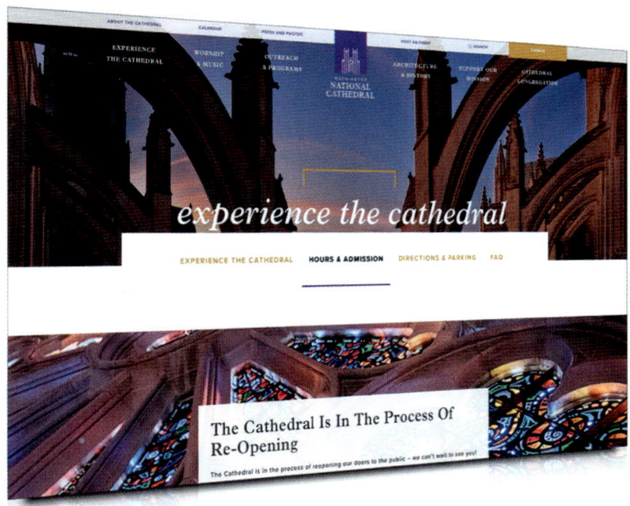

Okay, you've found a great location that you want to shoot—let's say it's a famous cathedral—and you show up there and the doors are locked. That's because they're closed every Sunday (this just happened to me—I drove 30 minutes to visit a famous cathedral and, sure enough, it's closed every Sunday. I know. I was surprised). A quick check of their website before I got there (not while I was standing outside their locked doors, which is what happened) would have given me a heads-up and saved me an hour-long round trip with nothing to show for it. Another example happened on my previous trip to this city. I wanted to photograph their famous spiral staircase, and since it's just in an office building, I figured I'd just walk into the building and get the shot. The problem was, you can only access the area where the spiral staircase is located by either: (a) being a tenant of the building, (b) being the client of a tenant in the building, or (c) taking the historical walking tour that only happens in the morning, at one certain time, on certain days. So, I went there, and couldn't shoot it. All of these places have their own websites (and their own rules), so take just a minute to research the times they are open and any ticket costs or fees (sometimes it's shockingly high and other times it's completely free, but you still need to register in advance for a ticket). Make visiting individual websites for places you want to shoot part of your travel photography research plan.

Search Stock Photo Sites for Ideas

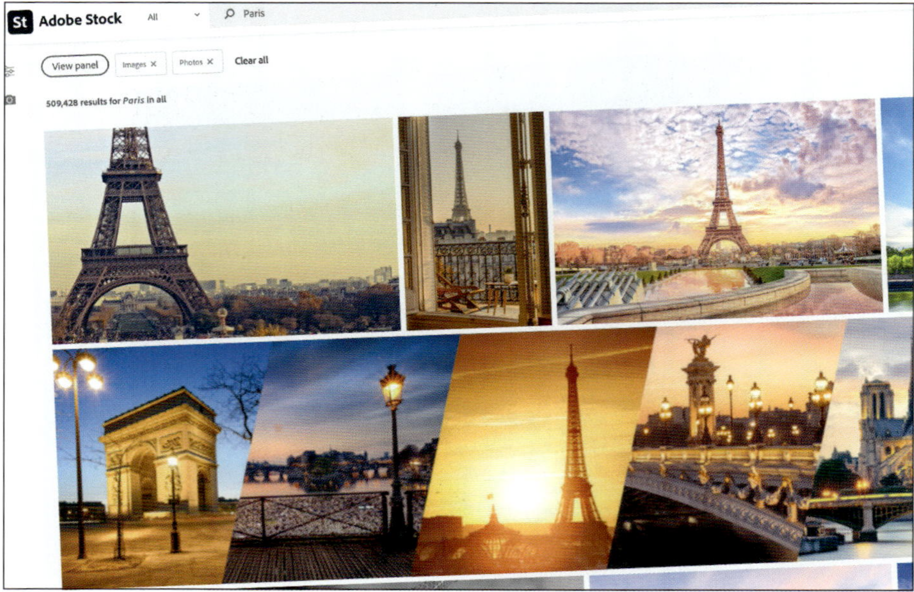

Another helpful travel photography research resource is to go to big stock photo websites (anything from Getty Images, to Shutterstock, to Adobe Stock) and search for images from the region you're traveling to. There's no charge to search, and once you're on their website, you can sometimes request to view only their premium images (their best, most-expensive shots to license). Remember, you're not going to buy these images—you're just looking for ideas, shooting locations, and inspiration, and you'll find all three on these stock sites.

Buy an eBook Photo Guide

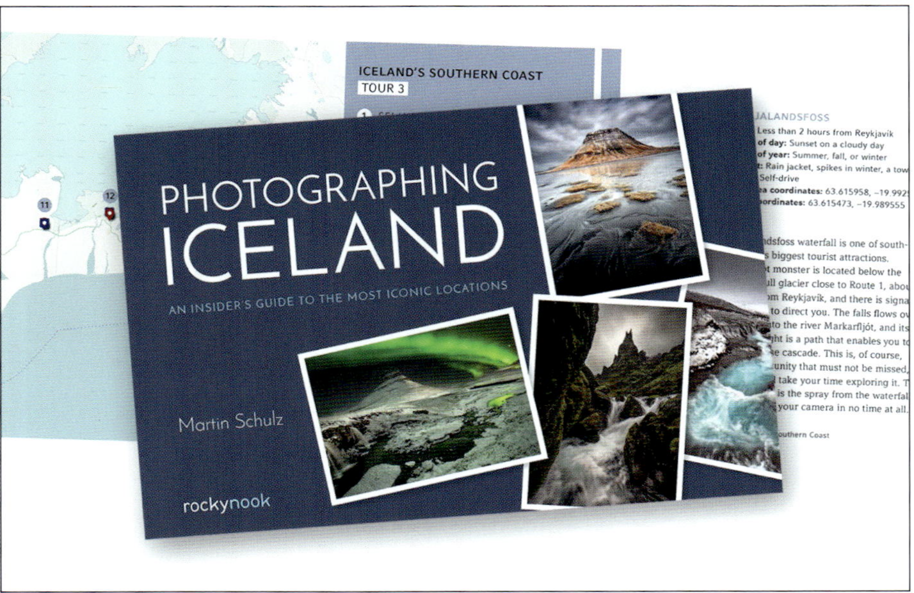

If an area is popular with photographers, you can almost bet a local photographer is selling a photo guide of popular places to shoot in that area. I've had pretty decent luck with these, as they're usually pretty inexpensive, they're all available in digital format so you get an instant download (usually, they're in PDF format), and some are very detailed, very well-researched, and worth the small amount they charge for them. You'll have to do a Google search to find a guidebook for where you're going, but that's usually all it will take. Hang on, and we'll do one now. Iceland is a really popular destination for photographers these days (has been for a few years now, which is why you'll never be alone at a photo location in Iceland. Expect 50 or more other photographers already there when you pull up in your rental car), so let's do a quick search for "Iceland Photo Guidebook" and it returns a link (one of many) to a book on Amazon called *Photographing Iceland: An Insider's Guide to the Most Iconic Locations*, by Martin Schulz. Now that sounds right up our alley (and the eBook version is only $20). It has 64 ratings and is rated at 4.5 stars (it's not easy to keep that high of a rating, so it's probably a safe bet). Of course, there are others, as well, but it's that easy to find a printed or digital photo guidebook to any place lots of photographers want to visit.

Keep an Eye Out for Special Events

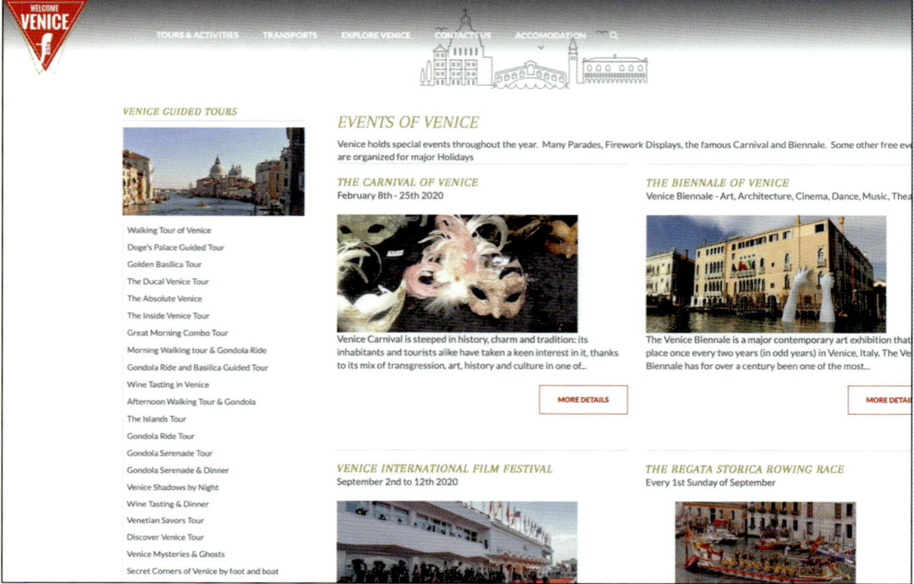

Special events taking place in the area you're visiting, like local festivals, carnivals, parades, and ceremonies, can present some especially awesome opportunities for photos. One way to find out when these are taking place (and if one is taking place while you're going to be there) is to visit the official website of the city you're going to visit (yup, they pretty much all have official websites these days, or at the very least, a tourism board website), and you'll find a calendar of what's coming up. Also, many tour operators have event information on their websites (like this one from venicewelcome.com). So, a quick search for "special events in Venice" will turn up lots of local calendars and lists of events. *Tip:* Once you find the name of an event, do a Google search to see other photographers' images from that event in previous years, so you can get an idea of whether or not it's worth attending from a photographic point of view.

Watch Movies to Find Locations

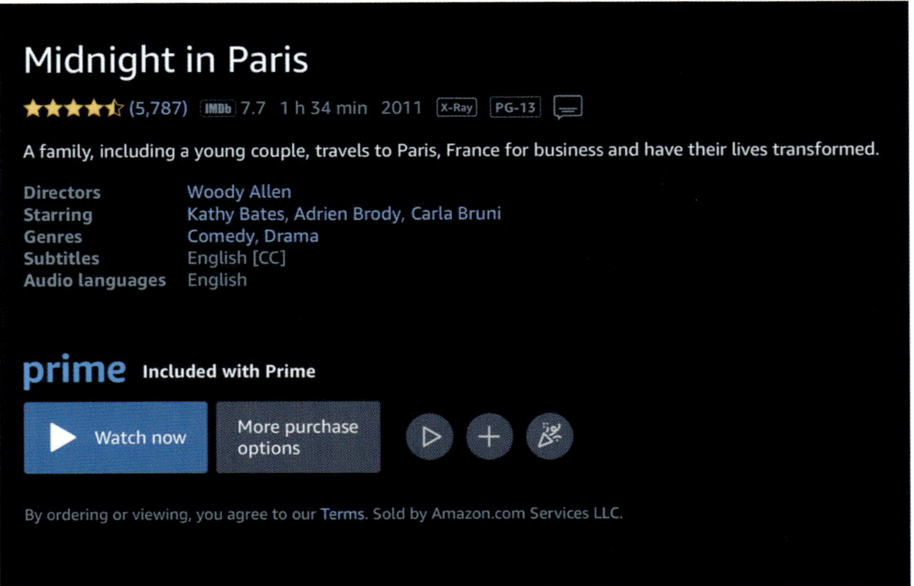

I love doing this for so many reasons, the first being that seeing a movie based on the location you're traveling to is just so inspiring. It makes you want to go there even more. Second, the directors and cinematographers for movies have hired local location scouts to help them find their locations, so you're already going to see some locations that capture the local flavor perfectly. There are just so many things you can glean from these movies, not to mention a great collection of background music you might consider if you're going to show a slide show of your trip when you return. Here's an example: Before my Paris workshop, I asked all my participants to watch the wonderful movie *Midnight in Paris*, and all of them that hadn't already seen it, watched it before the trip. In the movie, they eat dinner in a charming Parisian cafe, and I was not only able to find that same restaurant, but I booked a table for 16 for the opening night dinner at my workshop. The exact same restaurant they used in the film. It made the evening that much more special (and the food was, of course, fantastic!). So, before your trip, watch a few of the best movies from that region—you never know what ideas or inspiration will grow out of that experience (and worst case scenario, you don't glean anything, but you saw a great movie that got you even more in the mood for your trip).

The Ol' Postcard Rack Trick

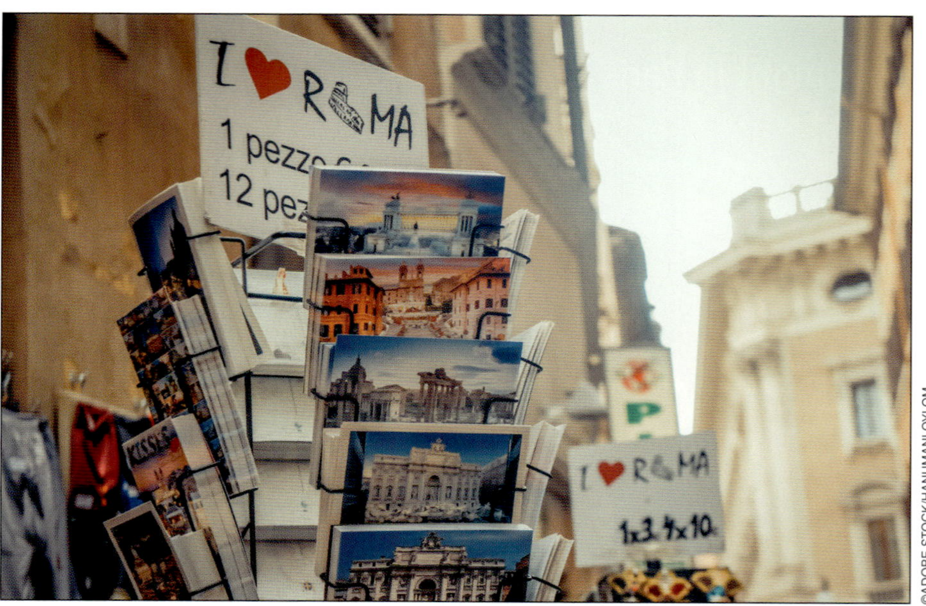

Okay, we're photographers, we're not going to buy any postcards, but when we go past a gift shop or two, we are going to peek at the postcards in the postcard rack. Sometimes, you'll find a nearby location that you didn't find in your research (that has happened to me), and all you usually have to do to find out where that location is, is to flip the postcard over and read the description. Now, they don't always 100% of the time list the location, and when that's happened, I've walked over to the counter, showed the gift shop clerk the postcard, and asked if they knew where the photo was taken. In those cases (well, except for one), they knew exactly where it was taken (in one case, it was a local castle, but I had missed it in my research). So, the ol' postcard trick can pay off, and at the very least, you get to look at some pretty pictures, so there's very little downside.

Hire a Driver for the Day

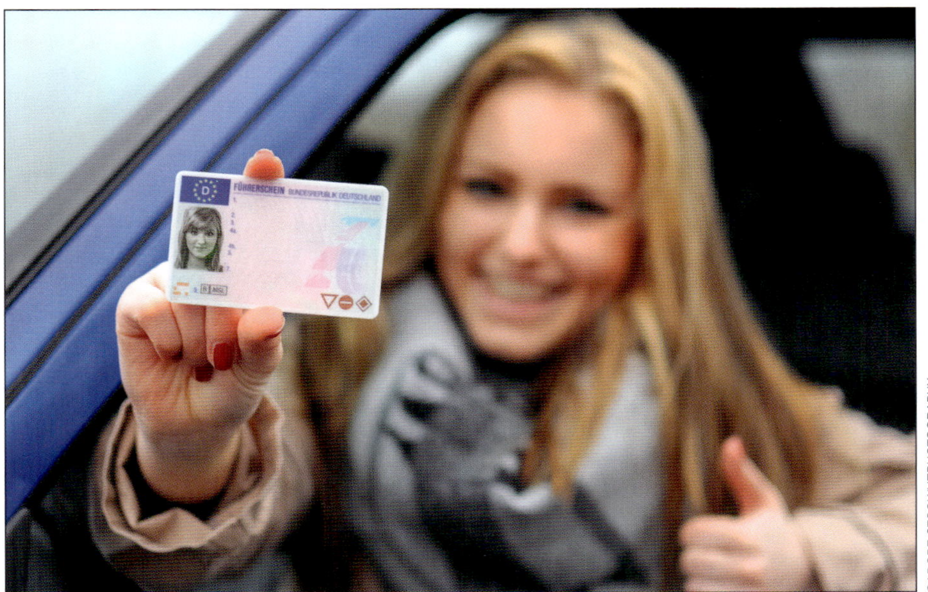

Imagine how many locations in a city you could hit if you hired your own private driver for the day. I know, it sounds expensive, but it's usually shockingly inexpensive as long as your hotel doesn't arrange it for you (because they take a big commission, so the cost is often prohibitive. Well, it was for me anyway). Instead, just grab a local Uber or Lyft, or even a taxi, and if you hit it off with the driver while chatting with them, tell them you're a photographer and ask what it would cost to hire them for the day. Using this method, I've hired a private driver, all day, numerous times, for anywhere between $60 to $100 for the day. That's not cheap, but when you add up how much a bunch of individual taxis or Uber rides are, each with its own tip, it's not that bad. Plus, since you have a driver (and this is a big plus for photographers), you can jump out while your driver circles the block—they don't have to find a parking space (which can be notoriously hard to find in many big cities), so you don't waste a bunch of time. You hop out, get your shots, and hop right back in. It's amazing how much you can cover like this—you'll be stunned at how many places on your shot list you'll hit. If it's a smaller area, you might even try a bike taxi, where they pedal you around. I've done this numerous times and because you can just say, "Stop right here" and they can usually just stop right there, you'll have loads of opportunities to shoot along the way. Give this one a try, and you'll be looking to do this as often as you can.

Keeping Your Gear Safe

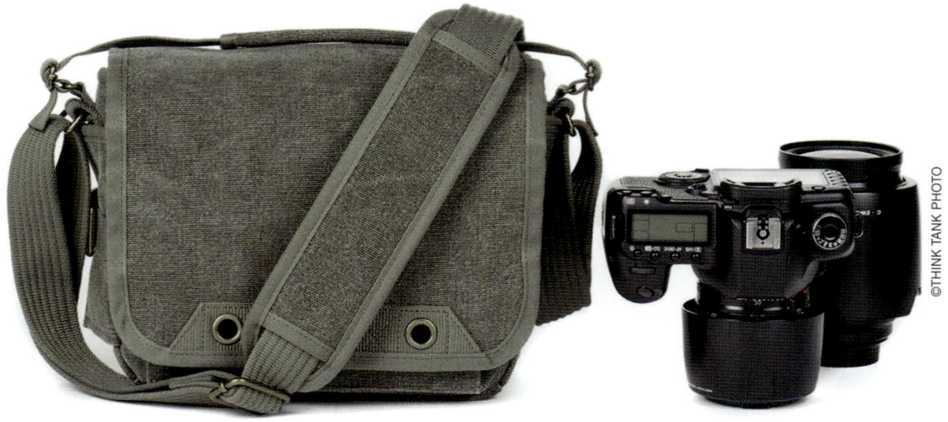

This is something you need to have a plan for before you take your trip. The first thing you might consider is insuring your photo gear before you leave. It's cheaper than you might think, but check to see if your homeowner's policy already covers you if your gear gets lost or stolen while on vacation (many do). Insurance is definitely worth looking into (I've got horror stories like you cannot believe about people getting *all* their gear stolen in the blink of an eye). One thing to consider is taking a camera bag that doesn't look like a camera bag, so it's not such an obvious target. Think Tank Photo makes a line of camera shoulder bags, called "Retrospective," that look more like messenger bags or totes than camera bags, but look and work like regular camera bags inside. Also, if you leave your hotel room, don't leave your gear out in plain sight—at the very least, tuck it out of sight, or ideally, take your body and lenses out of your camera bag and put them in your room's safe (or in the hotel's safe at the front desk if your room doesn't have one). I have a friend who had all of his gear stolen because he left it out in his room. It was a reputable hotel chain, but apparently a housekeeper told a friend about this room packed full of camera gear, slipped him a duplicate key, and well…before he knew it, thousands of dollars worth of his gear was gone (they wiped him out, taking everything, including his laptop and tablet). This stuff happens (more than you know), and not just in your hotel. It happened to another friend of mine on a subway. He had the bag right between his legs, so no one could easily grab it, but as they were about to pull out of a station, a man walked by, grabbed his bag, and stepped off the train just as the doors closed and the train pulled away. He said it was so perfectly timed, and it all happened in a split second. All his gear, instantly gone. Of course, his camera bag looked like a camera bag, so keep this in mind.

Flying with Your Gear

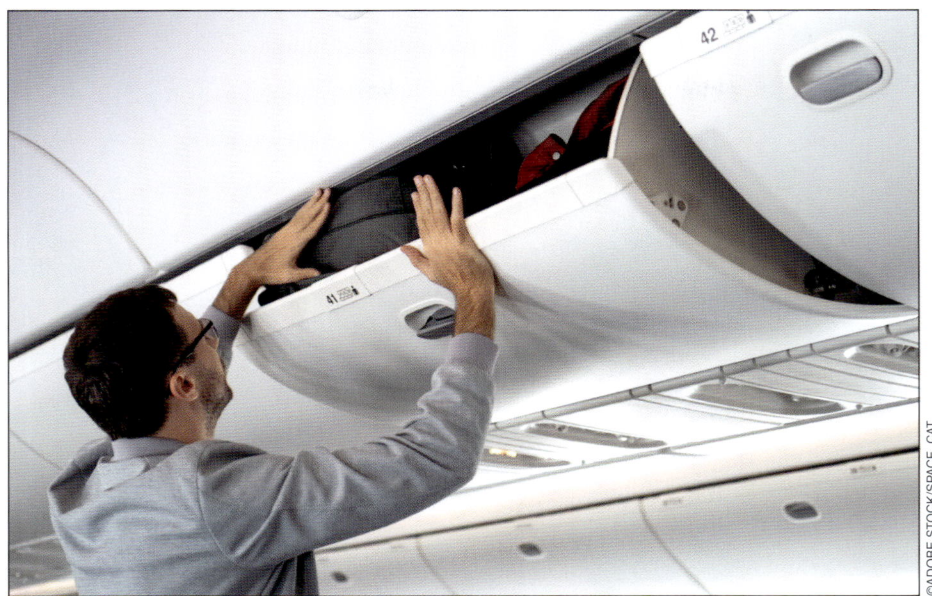

This one always makes be a bit queasy because I never want to get in a situation where I can't have my camera gear with me on the plane. I don't ever want to check it because we've seen the way baggage is often handled, and we've all heard stories of people opening their camera bags after they land to find their cameras and lenses are missing (it happens). This is why it pays to take a small camera bag that can fit under the seat in front of you, or if you wind up on a small 12-person puddle jumper prop plane, like I did on a trip to Norway. My bag was still small enough to come on board with me. Also, if you stow your camera bag in the overhead bin, put it in the bin directly across from your seat, so you can keep an eye on it. I know a guy who had his camera body stolen right out of his bag during the flight because he put it in a bin behind him on the same side. During the night, someone got up and snagged his expensive camera body, and there's really nothing you can do at that point. You call the flight attendant, tell them your gear was stolen, and they say they're sorry, but they're not about to launch an in-air investigation or start interrogating passengers. Also, if you're concerned you might wind up on a small commuter plane, consider getting a soft-sided camera bag—you can stuff them inside the smallest overhead compartments, rather than having them gate checked. You might also consider putting some larger things in your regular checked suitcase to get the size of your camera bag down. I've packed my travel tripod, and/or Platypod and ballhead, and even a flash inside my regular suitcase. If my luggage gets lost or delayed, it won't kill my trip (I don't put critical stuff in there). *One last tip:* If a flight attendant asks you to check your camera bag, this is the time to be super-nice, super-patient, and super-friendly. Don't get cranky or demanding or your gear is definitely going in the cargo hold and then all bets are off.

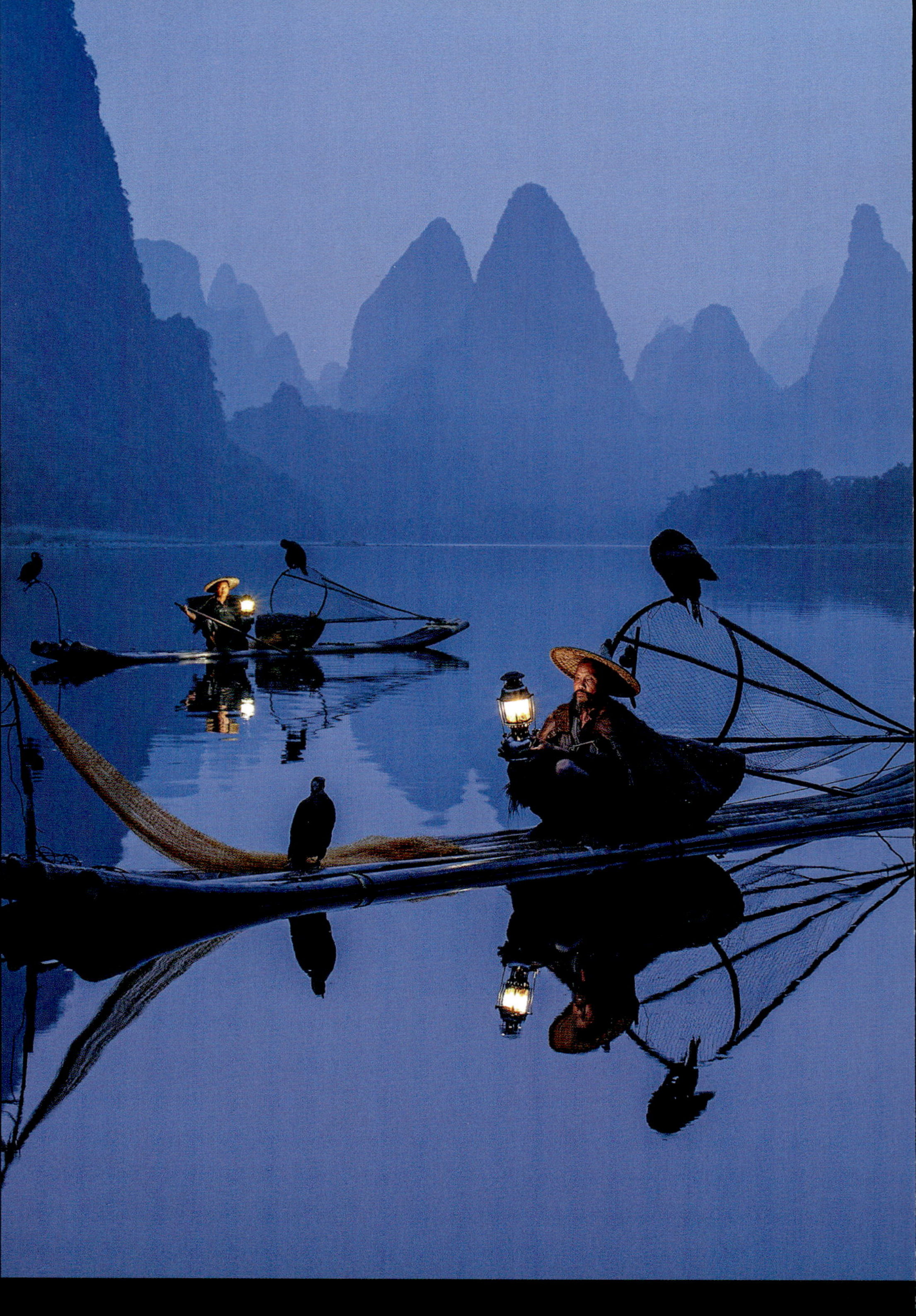
SHUTTER SPEED: 1/5 sec | F-STOP: F/5.6 | ISO: 800 | FOCAL LENGTH: 35mm
LOCATION: Yangshuo Rice Terrace, Guilin, China

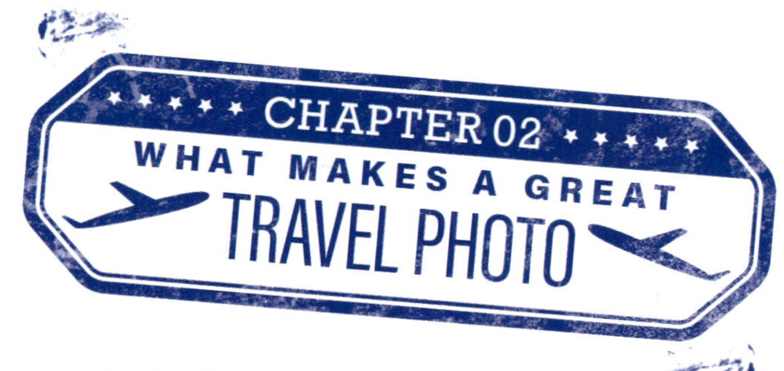

What Makes a Great Travel Photo? It...

Tips and Insights for Making Truly Captivating Travel Images

If I had to boil it down to its basics, a great travel photo is a photo that goes beyond just showing the place. I mean, you can go to Google and see a photo of just about any place, but a lot of them are what you might call "reference photos." Yup, that's Cinque Terre. It shows the place. But there are fabulous, beautiful, just amazing photos of Cinque Terre, and when you see those...that's when you realize what makes a great travel photo. It's showing a great place at its greatest. It's capturing the magic, the romance, the beautiful light, the color, the culture, the story, often combining several of those in one image and taking it over the top. When it happens, you know it, and when people see your image, they react to it. So, why do we see so many reference-quality photos? Two reasons: (1) Every other photographer out there (besides you and me, of course) stinks. However, you and I have magical visual storytelling powers that make us magical unicorns when everyone else is a donkey, and not like the cool one in *Shrek*. And, (2) they didn't have the most powerful secret weapon for making amazing travel images (which, by the way, is the book you're holding), and I'm not just telling you this to get you to buy the book because you already own it. Unless, of course, you shoplifted it, and...holy cow, you *did* shoplift it, didn't you? I have to tell you, I'm a bit shocked (and more than a bit disappointed) because I thought you and I, the only two magical-unicorn-level photographers out there, had a special sacred bond, bound together by our united disdain for everyone that is not us, but now...now I realize this was all just some sort of scam, and here I am alone with my special flying-horse self and no one to go shooting with except hordes of reference-shooting losers, and...well, now I have to rethink everything. I'm so upset, I don't think I'm going to finish the rest of this chapter opener. There, I stopped. Well, not there, but now. I'm stopping. I mean it. I'm not joking...I'll do it! P.S. You're back to being a donkey. Just so you know.

...Is Shot in Beautiful Light

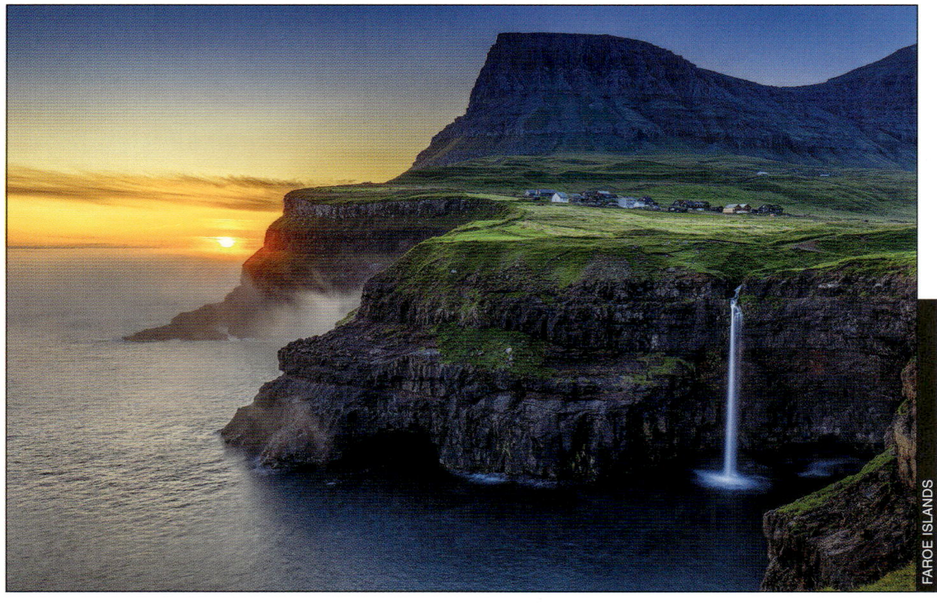

Everything looks better in beautiful light. Product shots, food photography, and people look their best in soft, beautiful light, and so do travel photos. Midday photos with hard shadows and washed-out colors generally aren't going to make the most flattering travel photos. That's why, if you can shoot really early in the day, right before the sun comes up or while it's still low in the sky (which, of course, also happens near sunset), you'll get beautiful light that flatters almost any scene. If the Taj Mahal looks great in the harsh midday sun, imagine how it would look later in the day—when the sun is lower, the shadows are soft, and the light is flattering. The image you see above, taken near sunset, not only has everything bathed in soft, beautiful light, the colors are much more vivid and saturated than they would be in the middle of the day. We have a wide range of colors in the sky—it's not just blue, as it was earlier in the day. I remember a portfolio review I did at a photography conference. One of the attendees said to me, "Mr. Kelby, I know you're very big on shooting in great light around dawn or sunset, but I want you to see this photo I took at 2:00 p.m. right in direct sun. I think it's pretty good." He turned the page, and sure enough, it was pretty good. I said, "You're right. This is pretty good for a shot taken in the day, but all I can think of is how awesome this exact same scene would've looked if you took it at the right time, in beautiful light." If you want your travel photos to look stunning, shoot them in beautiful early morning or near-sunset light that flatters the scene. It makes all the difference in the world (it's not always easy to get up that early, or plan your day so you're in a great location around sunset, but it can really, really pay off). *Note:* I'm not saying not to shoot in the day, but if you find an epic scene during the day, try to get back there to shoot it again when there's beautiful, magical light.

…Can Have Charm and Romance

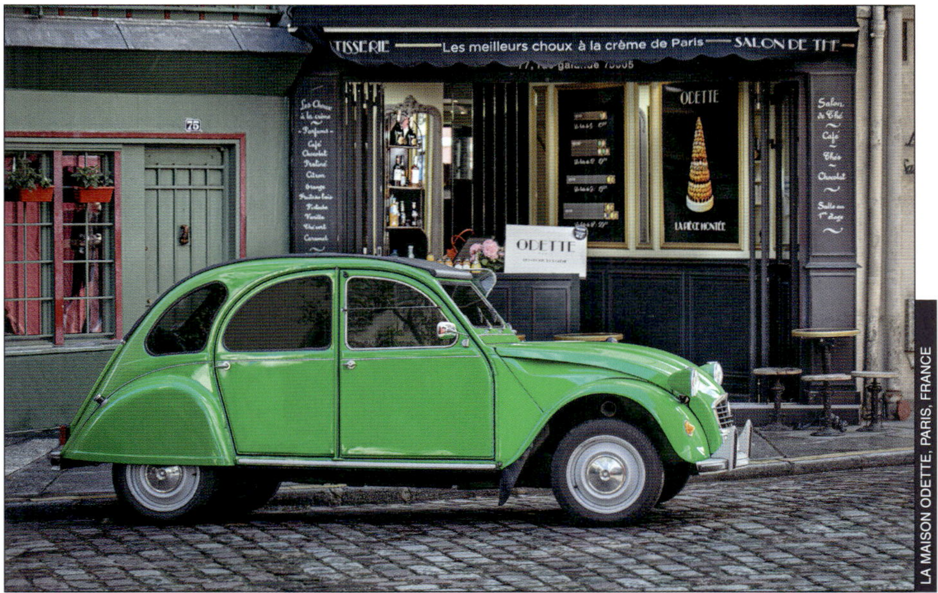

I remember walking with my wife along a small harbor full of little boats, but instead of shooting, I kept walking farther and farther down the pier, passing dozens and dozens of boats. My wife stopped, pointed at a nearby boat and asked, "What's wrong with this boat? It's cute." I agreed—it was cute—but I said, "See that big Mercury Marine outboard motor hanging off the back? That's killing the charm and romance of the scene. I'm looking for a quaint, simple rowboat. Just oars. No big engine. No plastic bottles lying inside. No radios. No plastic bags. Nothing that would give a hint to when it was taken." She totally got it and started looking for that charming boat with me. Now, of course, you can make great, very modern photos, but it's like putting a time stamp on your photo. When you compose your shot so you can't see modern signs or modern cars in the background, or things that time-stamp your image, you have an opportunity to take your viewer to a different time—one filled with charm and romance and opportunity. Plus, seeking this out is just fun. It's not always easy, but when you compose that perfect timeless scene, it'll be worth the extra effort.

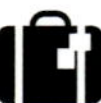
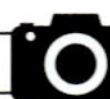

...Has Interesting Composition

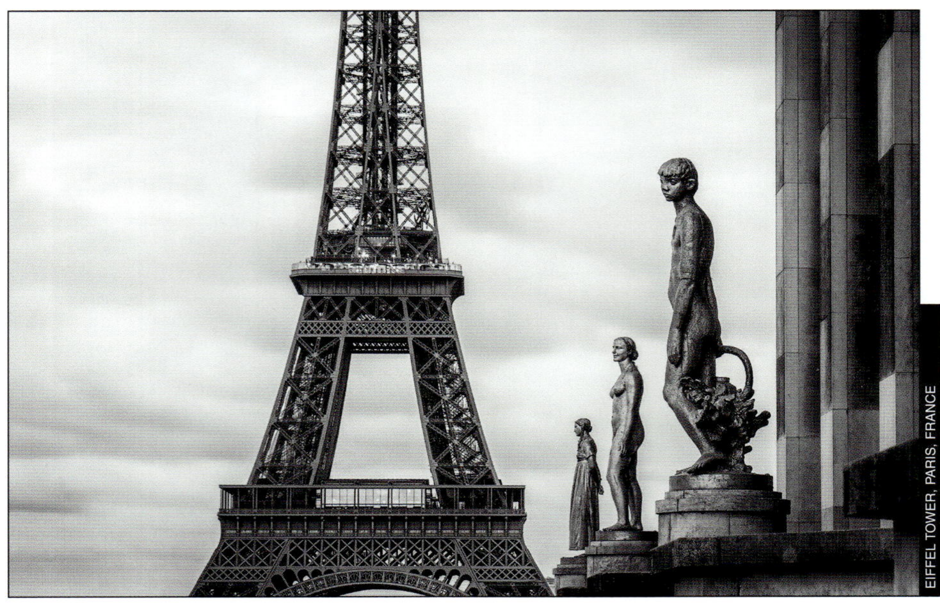

If I said to you, "Picture the Eiffel Tower in your mind," you wouldn't be like, "Uh, I'm not familiar with this Eiffel Tower thing." Nope, we've all seen it hundreds, if not thousands, of times in pictures and movies, and if I had to guess, I would say you pictured it shot from directly in front, seeing the full tower from top to bottom, with a blue sky behind it. Sound about right? That's probably exactly what you'd see if you looked up the Eiffel Tower on Wikipedia. In fact, hang tight—I'll go check it myself right now. One sec. Yup. That's it exactly (I seriously did just go and check. You can Google it and see for yourself). That's what I would call a "reference shot," and if you take that same shot, you're basically just documenting the fact that you were there. Nothing wrong with that. So, since we all already know what the Eiffel Tower looks like, does the world need yet another photo of the Eiffel Tower? Well…yes. We need one that's different. Instead of showing us another reference shot, you know what I would be interested in? How *you* see the Eiffel Tower. Maybe you love how the ironwork on the base looks, so you'd frame up only one leg, or you'd show a child running up its stairs, or the tourists crowding into one of its elevators. Maybe you'd show it as a background element in your image and not the main subject, or maybe you'd show its massive scale by showing someone looking up at it. There are so many different ways to compose the shot (up high, down low, showing only part of it, getting in close for a detail shot, shooting it from a rooftop or from across the river) that are all very different from that Wikipedia shot. My wife took a shot where the foreground is all flowers and the Eiffel Tower is clearly in the background, but kind of out of focus. That's how she sees it, and when I saw it, I thought, "Yup, that's how she sees it" and I loved it! Compose the shot in an interesting way. Show us something we've seen, but in a new and interesting way, and we'll love you for it.

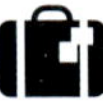
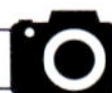

...Tells a Story

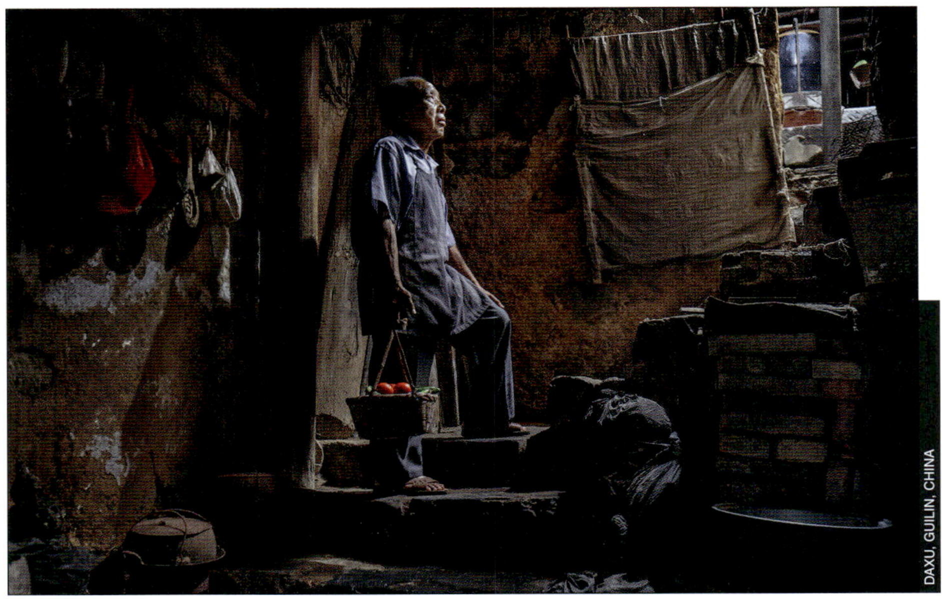

Who is this man? Where is he going? What's he carrying? Did he get what he's carrying down there? What's he looking at? Where is that light coming from? What's the story here? When the photo tells a story, it draws the viewer into the image as they try to quickly figure out what's happening there. If the image makes the viewer want to know more, you've nailed a storytelling image, and one of the Holy Grails of travel photography. Telling a story is one of the strongest things we can do with our images—it captivates the viewer, draws them in, and makes them want to learn more.

...Can Have Color as the Main Subject

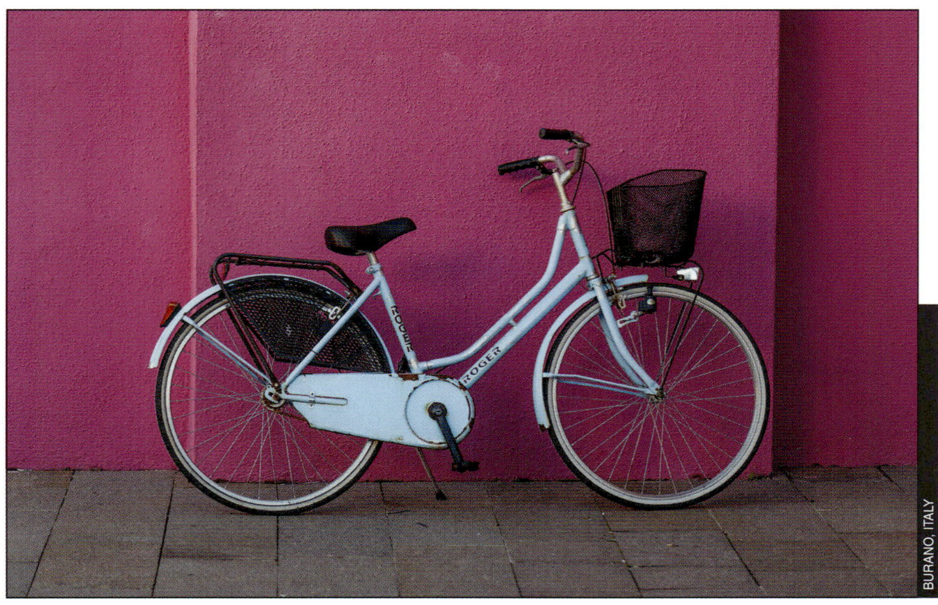

I love shots where the subject is color. At the heart of it, this photo is just an old bike leaning on a wall, but because of the bright, splashy colors, and the contrast of colors, there was no way I could walk by it and not take the shot. The colors are the shot! That's why you should keep an eye out for eye-catching color. I can't tell you how many images I've seen over the years that have won or been finalists in photography competitions where the subject was, or focus of the image was on, the colors. Once you start keeping an eye out for these contrasting color scenes, you'll be surprised how many awesome opportunities will pop up for you. By the way, this shot was taken on the island of Burano, which is just a short water taxi ride from Venice. The "official" story was each building was painted a different vibrant color to help the fishermen find their way home late at night in the fog, etc. The story as I heard it was that to get visitors visiting Venice to leave Venice and visit their island, the people living in Burano decided to paint everything in bright, vivid colors to make it kind of a tourist attraction, and I have to say—it worked! That's why I went to Burano—I heard it was the "most colorful place on earth," and that might be right. It's a color photographer's dream come true. Whichever story is true (a third version is out there, as well), I'm just glad it always looks like they just painted the place, and I love it! If you're thinking you might like shooting color as your subject, I'm not sure there's a better place to start.

...Can Be Very Simple

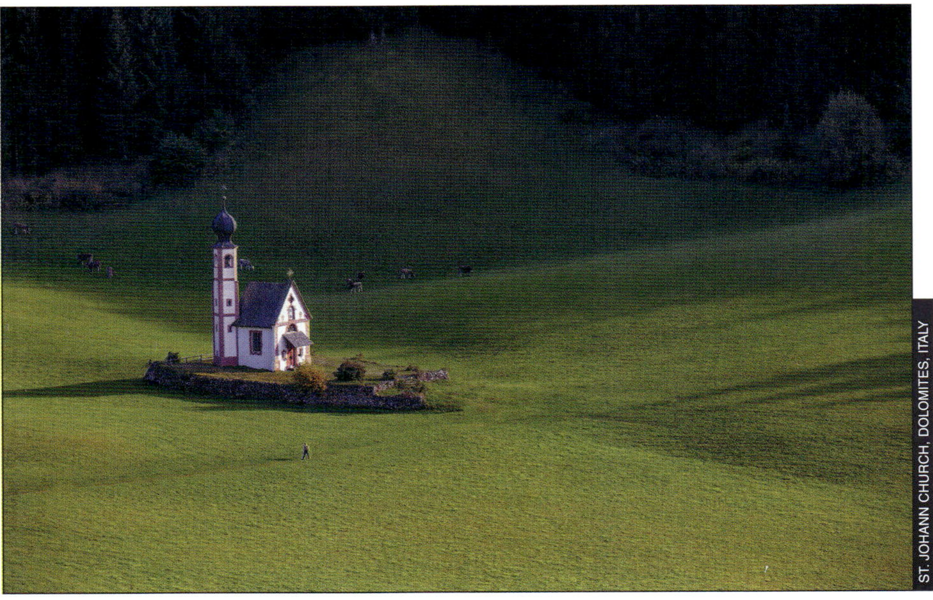

This is one of the most important concepts in the book, and one that can change the way you shoot forever, and it doesn't cost you a cent. If you want to make stronger, more impactful travel images, try to simplify the image. It's the whole "less is more" idea. I feel silly that I spent so many years looking through my viewfinder and thinking, "This doesn't look all that interesting," so I'd set out to find more things to add to an image to make it more interesting, and it rarely worked. That's because instead of searching for things to add, I needed to be looking to limit what was in my frame. What non-essential stuff could I leave out that would make this image stronger? That was the secret. I didn't really realize this until a friend and mentor told me to study the images of photographers I loved, and see if their images were busy and full of elements, or strong, simple, and clear. Son-of-a-gun, I was floored! It was right there in front of me all those years. I thought the secret was adding more, when all along it was showing less. When you only have elements that support the image, your message is stronger, your story is clearer, you've limited distractions, and it gives your image strength and depth. The famous artist Henri Matisse once said that if something in our image isn't adding to the image, it must be taking away from the image. He seems to have done all right with it. Anyway, this is such a huge, huge thing, and if you embrace this concept of simplicity, you'll come away with stronger and more interesting images.

...Shows Something Unique

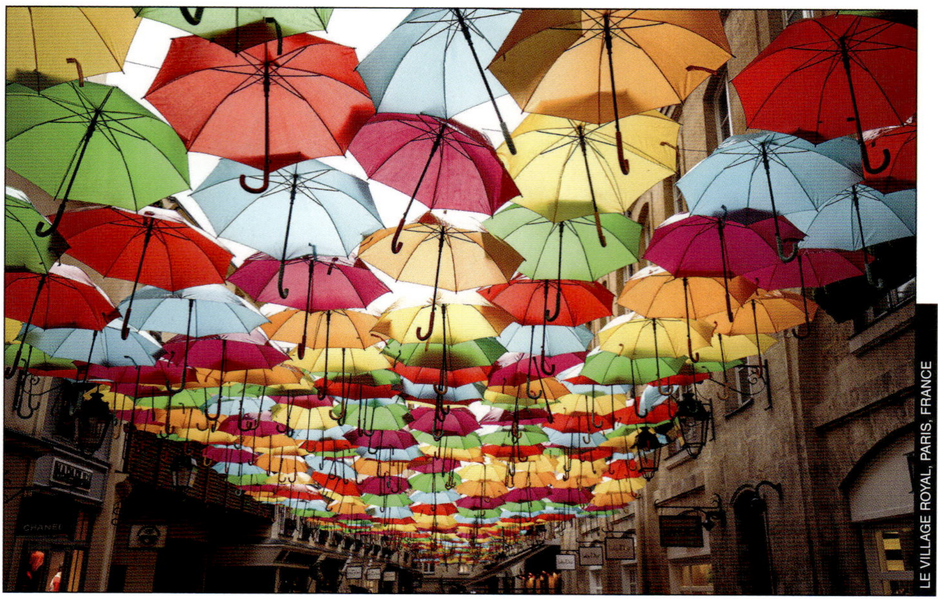

Anytime you can show something unique, something people don't see every day, like this street covered with colorful umbrellas, it has a good chance of being a winner. People love seeing things and places they haven't seen before, so if you can show them something like that, it just makes the image more interesting. It doesn't have to be mind-blowing to make a great shot, just something different or unusual—a bit out of the ordinary, and you're off and running. Now, don't fall into the trap that many photographers fall into thinking a scene is different or unusual just because it's in a different country than yours. Yes, a cobblestone street in a small village in Germany is very different than home, but that doesn't make it unique—there are lots of charming village streets all over Europe. Look for something really unique and interesting—not just something different than what we usually see every day.

...Can Have Interesting or Dramatic Light

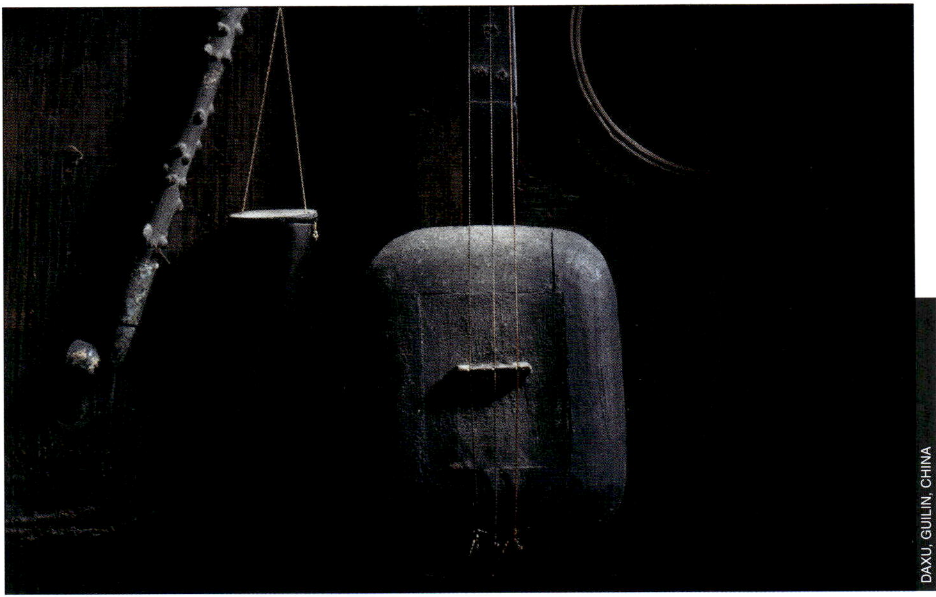

Light is so powerful that sometimes just a hint of it can create an interesting image, taking something very regular and making it look mysterious or exotic, like this musical instrument and tools hanging on a wall in a man's home in rural China. It was the light that caught my eye—it's just a hint of soft light streaming through a space in the tin roof above them, but that little bit of light created the drama and mood. These little hints of dramatic light falling on a scene are something you can always be on the lookout for while you wander through a city, because they're not as dependent on having an interesting subject. The light is the subject itself.

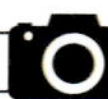

...Has Effective Post-Processing

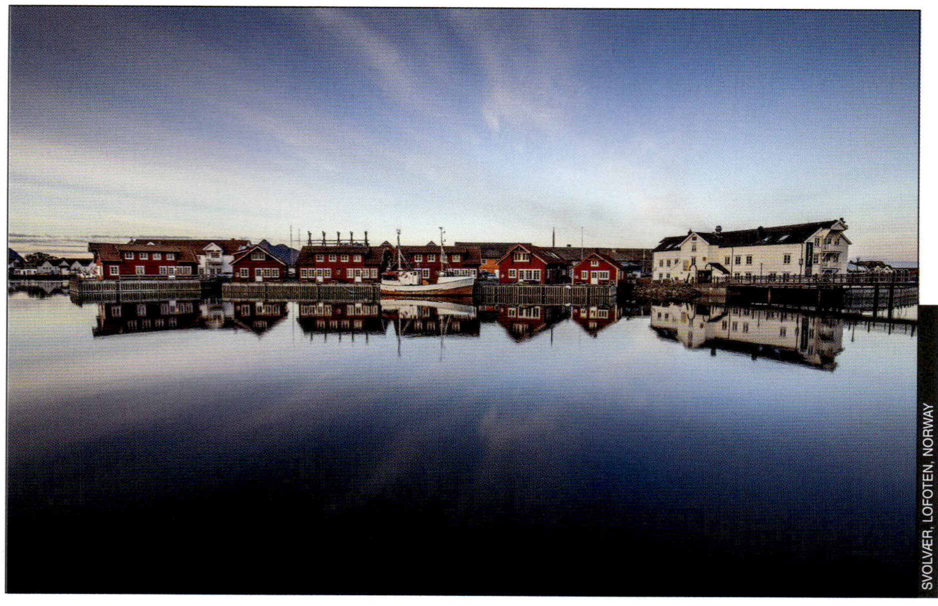

Shots like you see above don't come out of the camera like that. They're not nearly as sharp as what you see here (even if you're using a very sharp lens, which I was), they're not quite as colorful, and they don't have as much contrast or as much detail in the shadow areas. Great travel shots have the appropriate amount of post-processing. It doesn't have to go over the top, and you don't have to be a Photoshop shark to get great results, but you do have to know the basics of post-processing, and when you get those down, your images will come alive. They'll have that sharpness and dimension and detail, and you'll be able to make that shot—that is limited by what your camera's sensor can capture—look more like what it did when you were standing there. Heck, you might be able to make it look much better than it did when you were standing there, and that's great, too! Effective post-processing (that doesn't scream "I've been post-processed") can help you make the most out of your travel images, and all the top pros post-process their images. All of them—it's what separates us from the animals. Anyway, I'll try to help you down the road a bit in Chapter 12, which is all about post-processing, but our goal should be to, at the very least, make our images look at least as good as they did when we took them, if not better, and still leave the door open to artistic interpretation and experimentation if we're so inclined. That's a very stiff, formal-sounding last sentence, but you know what I mean. By the way, when you run into someone who smugly tells you, "I don't believe in post-processing my images," what they really mean is: "I'm not any good at Photoshop or Lightroom." I've never met anyone who was negative about post-processing that was any good at it.

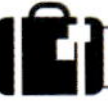
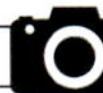

...Shows an Interesting Place

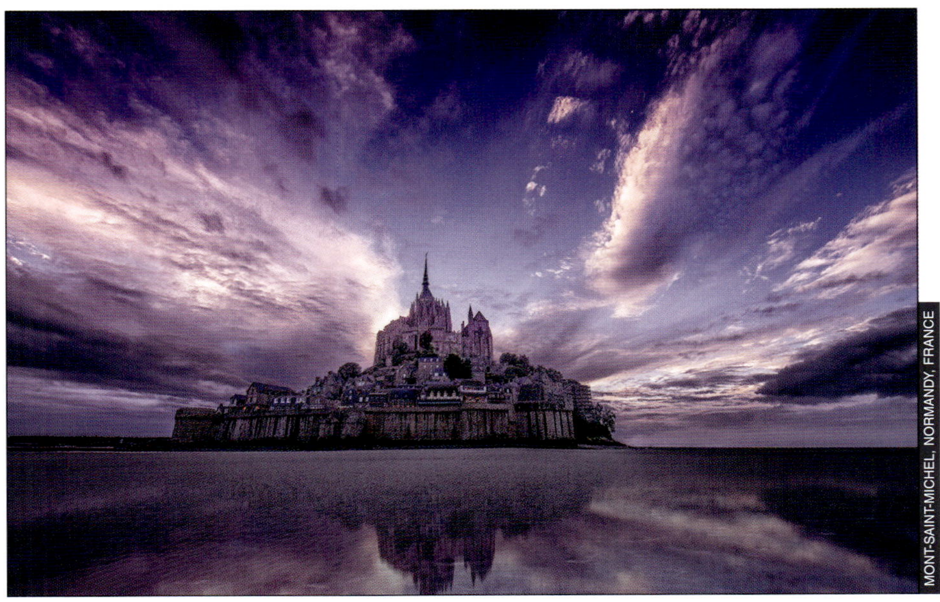

I'll never forget a quote I heard from photographer Joe McNally. We were teaching at a workshop, and Joe was on stage relating a story about something his photo editor (I believe at *Life* magazine) and editor said (I'm paraphrasing here): Joe, if you want to take more interesting pictures, stand in front of more interesting things. That right there—that nailed it, and it stuck with me all these years. We've all seen the Empire State Building. We've seen it to death, so showing me another Empire State Building shot, even one shot in great light, with great composition, probably isn't going to elicit a "Wow!" But, show me a shot of some place I've never been, or something I haven't seen before, and I'm fascinated. I remember the first time I saw a shot of the island you see above—that's Mont-Saint-Michel in France—I was so intrigued. I wanted to go where this was (how had I never heard of it before?), and then I wanted to figure out how I was going to get there to see it, and photograph it, myself. It took many years before I got an opportunity to go there, and I've only been there once, but I'll never forget the feeling of standing in front of something so unique on this planet. It looks like Disney built it for one of their parks, but there it was right in front of me, and I got lucky enough to have a fantastic sky show up, as well. When you can show something out of the ordinary, or something we haven't already seen a thousand times, you have the makings of a great travel photo. Show the viewer something new, something interesting, something that makes them say, "That's amazing! Where is that?" and you're on your way.

...Makes the Viewer Want to Go There

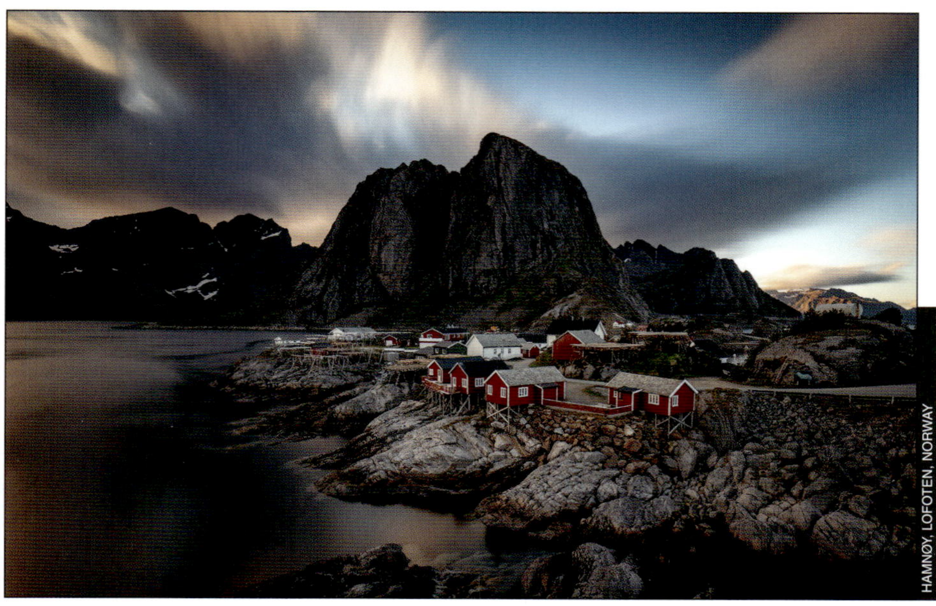

If you asked me what the #1 thing is that determines whether a travel photo is successful or not, it would be that a great travel photo makes the person viewing it want to go there themselves. It's exactly how I felt when I first saw a picture of the place you see above (which I later learned was in Norway's Lofoten islands, way up north in one of the least populated regions on the planet). The first time I saw that scene I wanted to go there. I was like "Wow—where's that?" But, I didn't want to go there just to take the photo you see above—I wanted to see and experience this incredible place (and we wound up having dinner in one of those little red houses you see above). I remember thinking to myself, "In this modern age, I can't believe places like this still exist" and that made me want to go there all the more. We planned a family trip to visit these islands (me, my wife, and my daughter), along with the rest of Norway (we had never been), and let me tell you, it was a massive pain in the butt getting there from our home in Florida. The trip included five flights (including one on a very old, very small prop plane), a bus, and a car, but we finally got there, and all that pain-in-the-butt stuff was totally worth it. I'd do it all again, even if I didn't take a camera, just to see it in person once again. That's the impact a great travel photo can have. If people look at your image and it inspires them to travel to that very location, and it captures their imagination, you know you nailed it.

...Has Motion or Action

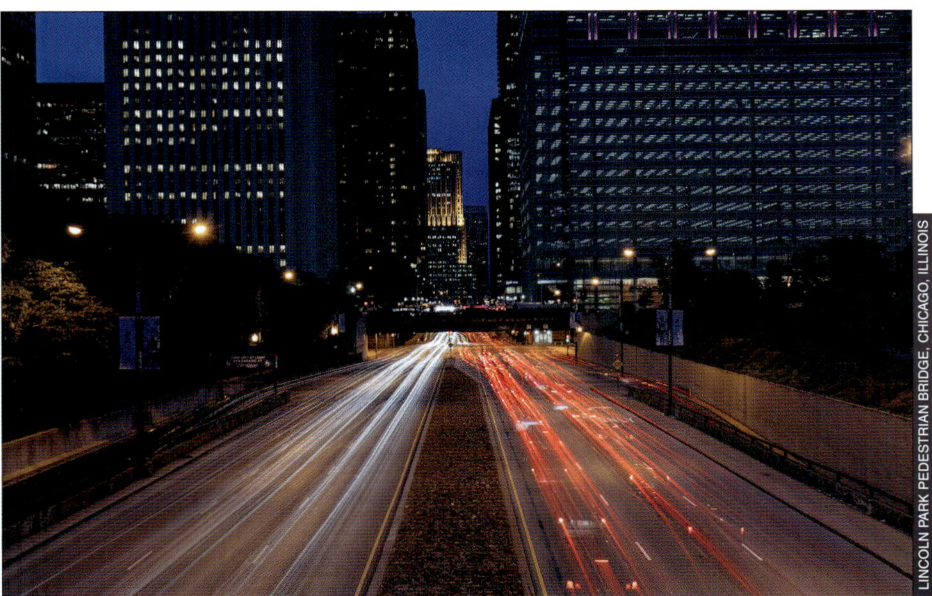

Anytime you can add some motion or action to your image, you have an opportunity to capture the viewer's attention. In this image, we have a long exposure (the shutter stays open a long time), taken while cars are whizzing down the highway. But, it could be anything from a small tuk-tuk (a tiny, three-wheeled taxi), to a kayak going down the river, to a horse and buggy trotting by, to kids playing basketball in the park. Freezing the action or showing the motion—they are additional tools you can use to help make great travel photos.

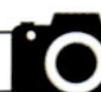

...Is Sharp

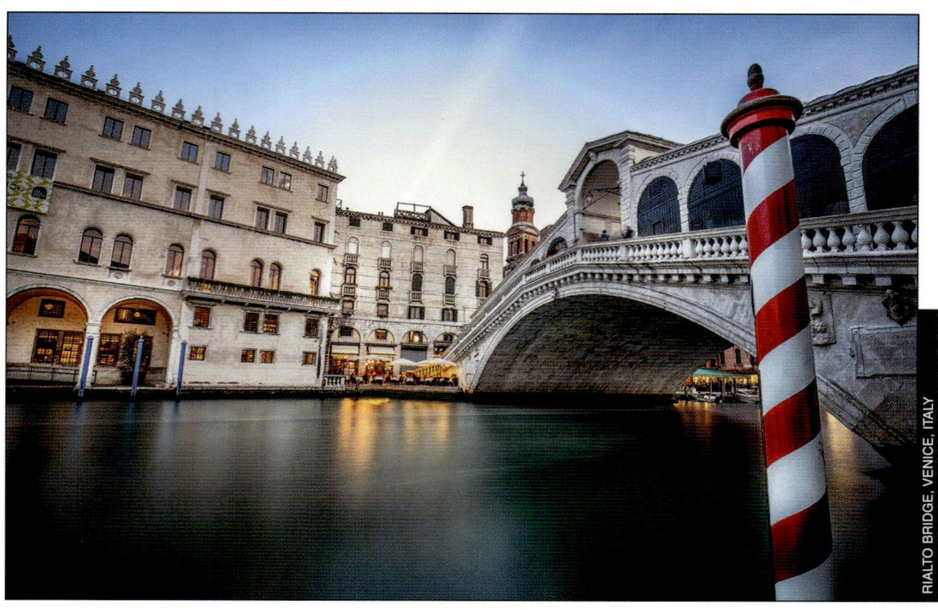

Great travel photos aren't blurry. The aren't "a bit soft." If you find yourself asking the question, "Is this photo sharp?" you know right then, it's not. Great travel photos can have a soft nature, like a foggy or misty morning shot, but they can't be out of focus. Take a look on Instagram at any of the great travel photographers there. Do you ever say, "Hey, that shot looks kind of out of focus?" Nope. They nail the focus because (say it with me), "Great travel photos are sharp." You might need to carry a lightweight tripod or a Platypod with you to get super-sharp travel shots when the light is lower and shutter speeds are slower (it's not really an issue shooting outdoors on a sunny day), but when you see how sharp and crisp your shots come out of the camera, you'll know it was worth taking that extra piece of gear. Now, you can definitely take a reasonably sharp photo and make it absolutely sharp as a tack by sharpening it in Photoshop or Lightroom—their sharpening tools are amazing (more on this in Chapter 12). However, if you start with a blurry photo, those programs will really only make it less blurry—they won't make them sharp and crisp. That starts in your camera.

...Has Limited Distractions

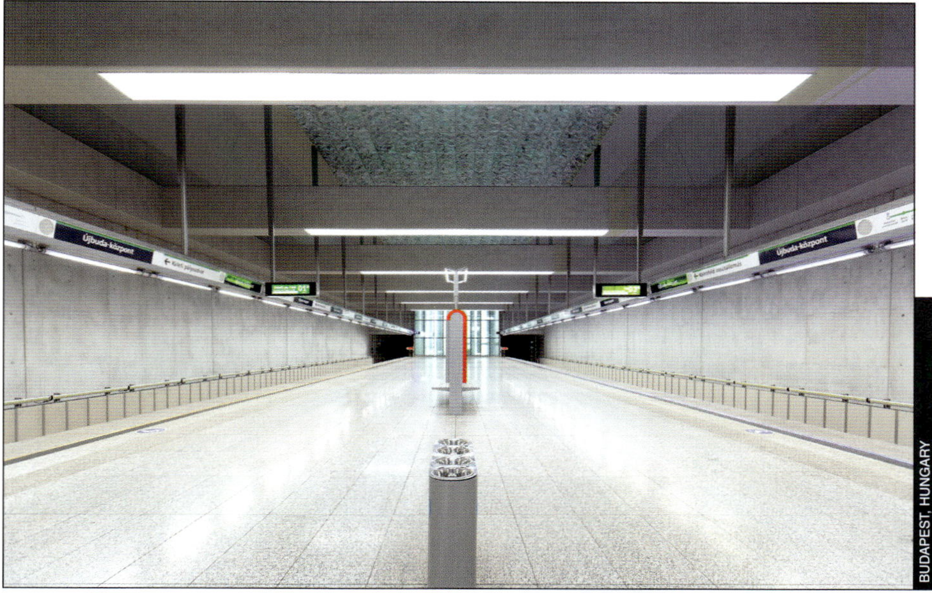

Great travel photos are clean, and don't have distracting things in the photo pulling the viewer's eye away from where you want them to look. There aren't tree branches sneaking into the sides of the image, or a beer can on the ground, or a big ugly trash can in the shot (this is a subway station in Budapest, Hungary. I had to wait patiently until there were no tourists milling around the platform, and we had to pick up some trash someone left on the ground, and I had to remove a few other distracting things in Photoshop. But, that's all part of the job of creating a clean travel image, with as few distractions as possible). Part of it can be achieved by how you frame the photo (aiming your camera to avoid distracting parts of the scene), part of it can be done physically (picking up some trash on the ground), and part of it can be done in post-production. Keep these things in mind—limiting those distracting things (often in the background)—and you'll wind up with much better, and cleaner, travel photos.

...Has a Straight Horizon Line

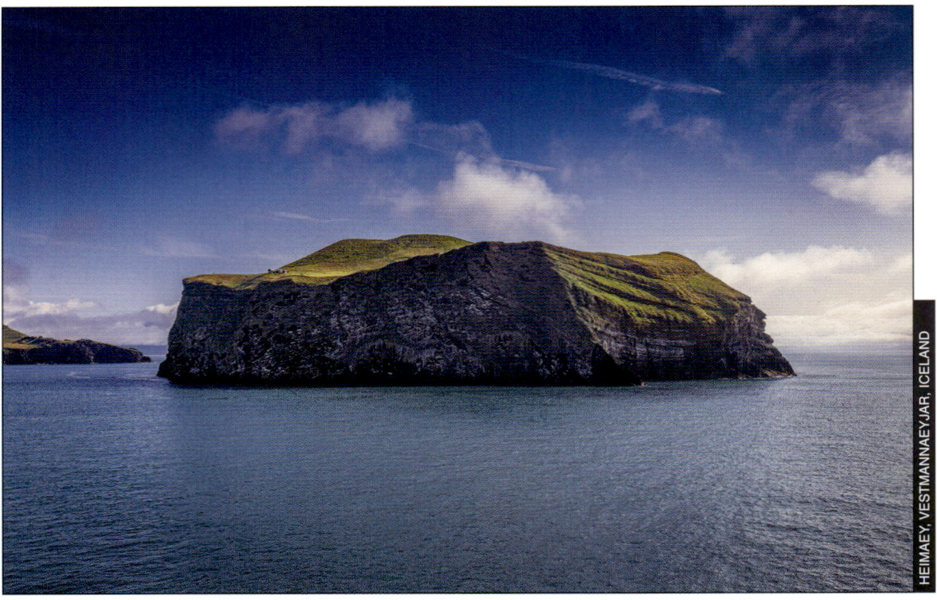

One of the most common mistakes I see in travel and landscape photography is a crooked horizon line, and yet it's one of the easiest to fix. A crooked horizon line is bad simply because it's so distracting. Ever been in someone's home or office, and the framed picture behind them on the wall is crooked? You can't enjoy the picture because all you want to do is jump up and straighten that darn picture. Well, a crooked horizon line is the digital equivalent and it ruins so many pictures. Sometimes, when you're out shooting, it is hard to get a perfectly straight shot—especially if you're hand-holding—but since Lightroom and Photoshop can both straighten your photo for you with just one click, there's no reason to have a crooked photo these days. Great travel photos aren't crooked. Fix that horizon line (before I walk behind your desk and straighten that picture on the wall myself. Well, I'd probably wait until you're out of the room for a minute, but as soon you're out of sight, I'm jumping up to fix it!).

...Has Color That Looks About Right

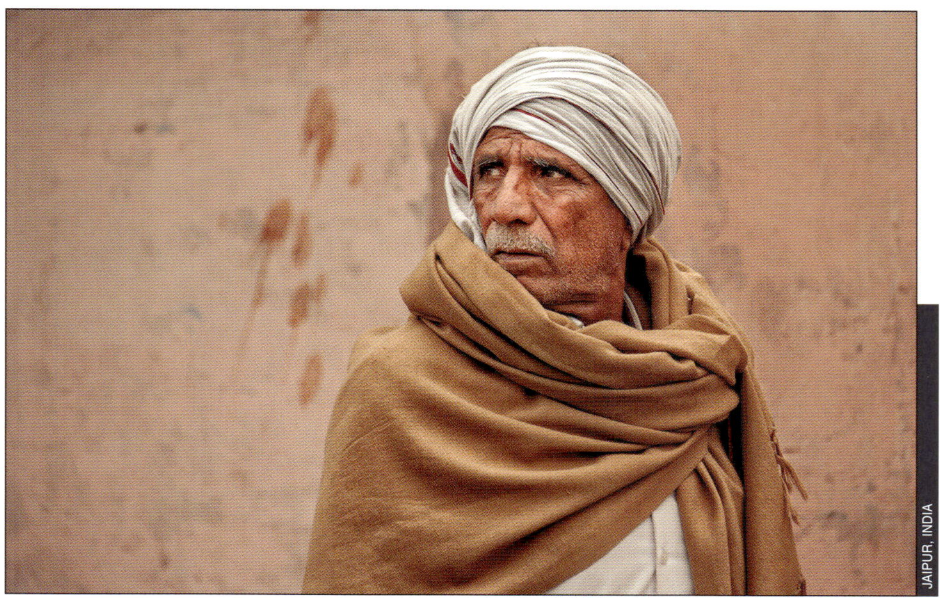

People in your photos shouldn't have a blue skin tone, but you'll see this often in travel photos. That's because when we shoot with our camera's white balance set to Auto (which works well in most situations), and our subject is in the shade or the shot was taken on a cloudy day, their skin tone, and the whole scene in fact, is going to look kinda blue. That is not a flattering look. When they want to make somebody look dead on a TV show or in a movie, they apply blue makeup, like their body has gone cold. You don't want that. You want your people and the scene to look alive. All you have to do is keep an eye on the color—not just for skin tone, but the overall color. Grass shouldn't have a blue tint and scenes shouldn't have a green tint to them or look too red. The fix is simple: to get your color on point, in your camera, simply choose the right white balance setting for the lighting situation you're shooting in (see page 48 on this). Great travel photos should have accurate color because if your color's not right...it's wrong.

...Includes the Human Element

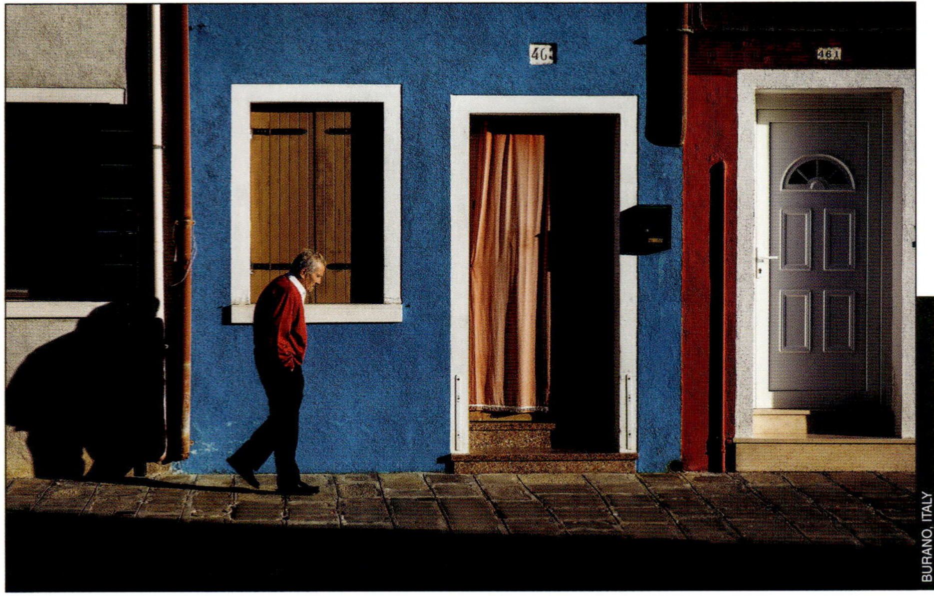

Don't come back from your trip with a bunch of photos of buildings, fountains, and monuments. Adding people into your photos, even if they aren't the main subject of the image, will not only expand the range of your travel photos, but it tells the viewer more about that location than just a static photo of a building. One of the reasons we love to travel is to learn about people from different places—to learn about their culture, their art, their lifestyle, and to learn their stories. If we don't include people in some of our shots (not tourists, if you can help it, but the locals), we're leaving out one of the most important aspects of any location and one of the reasons we love to travel in the first place.

...Can Combine More Than One of These

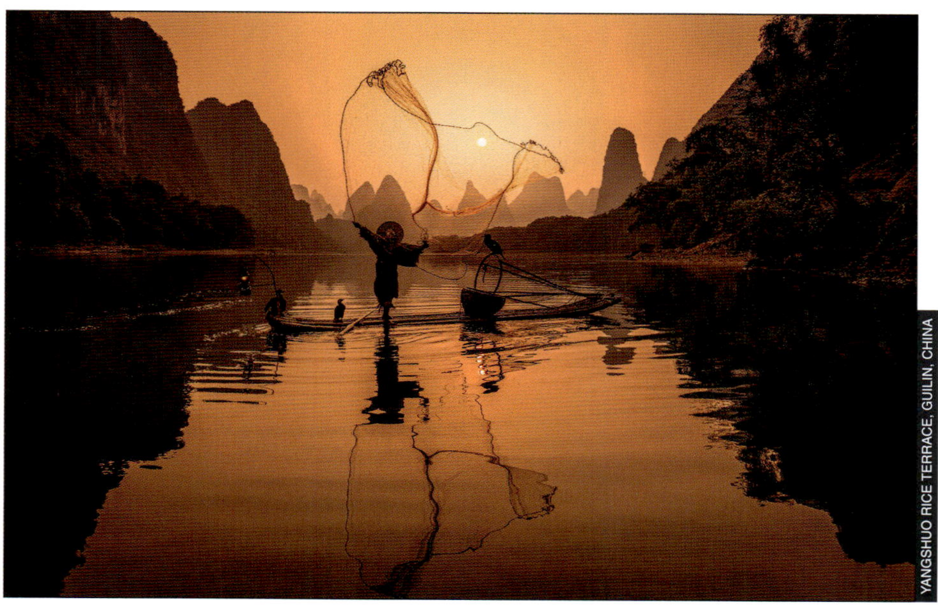

YANGSHUO RICE TERRACE, GUILIN, CHINA

Can a great travel photo be one where the subject is color? Yup. What about one where there's beautiful morning light? Absolutely. Or a human element? Sure. Okay, so as you've learned in this chapter, there are many things that make a great travel photo, but if you want to take things up a notch, how about combining some of these concepts in the same shot? Like a location taken in beautiful light, with interesting color, and you have one of the locals in the shot. Now you're creating even stronger travel photos. When you combine the things you've learned that make great travel photos, you're giving the image layers of things for the viewer to fall in love with. Take the image above. It has so much going on, all in one photo: great vivid color; it was taken shortly after sunrise, so the shadows are still somewhat soft; you've got atmospheric effects (the haze in the sky); and you've got the human element with a local fisherman casting his net (action) in a really interesting location with effective post-processing (I tweaked the white balance to make the scene warmer, and I added contrast, and then I removed any distracting things from the shot). When you combine these things, your image gets more depth and dimension and draws the viewer in.

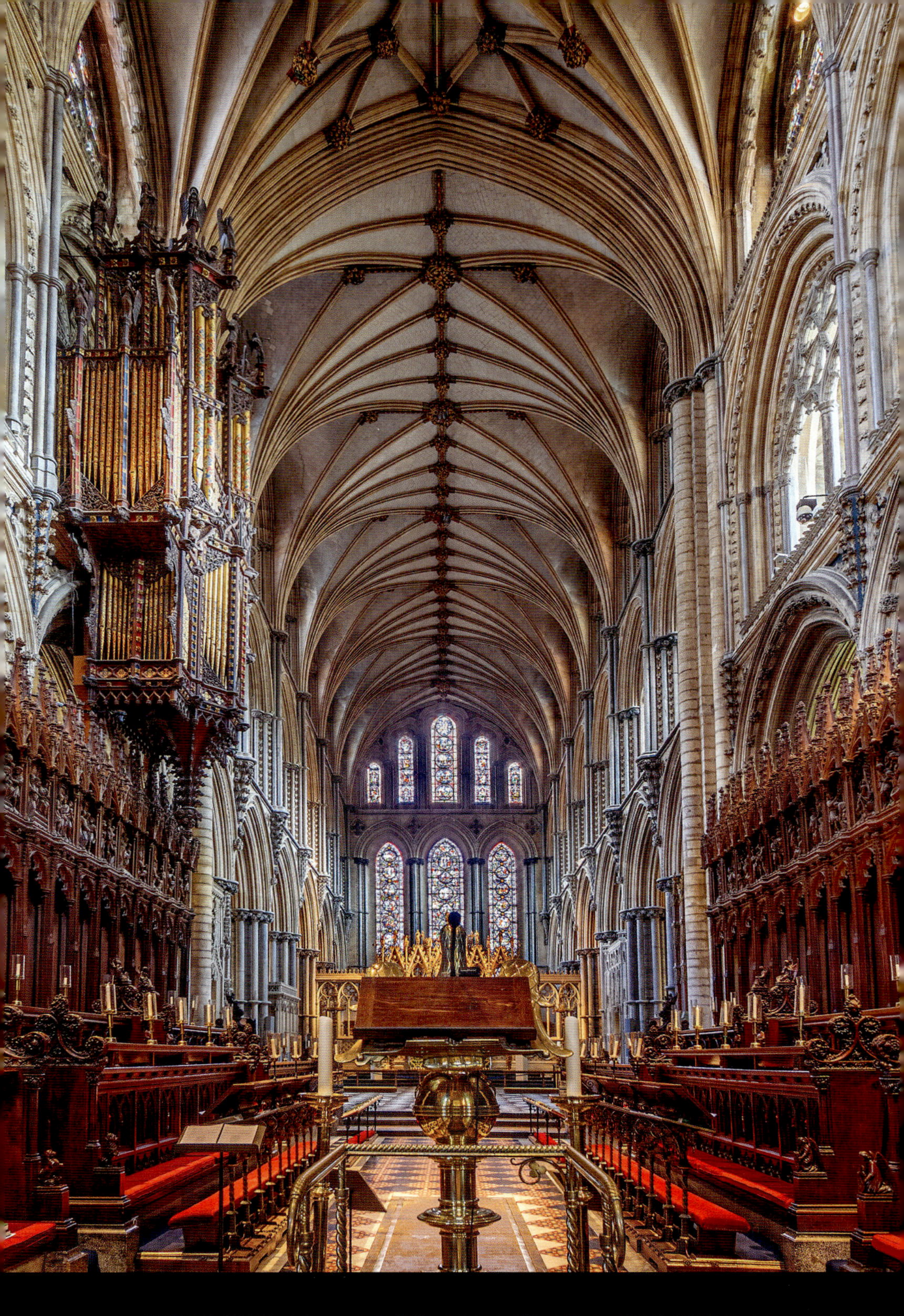

SHUTTER SPEED: 1.6 sec | F-STOP: F/11 | ISO: 100 | FOCAL LENGTH: 14mm
LOCATION: Ely Cathedral, Ely, Cambridgeshire, England

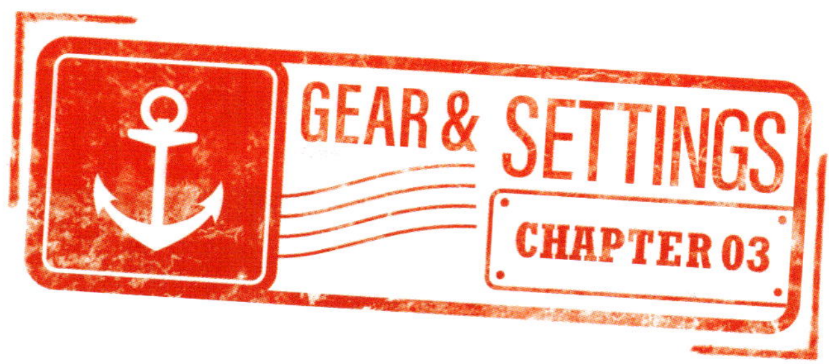

Gear & Settings

*What to Take (What to Leave Behind)
and Which Settings to Use*

When you're planning your trip, you might be tempted to travel light, with just a small camera bag and maybe one or two lenses, so you're able to take great photos and still enjoy your trip. You might be thinking how much easier and more convenient it would be if you didn't have to lug a bunch of gear around, and worry about it getting stolen, and how much easier hopping on and off of buses, subways, or trolleys would be. Heck, it would probably make your entire travel experience better and you'd still come home with some fantastic shots! But, what if you're on your trip—let's say you went to Vienna, Austria (make sure you try the McDonald's at Singerstraße 4. Their Big Mac tastes exactly like it does back home. Amazing, and totally worth the whole trip)—and you're taking photos of the Hofburg Palace, and you think to yourself, "Ya know, I could use a wider lens"? Yeah, then what, right? So, you'd better bring another, even wider lens, but then what if you see something far off, like the bell tower at Stephansdom, now what? Shoulda brought that longer lens, too. And, even though you did bring a backup body (just in case), what if that backup goes down? Then what? That's right, you'll need a third body as a backup to your backup. Well, it looks like you're going to need one of those big backpack-style camera bags so you can stuff it full with all your lenses and gadgets, and a ton of accessories. This is exactly what I recommend. Yes! Load that sucker up to where you can barely move once you hoist it on your shoulders, so at the end of each day of lugging that thing around, it has totally kicked your butt. Plus, it won't fit in the overhead bin on that one leg of your trip where you have to go on a smaller jet, so you have to gate check it, and then some of your stuff gets damaged, but it's okay because you have a backup, right? Yes, this sounds like a sensible plan. Let's totally go with this.

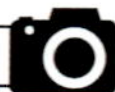

Which Camera Mode to Shoot In

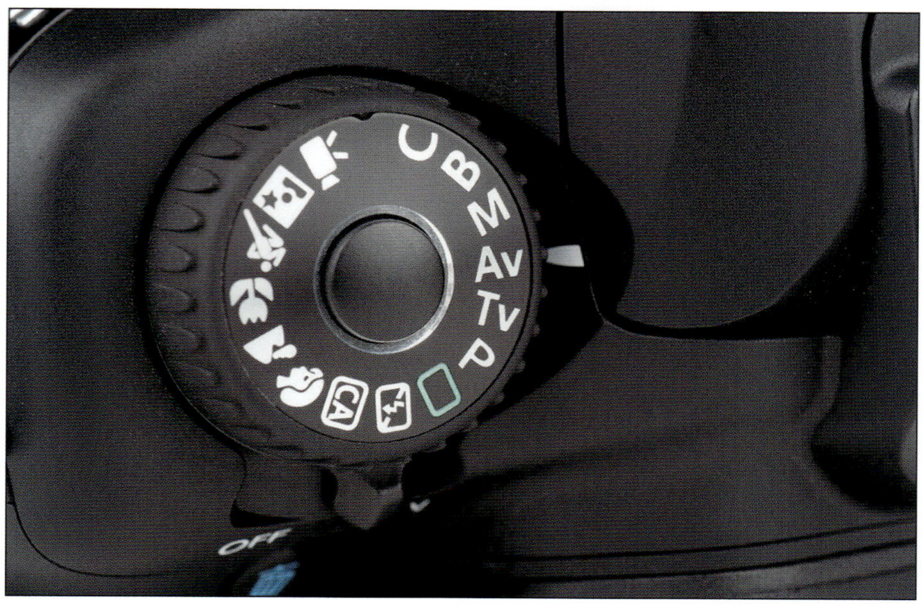

There is no official "right" mode to shoot in, but when it comes to travel, I always shoot in aperture priority mode (most of my pro travel shooting friends do, as well). On most cameras, if you have a mode dial on top, you would set it to A (not the green one that says "AUTO" or a green "A"—just "A") to shoot in aperture priority mode. On Canon cameras, you'd set the dial to Av. When you shoot in aperture priority mode, you choose the f-stop you want to shoot at, and the camera does the rest to get you a proper exposure. I love this mode because I only have to really worry about one thing (especially if I use the trick on page 46). So, I use one f-stop if I'm shooting travel portraits, and a different one if I'm shooting a cityscape or landscape, and my camera takes care of the rest. It's easy, it's efficient, and it leaves me free to get creative because I'm not messing with the settings a bunch. I don't change off of aperture priority mode at all during the trip—I set it before I leave, and I don't mess with it. I only change my f-stop—that's it (more on that in a minute).

Getting Sharp Hand-Held Shots

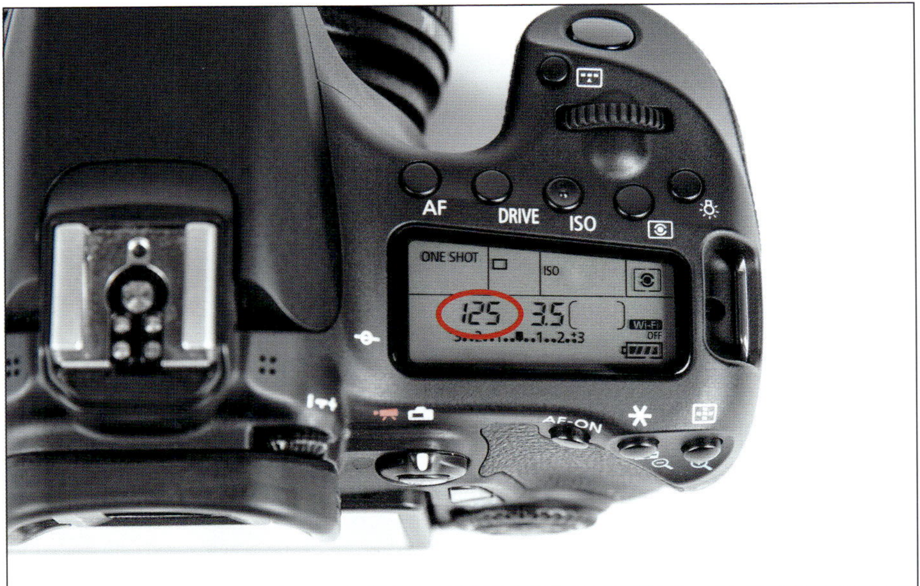

A woman once brought me her camera at a seminar. She was sure something was wrong with it because nearly all of her shots from her "trip of a lifetime" were either kind of, or really, out of focus. I looked at them, recognizing immediately what it was (it was heartbreaking to tell her). It wasn't her camera; it was her camera settings. When she was shooting outdoors in direct sun, the shots were sharp. Any other time (indoors, when it was overcast, in a cathedral or train station, when she was shooting in the shade, or in an alley, or a market, etc.), they were all blurry. In short, if it's sunny out, there's so much light that your camera uses really fast shutter speeds, which freezes everything (it even freezes movement from not holding it really still). But, when you shoot in less than bright light, it has to use slower shutter speeds, which means unless you're shooting on a tripod or you are an absolute wizard at holding your camera still (most folks aren't), you're going to have blurry, out-of-focus photos. So, how do we get sharp shots in lower light? We use a tripod (see page 65). But, that's not always convenient, and in many situations, it's simply not allowed, so we raise our ISO setting. This makes your camera more sensitive to light, which raises your shutter speed. How high do you need to raise your shutter speed, so you can hand-hold and not get blurry shots? For most folks, it's 1/125 of a second. You'll find people who can shoot at 1/60, and even 1/30, and still get sharp shots because they can hold their cameras incredibly still, but for most of us, our magic number is 1/125. So, start by raising your ISO to 200, then hold your camera up and look at the shutter speed in the viewfinder. If it's not to 1/125 yet, try raising the ISO to 400, 800, and so on until it gets there. Once there, you'll still need to hold your camera pretty steady, but you'll have enough shutter speed to freeze things even if you're not absolutely rock solid.

Insurance Against Blurry Shots

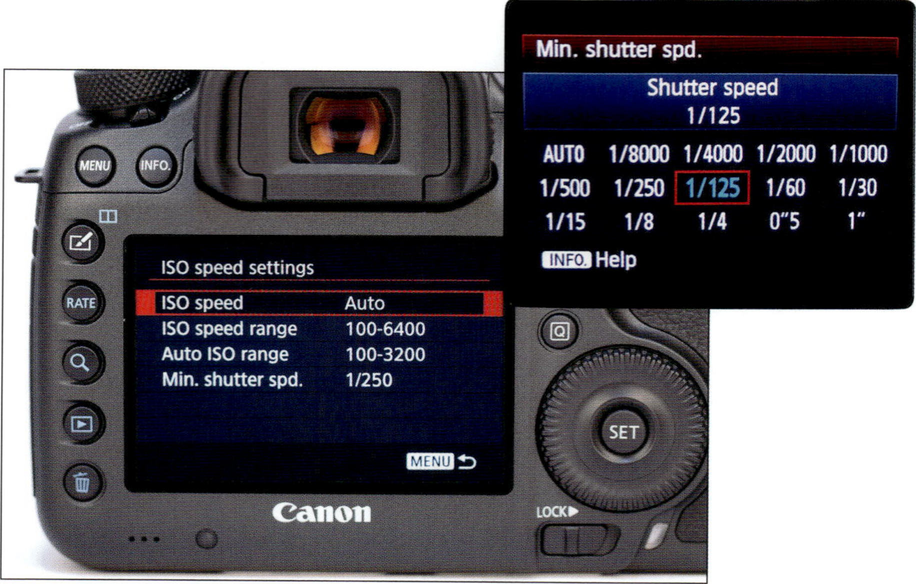

You just learned that you need to be at 1/125 of a second or higher to get sharp hand-held shots (well, most of us do anyway, right?). However, here's what's likely to happen: something really interesting or unusual happens while we're walking through town, and we quickly turn to capture the shot without actually looking to see if our shutter speed is high enough, and…we experience total heartbreak when we open that image later on our computer and it's soft (a bit out of focus). I've had it happen too many times. Well, at least I used to, until I turned this feature on that makes sure, no matter what, I never shoot a shot at below 1/125 of a second. It's called "Auto ISO" and when you turn this on, if you take a photo where your shutter speed would fall below 1/125 of a second, your camera instantly boosts your ISO to get it back to 1/125 of a second. It's brilliant, and it has saved my butt more times than I can count because I don't get any hand-held travel shots at 1/60 or 1/30 or 1/15 or slower. They're all at least 1/125. Turning this feature on is a simple two-step process: (1) go to your ISO menu and choose Auto, then (2) go to your Minimum Shutter Speed menu and choose 1/125 of a second, and now your camera won't take a shot slower than that. This means your ISO will be increased, which means you might have more noise visible in your image than normal, but if you have a choice between (a) a sharp shot with a little noise, or (b) a blurry shot with no noise, I think you'll take the sharp shot every time. Also, a bit of good news: unlike your ISO menu, where you can only choose 100, 200, 400, 800, 1600, 3200, and so on, when you use Auto ISO, it only uses the exact amount of ISO needed to get you to 1/125 of a second. So, if you look at the camera data after you take the shot, you'll see weird ISOs, like 140 or 365—these choices don't appear in the menu, but the camera can choose just what it needs to get you to 1/125 of a second. How cool is that?!

Which F-Stop to Use

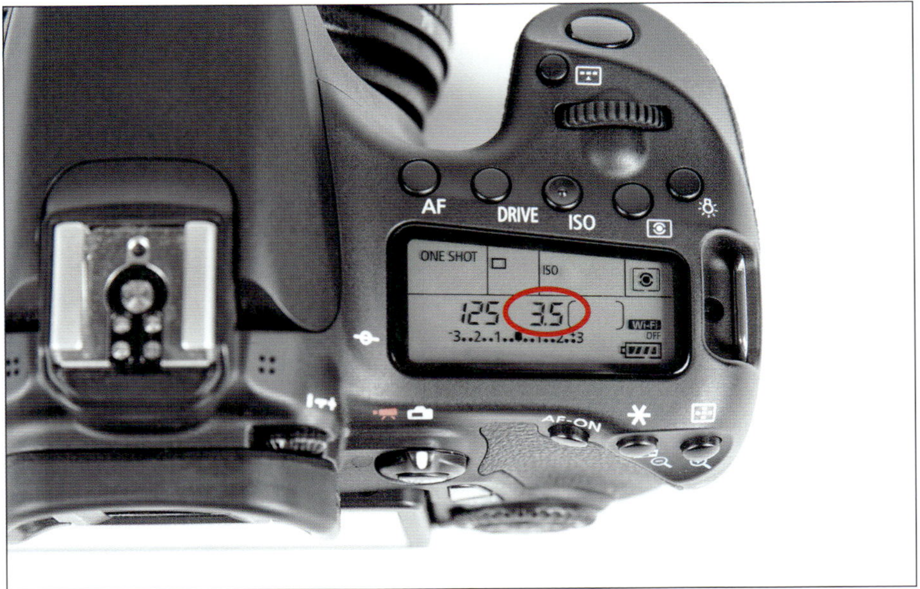

This is one of those things that photographers tend to overthink to death, but it's actually pretty simple because this is actually a creative decision you get to make. Let's say you're in a museum, and you see a stand with a beautiful vase on top, and you want to take a photo. The creative question is: "Do you want the background out of focus and blurry, or do you want everything behind the vase in focus?" There is no wrong answer here—it's totally up to you. Let's say you decide you want the background out of focus. Easy. You'd use the lowest-numbered f-stop your lens will allow, like f/2.8, f/3.5, f/4, or f/5.6. If, instead, you decide you want everything in focus behind the vase, you'd choose a high-numbered f-stop, like f/11 or f/16. So, since higher numbers put everything in focus from front to back, is that what you would use for cityscape or landscape shots? Yup. I actually use f/11 for all those types of shots where I want everything in focus. Well, why don't we use even higher numbers, like f/22 or f/32? While technically they should provide even more depth, there's a technical trade off that happens at those really high numbers that actually winds up making the images a bit softer. So, f/11 is my sweet spot, but some folks prefer f/16, and either one will definitely do the trick without a visible loss of quality. Okay, what if you're just walking around a town, shooting street scenes? Then, I would set my f-stop to my lowest number and leave it there. If I'm shooting wide with my travel lens, like my 24mm or 35mm, even with a low-numbered f-stop, everything will be in focus. But, if I see something interesting (maybe a flower) and I zoom in tight on it, that low-numbered f-stop will make the background behind it out of focus. I get the best of both worlds.

Getting Your Color Right

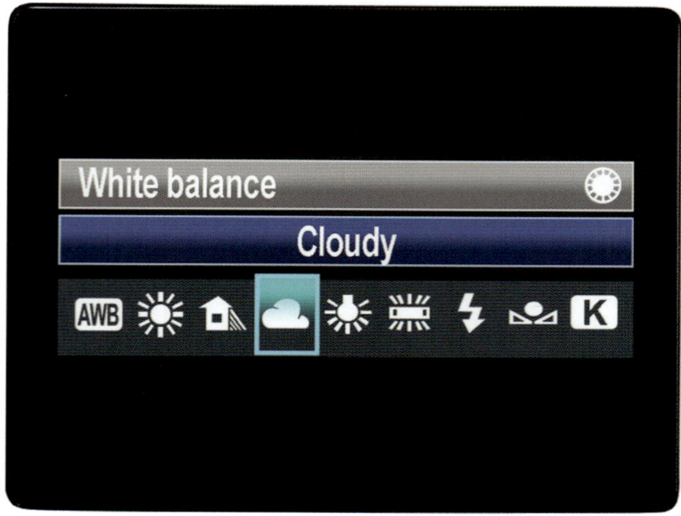

You don't want to get back from your trip and see that in lots of your photos people look kind of blue, or in indoor shots, everything looks really yellow. You want your color to be right, and most of the time just keeping your camera's white balance (it's what controls the color of your photo) set to Auto will do the trick. However, if you take photos on a cloudy day, or in the shade, or indoors, it fools the Auto white balance feature and you wind up with blueish tints if you shoot in the shade, or lots of yellow indoors, or even green in an office with fluorescent lighting. Luckily, fixing these color problems is easy while you're shooting (yes, in many cases, you can fix white balance problems later in Lightroom or Photoshop, but it's easier if you fix it now in-camera). If you notice your color doesn't look right, simply change your White Balance setting to match the lighting you're shooting under, and the secret to that is simply to look up. If you look up and you see tree branches or you're standing under an awning, choose Shade (your White Balance settings are in your camera's menu, but we use these so often that most cameras have a shortcut, using the buttons on the back of your camera). If you look up and see clouds, change your white balance to Cloudy. If you're shooting indoors, like at a restaurant, switch your white balance to Incandescent (Tungsten). In a factory or office, switch it to Fluorescent and it gets rid of the color cast from that lighting. Usually, this is all you have to do to get your color right all the time. So, what's the big thing to watch out for? Remembering to switch your white balance back to Auto once you go back outside. For some reason, the older we get, the harder it is. Not for me, of course, because I'm very young and youthful and youngish, but you know, other people. ;-)

How to Check Your Sharpness

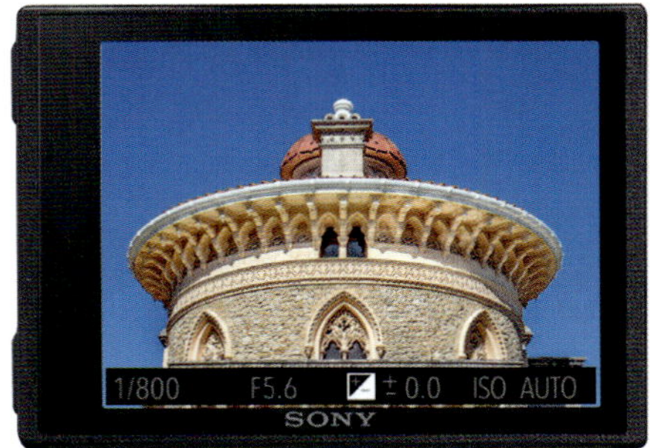

Normal View

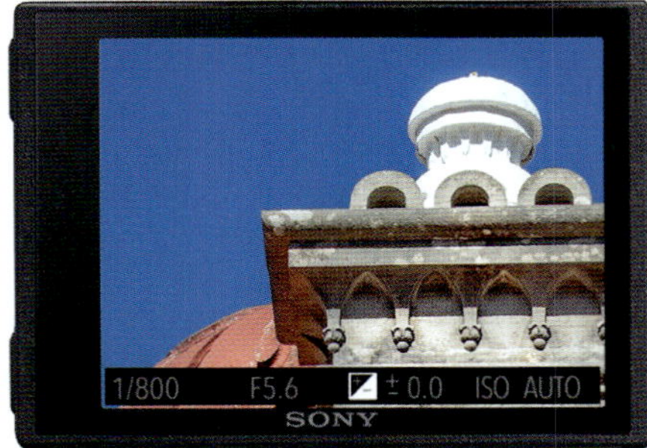

Zoomed In

Just about every shot looks in focus on that tiny 3" screen on the back of your camera, but then later, when you open it on your computer and see it at a larger size, the heartbreak begins because now it's too late—you're not at that amazing location, in that amazing light, while that amazing thing happened. You're looking at a blurry image and your heart just sinks. I would love to tell you this happened to me once, but sadly, it has happened to me many, many times. Well, that is until I learned to check my sharpness right then and there, while I was still standing in front of that amazing location, in that amazing light, while that amazing thing was still happening. You do this by pressing the magnifying glass button on the back of your camera, which zooms in on your photo, so you can check to see if the photo actually is in focus. Each time you press that button, it zooms in further, and then you can use the joystick or rocker switch (or whatever they call that dial on the back of your camera) to move around the image once you're zoomed in tight (for portraits, make sure you check the eyes—that's the part that has to be sharp!). Now, most cameras will allow you to set the center button on the dial on the back of your camera so it zooms in to any magnification you want, which is better than having to press the magnifying glass button again and again to zoom in, and then again and again to zoom back out. It's just one press and it zooms in tight; one press and it zooms back out. I set mine to zoom in to 8x magnification (check your manual to find out how to set your button to be your zoom-to-a-specific-magnification button when you're in playback mode). This is a biggie and it will make a difference (and save you from so much heartbreak. Well, the photo kind anyway).

Which Type of Lens to Use

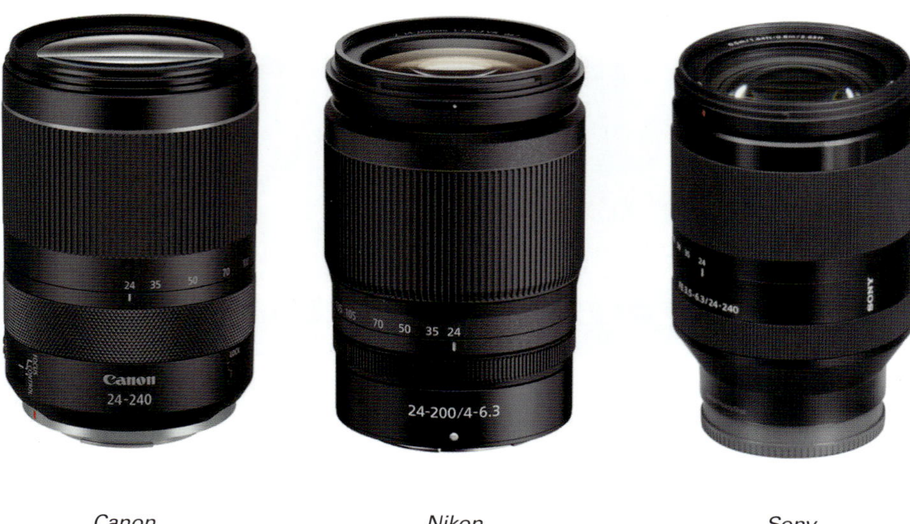

Canon   Nikon   Sony

If you and I were sitting at the bar, and you asked me which lens you should get for travel, I would, without hesitation, tell you to take just one lens. Take more than one, and you'll find this sad, sobering truth: whichever lens you have on your camera will always be the "wrong" one. You'll turn a corner and be like, "Oh man, I need my other lens!" So, you'll switch lenses to get that shot, then you'll keep walking and you'll see another shot, but (wait for it…) you'll think it would look better with the other lens, and now you're changing lenses again to take that shot. You turn the corner and…you see where this is going. I call it the "two-lens tango" and it's pretty brutal. However, if you have one lens that pretty much covers it all (from wide to portrait to telephoto), then you're not switching lenses—ever. In fact, you're not even lugging around a camera bag because you don't need one to carry your other lens. You can put a cleaning cloth in your pocket or purse, and if you need a filter, it'll fit in your pocket, too. Plus, they can't steal your camera bag because you're not carrying one. So, which lens would I tell you to buy? Either a 24–240mm or a 28–300mm. I prefer the 24–240mm because it's wider (Canon and Sony both make one), and you'd think that extra 4mm wider wouldn't make that big a difference, but it does. Plus, I can crop the 240mm to make it like I shot it with a longer lens. Just a small crop and I'm at a 300mm equivalent, but you can't make a shot wider, so I like the wider choice. If you're a Nikon mirrorless shooter, Nikon makes a 24–200mm that lots of folks like (I don't know why they didn't go to 240mm), and if you shoot a Nikon DSLR, they have an excellent 28–300mm (I used to have one when I shot Nikon—sharp, lightweight, and priced right). In short, if you have one lens, every-thing is easier, more convenient, you avoid the "two-lens tango," and you'll enjoy your vacation more without having to lug around, and worry about, that other lens.

When to Take Two Lenses

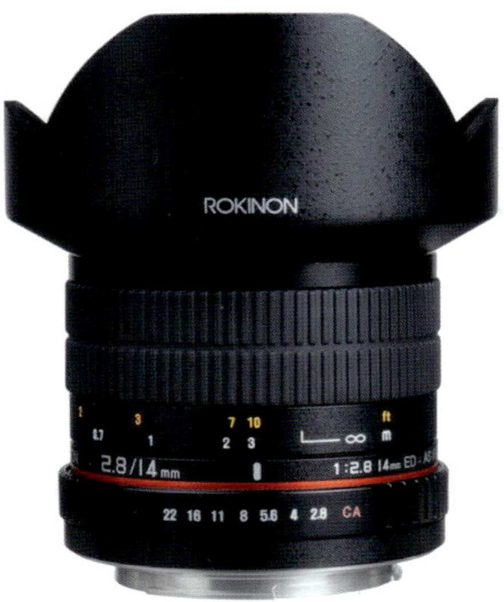

Okay, I will admit there may—*may*—possibly be times when a second lens is okay to take with you on a trip. So, what would be the scenario? Well, let's say that you're traveling to La Palma in the Spanish Canary Islands to shoot the Milky Way (it's supposed to be one of the top destinations for shooting the Milky Way). In that case, you'd need to take a specialized lens just for that (like the Rokinon 14mm f/2.8—a popular choice with Milky Way mavens). Or, if you're going to be shooting a particular interior, like an amazing cathedral or opera house, you might need something wider than a 24mm (like a 12mm or 14mm). In those cases, bringing a second lens makes sense, but it also ups the complexity of your trip because now you're carrying a camera bag (or a lens bag at the very least), and you have to worry about it getting snatched off your shoulder (oh man, I have stories), or leaving it somewhere, or dropping it or your lens (like I did in Lisbon, where I dropped my 70–200mm f/2.8 while changing lenses—it totally messed up the lens, with a repair to the tune of about $800). Anyway, I would need a seriously legitimate reason to haul another lens, and a bag, and all that entails, around anywhere. Now, if you're 24 years old, like my son, who can carry a packed backpack all day without breaking a sweat, all I can say is…that will change in time. LOL!!! But, for the rest of us, when it comes to lenses, less is more.

Picking the Right Focus Mode

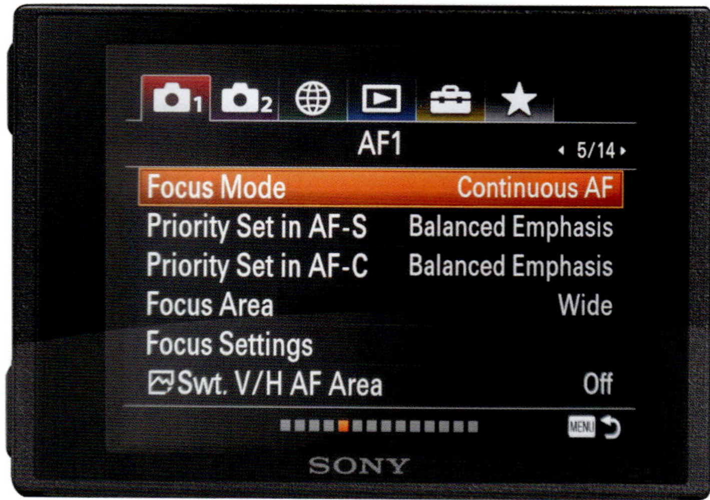

By default, your camera assumes you're photographing objects that are not moving, like a building, or your meal in a restaurant, or the person sitting across from you. This is called single focus mode (or something similar, depending on your camera's make and model). However, if you decide to shoot a moving object, like a taxi or tuk-tuk on a busy street, some horses running along the beach, or a bird flying by, you'll need to change your camera's focus mode to a mode expressly made for focusing on moving objects—not just focus on them, but automatically track along with the moving object. This mode is called "AI Servo" on Canons, "Continuous AF" on Sonys, and "Continuous Auto Focus" on Nikon cameras, and all you have to do is turn it on and it starts tracking the object as soon as you hold the shutter button halfway down. *Note:* While many cameras make an audible "beep" sound when you normally lock focus (letting you know it's locked on), when you turn on a continuous focus mode, it no longer beeps. Anyway, if your subject is moving, switch to this continuous mode. When you're done, switch back to single focus mode (these modes are found either in your camera's menus, or there's a shortcut button or dial on the back of your camera. To find exactly where, check the PDF version of your owner's manual).

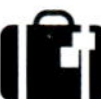
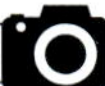

Turn Off Your Flash!

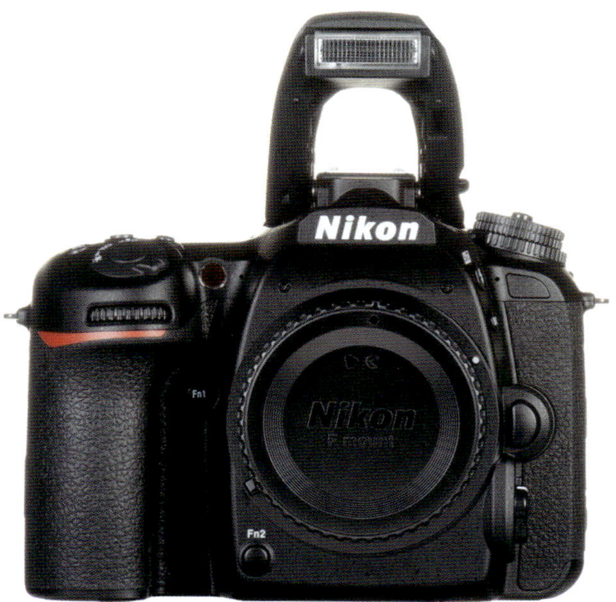

You know that pop-up flash you have on the top of your camera? You might think that's there for you to use. It is not. It's not to be used if there's not enough light. It's not to be used in an emergency situation. It's never to be used in any situation. It's trash. The only situation you should consider using that pop-up flash in is if you want to make your photo look as bad as possible, maybe as a gag. Better yet, if you see another photographer buddy leave their camera on the table when they go to the counter to get a coffee, pop up their flash, and take a quick shot of anything. They'll see the shot in their downloaded images and wonder if it's time to send their camera into the shop. Yes, it's that bad. Don't use that pop-up flash, no matter what, and you'll have better images.

An Easy Way to Brighten/Darken Your Photo

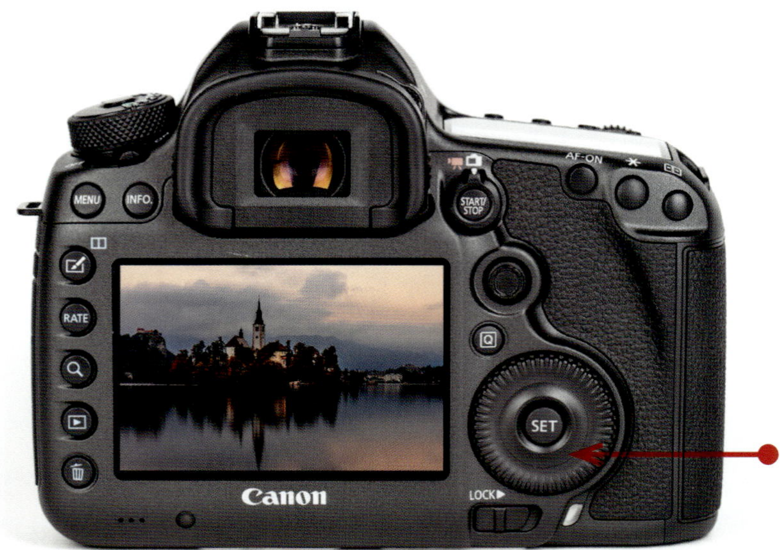

If you're out shooting and you take a shot that looks too dark to you (or too bright), there's a simple way to change the exposure. It's a dial, usually on the back of your camera, that controls exposure compensation, and it simply lets you make your image darker if you turn it one way, or brighter if you turn it the other way. This exposure compensation works perfectly if you shoot in a mode like aperture priority (like I do), where the camera makes the exposure for you. Once you take a shot, look at it on the back of your camera and if you think it's too dark or too bright, now you know what to do—move that dial, reshoot, and then look at the shot again to see if it's where you want it to be. If not, move the dial again, and try another shot. It's a process, but it's a quick and easy—and really important—one (especially if you get a highlight clipping warning, letting you know some parts of your image are so bright that there's a lack of pixels and detail. You can darken the image and retake the shot to see if that cured your clipped highlights issue). When I'm shooting travel, exposure compensation is a feature I use every day, all day.

Should You Shoot in RAW or JPEG?

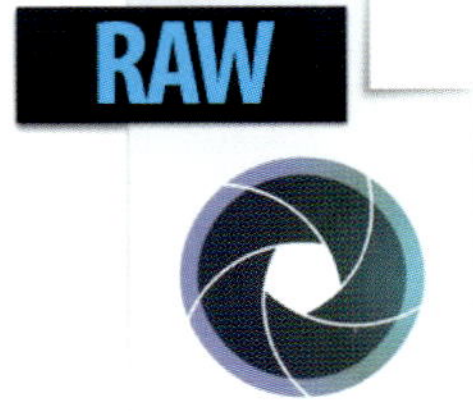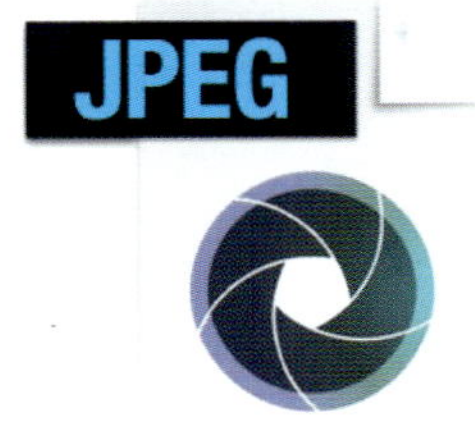

If an advanced user were to turn to this page, they might smirk and think, "Of, course, you shoot in RAW. No question," and that's because when you shoot in RAW your camera captures a greater range of tone (that right there is pretty big). Another advantage is that the RAW format is more forgiving if you're way off on your exposure and you need to make some big changes, or if you don't like your white balance, you can change it after the fact. There are a number of advantages, but those are the biggies. Now, shooting in RAW isn't for everyone because RAW photos don't look nearly as good as JPEG photos coming straight out of the camera. That's because when you shoot in JPEG, your camera sharpens your image, it adds contrast, noise reduction, color saturation, and so on. When you shoot in RAW, you're telling your camera to turn off all those wonderful things and just give you the flat-looking RAW image, and you'll add that stuff yourself in Lightroom, Photoshop, or a plug-in. That's great if you're really good at those programs, but if you're not really comfortable with your post-processing, then you might want to shoot in JPEG. The files look better (it helps if you nail your white balance—see page 48), they're sharper, more vivid, and you'll have much less to do in post, which some folks will forgo altogether because the images look pretty good. Plus, the file sizes are much smaller, so you can fit a ton more images on a memory card, and they take up less room on your computer, or iPad, or external hard drive. So, the decision comes down to this: If you're comfortable with your post-processing, I would shoot in RAW to take advantage of its benefits. If you're not comfortable with the post-processing end of things, shoot in JPEG and don't sweat it. Great images don't come from your choice of file format. Some of the greatest photos in history were shot in JPEG, including the covers of the biggest, most prestigious magazines.

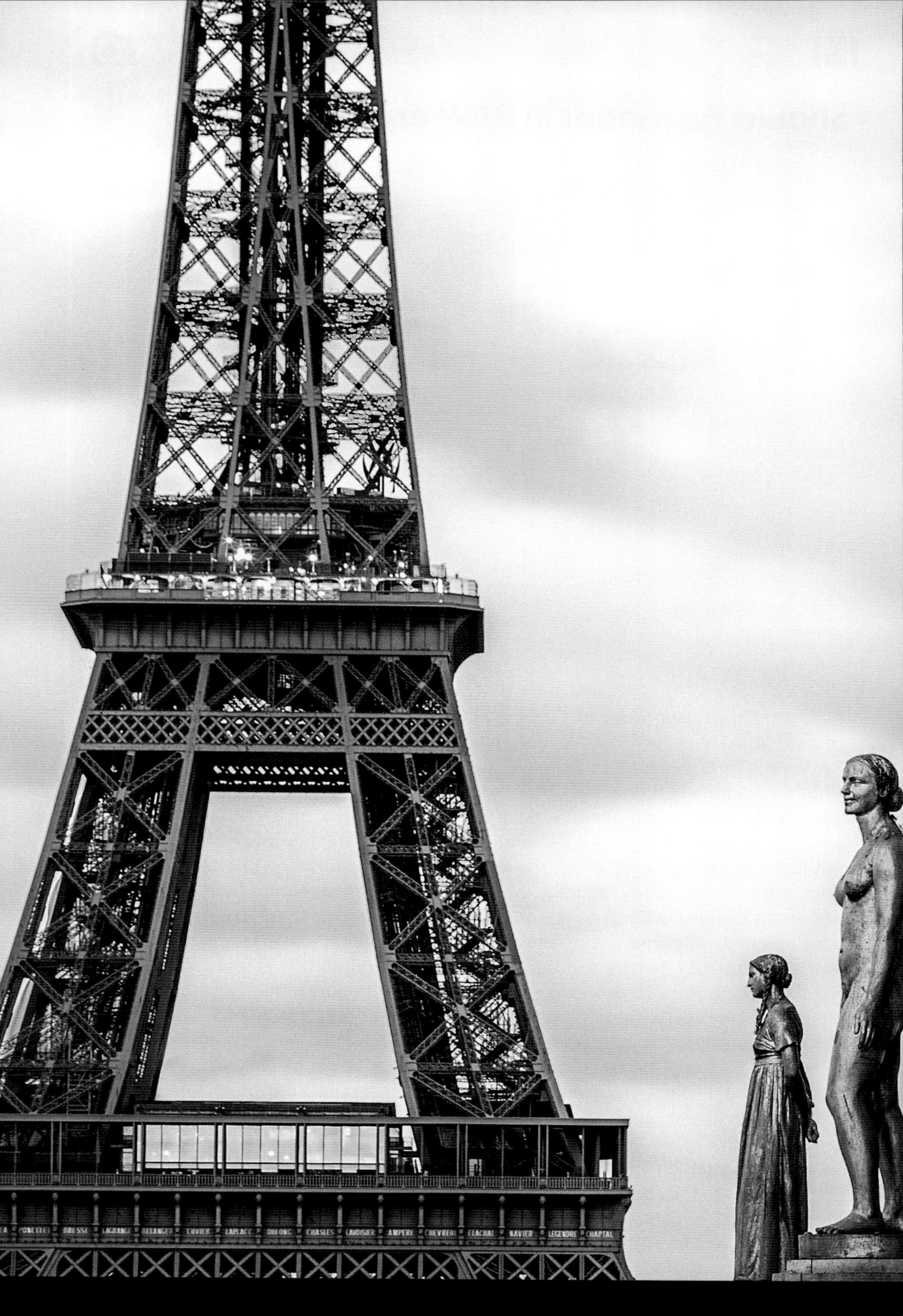

SHUTTER SPEED: 1.0 sec | F-STOP: F/11 | ISO: 100 | FOCAL LENGTH: 70mm
LOCATION: Eiffel Tower, Paris, France

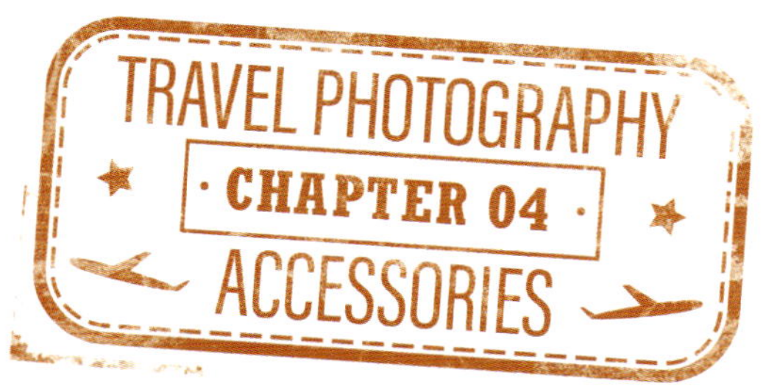

Travel Photography Accessories

Those Extra Little Gadgets That Can Really Make a Difference

You've probably already realized that I'm a big proponent of traveling light, but that's only because I've done so much of the opposite—I've flown to the ends of the earth carrying so much gear it would make Diana Ross say, "Okay, now that's too much stuff!" See, that's funny because Diana Ross is famous for traveling with a ton of outfits and bags upon bags, but I kinda get it when you're talking about Diana Ross because she is a living legend. If you get to Diana Ross's stature and you can't carry a ton of bags when you travel, what's the good of getting to that stature? She's got to "Go big or go home!" (a catch phrase my sports photography buddy Dave Black uses), but of course, that's easy for her to say (although I'm not 100% certain she ever said it) because she is an international superstar and I can't imagine that Diana Ross ever moves any of those bags herself. She probably has staff to carry all her bags for her, because if she had to move them herself, she'd probably say something like, "Okay, now that's too much stuff." However, if I were Diana Ross, not only would I have staff to help me move all those bags, I would have a special assistant just to hold my purse and stand near me at all times, similar to the military aide who accompanies the US president and holds a bag referred to as the "football," which was thought to contain the nuclear launch codes. In reality, the launch codes are on a laminated card carried by the president himself. The "football" is simply used to verify that the president is the real president, in case we are attacked and the president has to launch a retaliatory strike. As I was researching this, I ran across a great article in *Smithsonian* magazine talking about how one of the actual "football" bags is on display at the Smithsonian museum in Washington, DC, and when it was gifted to the museum and they opened it, they were shocked to find it packed with 10-stop ND filters, a cable release, a bunch of SD cards, and a lens cleaning cloth. True story.

Traveling Light Wins the Day!

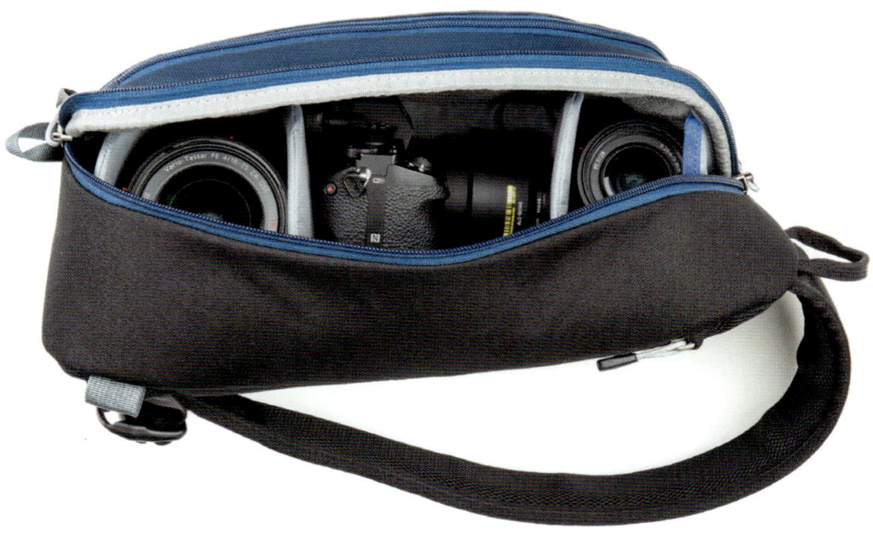

I used to lug large rolling bags of gear with me on trips, until I realized it wasn't actually making my photography any better—it was making my vacations worse. When I started traveling really light, I not only enjoyed the vacation more, I enjoyed the photography more because I wasn't lugging a bunch of junk everywhere (and worrying about keeping it safe). If I'm in a situation where I need to have a second lens with me, I carry a small sling bag, like the one you see above, which is the Think Tank Photo TurnStyle 10 Sling Camera Bag. It was made for making changing lenses easy—you swivel the bag in front of you, zip open the main pouch, and you can swap out your lenses easily. It has a number of pockets and it holds way more than you might think. In mine, I carry that second lens (up to a 70–200mm f/2.8), a Platypod Ultra and a ballhead, two ND filters, a cleaning cloth, and four backup batteries. That's all I really need. Plus, the bag slings safely across your body—kind of like a seat belt—not over your shoulder, so it's safer than a regular over-the-shoulder bag, which a thief can pull right off you as they run past (dislocating your shoulder in the process). It's really well made and cleverly designed all the way around. I love it!

Backing Up Your Images While You Travel

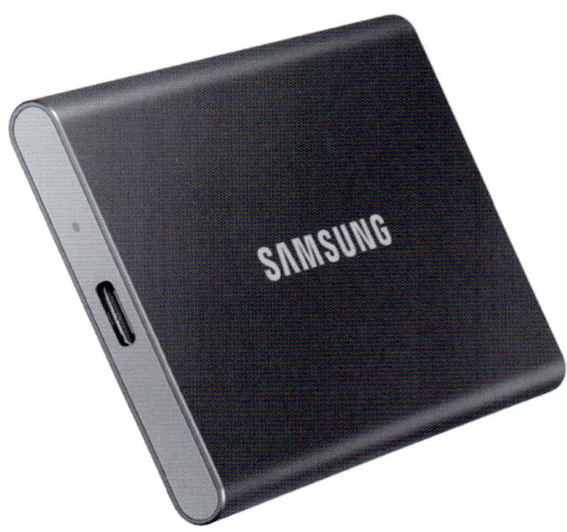

Can you imagine how heartbreaking it would be to travel to one of those "once-in-a-lifetime" destinations, take lots of great photos, and wind up losing them all? Your camera gets stolen or seriously damaged, or something technical goes way wrong, and all your shots are gone forever. I've heard sad story after sad story about folks who've lost most or all of their shots from a trip—they're just heartbreaking. That's why I'm pretty serious about my travel photography backup routine. Here's what I do: Every night, no matter how tired I am, I back up my images from my camera to an external hard drive, without fail. I also don't erase my memory cards because they act as a second backup for me (so I have one set of images on the external hard drive, and a second backup on the card). I take a lot of cards with me when I travel, but today's memory cards are so inexpensive (I just looked at B&H Photo and they have 32GB SD memory cards for $12). The good news is: external hard drives are so incredibly small and lightweight now (like the size of a pack of Dentyne gum), and you can get the same one I've been using for a few years now, the Samsung 500GB T7 Portable SSD for $79. It plugs into your laptop (yes, I take my laptop with me on trips, but it stays safely locked in my room safe), and it's very fast. Now, if you don't want to take a laptop, you can buy a hard drive with a built-in SD slot that can automatically back up your images for you (which I've done on several occasions). You just pop your card in it and it backs up the card's contents onto the drive, and you can even see the images using a wireless app on your phone (pretty cool, but the images display kinda slowish). I use the WD 500GB My Passport Wireless SSD mobile storage external drive. It's not as fast or as inexpensive as the Samsung I mentioned earlier, but at least you don't have to haul around your laptop.

If You Absolutely Need to Take More "Stuff"

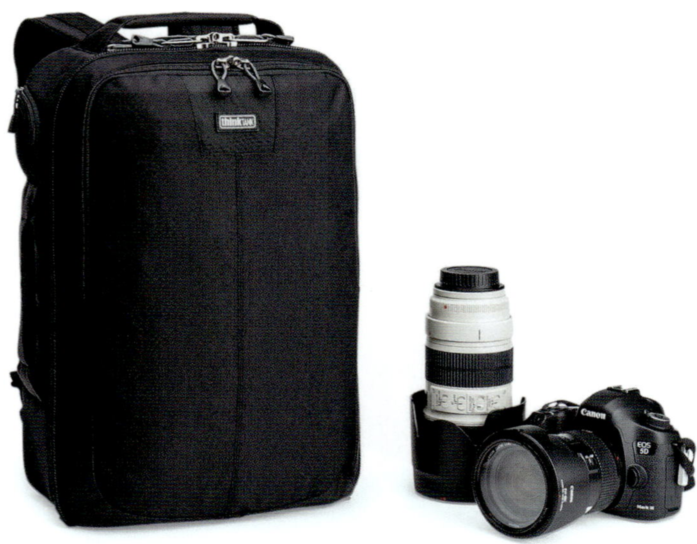

If you feel you just can't get down to a tiny sling bag for your trip, the next bag up in size I would recommend would be a small (key word here: small) backpack-style camera bag. I have the Think Tank Photo Airport Essentials Backpack, and it's not nearly as big as it looks in the photo above. It's actually quite small for a camera backpack, and it holds a bunch of stuff despite its relatively small size. It also fits in the overhead bins of even small commuter planes, so you won't have to worry about gate checking it in most cases. The only thing to look out for is that with a backpack, it's possible for a thief to walk behind you, open your backpack, and steal your gear, so make sure you keep a lock on it if you're in a sketchy area, any heavy tourist areas, or Barcelona (sorry, I had to say it). Outside of that (any time you carry a camera bag, you have to really keep a super-close eye out), it's the right size for those times when you don't mind messing up your vacation by carrying way more camera gear than you actually need (sorry, had to say that one, too).

You Might Want a Photo Vest

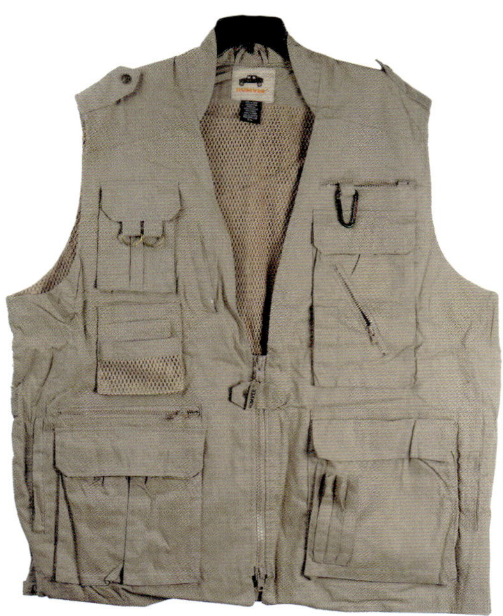

If you don't want to carry a camera bag, but need to keep a number of accessories with you when you're out shooting, like filters and cleaning cloths, batteries and memory cards, etc., you might want to consider a shooting vest. They have a ton of pockets with so much carrying room for stuff that the biggest issue you'll have is remembering which pockets you put your stuff in. They're fairly lightweight and comfortable, and they come in khaki, black (mine is black), and camo (don't get the camo for travel). Some of the most popular photo vests are from the Humvee line from Campco (they're around $50), so think of it as a camera bag without the bag.

Bring Spare Batteries

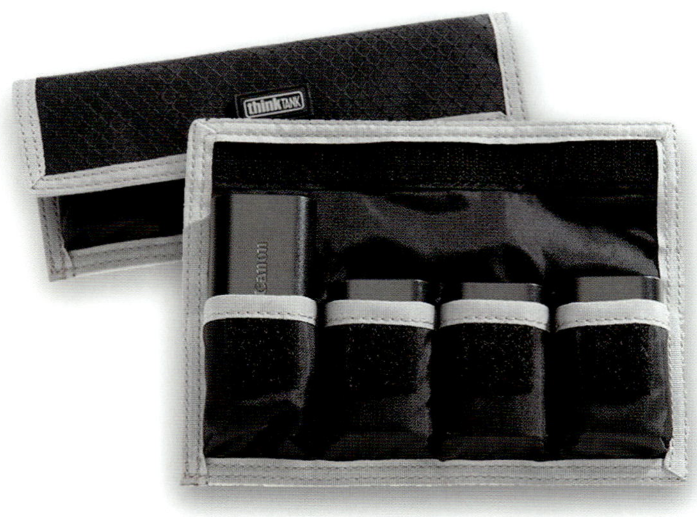

If you're off gallivanting (there's a word you don't get to use everyday) in some foreign land and your battery runs out, two things are likely to happen: (1) you'll spend the rest of the day searching for a camera battery that works with your camera, and (2) when you finally find one, the price will render you temporarily unconscious for two to three minutes. I've had to do this, and believe me, the throbbing pain in your head at the checkout counter will be something you'll always remember. So, take more batteries than you think you'll need (because batteries are now cheap too!). I travel with five camera batteries: one in the camera and four in a nifty little battery wallet, like the one you see above from Think Tank Photo (I know I sound like I'm sponsored by them or something, but I'm not—I'm just a big fan and have been using their gear for many years and swear by it), which is only $17 at B&H Photo. However, you can find a similar style battery wallet for around $8 online. Just sayin'. Anyway, I use the same method for managing batteries that you're about to learn on the facing page for managing memory cards, but the important thing is, don't run out of batteries (by the way, you can find rechargeable third-party batteries for most major cameras online for literally around $12 a battery, versus $60 or $70 each from the camera manufacturer. And, yes, they work fine—never had a problem).

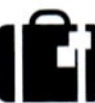
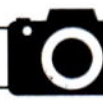

Memory Cards (and How to Organize Them)

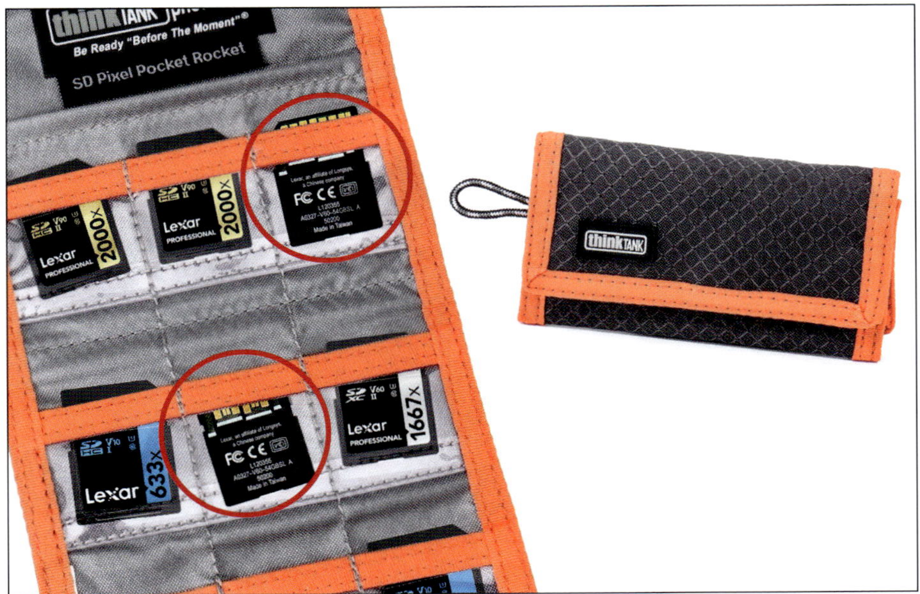

First, how many memory cards do you think you might need for a trip? I figure probably one 16GB to 32GB card a day. It depends on how much you shoot on an average day, and whether you're shooting in RAW or JPEG. A JPEG file is about 1MB in size and a RAW file is around 20MB to 30MB, so shooting in RAW will fill up memory cards faster. So, if you do shoot in RAW and you feel like you shoot a lot (1,000+ images per day), you might want to shoot on 64GB memory cards. The one thing you don't want to happen is the same thing you don't want to happen with batteries—you don't want to run out at the worst possible time and spend the day searching for expensive replacements. Memory cards are cheap now, so buy a bunch of them so you can use a new, fresh one every day (and leave the ones you've shot on untouched as backups of your images). There's a simple technique I use for keeping my memory cards sorted, so I know which ones are empty and which ones already have images on them that I don't want to accidentally erase. When I take a card out of the camera and put it in my card wallet (I use the Think Tank Photo SD Pixel Pocket Rocket memory card wallet seen above), I turn the card backward, so I can't see the label (as seen circled above) and know at a glance that card has been used, and not to use or erase it on the trip. I do the same thing with my camera batteries—I put used batteries in the wallet backward, so I know which ones are used, and which ones are fresh. Both of these help tremendously when you're racing to switch batteries or memory cards when something really cool is happening in front of you (by the way, memory cards and batteries have a way of going out when you need them most. I think they sense fear). Anyway, having a card wallet like this is more helpful than you'd imagine (this one is $16.75, but again, you can search online and find much cheaper alternatives that look and work pretty much the same).

My Go-To Camera Strap for Travel

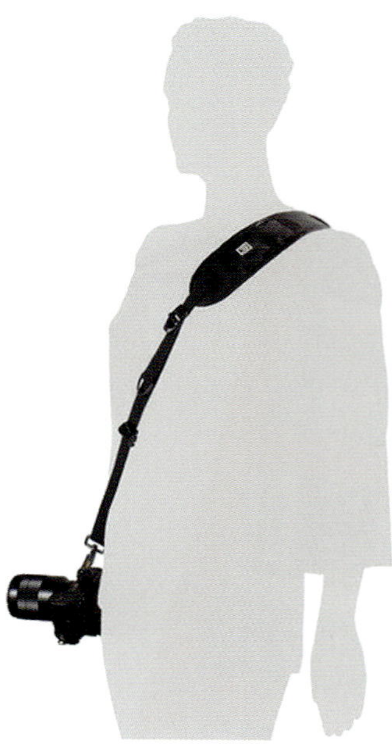

I use (and dearly love) the Black Rapid 10-Year Anniversary Edition Classic Retro RS-4 Camera Strap. It's my favorite camera strap ever (it's $64, but worth it) and one reason is safety. It goes across your body, like a seat belt, so someone can't just run by and rip your camera off your shoulder (it happens more often than you'd think) because well...you'd be going right along with them. But, there's another reason I love an across-the-body strap: your camera sits right at your side, so if you see something you need to shoot quickly, you just reach down and bring it straight to your eye. No having to take it off your shoulder first before you can shoot—it's awesome for never missing the shot. Plus, it has a little zipper pocket where you can keep extra memory cards or a battery (I put a battery in mine). Another benefit of this strap is how it distributes the weight across your body, so your shoulder doesn't get sore. It's a great strap—you'll super-dig it!

A Travel Tripod

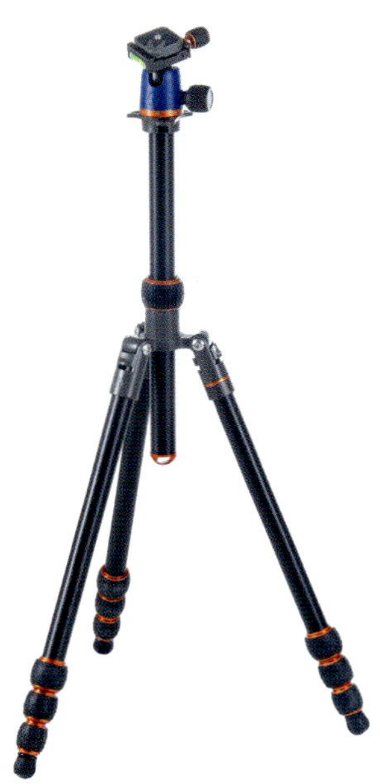

There are five times you really need a travel tripod: (1) When you're shooting at dawn or dusk, which are the ultimate times to get great shots of a city—the whole city is still sleeping and you're getting to shoot it bathed in beautiful light. However, that light isn't bright (which is one reason it's so beautiful), so you'll need something (a tripod) to keep your camera perfectly still in those low-light situations. (2) You're shooting an HDR image using exposure bracketing (see page 117). While you, technically, can hand-hold an HDR shot in some certain bright-light situations, it's much better if you're on a tripod to have the shots perfectly aligned with one another when they're combined. (3) You're shooting a long exposure, and your camera can't move—not a bit—while that shutter is open or it will trash your shot. (4) Almost anytime you're shooting indoors—this is a biggie—a palace, theater, museum, cathedral, small chapel, opera house, etc. And, (5) group shots where you want to be in the shot. Now, you can pretty much use any tripod for travel, but I recommend actually getting a travel tripod, which means it's super-small and lightweight (if it's not lightweight, after a day or so, you'll get tired of lugging it around, and it'll end up sitting in your room). The one I use is from British company 3-Legged Thing, and it's their lightweight, aluminum model, the Travis. It folds up really small, it's lightweight, and it comes with a pretty nice ballhead. They actually make a smaller one called the "Corey," which folds up even smaller and weighs less, but it doesn't extend as high as the Travis, which extends up to 65", so I went with that one. These are very popular, cleverly designed, and well-built, but the brand you get doesn't matter as much as having one, and having a lightweight one that folds up small. Some other popular travel tripods are from MeFOTO, Oben's AT-3586 tripod with BZ-226T ballhead, and Manfrotto's Befree GT travel tripod, which is nice, but pricey.

Or Take a Platypod Instead of a Tripod

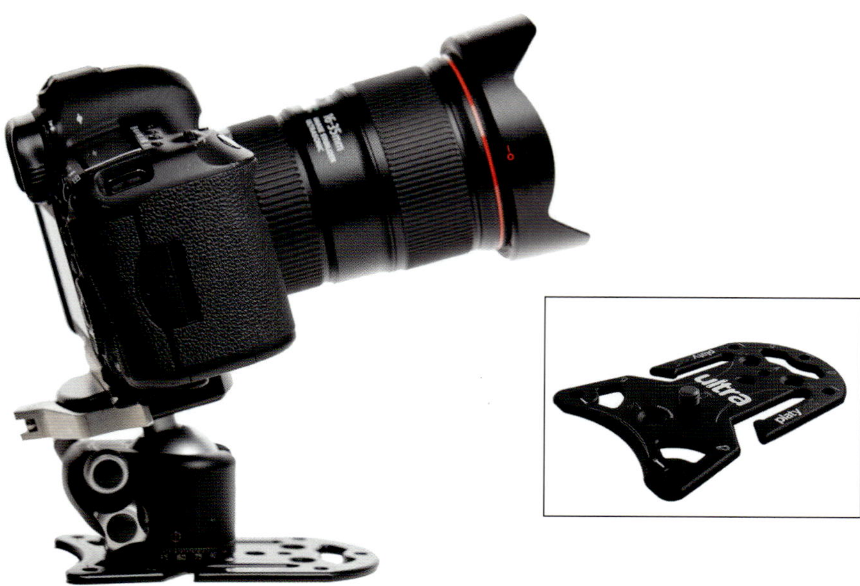

One of the big downsides to tripods is that in more and more places, they're simply not allowed (especially indoors). A number of monuments and attractions post "No tripods" signs all over and even if they don't expressly say it, when you set yours up, a lot of times, a security guard will come over and tell you they're not allowed. That's one reason why, for the past few years, my secret weapon has been the Platypod Ultra. It's kind of a tripod without legs because it's a super-solid base that holds your camera very, very still, so you can use it for long exposures and shooting indoors where tripods aren't allowed (in all these years, I've only been stopped a single time using one of these indoors. Security guards look at it and just walk right by). It's made of commercial aircraft aluminum, it's super-lightweight, but crazy sturdy (I've used it with my 70–200mm f/2.8 hundreds of times), and it's so small you can literally fit it in your shirt or jacket pocket. When you take it out, you screw a ballhead into the plate, put your camera on the ballhead, and now you can put your rig on the floor (which I do often, especially in cathedrals or palaces where I can use my wide-angle lens, since seeing the ceiling is important). It comes with metal spikes, in case you want to put it on some rocks or another unlevel surface, and it's made so you can strap it to a railing or a pole (I did this in Hallstatt, Austria, and it worked amazingly). You can not only use it in places where tripods aren't allowed, but you can use it in places tripods can't fit. Full disclosure: Platypod is one of the sponsors of my weekly photography podcast, *The Grid*, and I've become friends with its inventor Larry, who is a pediatrician and avid photographer. I don't get a kickback or a fee or anything if you buy one, but I can tell you they have fans all over the world who dearly love their Platypods like I do, for the same reasons I love it. You'll dig it, too.

Using a Tripod? You're Gonna Need a Ballhead

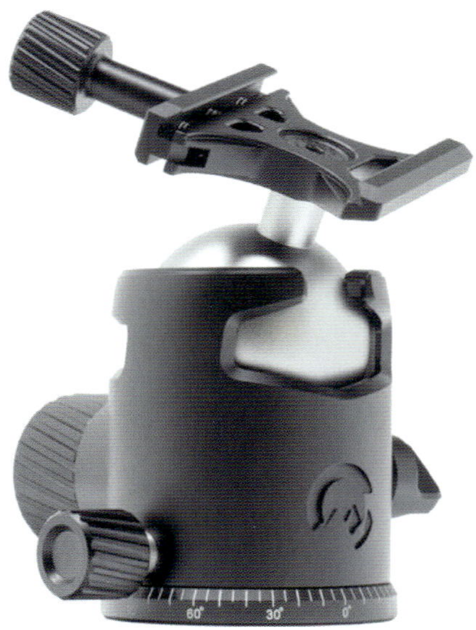

A ballhead goes on top of a tripod. It's the thing that goes between the tripod and your camera. Your camera attaches to it, and it's what you use to aim your camera. Without a ballhead, your camera would just aim straight ahead. You wouldn't be able to tilt it up and down—you'd screw it onto the top of the tripod and it would stay stuck there, so ballheads are an important part of this whole "keeping your camera steady" scenario. If you're buying your first travel tripod, you can find lots that come with a ballhead as part of the package price (like 3-Legged Thing's travel tripods), but if you don't get one included with your tripod…well…you're going to need to buy one. I have a number of different ballheads I've picked up over the years (some came with the tripods I bought). The one I'm using right now is really nice—it's from the Colorado Tripod Company, and it's their Highline ballhead. It works great on my tripod or on my Platypod Ultra, it's light, and it's really well made (especially for the price—around $129, which is pretty reasonable for a nice, quality ballhead because you can spend $650 on a ballhead without breaking a sweat. Well, I'd be sweating that my wife would find out I spent $650 on a ballhead, but you know what I mean).

Some Kind of Cable Release

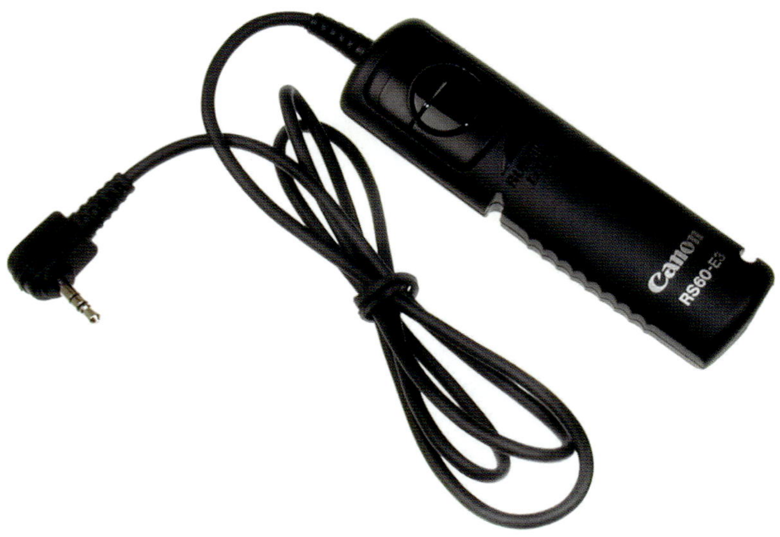

The whole idea behind a tripod or a Platypod Ultra is that it holds your camera absolutely, perfectly still. Any little movement, any minor bit of shaking while the shutter is open, and you'll wind up with a soft or blurry photo. You know what causes your camera to shake a little when it's on a tripod or Platypod? Your finger. When you press the shutter button, it literally shakes the camera a tiny bit—just enough to make sure you don't get a super-sharp shot. How do you get around this? You don't touch the camera. You use either a wireless shutter release or a cable release, which attaches with a cable to your camera, so you don't actually touch the camera, but instead, you touch the shutter button on the end of a cable that takes the picture for you without you ever touching the camera body itself. It's a must, must, must if you're going to use a tripod or Platypod. You can get name brand ones, like Canon or Sony or Nikon, but they cost a lot, or you can do what I do, which is buy a simple release—no fancy LED readouts, no long list of features, just a cable and button. Plus, it's small and super-lightweight, which gets lots of points in my book. The one you see above is the Canon version (for around $21), but most major brands make their own cable releases, and you can spend nearly $100 if you want. However, unless you have a particular need for more features (like you want to do time lapses and that feature isn't built into your camera), just keep it simple (and cheap). Also, besides releases that attach with a cable, there are also wireless remotes that are small and very lightweight, but make sure the one you buy works with your exact make and model of camera.

Shooting with an App Instead

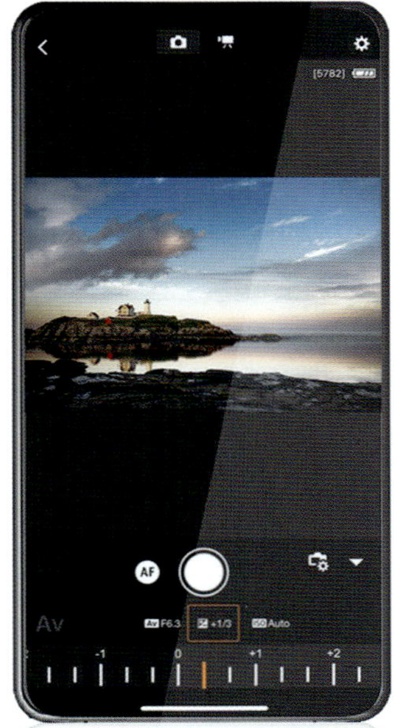

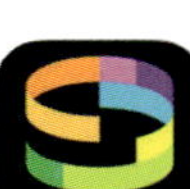
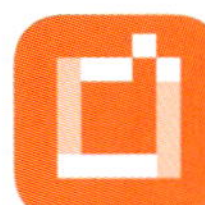
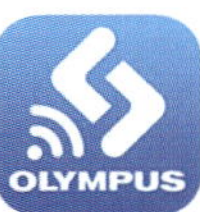
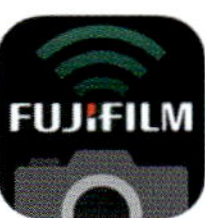

If your camera has built-in wireless and Bluetooth (most cameras these days do), here's something you might consider instead of using a cable release, as it has its own distinct advantages, one of them being it's free. That's right—F, R, double-E, free! You simply download the free app from your camera manufacturer onto your phone (a few are shown above), connect it to your camera, and now you can not only fire your shutter button wirelessly without touching your camera, you can change your camera's settings and even see a preview of what the camera's seeing right from within the app. Download them where fine apps are sold (or, well…given away in this case).

Why You Might Want a Polarizer

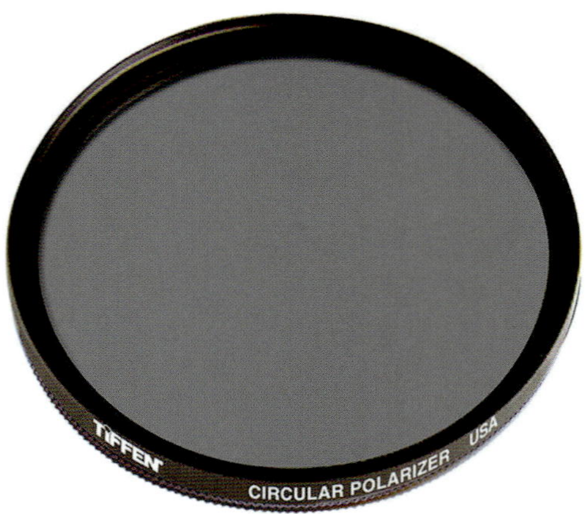

You might be wondering why you'd need to bring a circular polarizing filter on a trip if you're not going to be shooting landscapes. Say you're going to Berlin or Prague or Toyko, and you're thinking you're going to leave yours at home because you won't be shooting that many scenes with big skies, right? That's probably true—you won't be doing a lot of landscape-type shots (unless you head out to the countryside)—but that's because you're thinking of a polarizer as a filter that makes your skies bluer, instead of what it does for travel photographers, which is cuts reflections. It's brilliant at it, in fact—it cuts reflections in windows (including shop, store, restaurant, and car and bus windows), in water and metal, anything that reflects the sun, and it can come in really handy in so many instances. They're small, lightweight, they screw right onto your lens, and you don't need some crazy expensive one (you can get 'em for around $28 at B&H Photo). So, toss one in your bag because hey, ya never know, you might wind up shooting one of those big sky landscape images, and then you'll have a polarizer with you anyway.

An ND Filter for Taking Long Exposures

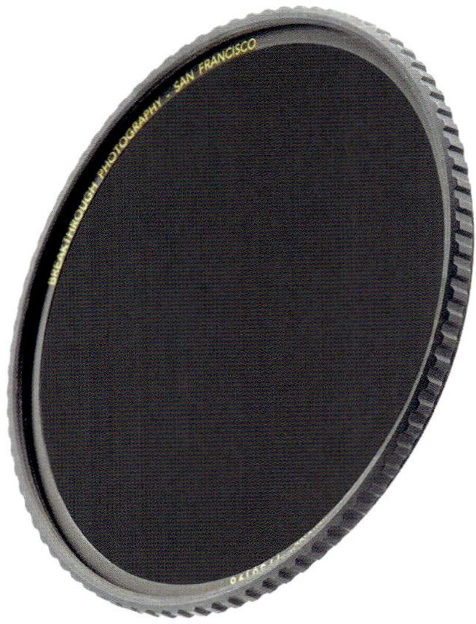

I've fallen madly in love with long exposures for travel. I used to just think of them for waterfalls and streams, or for streaking car lights in a city, but there are so many wonderful things you can do with them—from getting rid of tourists (see page 187), to creating wonderfully streaky skies, to making choppy water in a lake or harbor smooth as silk. To get your camera to keep its shutter open long enough to make a long exposure without overexposing your shot to death, we use a neutral density filter (I use Breakthrough Photography's, seen above. They're fantastic quality!). Now, we don't call them "neutral density" filters because we don't have time to say such a fancy name—we're too busy charging batteries and backing up images. We call them "ND" filters. These ND filters are super-dark, like tinted-windows-on-a-limo dark, and that's all they do—screw it on the end of your lens and it makes everything really, really dark. Because your camera sees the scene is now so dark, you can leave your shutter open for a long time before creating a proper exposure (in short, before the images look bright enough). ND filters come in different darkness levels. For example, a 3-stop filter makes things a little darker, so it'd be fine to use on an overcast or really cloudy day to get a longer exposure, but I prefer a 10-stop filter when shooting in the day, so you can keep your shutter open longer even in bright sunlight. I have both filters—a 3-stop and a 10-stop—so I can use the right one based on how bright, or not bright, it is outside. But, there's another advantage: you can screw the 3-stop on top of the 10-stop and it has a multiplier effect where I've been able to leave my shutter open, in the middle of the day, for 14 minutes (crazy, I know). An ND filter is one of those "must have" filters for travel and once you start using one, it opens a whole new world (well, at least a new world of sitting there waiting for your long exposure to be finished anyway).

The PhotoPills App

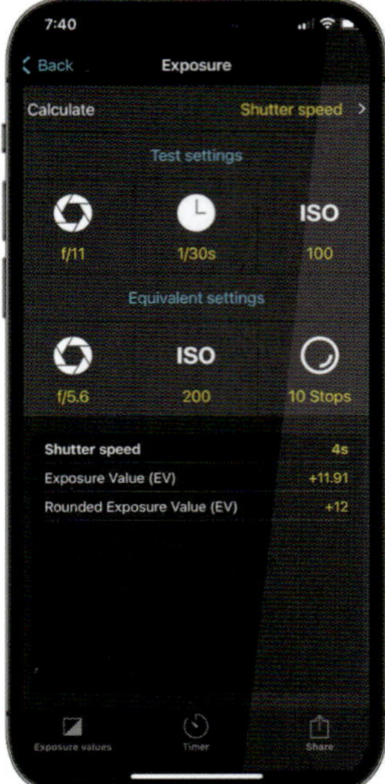
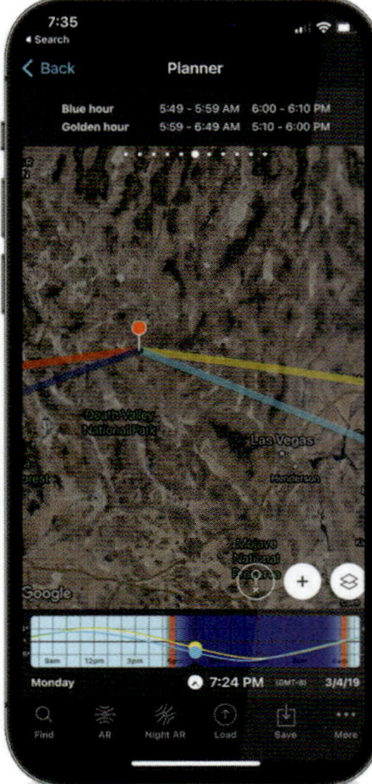
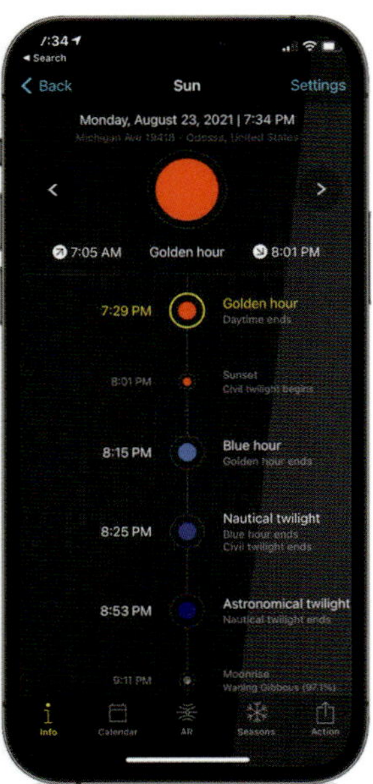

If there is one app that every photographer on the planet needs, it's the PhotoPills app. It's not for shooting on your phone—it's for helping you make better images with your DSLR or mirrorless camera, and it has so much information packed into it, it's insane. It does everything from telling you exactly where the Milky Way is going to be in the sky on any given night (now, or in the future), so you can plan out your shots in advance (along with an Augmented Reality overlay of the Milky Way on your current scene. It's crazy!), to timers for taking long exposures, to all the exact info for sunrise, sunset, blue hour, and twilight every day, to a calculator for doing time lapse photography. But, it's so much more than that—it's just packed with so much stuff, it's like having a really smart photo assistant right there with you (except it won't lift heavy stuff like a real assistant).

You're Gonna Need a Cleaning Cloth

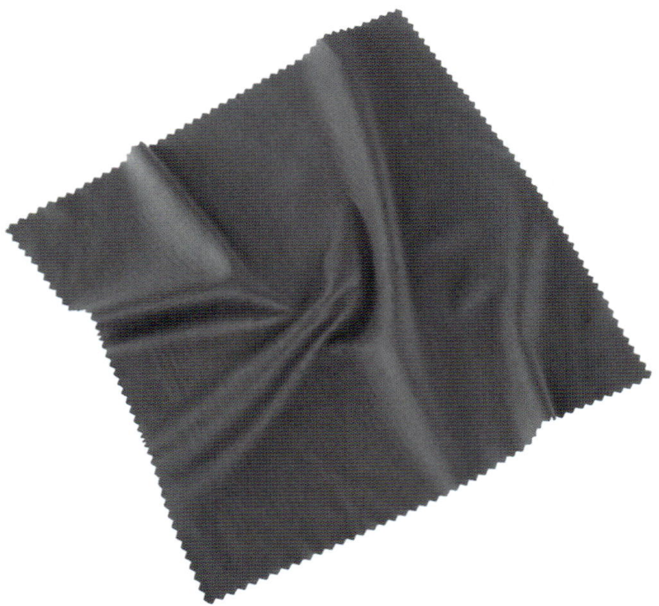

This is such an overlooked thing, but it's so important, and I have photographers show me shots where I can tell they haven't cleaned their lens in a long time (maybe ever). The whole image just looks a bit soft, and they think something's wrong with their lens. There is. It's dirty. And, it's not just the front of the lens that gets dirty and needs cleaning—it's the rear element (that small, round glass area inside the tube that fits into your camera body) that needs cleaning. You need to carry a microfiber cleaning cloth with you. Keep it in your back pocket or sling bag or purse or photo vest—just have it on you. The Sensei Microfiber Lens Cleaning Cloth is 5 bucks at B&H Photo. Get two because you'll probably lose one. Well, I did.

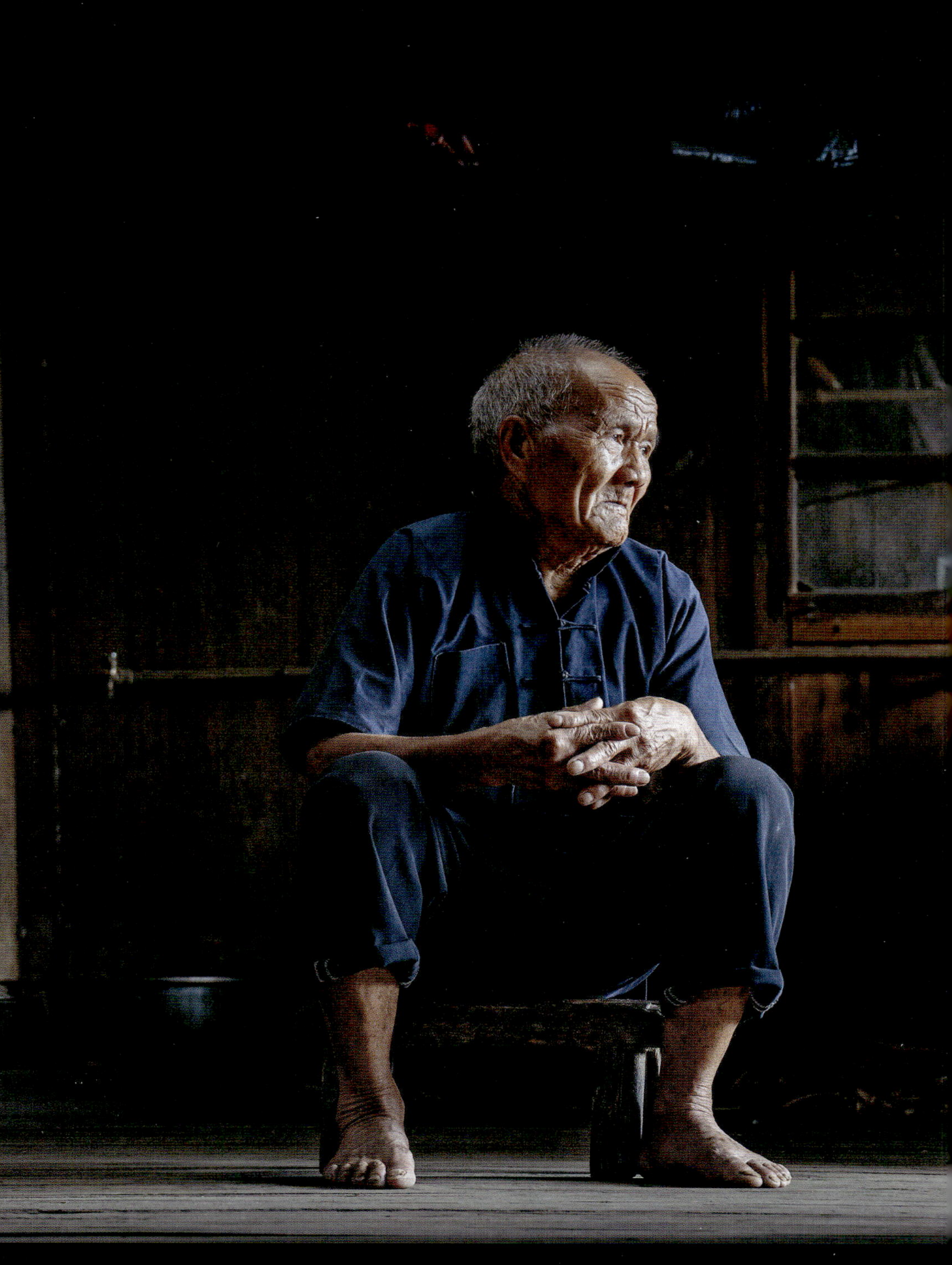

SHUTTER SPEED: 1/10 sec | F-STOP: F/6.3 | ISO: 800 | FOCAL LENGTH: 94mm
LOCATION: Dazhai Village, Shanxi, China

Capturing Images of People

Coming Home with More Than Just Images of Buildings and Monuments

One of the challenges of getting locals in a foreign land to pose for you is the language barrier. Of course, here in the United States, getting strangers you approach on the street to pose for you is easy. Let's say, for example, you're on the busy streets of New York City, or perhaps Newark, New Jersey, and you see someone you'd like to photograph. You just walk up, stop them, and say, "Hi. You don't know me, but I'd like to take some photos of you and post them on the internet." Now, what is the most likely scenario for their response? Is it: (a) "Sure, that sounds like fun. Where would you like me stand? Is over here okay, or would the light be better over there?" Or, is it: (b) the next sound you hear is their fist connecting with your face, or perhaps the sound of pepper spray being aggressively sprayed into your eyes? If you guessed (b), that's correct, and earns you 10 points and a chance to move on to our bonus round. There is a third, less likely scenario where they stab you, but that only happens in Newark. Anyway, when you think of those made-up, but sadly all too real, possible scenarios here in the US, you have to imagine that getting someone on the street to pose for you would be easier in almost every place else on earth, and I can tell you from experience, it is. First off, outside of New York and Newark, virtually nobody carries pepper spray, but beyond that, there is another proven method for getting people to pose, but you'll need the Google Translate app on your phone, with the feature where you type in English and it says back the translation out loud using your phone's speaker, so the person can hear and respond. The trick is what you write into the translator. I generally go with this, "I'm an eccentric billionaire from France, and I would gladly pay €1,000 if you let me take a quick photo of you." Once you take the shot, you quickly type into the translator, "Hey, isn't that Beyoncé?" you point behind them, and when they turn to look, you run like hell in the opposite direction. Works every time.

Getting People to Pose for You

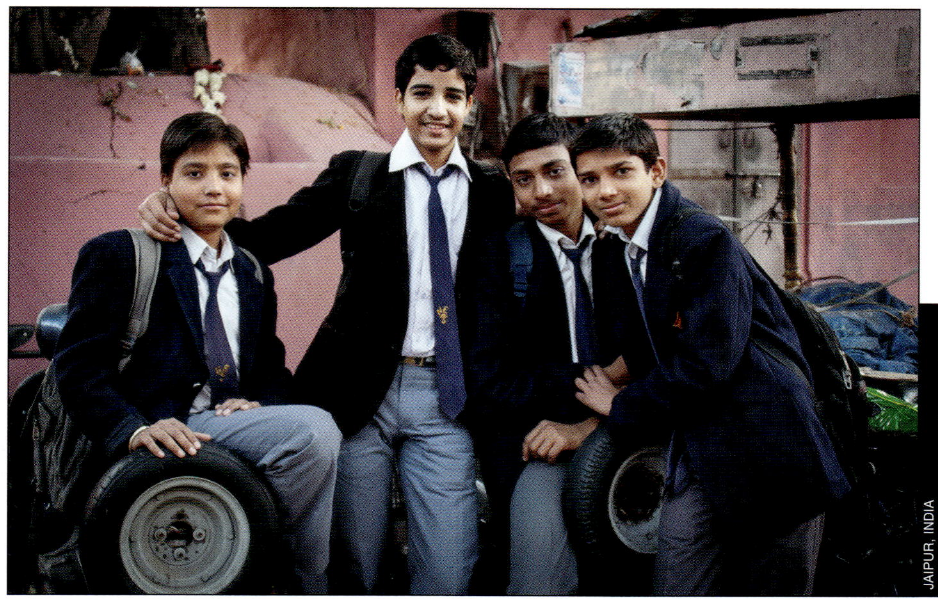

If you're like me, you're a little uncomfortable approaching a stranger and asking them to pose for a portrait. Okay, I'm more than a little uncomfortable, which is probably why I do it so rarely. So, how do you get people to pose for you? Well, I'm going to share a technique that has worked for me many, many times. You're kind of going to ask their permission, but that happens after you take the shot. Here's how it works: If you see someone on the street you want to photograph, get in their line of sight, make eye contact, hold your camera up near your face like you're saying, "I want to take your picture with this camera," then give them a big smile and quickly take their picture. Usually, your big smile will get some sort of smile back. As soon as you take the shot, turn your camera around so that they can see the back of it and walk over and show them the shot of them you just took. I've never had anyone not look at it. They always look. Now, if they speak your same language, you could say something along the lines of, "You have such a great face! Do you mind if I take just a couple more?" You say that with a big, friendly smile and chances are they'll say sure, and now you've got somebody posing for a portrait. If you don't speak their language, just hold up your camera again, smile and nod, like you're saying, "Is it okay?" (remember the big smile) and chances are they'll nod yes. See the school boys in the shot above? They were waiting for a bus in Jaipur, India, when I came across them. I don't speak Hindi, so I held up my camera, nodded like, "Is it okay?" and they immediately jumped into a group pose. Once they heard the shutter click, they raced behind me to see the shot on my camera. They laughed, and then went back, reposed, and they did this again and again. If their bus hadn't finally arrived, I'd probably still be there shooting. Remember: Smile. Shoot. And share.

Have Your Guide Ask Them for You

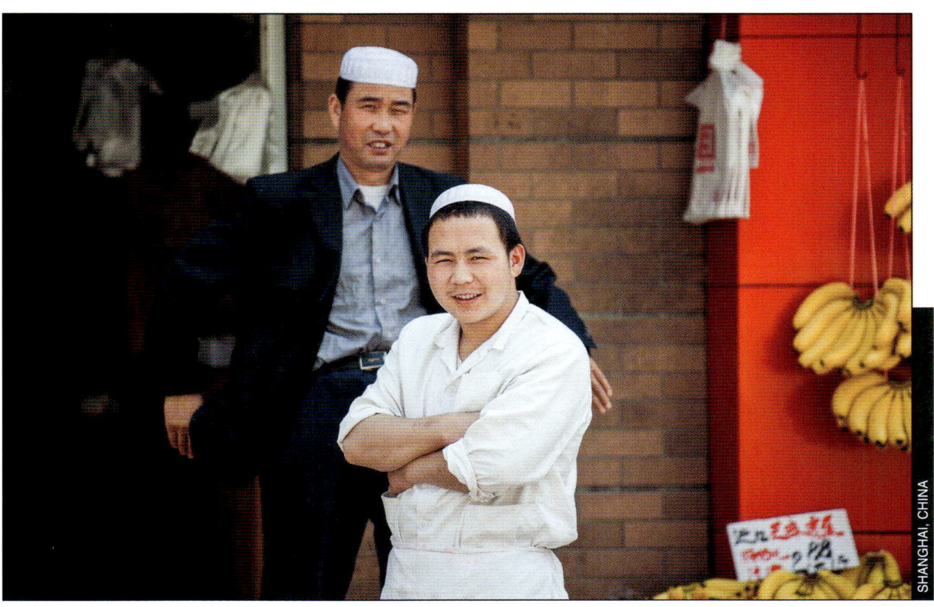

One terrific way to get people to pose for you when you're in a foreign country is to hire a tour guide or a walking guide, and when you come across someone you want to take a photo of, ask the guide to ask them if it's okay. This works amazingly well, and I can't even remember a time when it didn't work. I imagine they say something to them like, "This guy is a tourist and he's driving me crazy. Will you let him take a quick photo of you, so he'll stop bothering me?" Whatever they say, it works, and I've gotten some nice portraits I wouldn't have gotten thanks to them asking. So, their part is to ask people if it's okay, and your job is to smile and look as friendly as humanly possible, so they're more likely to say okay.

WHY A 50mm LENS MIGHT NOT BE THE BEST CHOICE

I know, I know…they're small, lightweight, inexpensive, and they can shoot at f/1.8, so you can get really out-of-focus backgrounds and shoot in low light. They also are one of the least flattering lenses for photographing people because of the facial distortion it causes if you're up close shooting a portrait. To get the background out of focus, you'll need to be pretty darn close, which when you're shooting candid travel portraits, is really tricky/awkward and might be impossible in many cases. That's why I leave my 50mm at home when I'm traveling. There are some travel photographers out there that swear by their 50mm. They've mastered the nuances of shooting with that lens, and they're after a particular look, and they've learned how to get it. If you haven't fully mastered that technique, I'd leave that 50mm at home.

The Art of Taking Candid Portraits

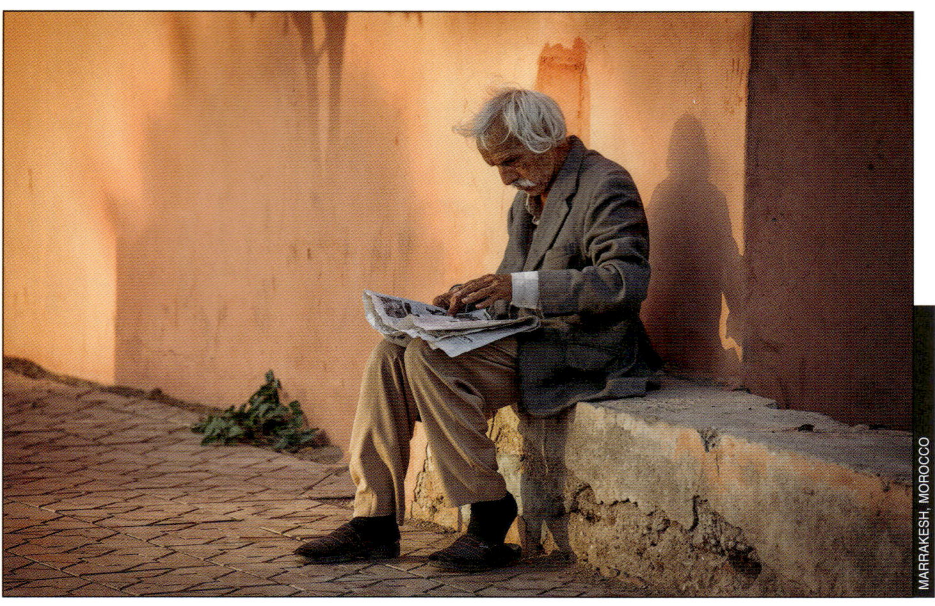

For most of us, our travel photos of people will mostly be shots that we take while our subject isn't aware we're taking their photo, like the shot you see above. These are the easiest types of people shots, since there's little worry they'll object or say anything because they don't even know you're there. There's a tricky "dance" to shooting discreetly like this because if you get a little too close, or stay aimed at them a little too long, they sense that someone is looking at them, and suddenly they're looking straight at you. Sometimes, that can make for a good shot, but often, their facial expression lets you know they're not up for it. So, our goal (for the most part) when shooting candids is to be so discreet that our subject doesn't notice we're photographing them. Here are a few tips that can help you get better candids: The first is to stand far away from your subject and zoom in tight with your lens. This is when it's great to have one of those 28–300mm lenses, or a 24–240mm, where you can stand so far back that not only will you have a better chance of cranking off a few shots without them noticing, but zooming in tight on them will make the background either a little or a lot out of focus, which helps separate your subject from the scene and adds more depth to the image. Another big tip is to find a spot to sit for a while—maybe at an outdoor cafe or on a bench—and just patiently wait for opportunities. This is often the best way to get candids, because after a few minutes of being in that location, you start to blend in with the surroundings, so you don't stand out as much or garner nearly the attention you would when leaning against a wall, where you might get a, "Hey, what's that guy up to over there?" Find a busy area, find a place to sit, watch, use a long lens, and you'll have lots of opportunities for great candid people shots.

Keep an Eye Out for Dramatic Light

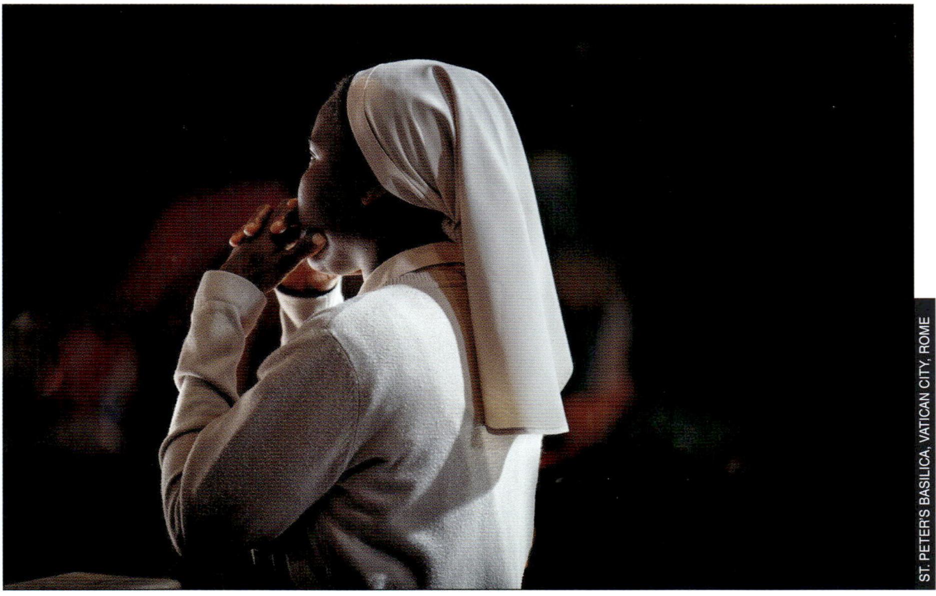

This one is always on my checklist for things to watch for when I'm visiting an area: I'm always on the lookout for dramatic light, and by that, I mean a scene lit with just a sliver of light, or a beam of light. A hint of light falling on your subject usually makes for a really interesting shot. I'll never forget something renown people photographer Joe McNally said: "If you want to make something more interesting, only light part of it." Man, is that on the money! That's why, if I see a sliver of light coming in through a window, or between some buildings, etc., I stand back and wait for someone to walk into that light and I take the picture. Now, the angle you choose at first might not be the right one to make the kind of shot you want, so be prepared to move around a bit until the light hits your subject in an interesting way. But, when you find this dramatic light, and you find the right angle to capture someone in it, it'll be worth the wait.

A GREAT WAY TO GIVE BACK

One of the best things you can do for yourself, for your subject, and for the next photographer that comes along is to offer to email your subject your favorite shot of them. That way, you're repaying their kindness with some of your own, and you're paving the way for the next photographer who might ask them to pose for a portrait.

Another Tip for Getting People Portraits

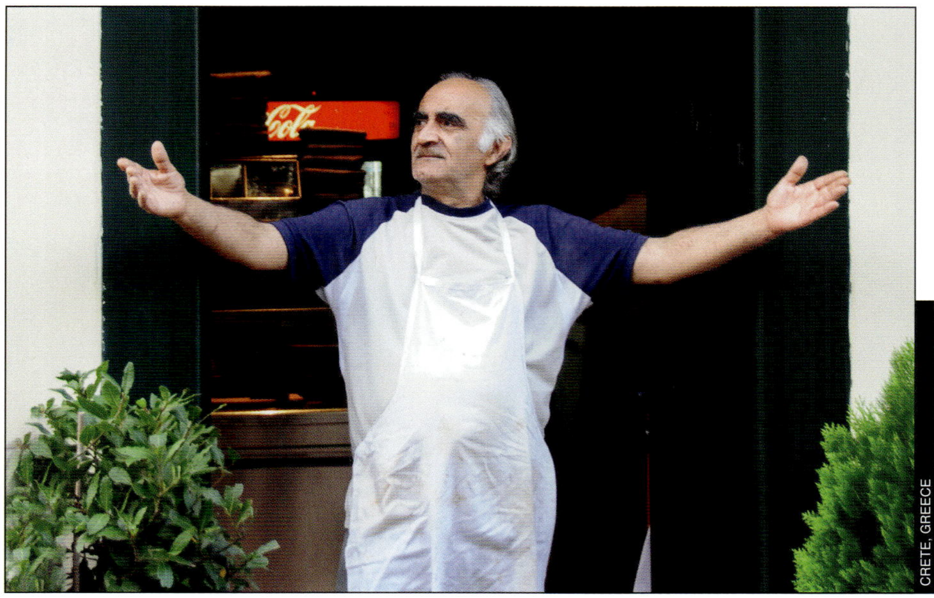

If you're uncomfortable getting people to pose, but you want something more than just candids, here's a tip I've used many times that works like a charm, and that is to buy something small from a street vendor (maybe just a piece of fruit or a small trinket), and then ask them if it's okay if you take their photo. If you walk up to a vendor without buying something, you're a stranger. You're somebody who is taking them away from their job of selling to feed their family. However, once you buy something, no matter how small, you're not a random stranger anymore. You're a customer. Once you're a customer, and ask, "Hey, is it okay if I grab a quick photo?" they will almost always pause for a quick moment to let you get a shot (as long as you don't break the rule on page 89, you'll be in good shape).

IF THINGS GO WRONG...

If you take a candid photo of someone and they get upset, apologize immediately and offer to delete the photo right in front of them. Don't argue with them about why it's okay for you to keep it. It's just one photo and not worth hurting or angering someone (plus, it poisons the water for the next photographer to come along).

Shooting with Window Light

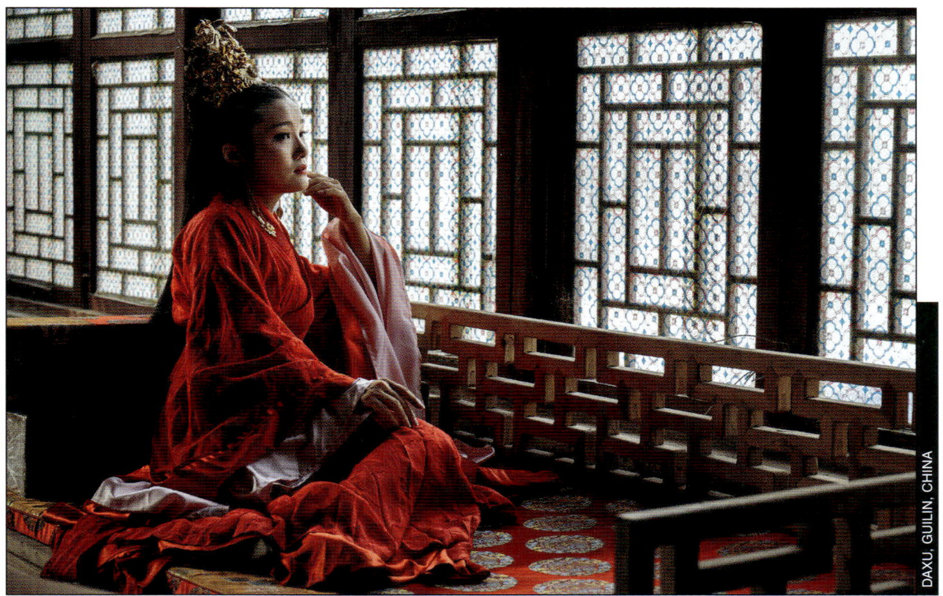

If you get the chance to pose a subject indoors, one of the most flattering light sources is window light, and there are a couple of important tricks you can use to make sure your window light shots look awesome. The first is: You want to shoot parallel to the window, so you and your subject are beside the window. You don't want to be at the window shooting back toward your subject because the light will be very flat. You want shadows on one side of your subject's face (the side farthest away from the window) to add depth and dimension, so shoot parallel to the window. Also, you don't want your subject right up close to the window—that's where the light is its harshest. If you can move your subject a few feet back from the window, the light will be much softer and more flattering (the farther they are from the window, the softer the light will be, but it also won't be as bright, so you don't want them to get back too far). There's a rule, too: The dirtier the window, the better the light. So, if you see a window that needs cleaning, it'll probably make a great window light window. That dirt diffuses the light and makes it very flattering. In this shot, there's a fabric pattern over the window, which is why I asked our subject to sit near it for this shot—that pattern helped soften the light. One more thing: If you have your choice of windows, choose one that's facing north, as north-facing windows are softer and more beautiful (that's the trick the old Dutch Master painters used for their portraits—a north-facing window, which doesn't get direct light, is some of the most flattering light you can get). Soft light adds glamour; direct light is like a hammer. I just made that up, and granted, it's pretty lame, but it might help you remember how important great light is for flattering portraits.

Choosing Your Background for Portraits

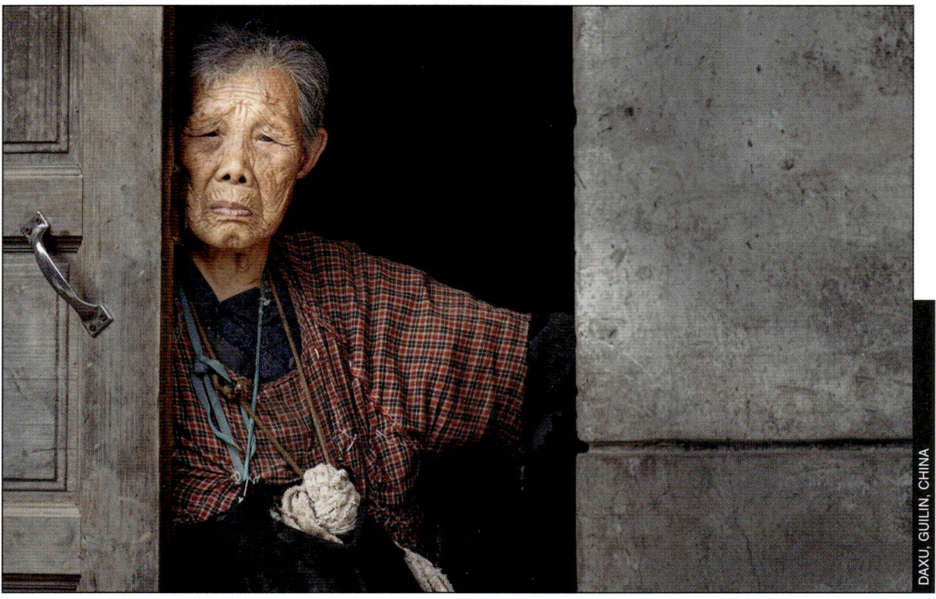

When you shoot a portrait with your subject on a busy background, it's easy for them to get "lost" in the image. That's why, when we're shooting travel portraits, we generally try to keep the background very simple, with the least amount of distracting things back there as possible. The simpler the background, the stronger your portrait will be. That's why we often try to put the background behind our subjects out of focus, so it separates them from the background, which limits any distractions behind them. Now, we don't always have the luxury of being able to move our subject onto the perfect simple background, so what we have to do is be really cognizant of how the background looks and change our shooting angle so we see as little background clutter as possible. As I mentioned, blurring the background behind them can help simplify it (more on this on page 90), but it may come down to where you stand and how you frame up the shot. If you do have the option of choosing the background your subject stands in front of, try to choose a darker background, or one that's a darker color than what they're wearing, so they'll stand out from it. If the background behind them is bright, it will draw the viewer's eye away from your subject because our eyes are immediately drawn to the brightest thing in the photo. When you start really seeking out simple backgrounds, or framing things up to keep your backgrounds as simple as possible, you'll see the quality of your travel portraits soar!

Where to Focus for People Shots

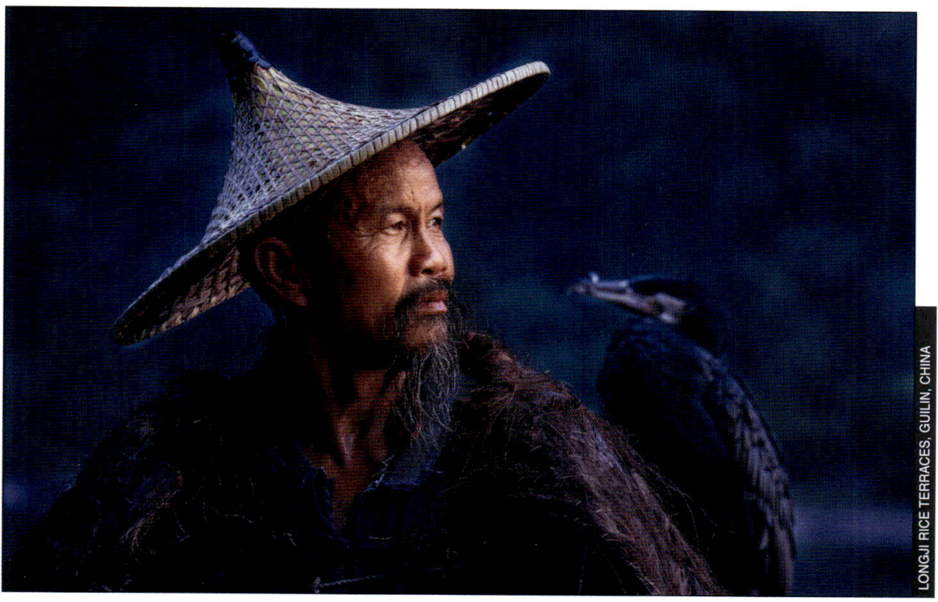

This is an easy one: when it comes to photos of people, you need to focus on their eyes. If their eyes appear in focus, then everything looks sharp. If their eyes are out of focus, the shot goes in the trash, so it's important to get your focus right. If their head is turned to the side (like you see above), you'll want to focus on the eye that is closest to the camera (so, in this case, his eye on the left here). Now, most of today's new mirrorless cameras come with an incredible feature that makes this "focus on the eyes" absolutely effortless because they use AI facial-recognition to find your subject's eyes and lock focus on them automatically. It's called Eye Autofocus (on Canon), or Eye AF (on Sony), or Eye-Detection AF (on Nikon), or Face/Eye Detection (on Panasonic and Olympus), and it works shockingly well. You'll see it activate while you're looking through the viewfinder: as soon as you hold the shutter button halfway down to engage the autofocus, you'll see the focus point instantly snap to their eye. Now, if you don't have one of these newer cameras, no problem—you'll just do it manually (like we always have). You see that center point when you look through your viewfinder (or on your screen, if you shoot that way)? Position that point right over your subject's eye, and then hold the shutter button halfway down to lock the focus on their eye. Keep that button held halfway down, but now you can move the camera where you want it to compose the shot however you'd like, knowing the focus is locked on their eye. When their expression looks good, just press the shutter button the rest of the way down to take the shot, and their eyes will be sharp and in focus. That's all there is to it.

Paying Locals to Pose

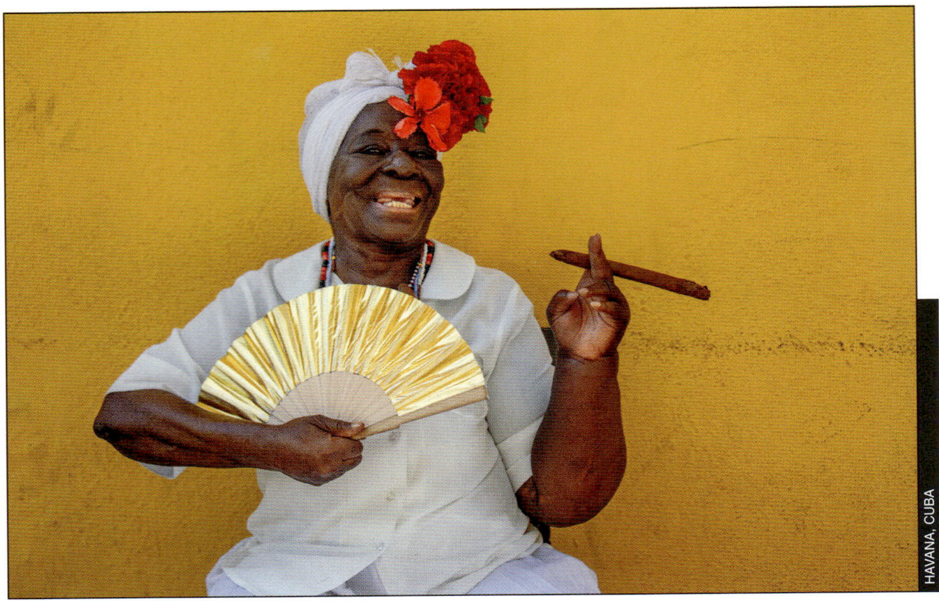

Just like there are street musicians and street performers out there performing for donations, in more and more places, you'll have people who dress up in colorful local costumes for tourists to photograph them for a fee. Don't worry, you won't have to ask if they're willing to be paid to take their portrait—if they see you walking past with a nice camera, they will ask you if you want to take their portrait! It's usually a surprisingly little amount for a quick photo (often just $1). What I've found is, most tourists want to have their photo taken *with* the subject, rather than just taking a photo *of* the subject (so, they essentially want a selfie with the subject), whereas you and I would prefer to just have a photo of the subject. They usually stand in an area with a background that makes sense for a photo with what they're wearing, but once I've "hired" a subject, I'll have them move 25 or so feet one way or another, so I can have them on the background I want (and if I ask them to move, I always increase my tip). My experience has been they are very friendly, accommodating, and patient (though I don't take too long with them because theirs is a volume business and I don't want to take too much of their time. So, I get my camera settings all dialed in and I'm ready to shoot before I ask, "How much?"). Now, you'll sometimes see photographers arguing online that you shouldn't pay locals to pose like this (photographers love to argue in online forums), but some of the world's most famous travel images you've seen in and on the cover of famous magazines are with a local subject that was paid to pose. But, if you want to get into a "lively" discussion on this topic, pop into a forum and post a question asking if it's okay. Then, just sit back and watch the fireworks.

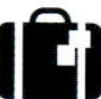
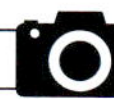

Shooting in Direct Sun

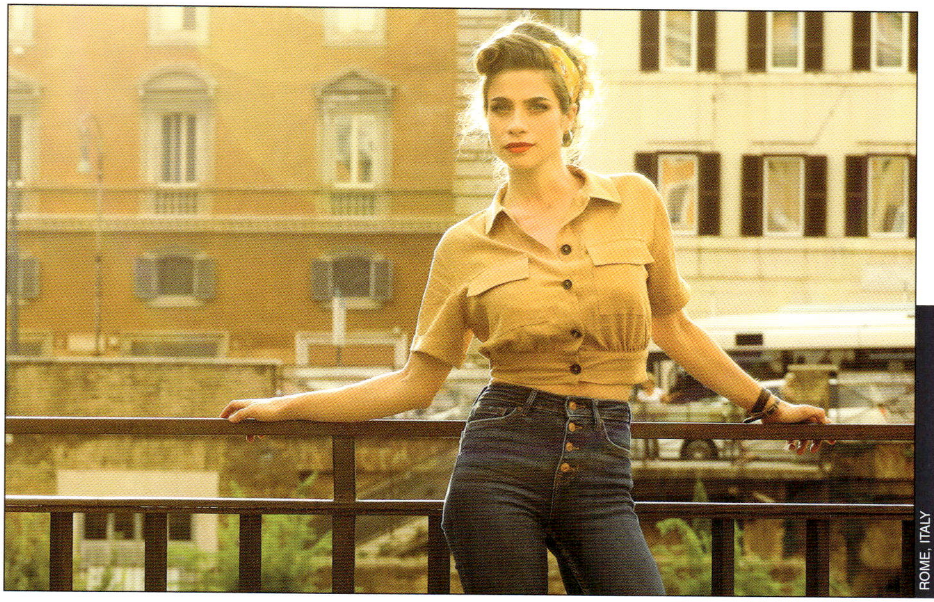

If you're shooting portraits out in direct sun, there's a technique you can use that works wonders because it keeps your subject out of hard, direct light and instead, they wind up in nice, soft light. The first part is to put your subject's back to the sun. This works nicely because now the sun acts as your second light, lighting their hair with a nice rim light (like you see above). Now, when you put your subject's back to the sun, this usually creates almost a silhouette, where your subject is very dark against that backlit background. So, the second part of this technique is to brighten the scene, so your subject isn't in the shadows anymore. That's right—we intentionally overexpose (make the scene too bright), and while it makes the background behind your subject brighter, at the same time, it brightens your subject so they're not in the shadows any longer. I shoot all my travel photos in aperture priority mode (see page 44), so for me, all I have to do is use the Exposure Compensation dial on my camera (every camera has one) to brighten the image, making it brighter than my camera thinks the scene should be. I usually have to brighten by around 1 to 1-1/2 stops, but I don't really go by the number—I look at my subject and brighten the scene until they look properly lit. This looks so good because your subject's face and body is in the shade (it's facing away from the sun), so there's no squinting or harsh shadows or any of the bad stuff that comes from shooting in direct light. Now, if the background gets too bright, move your subject so the background behind them is darker, so if you brighten the whole photo, you don't notice it as much (I rarely have to do this). In short, put their back to the sun, brighten the scene until they look fairly well lit, and you're done.

More Flattering Portraits

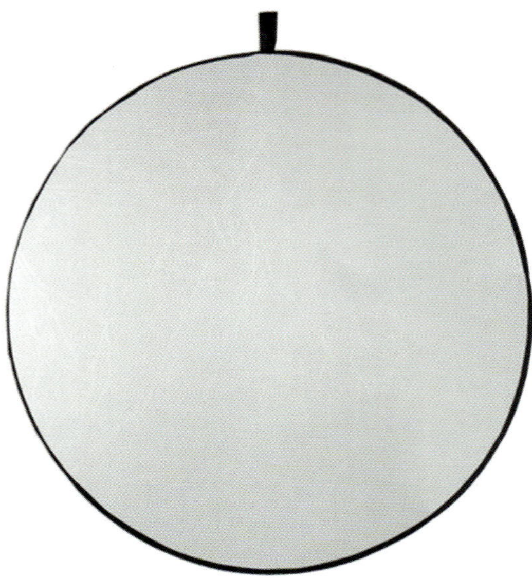

If you think getting portraits of the locals is going to be your focus, there's an accessory you'll want to pick up that will help you make better outdoor portraits. It's small, lightweight, inexpensive (I've seen it online for $9), and it works wonders. It's called a "1-stop diffuser," and it's a trick pro photographers have been using for years to make beautiful outdoor portraits. You simply put this diffuser between the sun and your subject (holding it over their head), and it takes that harsh, nasty, direct light and turns it into soft, beautiful, incredibly flattering light that makes people look great (that's a lot of magic for $9). Also, it folds down into a small circle, so it fits in your camera bag, and then when you take it out, it pops open into a large circle and it's ready to go. You won't be able to use it in every situation (like candid photos), but when you do get to use it, you'll be amazed at the results you can get shooting right out in the harsh sun.

Portrait Composition Essentials

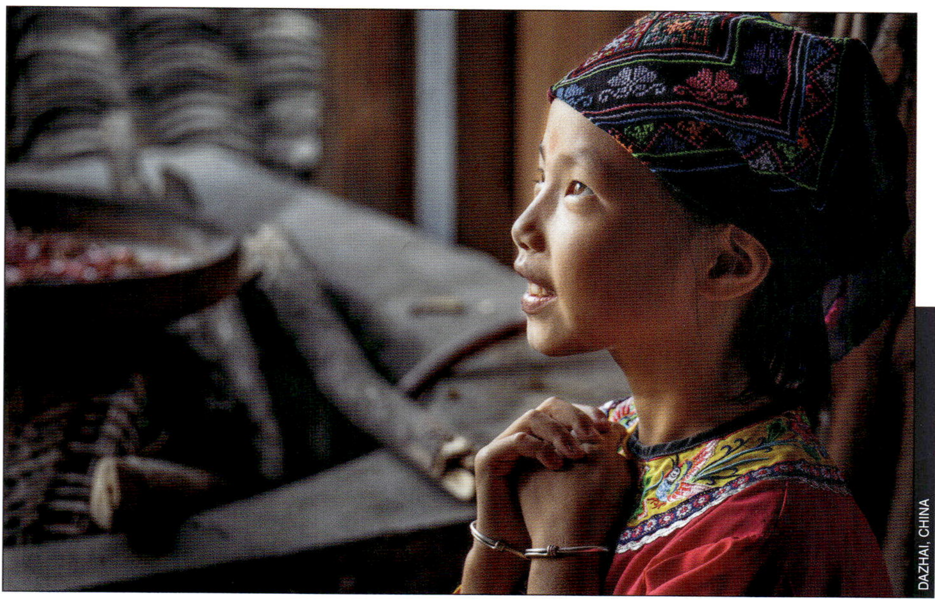

There are a few simple rules for composition to keep in mind when you're shooting travel portraits so your shots look like the pros. The first is where to position your subject's eyes in the frame. The general rule is to place their eyes in the top 1/3 of the frame. If you want a more intimate portrait, it's very popular to move in close enough so that you crop off the top of their head, but if you do this, crop off at least 1/3 of their head, so it doesn't look like an accident—it should look like you intentionally framed up the shot that way. Also, for a more flattering look overall, have your subject turn their shoulders so they're not facing the camera flat on. That way, when they're turned a bit sideways, they don't look as wide on-camera. Also, if you can shoot from a little higher angle, so you're aiming slightly down on your subject, you'll wind up with a more flattering portrait (it's why "selfie pros" always hold their cameras up high when they take selfies—it's because when they look up at the camera like that, it strengthens their jawline, pulls their skin tighter, and everything looks better). Now, of course, depending on the situation, you might not be able to pose your subject just the way you want to, to get the perfect portrait, but try to put as many of these compositional tips into play as you can (especially the positioning of the eyes in the frame).

They Don't Always Have to Be Smiling

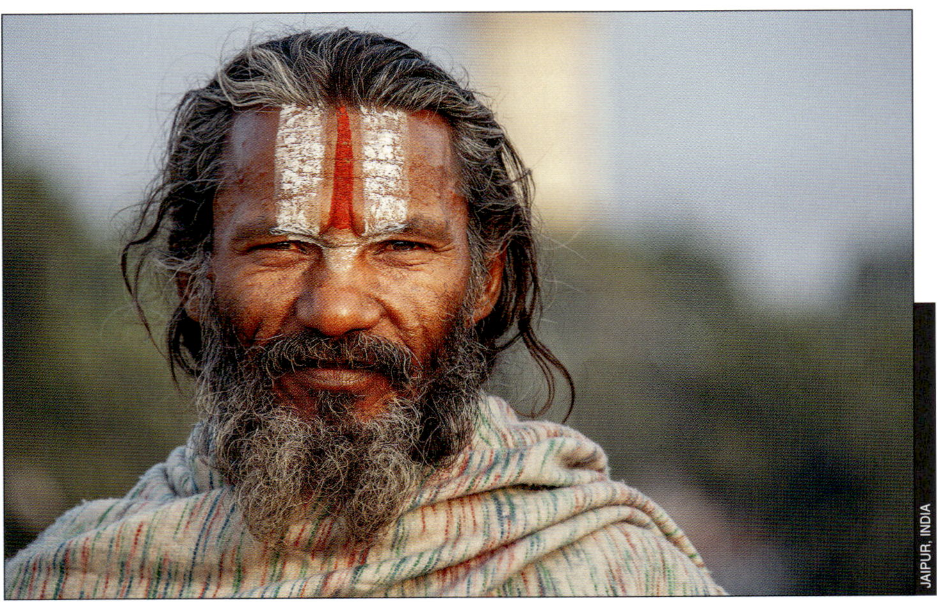
JAIPUR, INDIA

If you do get someone to pose for you, whether it's someone on the street, or a vendor, or even your tour guide, you'll get more impactful and emotional-looking shots if they're not smiling in every photo. If they're always smiling, it looks like an ad for the local tourist board, so I encourage them to start with a smile, and then just relax. Now, I'll tell you this: this is harder than it sounds because it's most people's natural inclination to smile when someone's taking their picture. So, once I get the first smiling shot out of the way, I just try talking to them, asking them questions, or if I don't speak their language, I ask the tour guide or fixer or photo guide with me to ask them questions. Another tip is to thank them for letting you take their portrait (and you got lots of smiling shots), but ask if it's okay if you take a few more shots while they get back to doing whatever it was they were doing before they posed for you. Whether they're working in a shop or a business, or they're working a vendor cart, etc., you can wind up with some very natural-looking shots.

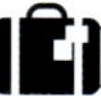
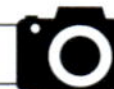

Shoot and Move On

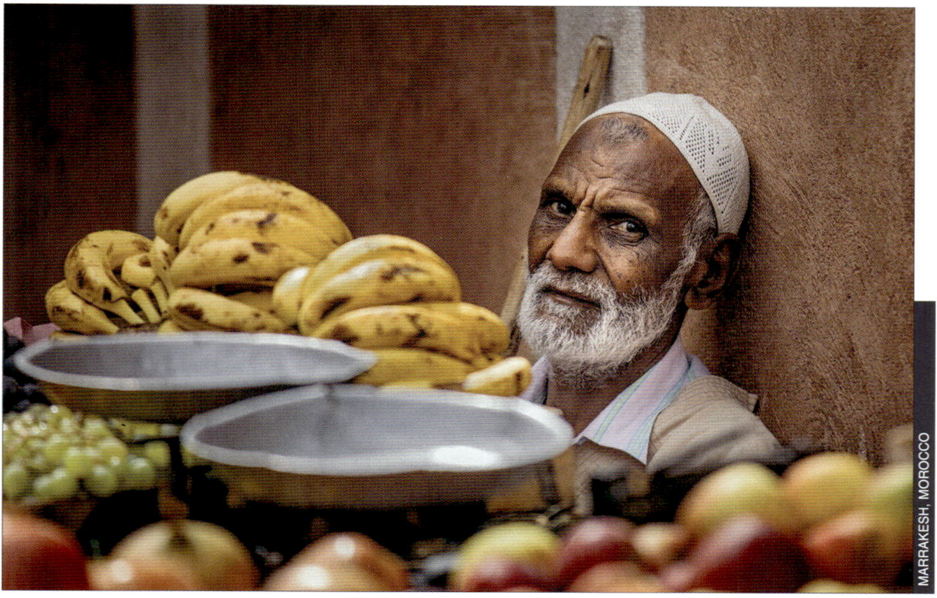

If you get the opportunity to have someone stop and pose for you, you need to do this quickly and move on. If they agree to pose for you, we're talking 30 seconds or 60 seconds, tops. After that point, you can start to see their facial expression change from happy or thoughtful to annoyed. Get in, get your shots, and get out. Now, there will be times when you strike up a conversation and you can tell they're willing to let you shoot much longer, but just be aware of their facial expressions and body language to let you know how long you can shoot without taking advantage of their kindness.

Camera Settings for Outdoor Portraits

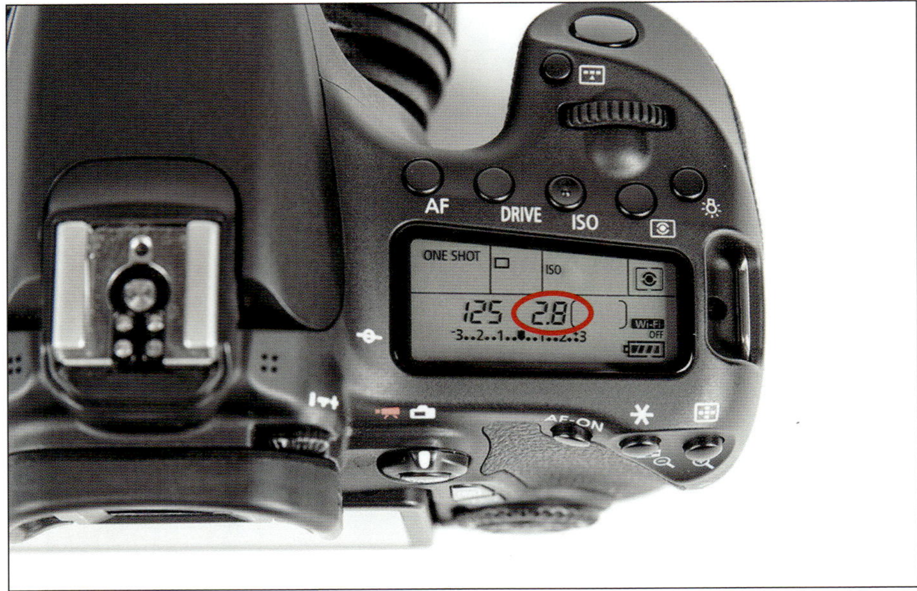

When it comes to taking portraits, I have a "go to" set of settings that work really well when shooting outdoors. These settings (along with using the right lens setting) will help separate your subject from the background (so important, as I mentioned on page 82) and limit distractions. For this to work, you're generally going to need somewhat of a zoom lens (at least one that goes to 100mm, or ideally longer) because it's the "zoom in close on your subject" part that is the most important part of getting the background out of focus. So, the first part of this is to stand back and zoom in tight on your subject. The tighter you zoom in, the blurrier the background will be. It's much harder to get a full-length shot and have the background look blurry than it is a headshot, because you would have to stand so far back to get their whole body in the shot while zoomed in tight. It can be done, but especially indoors, you usually won't be able to get back that far, so think shots from the waist up, or head-and-shoulders type of shots. Okay, so part one is to stand back and zoom in tight. Part two is to use an f-stop that helps make the background out of focus, and that will be the lowest-numbered f-stop your lens will allow. That might be f/2.8, or f/4, or even as high as f/5.6 or f/6.3—that's okay, the background will still be out of focus if you've zoomed in tight. There's a third part to this: for a background to be really out of focus, it can't be directly behind your subject (in other words, if they're standing right in front of a wall that's 8" behind them, it's not going to be out of focus). The more distance there is between your subject and the background, the blurrier that background will be (provided, of course, you did the zooming in and using a low-numbered f-stop things). So, that's my "go to" for travel portraits shot outdoors: zoom in tight, use a low-numbered f-stop, and try to get some space between your subject and the background behind them.

Camera Settings for Indoor Portraits

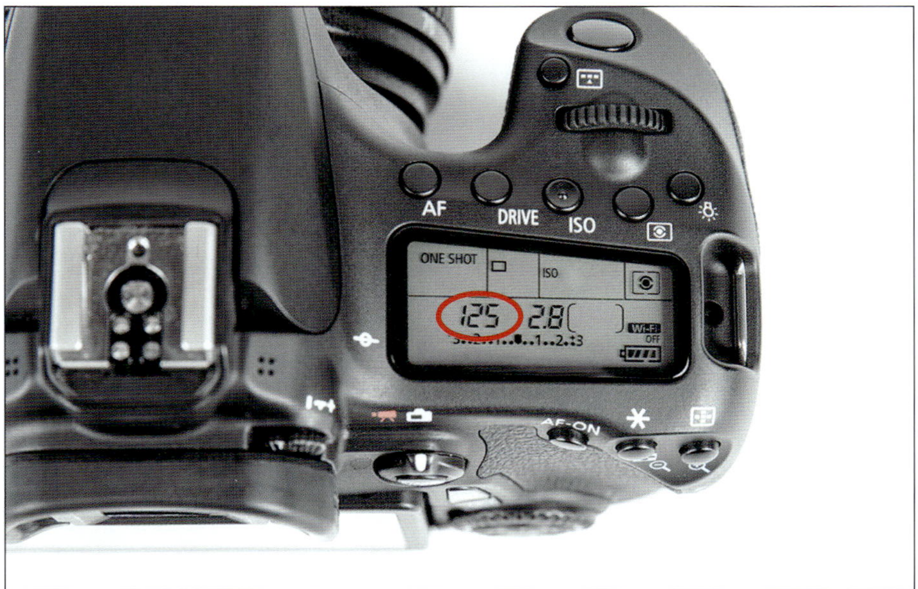

Your challenge shooting indoors will mostly be this: Is there enough light for your camera to use a high enough shutter speed so your shot won't be blurry? If there's lots of light indoors where you're shooting—no problem. If there's not bright light where you're shooting indoors, that's where it becomes an issue. You might be tempted to use your camera's built-in flash, but don't do it. That pop-up flash should never be used for anything ever. It's the "ugly maker," so just pretend it doesn't exist and you'll make better photos. So, what can you do in these low-light situations? Well, one thing is to use a small tripod, even a tabletop tripod (see page 65), to hold your camera perfectly still while you take the shot. But, if you don't have one handy, and you have to hand-hold your shot, then you'll need to get your shutter speed up to around 1/125 of a second to ensure you get a sharp shot (there's a setting on page 46 that will help with this big time). Even when we raise our ISO enough to hit that magic 1/125 of a second number, you'll still have to hold your camera as still and steady as you can because if you don't hold it really still, you can wind up with slightly blurry photos or shots that aren't really nice and sharp. One thing that will help get you that faster shutter speed is to use the lowest-numbered f-stop on your camera. The lower the number, the more light it lets into your camera, and you need lots of light to get higher shutter speeds, so this helps a ton (the more light, the higher the shutter speed, and fast shutter speeds freeze any movement, so we love fast shutters speeds). The whole trick to shooting portraits indoors in low-light situations is to find ways to either: (a) keep your camera super-still (small tripod; lean it on something to keep it still, etc.), or (b) raise your ISO enough that it raises the shutter speed enough (1/125 of a second or higher), so you can hand-hold your camera and still get a sharp shot.

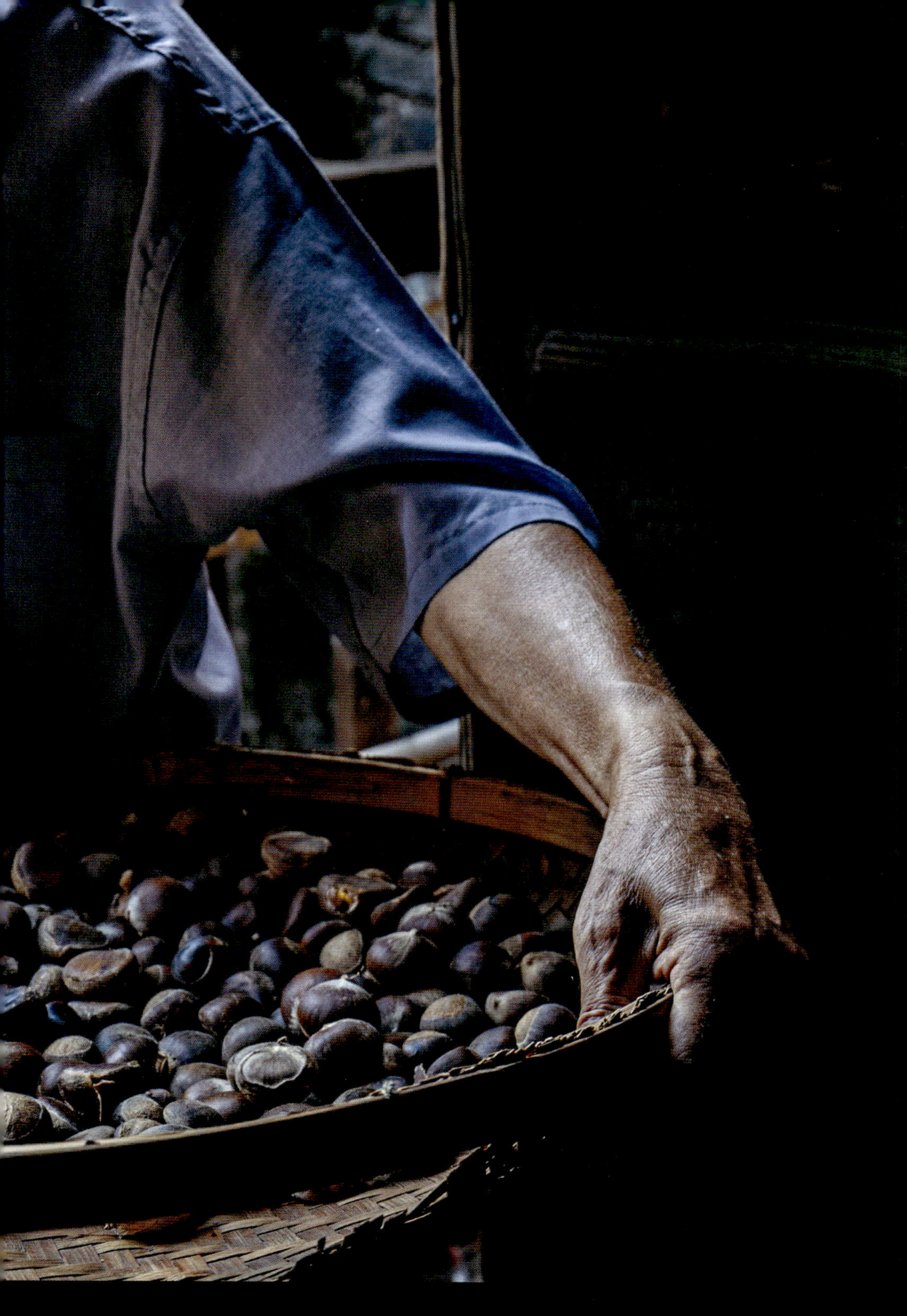

SHUTTER SPEED: 1/13 sec | F-STOP: F/5.6 | ISO: 800 | FOCAL LENGTH: 35mm
LOCATION: Daxu, Guangxi, China

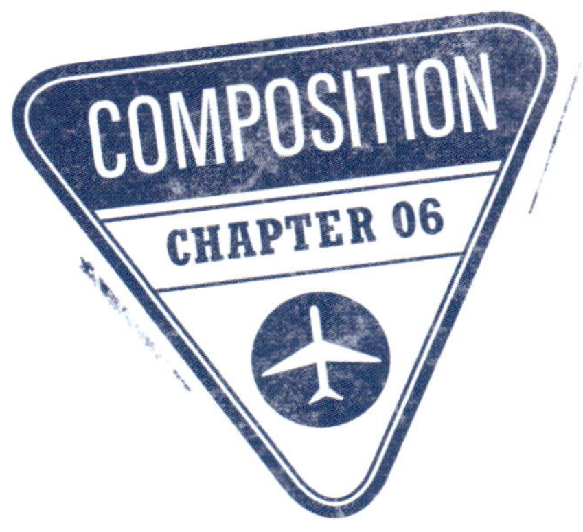

Composition

How to Arrange Things for More Compelling Photos

There is so much talk about the importance of composing your image in-camera, but of course, with our high-megapixel cameras these days, we can easily recompose our shots after the fact in Photoshop or Lightroom, or whatever. Anyway, with all this talk about composing and recomposing, one often overlooked topic by photographers, one we seem to avoid for reasons I can't seem to grasp, is the art of decomposing. I know this topic is kind of a dead end, but I feel like many photographers could make a grave mistake by not digging this topic up. It kills me to even talk about it, but working in a darkroom is probably a dying profession. Anyway, before we dig down too deep into a hole, I think it's important that we realize that some of the aspects of discussing decomposing are a dead giveaway, but every good story (and person, as well) needs a good plot. Some of these ideas have obviously expired, but some are still a dead ringer. Okay, at this point I've totally run out of decomposing puns as they relate (in some vague way) to photography, but since this is supposed to be a mental break anyway, let's wrap up with some stupid one-liners that'll help put the "fun" back in "funeral." Here goes: Why do they put a fence around a cemetery? Because people are dying to get in (ba doomp, crash!). Or how about this one: Cremation is my only hope of having a smoking hot body! (Bazinga!) Or how about: Why do ghosts ride elevators? To lift their spirits! (I'm here all week, folks. Don't forget to tip your bartenders.) Okay, that last one was kind of a Halloween joke, but the problem is, as you've already learned, there just aren't enough death and decomposing jokes. Well, there are more, but if you can believe it, they're actually worse than the ones I just shared, which were not exactly hall of famers. Hey, look over there! Is that Beyoncé? (Hey, it worked before.)

Don't Forget to Shoot Details

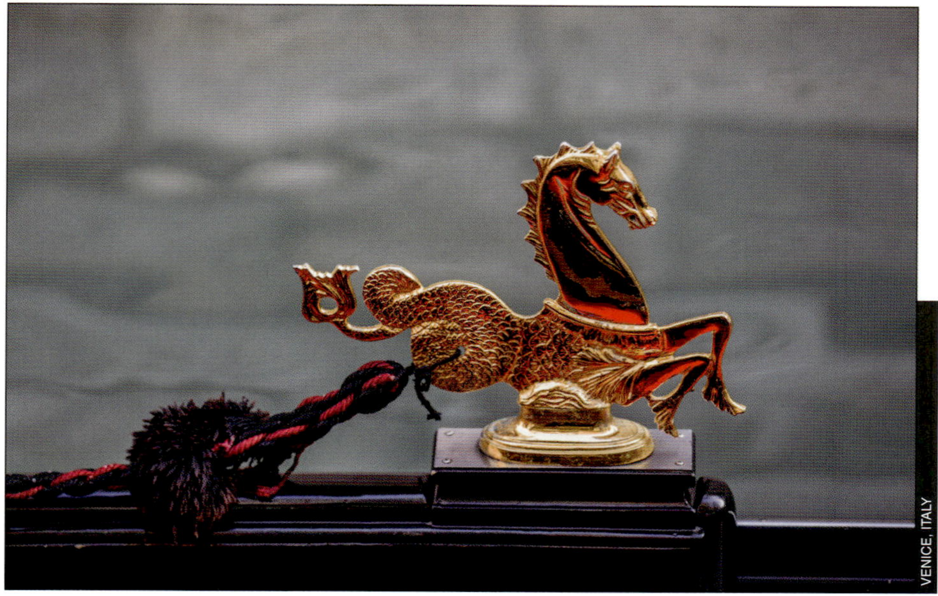

When you're standing in front of a beautiful opera house, or a palace, or a cathedral, your first inclination is to try to capture a photo of the entire building. Depending on the location of the building, this can be really tricky because a lot of the time there are distracting things around it, like signs for businesses, or billboards, or posters. There may be power lines, or vendor carts, or even distracting directional signs, like a large sign pointing toward the ticket office. That's why I feel it's so important to shoot detail shots that don't show the entire building, but give you an up-close glimpse of its beauty. Maybe it's an intricate pattern on the ceiling, or a statute along the roof line, or any one of the building embellishments that you miss with a wider shot, but can really enjoy with a tight, zoomed-in detail shot. This doesn't just go for buildings, of course—I always include detail shots wherever I go, whether it's just an ornament on a gondola in Venice (as seen above), or an interesting door handle on the entrance of an old building. These detail shots are wonderful for helping tell your story, and for giving your viewers a different view of a place they, perhaps, had seen before or maybe even visited themselves. Add detail shots to your trip, and you'll love the different, close-up view it delivers.

Getting the Most from Your Wide-Angle Lens

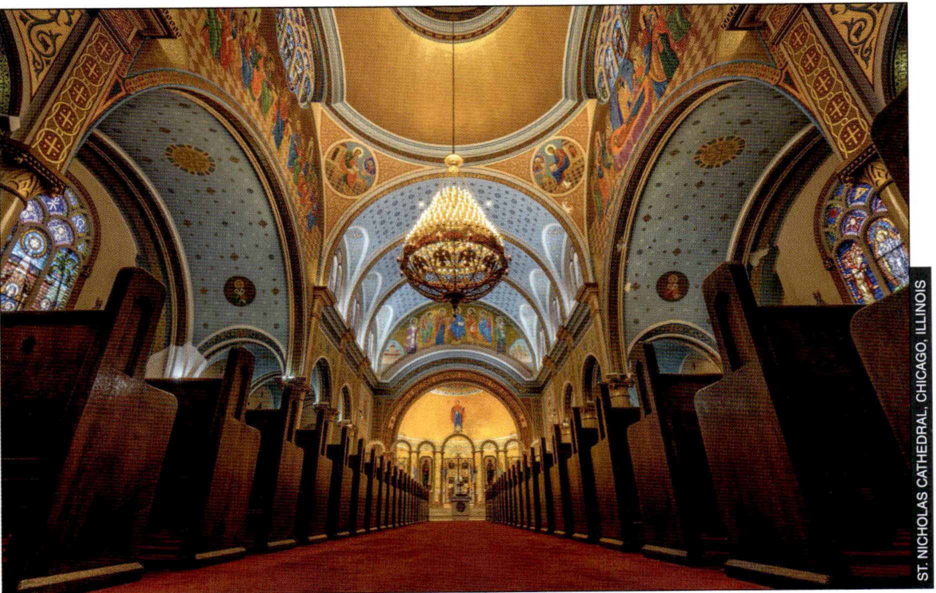

If you wind up shooting a lot of wide-angle shots, especially in places like palaces or libraries, old hotels, cathedrals, etc., there's a technique you can use to help add more depth and interest to your photos. The trick when using a wide-angle lens (in my case, it would either be the 24mm end of my 24–240mm, or if I brought a second lens and I'm doing the "two-lens tango," then it's my 14mm) is to put something near you right in the foreground. This helps to add depth to the image, so you have a foreground, a middle ground, and a background (most new photographers just have a middle ground and background, so their shots don't have nearly the depth). Another technique is to get down low with that wide-angle and shoot from a low perspective (see page 188 for a great way to do this). Couple that wide-angle lens low-shooting angle with placing some object of interest in the foreground, and you're going to have a shot with lots of depth and an epic feel.

Capturing the Moment vs. Composition

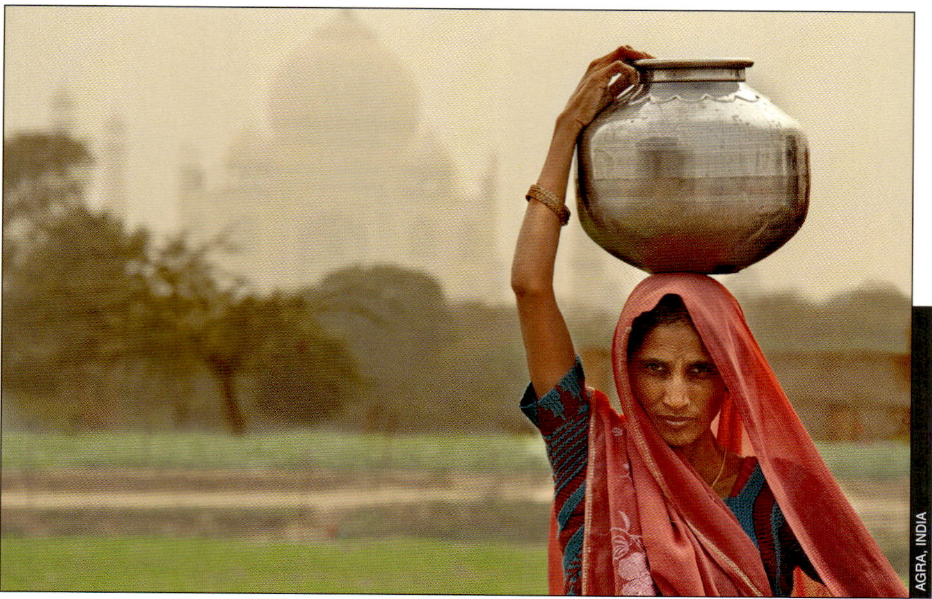

We all want to make great compositions when we're out shooting, but there's one time when worrying about composition kind of goes out the window, and that's when you're right there when something interesting/fascinating/funny or unusual happens. That's when the composition part goes out the window and the most important thing is to capture that moment (and, of course, try to capture it so it's nice and in focus). We can re-crop the photo later in Lightroom or Photoshop, or whatever, to make the composition look the way we want, but there's no filter or feature in any of those that recreates a special moment. Capture the moment—that's the goal—then worry about the composition later.

Shooting Skyscrapers

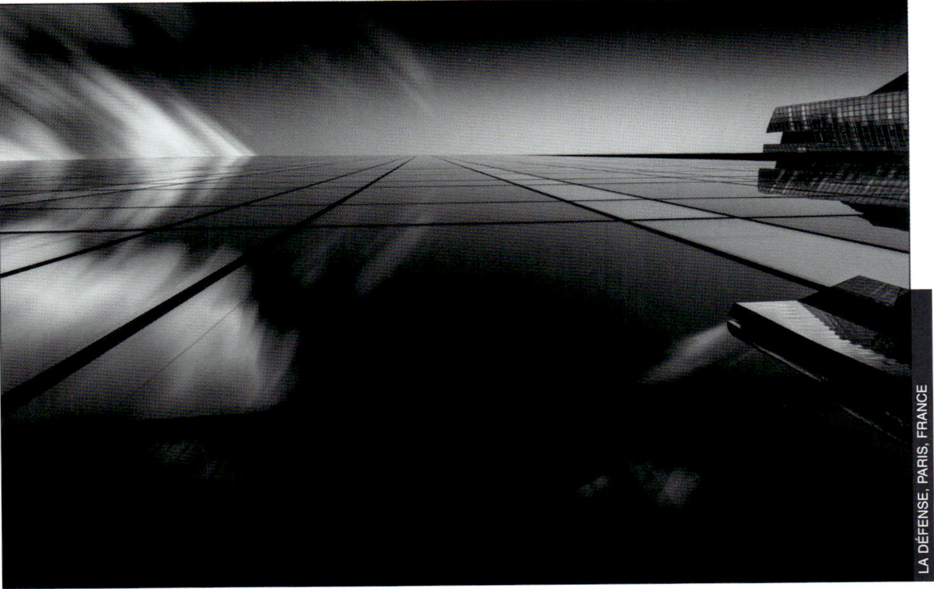

It's harder than you'd think to make a compelling shot of a skyscraper, or a soaring cityscape of tall buildings, and there are a couple of reasons for this, but I think one of the biggest is that most of the images we see of skyscrapers are taken from the same vantage point we always see them: from the street level looking up at them. You're not showing the viewer anything new, it's just kind of "Yup, that's what it looks like." That's why you can get much more interesting photos of tall buildings by shooting from another tall building. It's why photographers love shooting from the Top of the Rock (the observatory on top of 30 Rockefeller Plaza in New York City). You can shoot some of the most iconic buildings in the world from there, like the Empire State Building and the Chrysler Building, along with lots of very modern buildings, and you're showing all of this from a different view than the standard street level. If you don't have access to a high building to shoot from, one street-level technique you can use is to get very close to the building, preferably at a corner or edge, and shoot straight up alongside it. It creates a soaring feeling, and since most folks step out on the street corner, or across the street to shoot the skyscraper, you'll be bringing a very different and much more dynamic view. If you have some reasonably fast-moving clouds in the sky, you can take things up a notch by shooting a long exposure (with an ND filter; see page 115), so you get wonderful streaky clouds stretching across the sky. Try to position yourself so the clouds are either heading in your direction, or moving away from you for the best results, and of course, if you're doing a long exposure like this, it helps if you're on a tripod. One last tip: once you've got your shot, and you're post-processing, try converting your image to black and white. Architectural shots can really take on a whole new feel, so it's worth giving it a quick try. You can always undo.

Where to Put the Horizon Line

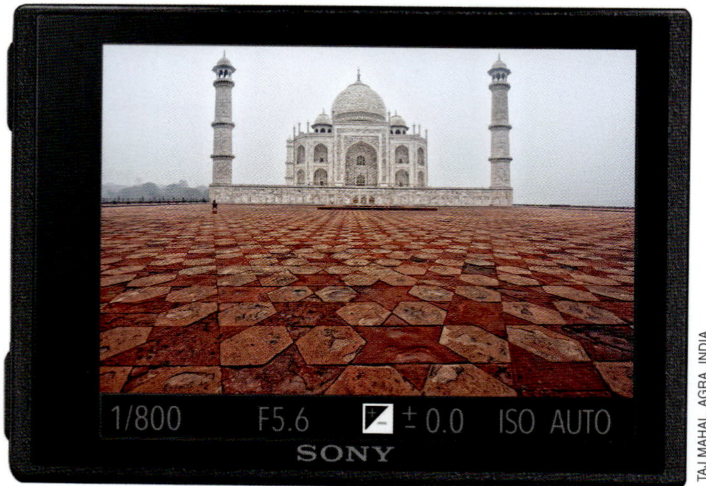

If you're shooting in a situation where you can see the horizon line, we have a simple, but powerful compositional rule we use to determine where the horizon line should go in our image (spoiler alert: it never goes in the middle. Dull. Boring. Predictable. Meh). Here's the rule: If the sky is really interesting (you have great clouds that day), then show more of the sky by putting your horizon line in the lower 1/3 of the image. That way, you see more sky (more of the most interesting part) and less of the foreground. However, if you have a boring, cloudless sky (like I do here, in my shot above), then we hide most of the boring part (in this case, the sky) by putting the horizon line up near the top 1/3 of the frame, so you don't see that much sky at all. Depending on the image, you might even get away with just showing 1/4 of the sky by moving your horizon line up even higher. To sum it up: Hide the boring 1/3 and show the more interesting 2/3. If the sky looks best, we show more of it (by putting the horizon line down low). If the sky is boring (like you see above), we show more foreground by putting the horizon line up higher. Easy enough.

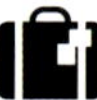
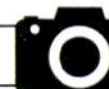

Shooting Level Matters

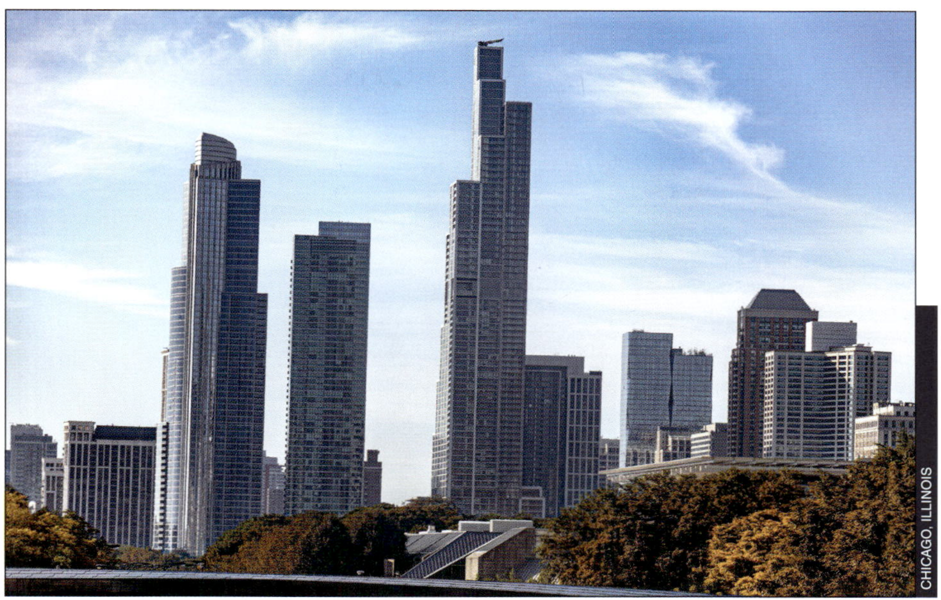

If you shoot a crooked photo where your horizon line isn't straight, or your buildings are tilted left or right (like in the image above), or the table in the restaurant looks like the plates are about to go sliding off onto the floor, you can definitely straighten your image later in Lightroom, Photoshop, or whatever. But, when you do that, it will require you to recrop the image because when you rotate your photo, it will leave little white gaps in all the corners. This changes your original composition, which is fine if you didn't particularly like your original composition, but you won't have to go through any of these annoying things if you just get a straight, level shot in the first place. It's not that hard anymore because nearly all new cameras have a built-in level feature that shows you if your camera is straight. Also, there are now many ballheads and/or tripods that have a built-in level (though the ones on tripods are somewhat less useful because your tripod can be perfectly level, but then your ballhead can be tilted and your photos winds up tilted. So, I usually ignore the one on my tripod). For travel photography, I have a Vello Low Profile Bubble Level that works great. It's small, super-lightweight, and inexpensive, and you don't have to take it off/put it on—it just stays in place. Pretty brilliant. It doesn't matter which method you use, but I can tell you this is one of those things that is better to fix in-camera when you're shooting than to try to fix later in post.

You Don't Have to Show the Scene as It Is

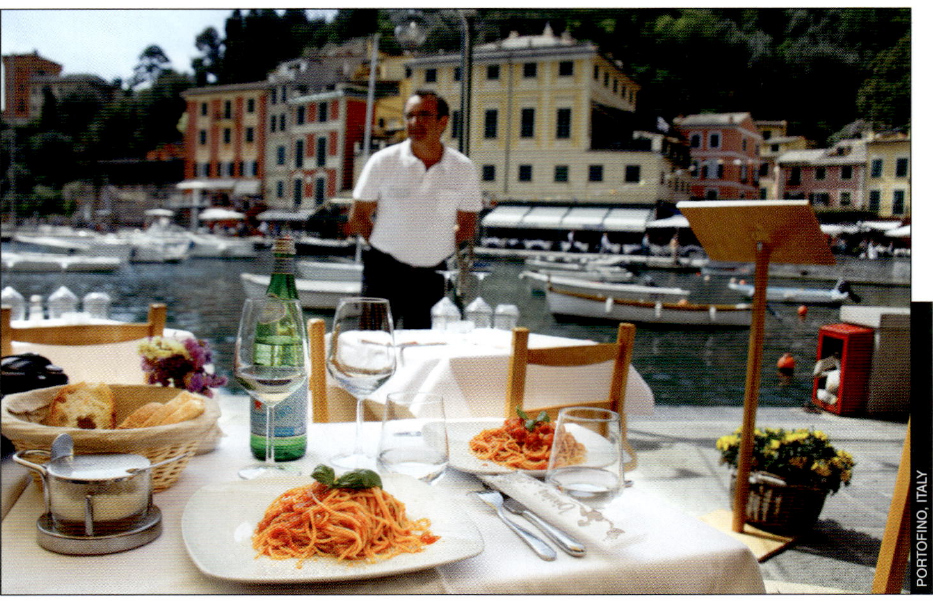

An important part of our job as a travel photographer (heck, as any kind of photographer) is deciding what story we want to tell with our image, and that essentially means we make a decision about what goes in our frame (in our image) and what we leave out. This is a very intentional decision—a creative one—and what you decide to include or leave out is literally what tells the story. So, there's something I want you to consider when you're doing all this: you don't have to show the scene as it is. If we're not on assignment for a news agency, then we can use our camera to be selective about what we show and what we don't show. For example, let's say you and your spouse are having a romantic dinner in a quaint restaurant, which could make a lovely image, but there are only the two of you and two other couples in the restaurant. You could choose to show the mostly empty restaurant in your image, which tells one story (maybe you picked the wrong place to eat?), or you can frame the shot so you see the other couples in the shot, so it looks like the restaurant is busy, which tells a more romantic story—one of a bustling restaurant full of life. Maybe you choose to only show you and the waiter, and it's assumed that it's a bustling place. The important thing to keep in mind: you get to choose what appears in the frame, so use this power to tell the story you want to tell. You don't have to show reality, with all its bumps and bruises (or empty tables). You're an artist, so go create your art.

Leading Lines (and How to Use Them)

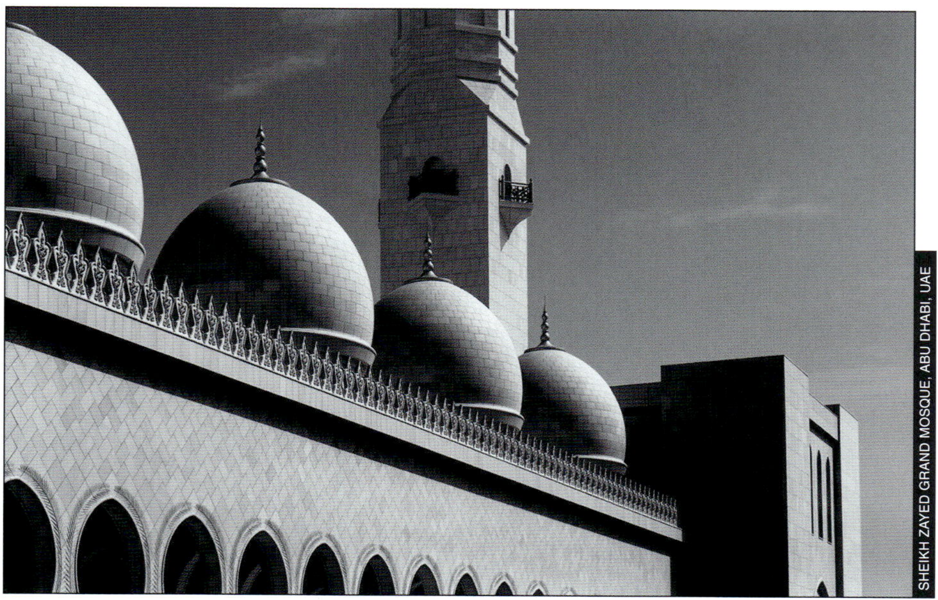

One thing we generally try to do with our composition is to lead people into our image—to draw them in and lead them where we visually want them to go in the photo. That's why the compositional technique called "leading lines" is pretty popular because it leads the viewer's eyes right to the area you want them to find in your photo. A leading line can be anything that leads the viewer's eye, from a picket fence to a road winding around a hillside, to a row of sheep, to a railroad track leading their eye off into the horizon. When you're taking your shot, and you see something you might be able to use as a leading line, like perhaps a row of streetlights or a row of bushes, you have to position yourself so these things in the scene lead the viewer's eye into your scene (this is actually more fun than it sounds—finding that leading line and using it to your advantage). In the image above, taken at the Sheikh Zayed Grand Mosque in Abu Dhabi, I used the roof line of this side of the mosque to lead the viewer from the left of my image straight down to the right corner. Now, every image won't have a leading line opportunity in it, but be prepared when you do see one to use it to make your composition even stronger.

Changing Your Perspective

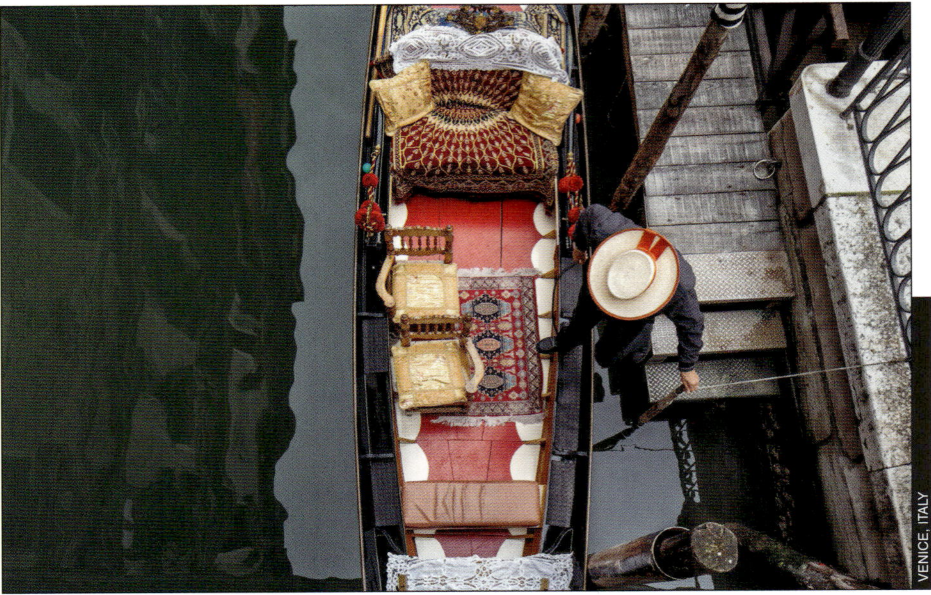

Think for a moment about how an amateur photographer photographs anything—they walk up to whatever it is they want to take a photo of and they take the photo. All of their shots would be, with a rare exception I imagine, taken at eye level. There's nothing wrong with eye-level shots; we all take them, right? But, there's nothing particularly exciting or intriguing about them either. It's the viewpoint most of the world's photos are taken from, so it's a very routine view. Want to take your photos up a notch really quickly without spending a dime? Change your perspective, and suddenly, even regular things become much more interesting because the person viewing your image is seeing things from a different view, a different perspective. This means getting down low, or even very, very low, or it can mean shooting from up high (or way up high) to show the view down on a scene. Think about food photography—the "shooting straight down" on food shot has become popular these days because it's a different view than we've seen for most of our lives. It's the same food we always see, but just changing the perspective (showing it from directly above) makes the scene more interesting. Shoot from a staircase or balcony down on a scene, or put your camera in a spot where you normally wouldn't put a camera and use your self-timer to take the shot, and you'll show someone a view they're not used to seeing, and they'll love you for it.

Working the Scene

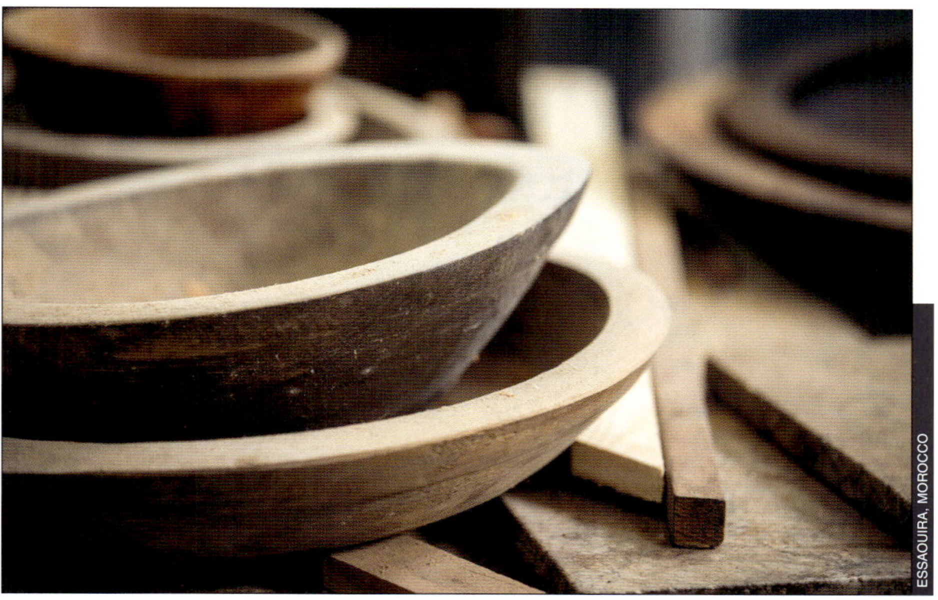

I'll bet you've had this experience dozens of times: You walk in a city and come across a scene and stop to take a few shots. You look at them on the back of your camera and they look pretty boring, so you take another shot or two and then move on. Here's what you're missing: if something made you stop there, that means something there caught your eye. There's a shot there—you just didn't stick around long enough to find it. You didn't stay and "work the scene" long enough to find out where that certain something that called out to you was, so you didn't get it. When you put your camera up to your eye, it doesn't automatically snap to the thing that made you stop. You have to seek it out. Working the scene like this is so critical because there is a particular angle, a particular view, a particular composition where everything comes together—the light, the angle, the structure—to make a great shot. But, if you just walk away from a scene that called out to you, you'll never find it. The secret is staying with it and "working the scene." Your job is to stick with it, try different angles, different perspectives, try zooming in tight, going out wide, shooting from different viewpoints, until you uncover that frame that called out to your artistic subconscious. It may take 10 minutes, it may take 30, or you could get lucky and all it takes is 2 more minutes, and yet sometimes, you'll still come away empty-handed, but that doesn't mean it was time wasted or that we shouldn't try. The image above was taken in the workshop of a gift shop in Morocco. The light was really nice, but it was just a big mess of tools and wood and...well, it was a mess, but something was drawing me there, so I stuck with it for like 15 minutes. I have a lot of really bad photos from that little shop, but I really like this simple one—its shapes and the softness of the light. Working the scene is a key technique and the more you try it, the more you'll uncover a hidden gem in a sea of what seemed like nothing.

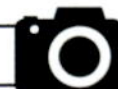

Avoid Junk around Your Edges

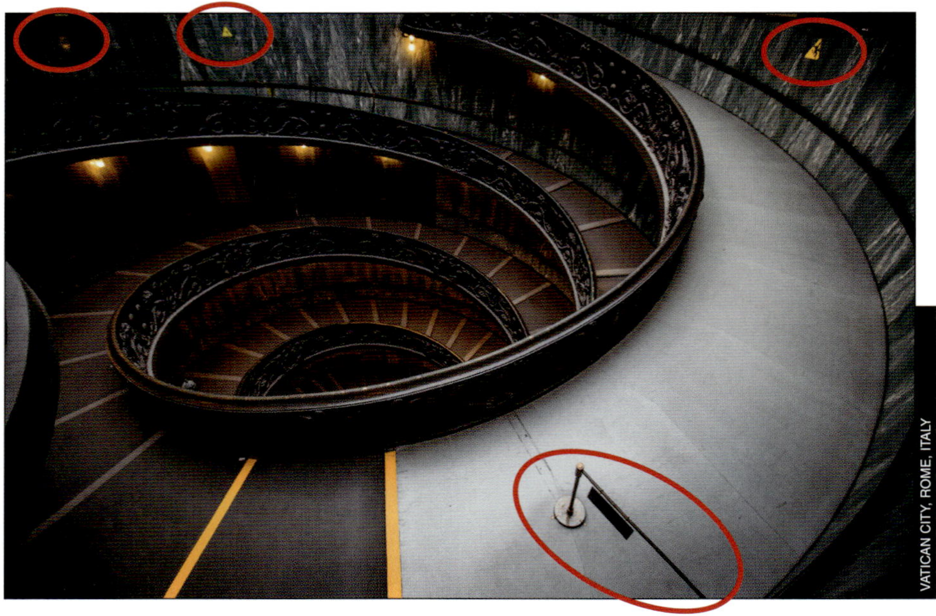

One of the most common compositional mistakes is one of the easiest to avoid because all you really have to do is be aware of it, and that is not letting things you don't want in your image to creep in from the sides of it. A tree branch, a sign, some weeds, an ugly bush, a telephone pole—there are a host of things that can sneak in and become a distraction if you're not looking out for them. One reason we get burned by this so often is that we're focused on the subject when we're taking the shot. Let's say it's a stream, and we're using an ND filter to make the water all nice and silky, so that's what we're focusing on—the stream and whether it's silky. We're not paying attention to the things along the edges that sneak in to ruin our shot. Start keeping an eye on the edges of your photos, so you can change your shooting position—sometimes just an inch or two will do the trick—to keep things from sneaking in and messing up your image (or at the very least, making you spend a bunch of time trying to remove them in Photoshop. You want to spend your time in Photoshop being creative and having fun, not fixing stuff you should have caught while you were shooting). Just add keeping an eye on the edges to your composition list and it will pay off for you.

Simplify the Scene

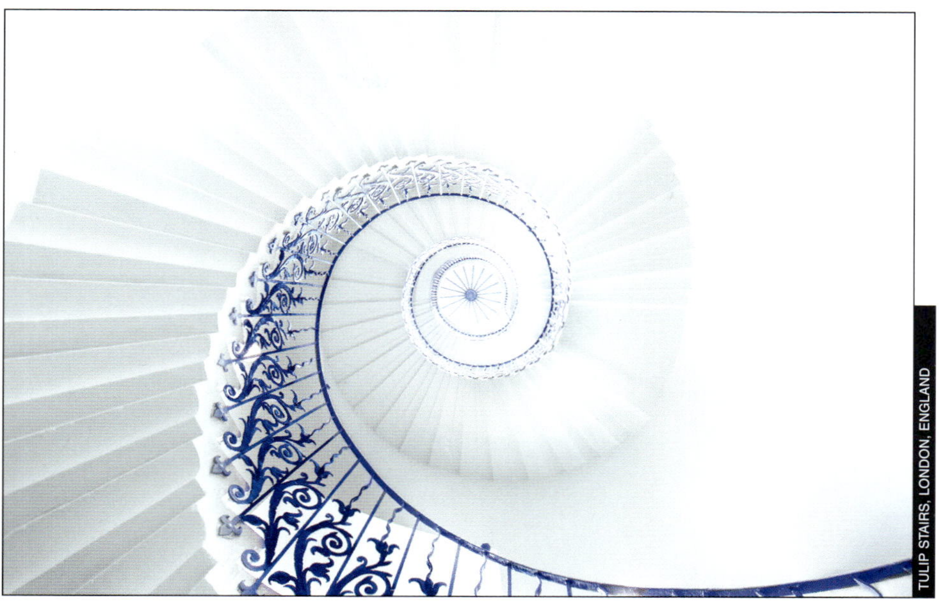

Of all the compositional techniques in this chapter, if I had to choose which one is the most important, it would be to work hard to keep your scene simple. To limit what you include in your framing, so your message, your story, is strong and clear. Don't make the mistake I did in looking through my viewfinder, not liking what I saw, and thinking the answer was to add more to my image, to include more to make the image more interesting, when the exact opposite was what I should have been doing. I needed to look through the viewfinder and ask myself if each element in that photo was making the image stronger or taking way from the image. When I learned to look for simplicity and clarity, not busy scenes with so much going on that the viewer didn't know where to look first, it was a turning point in my photography. When I'm composing a shot today, I'm trying to figure out what I can leave out. Is there a way I can zoom in/out, move left/right, tilt up/down to simplify the image I'm creating, which would help make my visual story that much clearer? This is definitely a case of less is more. Give this one a try. I think you'll dig it.

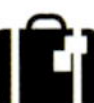
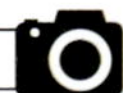

Odd Numbers Work Best

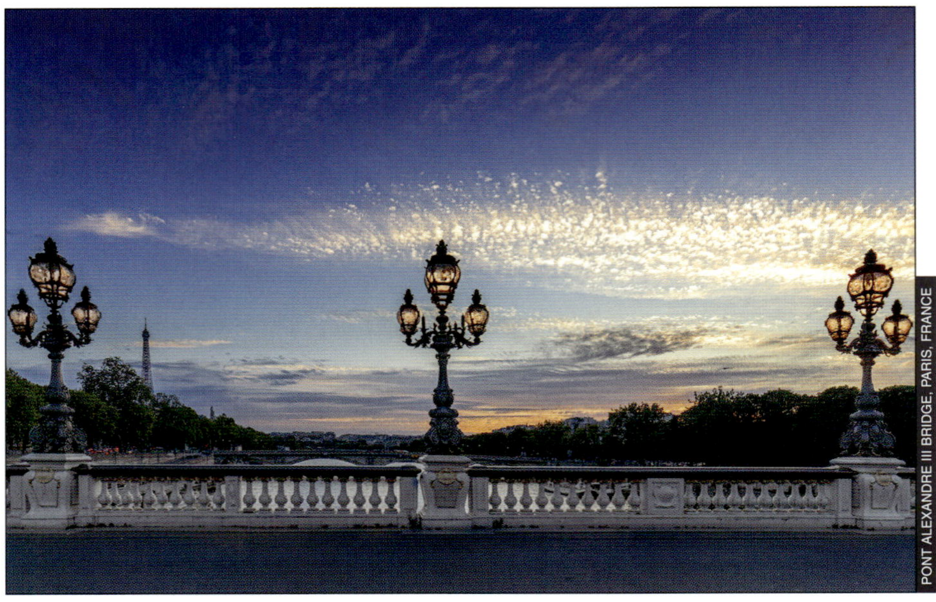

This is one of those tried-and-true techniques, and it's based on the psychological concept that people like things better when there are odd numbers (people are weird. I know. I'm one of them. Have been for a while). For example, if you're taking a photo on a bridge and you can include three or four lampposts along that bridge, always go with three. If there are lamps hanging in a restaurant, include three or five, but don't choose four. By the way, I know I just used two lamp examples, but it really has nothing to do with lamps, so don't let that get you (or me) off track. It's any object in your image. There's a row of shot glasses on the bar? Show one or three, or five or seven, but skip showing two or six. There…I broke the lamp curse. ;-)

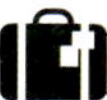 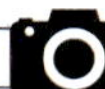

The Power of Negative Space

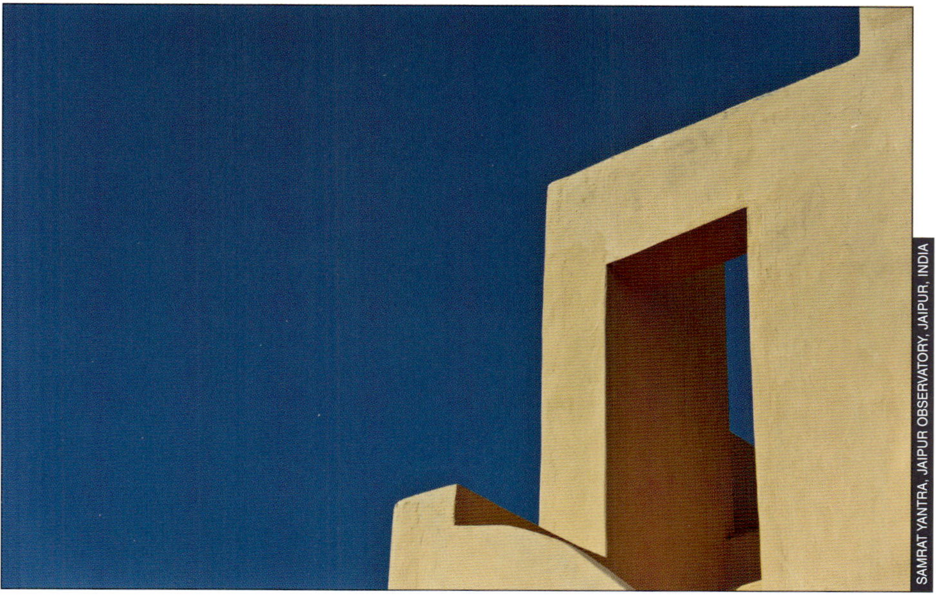

One of my favorite compositional techniques is called "negative space," and that simply just means leaving a large area of your image empty (or without anything important), so it immediately draws the viewer's eye to your subject. Negative space can be a solid color (like a wall), or a cloudless part of the sky (like you see here), or anything where there's nothing (so it's kind of empty), which brings strength and energy to your subject. This is an easy compositional technique to pull off. You just have to keep an eye out for negative space opportunities—situations where you can literally have your subject stand alone—and compose the shot so your subject is surrounded by nothing. It's a more powerful technique than it sounds. Give this one a try.

Shooting Patterns

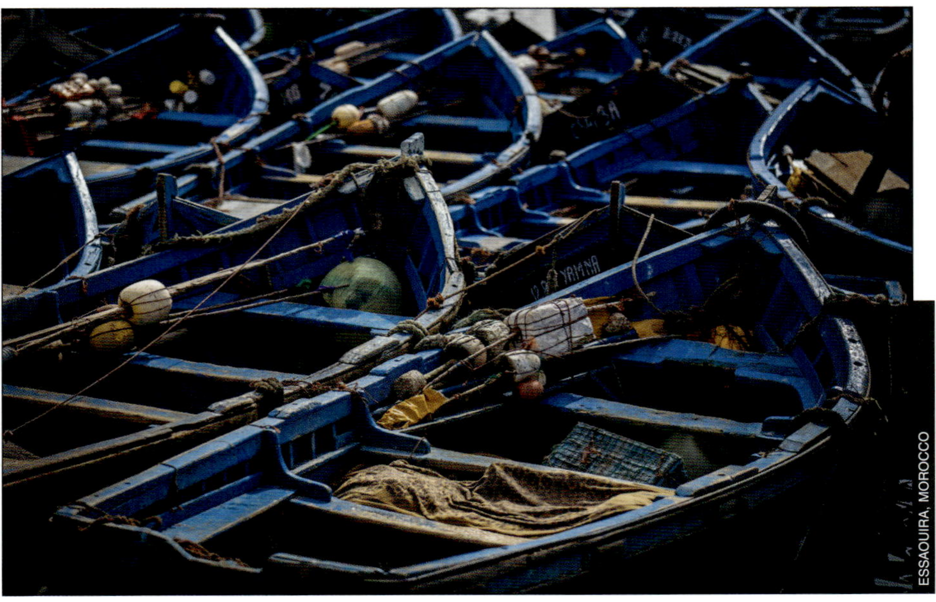

Humans love patterns. I have no idea how aliens feel about them, but speaking as a human (and an unofficial ambassador for this planet), I can tell you we love patterns. They're everywhere in our lives, from tile patterns in our kitchens and bathrooms, to repeating patterns in the carpets beneath our feet, to the repeating patterns in ceilings, and buildings, and pretty much everywhere. So, since we love patterns so much, why not show folks something in your photography you know they already love: patterns. It's a little trickier than it sounds because just a straight pattern of stuff can actually make for a fairly boring image, so to take things up a notch we do something I learned from legendary photographer Jay Maisel, who said (I'm paraphrasing here): patterns are interesting, but a pattern interrupted is even more interesting. He is so on the money! If you see a row of yellow umbrellas lining a sandy beach, that can be interesting. But, if just one of those umbrellas is a different color—maybe one of them is blue or red, interrupting the pattern—that takes it to a whole new level. Keep an eye out for patterns while you're traveling, and keep shooting them and finding interesting ways to show them. You might even get lucky and have that pattern interrupted, and if you don't have an interruption, well… there's always Photoshop, which will take one of those umbrellas and change its color in two seconds.

Using Frames in Your Composition

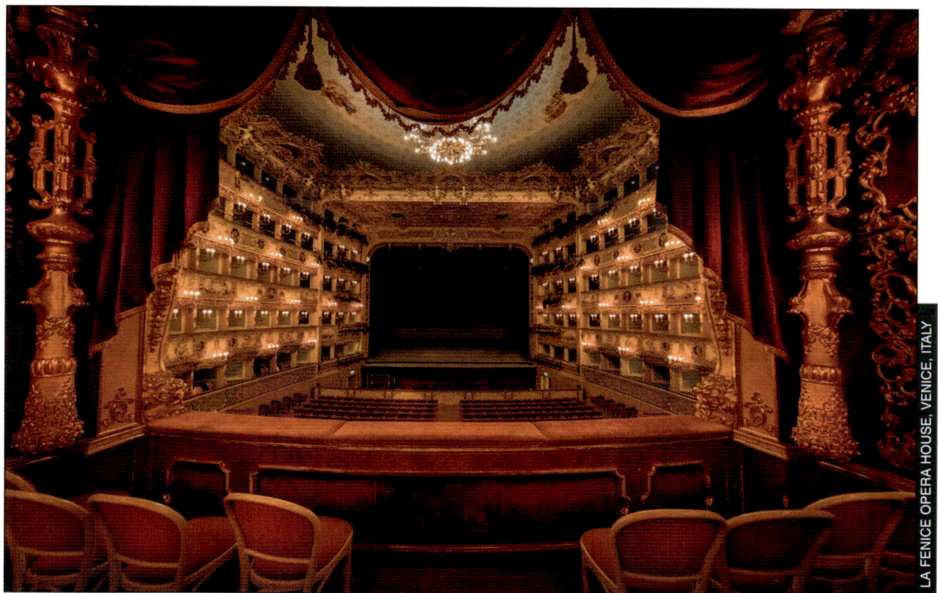

What do people do when they have a photo they really like? They frame it. They frame it and put it on their desk or hang it on the wall. We love putting frames around things. That's probably why "framing" a shot in-camera, where you're shooting through a doorway or a window or an arch (or, in this case, a set of curtains), and including those elements in your shot is so pleasing to people. I wasn't a big fan of this technique until I tried it a few times and saw the reactions of people who saw those framed-style shots. It's like they're drawn to them. So, if you want to create images people are drawn to, add this one to your bag of compositional tricks.

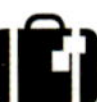
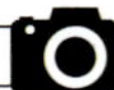

Symmetry: Why We Love It

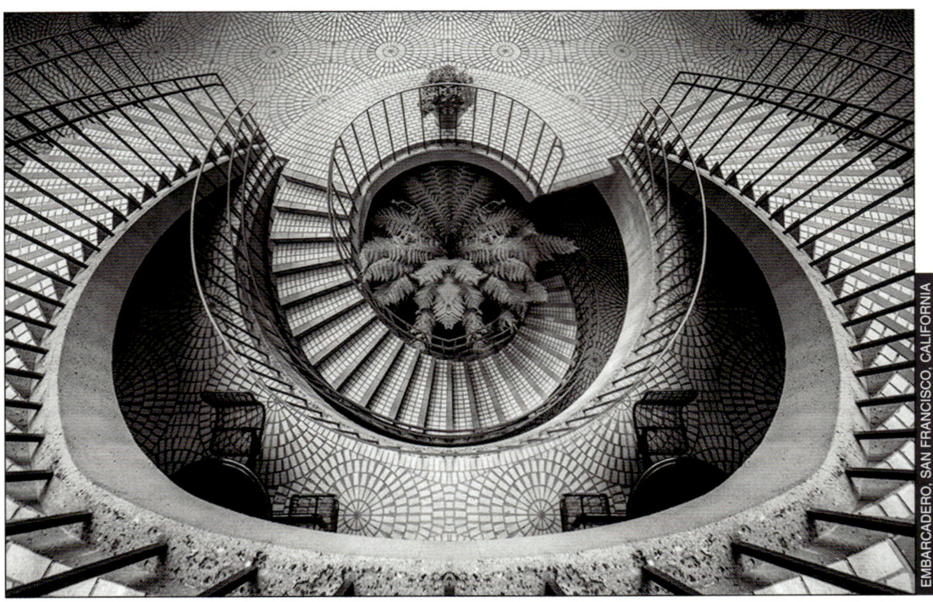

This is another one of those things that people seem to just love in photographs. We love symmetry in real life (they've even done studies that show that babies are drawn to adults and teens whose facial features are the most symmetrical—their eyes are perfectly aligned with each other, their smile extends the exact same amount on each side, their ears are perfectly aligned with one another, and so on). This is just something to be on the lookout for as you move through a city. But, in some cases, you can create symmetry artificially in Photoshop by selecting half of your image, putting it up on its own separate layer above the original image, and then using Photoshop's Free Transform feature to horizontally flip the copied half of your image, and—boom—you have symmetry (not sure why I said "boom," but I can't take it out. I get paid by the word). Anyway, this is something else to keep an eye out for, but I have one additional tip: when you're standing in front of something that's perfectly symmetrical, like the Taj Mahal or the Eiffel Tower, or a group of buildings downtown, take an extra moment to make sure you're shooting from the center of the object. If you're off by a foot or two in either direction, it throws everything off just enough to look not quite right. It's worth the extra few seconds to really make sure you're centered before you shoot.

The Rule of Thirds

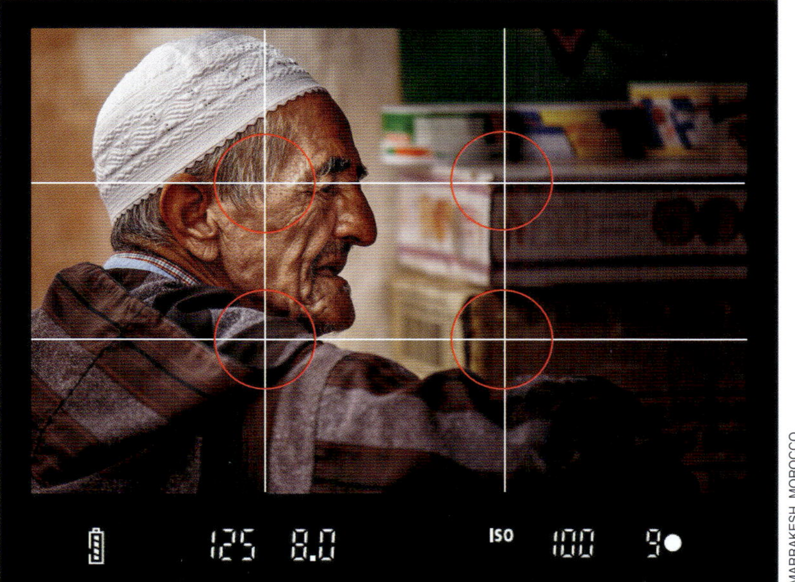

This is probably the most popular of all the compositional techniques. It was first created back in 1797, and not only do we still use it to this day, it's so popular that most cameras (along with the camera in your cellphone) have a feature built in to help you use it when you shoot. The rule of thirds starts with the idea that putting things in the center of your image is boring, and that you can create an image with greater strength and depth by applying this compositional rule ("rule" is actually a bad name for it because it's not a rule or a law. It should just be called the "rule-of-thirds tool" or something like that. It's a helper. Not written in stone). To use the "rule," you mentally divide what you're seeing through your viewfinder into thirds (as I just mentioned, most cameras allow you to put a visible rule-of-thirds grid over your scene in the viewfinder, like you see above, so you can use it while you're framing up your shot). Once you see the grid (either onscreen or in your mind), the idea is that the strongest place to put your subject is where the horizontal and vertical lines intersect. Any of those four places would add more dimension to your shot, versus putting your subject in the center (though, the reason this isn't a law is that sometimes the exact right place to put your subject is in the center. Just depends on the image, right?). There is also a rule-of-thirds rule for horizon lines (which is covered on page 98), but that's pretty much all there is to it. Put important elements where those lines intersect, and you'll have stronger, more interesting images.

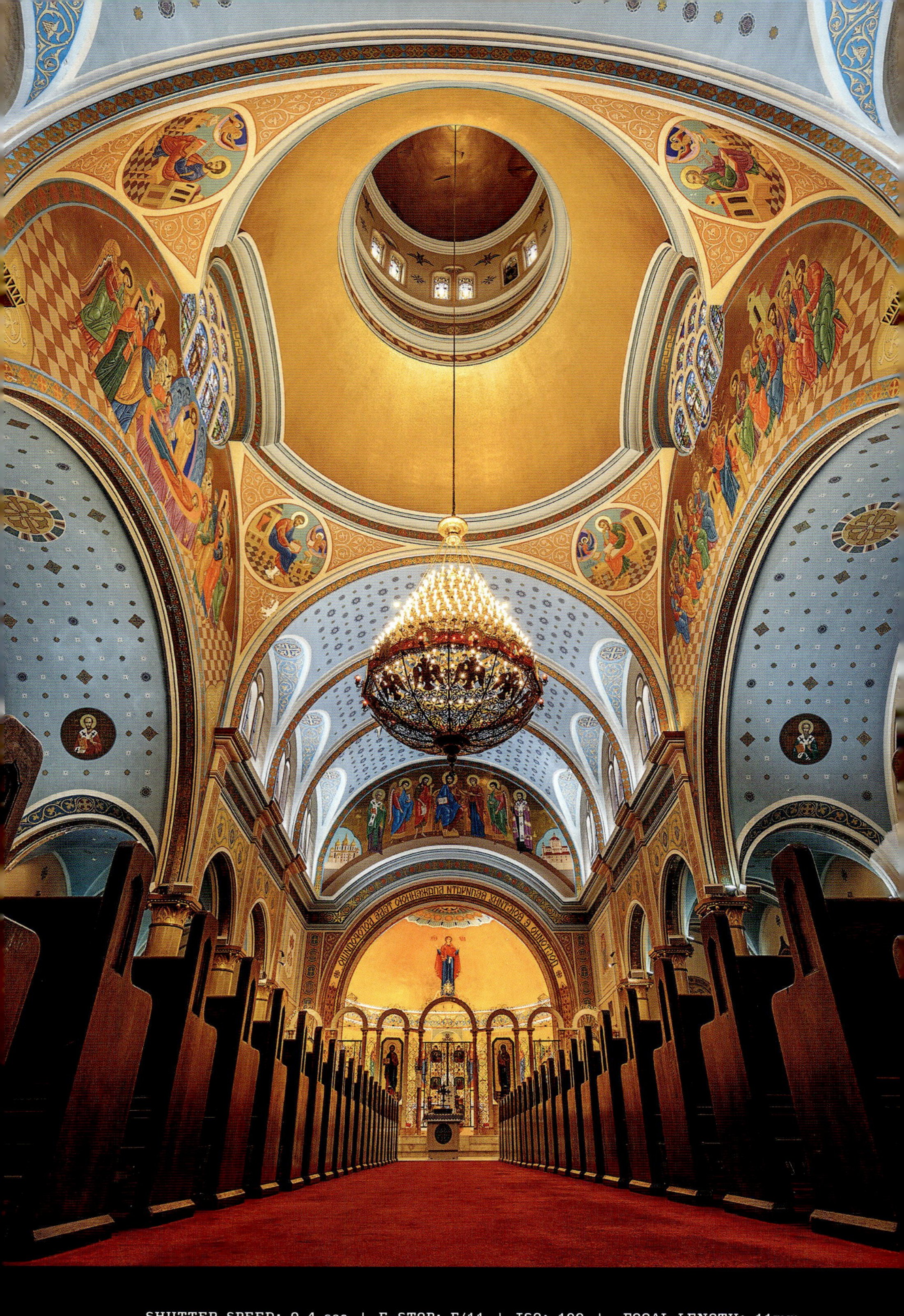

SHUTTER SPEED: 0.4 sec | F-STOP: F/11 | ISO: 100 | FOCAL LENGTH: 11mm
LOCATION: St. Nicholas Ukrainian Catholic Cathedral, Chicago, Illinois

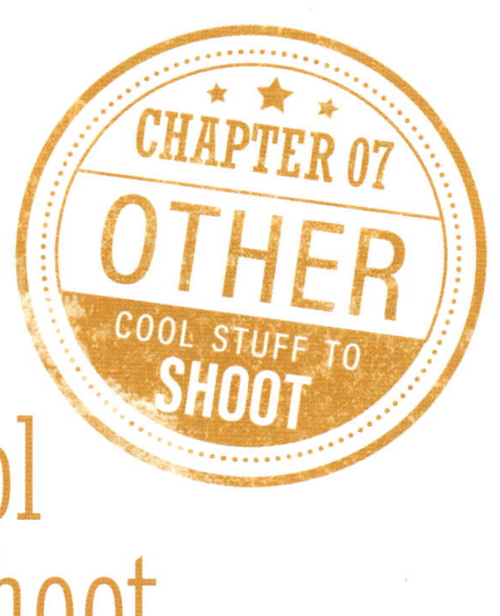

Other Cool Stuff to Shoot

Well, That Headline Kind of Kills the Need
for Me to Write a Subhead. Still Did, Though

When it comes to shooting travel, there are the obvious topics (monuments, tourist attractions, palaces, etc.) that you're definitely going to wind up shooting (you don't need a book to tell you that), but then there are the less obvious things, things you might not have thought of, and features on your camera that allow you to do things—especially as they relate to travel—that maybe you haven't tried. One feature that is found in more of today's mirrorless cameras is MMM, which is an acronym for "Make More Magical," and which essentially adds kind of a "fairy dust" overlay effect on your photo. Now, at first you might be thinking, "Well, that's kind of dumb" and "When am I going to use something like that?" But think about it: when Tinkerbell appeared onscreen and tapped her magic wand (I'm not certain why Tinkerbell had a wand in the first place, but let's not focus on that), and it added a bunch of fairy dust over the image of Sleeping Beauty's castle, did you ever stop to think, "Wow, that makes the shot look really bad!"? I bet that never crossed your mind, and the main reason is: "fairy dust makes everything better," which is probably why Sony first introduced this feature in their a7 II full-frame mirrorless back in 2014. Of course, it wasn't long before Canon introduced their version in the EOS 5D Mark II, which they called "Pixie Dust," followed by Nikon, who named their version "Sensor Dust," which really didn't catch on the way they thought it would. It's a shame, too, because they had the best implementation of a fairy dust overlay I've ever seen. Well, with the possible exception of Fuji, who released a version called "Grated Cheese." In the launch's press briefing, they said they chose the name because "like real grated cheese, anything you sprinkle it on is made better." It was removed from Fuji cameras, starting with the Fujiflim X-A2, and the company rep who came up with the name was subsequently fired and now owns a Chem-Dry Carpet Cleaning franchise in Sun Valley, Idaho.

Shooting a Time Lapse

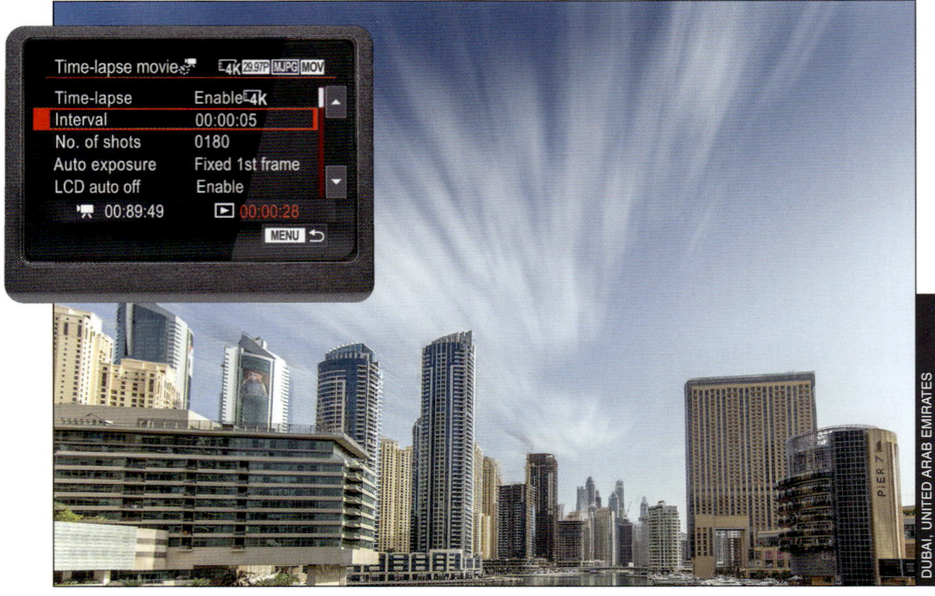

Time-lapse photography is awesome for combining movement with the passage of time, and a popular example would be setting up your camera on your hotel balcony and letting the time lapse run from sunset to sunrise. Your camera takes a photo at certain intervals, and it does this unattended, so you start it and let it run for the amount of time you choose (like one shot every 10 minutes, or one shot every minute, etc.). Once it's done, you compile your time-lapse images together so they display rapidly (usually no longer than 30 seconds), then save it as a video (you can do this right within Lightroom, or do it all on your phone, which can automatically compile the images into a video for you—see page 128), and you get this amazing movement over time which has a real documentary-style feel to it (it's easy to get hooked on doing these. They look awesome and some of the most amazing time lapses I've seen have been travel-based time lapses). Many cameras these days have a built-in time-lapse feature (though sometimes it's called "interval" shooting in the menus), and you essentially choose how many shots you want to take in total, over what period of time, and then put your camera on a tripod or another sturdy surface and let it do its thing. If your camera doesn't have this feature, you can buy a cable release that has an intervalometer (time-lapse) feature built right into it (they're around $45, but it's both a time-lapse controller and a cable release all in one, so that's a little easier to swallow).

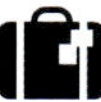
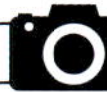

Shooting Long Exposures

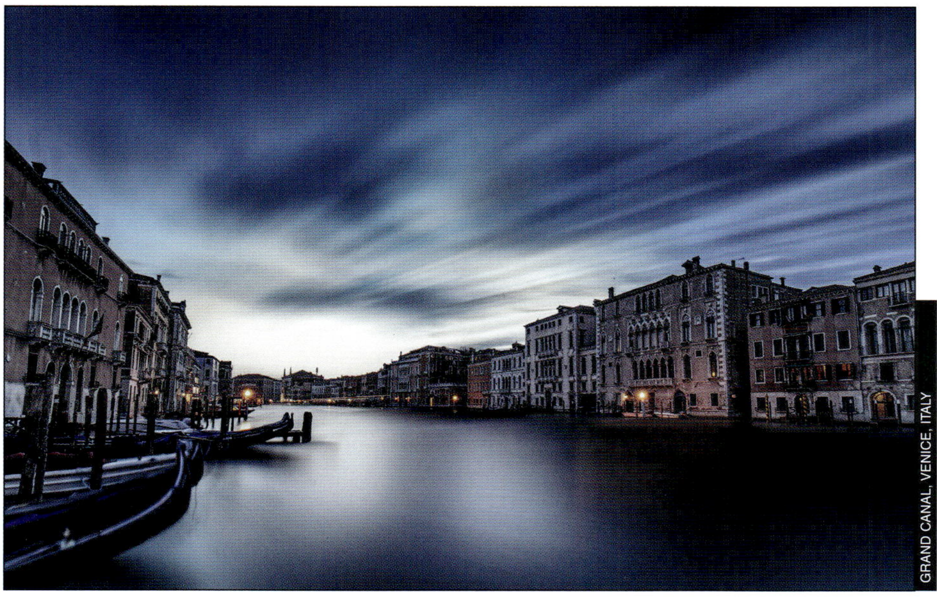

A long exposure with a neutral density (ND) filter is wonderful for showing movement. What probably comes to mind first is how awesome it looks on water—think fountains and waterfalls that are smooth and silky instead of frozen, or a lake that's smooth and misty instead of choppy—or on clouds. I also use it for getting rid of tourists (see page 187). There are so many great things you can do with one that an ND is usually the only filter I have when shooting travel. Using a high-numbered f-stop, like f/22, will force your shutter to stay open longer, but unless it's a cloudy, overcast day, or nearly sunset, that alone won't be enough. You'll need an ND filter (see page 71), which goes over your lens, darkening the scene to force your shutter open for long periods of time (from a few seconds to 10 or 15 minutes), so you can get that water really silky, or those clouds streaking across the sky. Using an ND filter is easier if you're shooting mirrorless. Just screw it on, and if you think your exposure is going to be longer than 30 seconds, switch to Bulb mode, which lets you keep your shutter open as long as you hold the shutter button down. Then, using a cable or wireless shutter release (see page 68), lock that button in place for as long as you need to make a proper exposure. How long do you need to keep that shutter open? There are apps that'll do the math for you. I use NDTimer (for iOS or ND Filter Timer for Android) and PhotoPills can also do this (see page 72). They're awesome. Tell the app what your shutter speed was before you screwed on the filter, then tell it how dark a filter you're using, and it tells you exactly how long, in minutes and/or seconds, you'll need to keep that shutter open. If you shoot DSLR, there are two extra things to do: (1) Set your focus before you screw the filter on, and switch the Auto Focus button on your lens off, so it doesn't try to refocus. Then, (2) cover your viewfinder with a piece of black tape, so light doesn't leak in and ruin your photo.

Shooting Panoramas

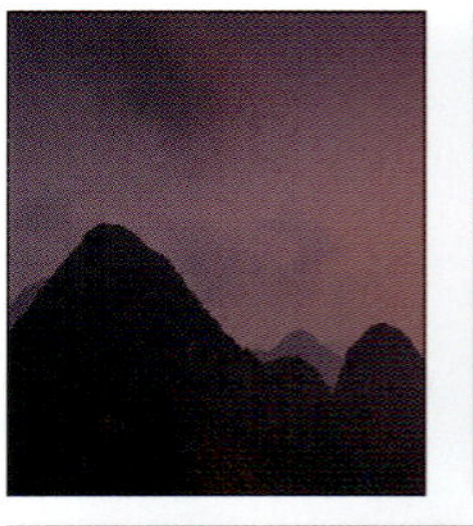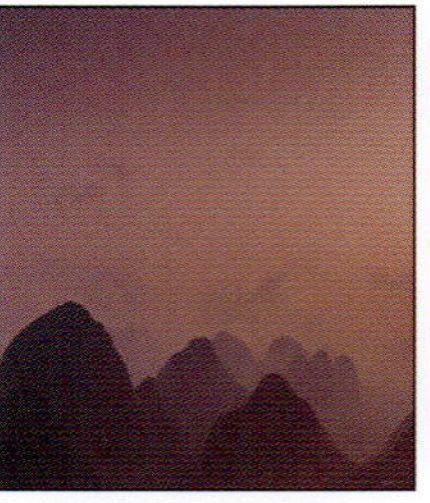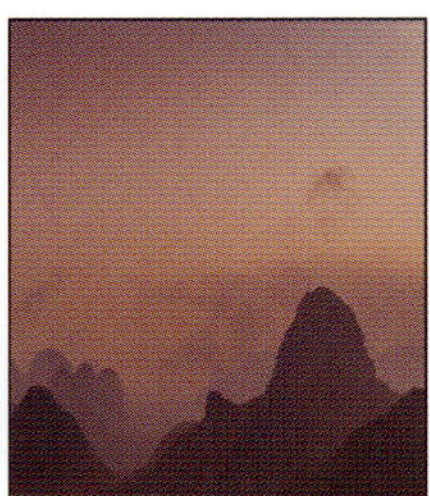

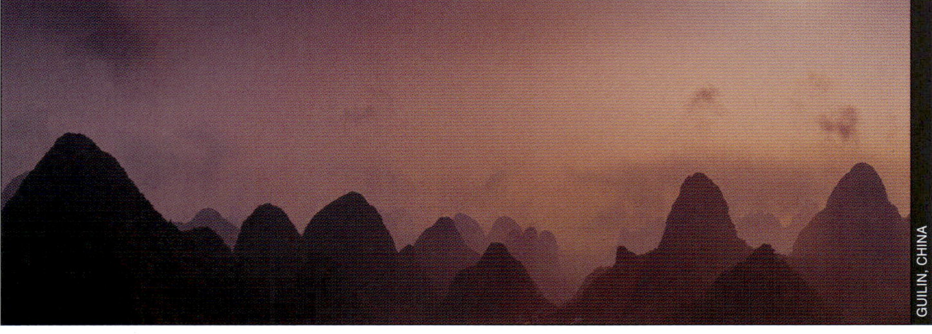

GUILIN, CHINA

I shoot a lot of hand-held panoramic shots (called "panos," for short) when I'm traveling, and not only is it easy to shoot a pano, Lightroom or Photoshop will do all the work of putting it together for you. It really couldn't be easier. First, the camera part. There are only two things to do setting-wise: (1) Set your focus on the scene, and then turn the Auto Focus button off (it's right on the side of your lens). (2) Set your f-stop at f/11, so everything's in focus, and then let the camera choose your shutter speed. Then, look in the viewfinder and make note of the shutter speed it chose for you. Now, switch your shooting mode to manual, and then dial in f/11 for your aperture, along with whatever shutter speed you just saw in your view-finder. Doing this ensures that neither your focus nor your exposure will change while you're making your pano. (*Note:* All that is not always necessary. I've shot literally 100+ panos where I didn't change either of those on my camera and they came out fine. But, if you want to be really serious about panos, technically, you should do those steps for the best results.) Now that your settings are in place, as far as shooting goes, just make sure each frame overlaps the previous frame by around 30%. That's it. That's all Lightroom or Photoshop needs to make the magic happen (I go into exactly what to do in Lightroom or Photoshop to combine these multiple images into a single panoramic image on page 228).

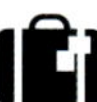
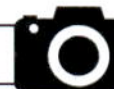

Shooting High Dynamic Range (HDR) Images

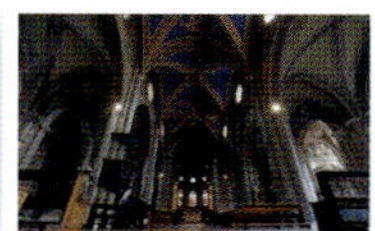

Normal

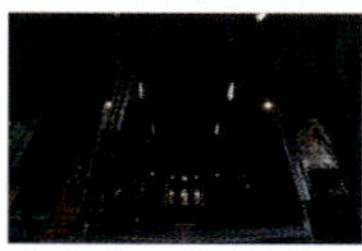

–2 Stops

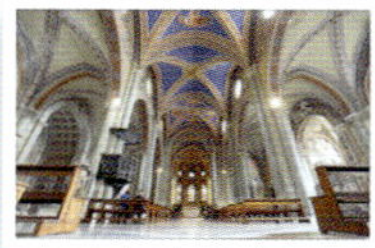

+2 Stops

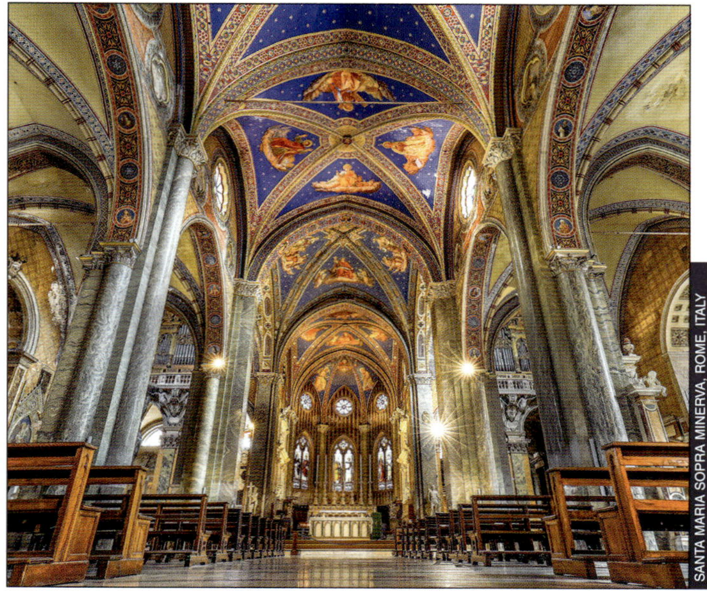

The human eye can see an incredible range of tones, from really dark areas to super-bright areas, and it automatically adjusts so we see everything. It's really remarkable. For example, let's say you're in a beautiful city, inside a towering Gothic cathedral with tall, stained glass windows on either side. You see everything perfectly as you're standing there, but when you take a picture, the stained glass windows are totally blown out—no detail, no color, no nuthin'. That's because your camera doesn't have nearly the range of the human eye—it can't handle that huge change in tones, so it either makes the windows blown out, or if you darken the exposure enough so the stained glass looks okay, then the cathedral is so dark you've lost all the detail. That's where HDR (high dynamic range) comes in. Your camera takes a series of shots with different exposures (for example, one normal, one two stops darker, and one two stops brighter), and then you combine them in Lightroom or Photoshop into one image with an incredible amount of range—more than any sensor can capture on its own. You turn this feature on by enabling Exposure Bracketing on your camera, and then you turn on the camera's self-timer, set to 2 seconds, press the shutter button once, and it takes all three photos for you (if you're in a low-light situation, like shooting in a cathedral, you'll get the best results if you shoot on a tripod). That's the camera part—I'll show you how to combine those three images into one HDR image on page 229 in the post-processing chapter.

Shooting HDR Panos

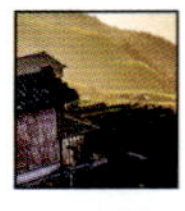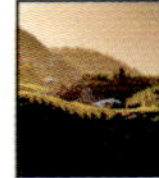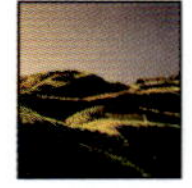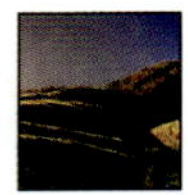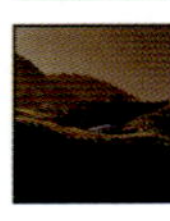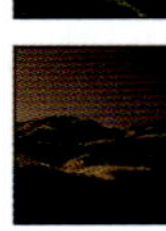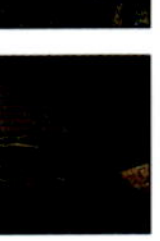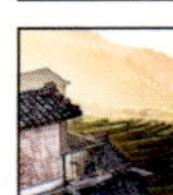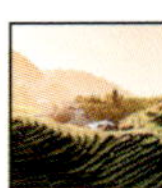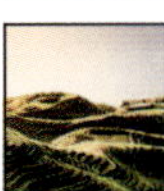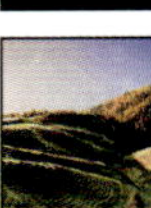

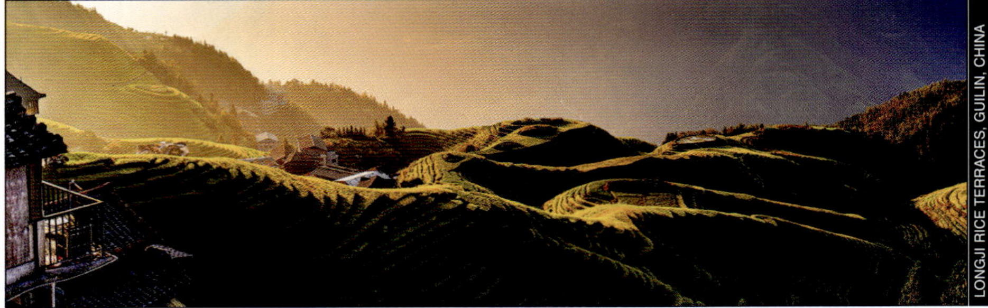

Okay, if you're feeling really adventurous, you can not only create a pano *or* an HDR, but you can have both all in one. Lightroom and Photoshop can both combine the multiple HDR frames into single HDR frames, and then take all the resulting frames and combine them into a single RAW image. But, before we get to the post-processing part (I cover that on page 228, and I also created a video for you, which you can find on the book's companion website mentioned on page xiii), here's what you need to do to get the shots you'll combine: (1) Turn on Exposure Bracketing in your camera (so it takes three shots: the normal exposure, one that's two stops darker, and one that's two stops brighter). And, (2) take your first set of three photos (see the previous page for how to shoot an HDR), then aim to the right a bit, making sure this second frame will overlap the first one by around 30%, and then take all three bracketed exposures. You keep repeating this process of aiming your camera to the right a bit, still overlapping by 30%, and then taking all three shots, before moving to the right again to repeat it. When you're done, you'll have a lot of frames, but you'll have a super-high-resolution image with an incredible tonal range.

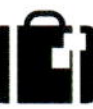
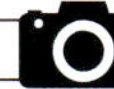

Shooting the Milky Way

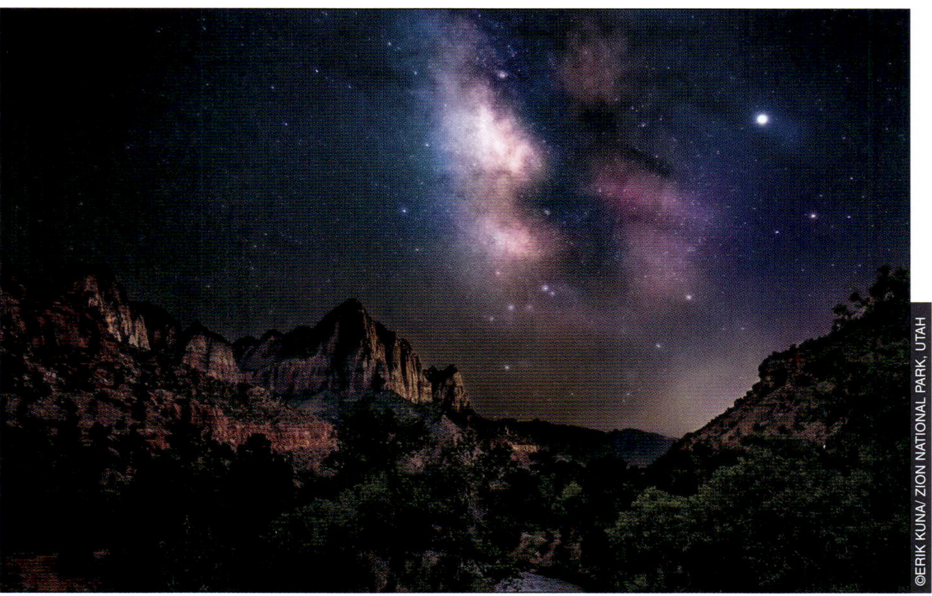

If you're somewhere far away from the lights of a city (known as "light pollution" in astrophotography circles), and it's a clear, cloudless night, you might have an opportunity to capture a stunning shot of the Milky Way. There are a few things you're going to need to make this happen: First and foremost, a tripod and some kind of cable release or wireless shutter release (see pages 65 and 68). Next, you'll need a wide-angle lens, preferably one that can shoot using a very low-numbered f-stop (like the Rokinon 14mm f/2.8 that I mentioned in Chapter 3. It's inexpensive and very popular with astrophotographers), because while you see the Milky Way looking very bright in photos, it's really not that bright in real life, and you'll need to get as much light into the camera as possible (that's why the low-numbered f-stop helps). You're still going to have to majorly crank up your ISO, but not as much if you have an f/2.8 lens. Okay, that's the gear part (and one of the camera settings—you'll shoot at f/2.8). Your shutter speed will probably be around 15 seconds (if it goes too much longer, all your stars will be blurry because of the rotation of the earth. You may be able to go a little longer, but not more than 30 seconds). As I mentioned, you'll have to crank up that ISO, probably to around 6,400 to get the stars bright enough, but don't freak out—on a solid black night sky, you won't see the noise like you normally would (just give it a try and you'll see). Also, you'll either focus your lens to Infinity (it's that little sideways 8 thing on your lens), or you can use your camera's Live View (on the back of your camera), and if your camera has a focus peaking feature, turn that on. So, the settings are simple. The "make it or break it" of whether you get a great Milky Way shot will be how clear the sky is at your location, and how far away you are from any light pollution from a city, or a gas station, or other cars.

Shooting at Night

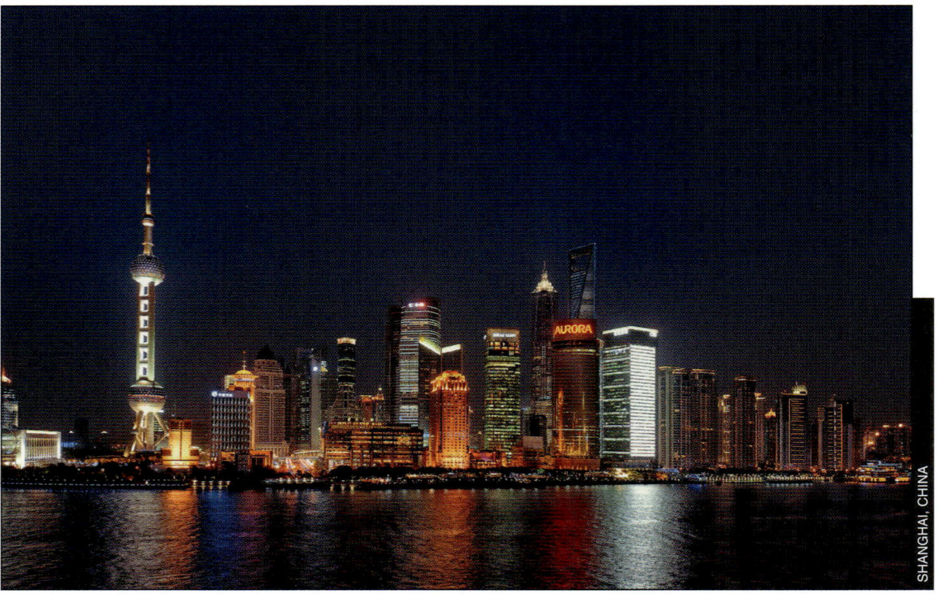

I have two tips for shooting travel at night, and the first one goes against something I've been saying in this whole book, which is to shoot in aperture priority mode, which almost always works great until it comes to shooting at night. The problem with shooting in aperture priority at night is that your camera tries to make a balanced exposure. When it sees a dark sky and dark scene overall, it thinks it needs to make things brighter, and…well, it usually overexposes the night sky and the shot looks kind of funky. That's why, when it comes to nighttime shots, I switch to manual mode. If that freaks you out, don't let it because we're going to use a trick to make this easy. Start in aperture priority mode and look at the settings it chose (knowing they're going to be a little too bright). Remember those settings, switch to manual mode, and dial in the same f-stop and shutter speed. Now, you know it's too bright, right? So, just darken the scene by choosing a higher-numbered f-stop. So, for example, if we know it's a little too bright with the f-stop set at f/5.6 and the shutter speed the camera chose, then try f/8 or f/11 and the whole scene gets darker. Just pick the f-stop that looks good to you (and looks like a normal night shot). The other tip is to try some of the different White Balance settings. In particular, try a cooler (blue) white balance and it'll make your black look a bit blue, giving kind of a futuristic look to the city at night. Give those two things a try—they'll make a difference.

Shooting Reflections

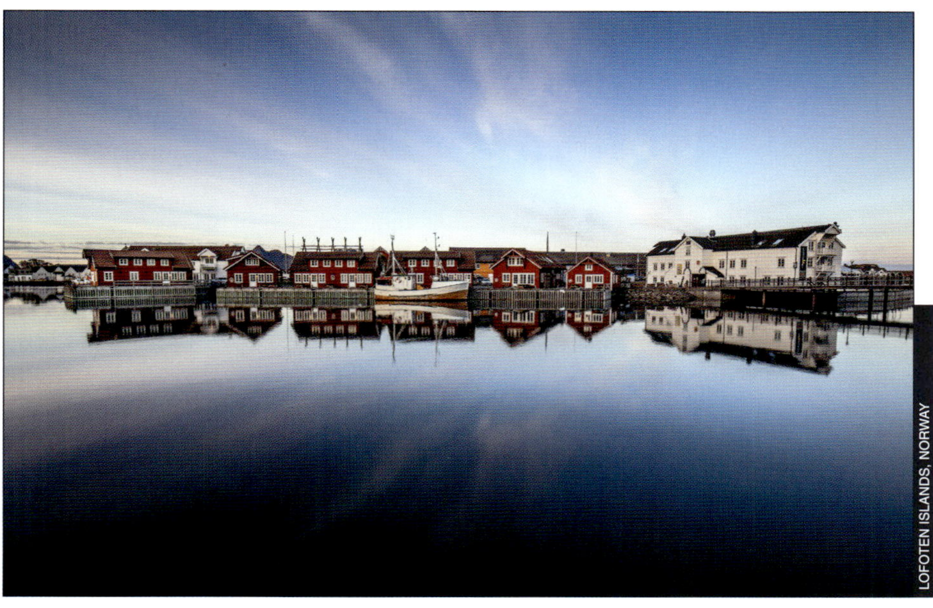

The secret to getting beautiful mirror-like reflections doesn't happen in your camera. There's no special technique for it. The secret happens in your alarm clock because the time of day that you're most likely to find glassy, still water like this is right around dawn. It's this calm time before the wind starts up and the water gets choppy that you can get these reflections on lakes and ponds and harbors. An hour after dawn and it's already too late, so set that alarm early to get those perfect glassy reflections. *Note:* This shot was taken in Norway's Lofoten Islands at a time of year when the sun actually never sets, so you get hours and hours of beautiful light (and in this case, still water) even though this was taken in the middle of the night.

A Twist on the Standard Vacation Photo

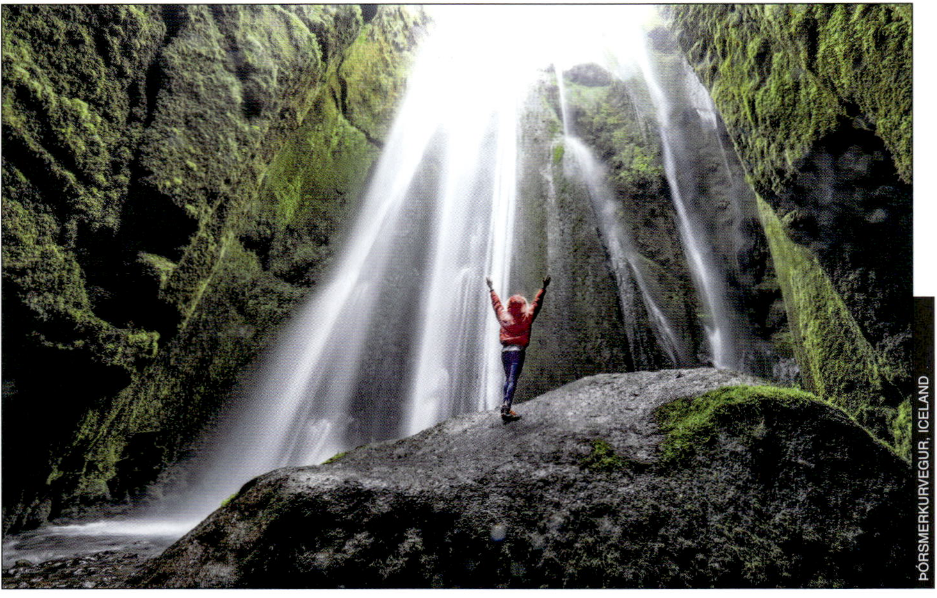

When we usually include someone from our group in a shot (a friend, family member, boyfriend/girlfriend, etc.) they're facing directly toward the camera, smiling, and essentially, posing in front of the scene. It's one of those, "Look I'm in London" type of shots we take, and while we do want to capture these types of shots (they're perfect for sharing on Facebook), they're not designed to capture the moment or feeling—they are essentially "vacation photos" (and there's nothing whatsoever wrong with that. I take them on every trip). However, there's a different type of shot that's very popular on Instagram right now, and that is to include someone from your group in the shot, but have them not look at the camera. Instead, they're part of scene, and you're seeing them enjoying the location (like you see above), rather than just posing in front of it. You get an entirely different feeling from these shots that often showcase the joy of travel in a way that just posing in front of the camera can't do. Give some of these a try next time and see what you think. I think you'll wind up doing them more often.

Showing Movement

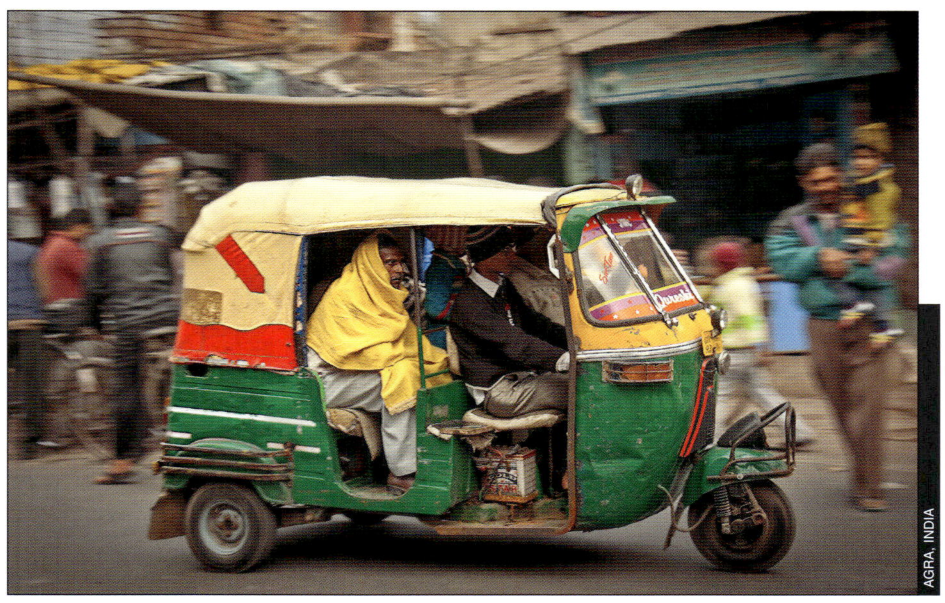

Generally, with travel photography, we're freezing everything (it's that whole "freezing a moment in time" thing), but there are times when not freezing everything and showing motion brings a photo to life (and shows a different view than we normally see). There are two camera techniques that work together to create this sense of motion: First, keep your shutter open longer than normal. Really fast shutter speeds (like you get on a sunny day) freeze motion, but slower shutter speeds blur anything moving (and the longer your shutter stays open, the blurrier it gets). The easiest way to get this motion effect is to shoot on a tripod (so it's perfectly still) on either a very cloudy day, or some place very shady, or sometime late in the day when your shutter, with less light, would have to stay open longer. You can also choose a high-numbered aperture, like f/16 or f/22, which will make it stay open longer if you're shooting in aperture priority mode. The darker it is where you're shooting, the longer that shutter will stay open to make a proper exposure, so you don't want direct sunlight (unless you have an ND filter—see page 71). Another technique is the one I used above where I switched to shutter priority mode (you choose the shutter speed and the camera picks your f-stop for you. It's usually an "S" on your camera's mode dial), chose a slow shutter speed (like 1/60 of a second, or even slower) and panned (followed along) with the moving object. The goal is to try to move at the same speed as the moving object, which keeps it mostly sharp and in focus, but the wheels will look like they're spinning, and the background will have blurry movement, too. This panning technique takes a bit of practice, so don't be surprised if you wind up with a *lot* of blurry shots. Within that bunch of blurry shots, you'll probably have one or two nice, sharp shots (I mean, how many shots are you going to show of a three-wheeled rickshaw driving by?).

Fine Art Style

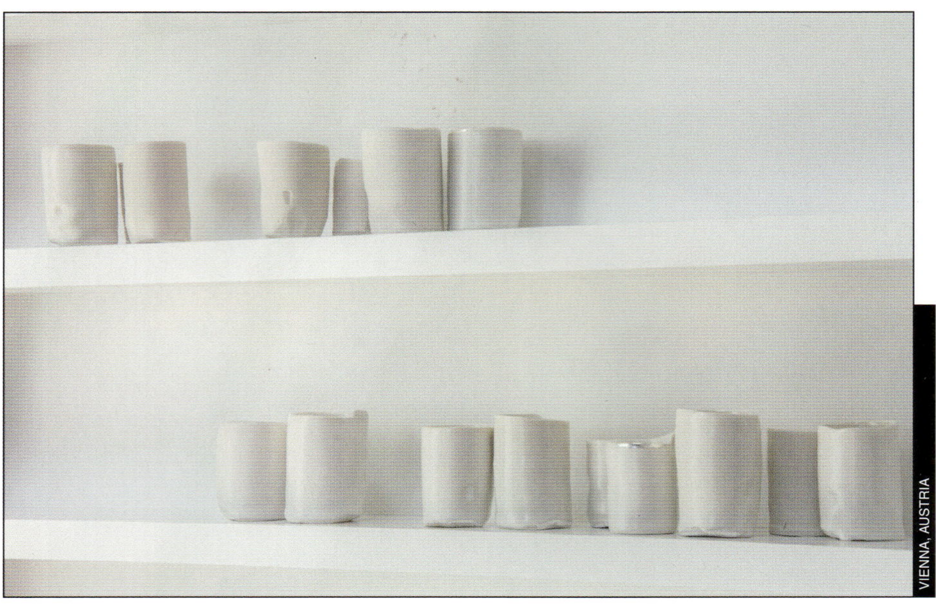

I always joke that if you can't really describe what's in the picture, then it's "fine art," but if I had to describe fine art travel photography, it's a particular style where you see something interesting and you capture it in a creative way. You're expressing more of an idea or a feeling than you are showing a place or a monument. You're not trying to show a scene or an object for what it is—you're interpreting that scene in an artistic way. All of this is why it's so hard to pinpoint what fine art is (but you'll know it when you see it). The image you see above was taken in Vienna, Austria, and I'm not certain where I saw it, but it really intrigued me, and I wanted to capture it in a way that made it interesting. But, at the end of the day, it's just a shelf with some white glasses (I'm not even sure they're glasses. Maybe they're mugs. Maybe they're made of clay. I can't really nail down what they are, so—boom—must be fine art). Keep an eye out for opportunities like this to step aside from the standard things we shoot in our travels and try something different.

Give Yourself a Magazine Assignment

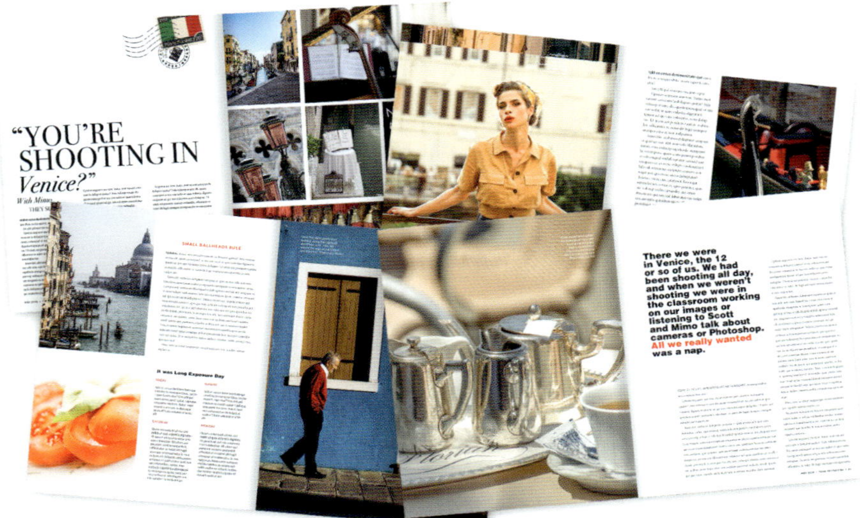

If you get to a city and you're stuck—you're not sure what to shoot, or you feel you're not coming away with the type of images you wanted—try this: imagine that you've been sent to this city on assignment for a magazine, and you have to come back with photos that make people want to visit that city. First, it makes you stop and think about the story you want to tell. What is this city famous for? Is it the food? The architecture? A particular monument? The fashion? Really give it some thought and it will give you a starting place and a game plan to keep you moving forward. This is a lot more fun than it sounds, and it will pull a different perspective out of you that you'll see in your images. When I do a hands-on workshop in a city, on one of the days, I send my students out for two hours on an assignment just like this for a fictional magazine. They choose their best images from those two hours, and then I lay them out travel-magazine style (like you see above), so they can see how their images work, and we're all always surprised at how great the shots come out. When you have a clear goal, and you have to deliver on time, it pushes you in a very creative and fun way.

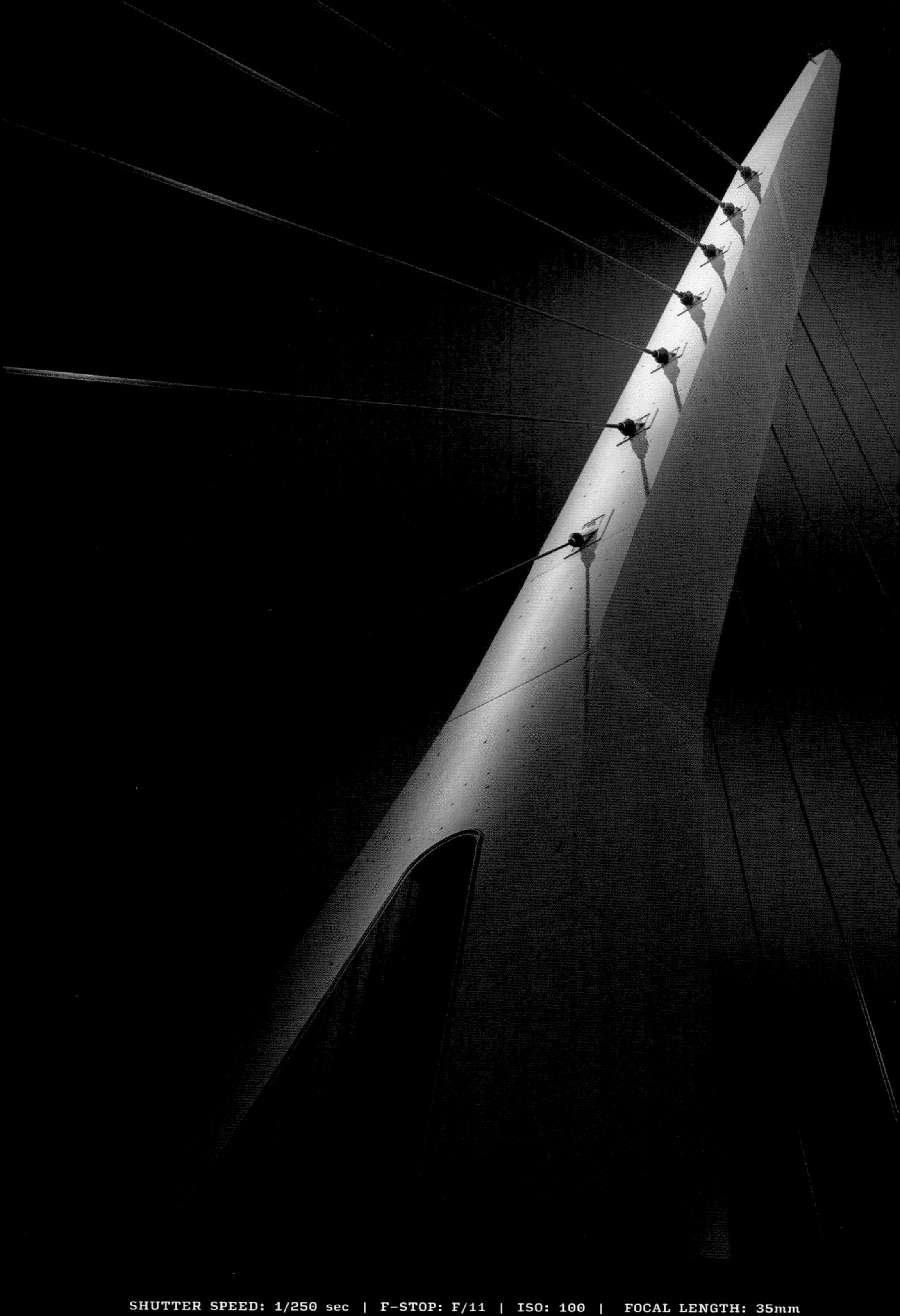

SHUTTER SPEED: 1/250 sec | F-STOP: F/11 | ISO: 100 | FOCAL LENGTH: 35mm
LOCATION: Teleport Bridge, Odaiba, Tokyo, Japan

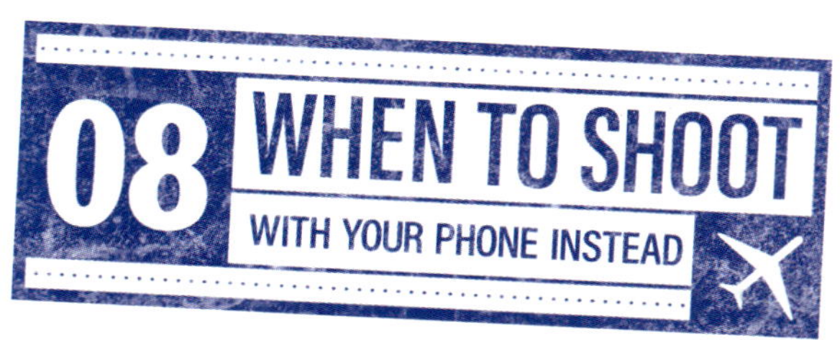

When to Shoot with Your Phone Instead

Sometimes It's Just Faster and Easier

So, Scott, let me get this straight: after all this—after weeks of careful research to choose the right DSLR or mirrorless camera, after toiling over DxO charts and graphs, and reading every lens review at DPReview.com, along with arguing with my friends at my local photo group, and then taking out a payday advance from AMSCOT to finally buy the perfect, thoroughly researched, painstakingly vetted camera body and lenses of my dreams—you're telling me there are times where my phone will actually work better than my "real" gear? Is that what you're telling me?????!!! No. I would never tell you that, because it would just make you angry, and the last thing an author wants is for the people who buy their book to be angry at them, with the possible exception of that guy who wrote the book *I Hate Everybody, But Especially People Who Buy This Book!* (Simon & Shoehorn, March 3, 2017, ISBN# 1681984849, 312 pages). No, I don't think it's a good idea to tell you that sometimes, just sometimes, it might be easier/better/faster to use your phone for what God intended it to be used for: a camera. Nope, that's not my intention. However, including a chapter like this in the book could be misconstrued as tacitly implying that perhaps, just perhaps, there are times when maybe, possibly, you might kinda maybe you know…well, you know. Now, I will say this in my defense, the proper title (and the original one I wrote) was simply: "When to Use Your Cell Phone Instead," and it's clearly a typo that the word "Shoot" was inserted into the title above, which I can only imagine is the result of an autocorrect error. But what I find amazing about all this is that I was able to determine, even before the printing and publication of this book, that a typo would indeed sneak its way into the headline of this chapter, which was supposed to be about when to use your cell phone to call B&H Photo to place a lens order, or how to call for pizza delivery, or how to call your publisher to ask why they're using autocorrect on your book.

Time Lapses Made Simple

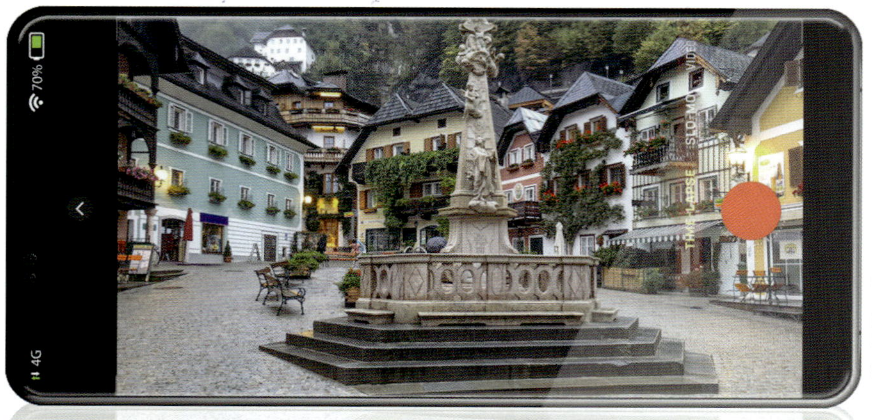

More and more new cameras these days are coming out with a built-in time-lapse feature, but there are many that don't have one (including lots and lots of DSLRs). Even if your camera has built-in time lapse, it's usually much easier and faster to just set it up on your phone (I've seen some beautiful time lapses of the sun coming up over the city taken from a hotel window). The iPhone camera's built-in time-lapse feature couldn't be easier to use. In the Camera app, swipe over to Time-Lapse and it takes a series of still images as long you keep the shutter button active. Then, it takes those images, compresses the amount of time between each photo, and stitches them together to make a cool little video (usually less than 30 seconds). If you want to do a long time lapse (20- or 30-minute time lapses look really good), you'll definitely want to be on a tripod (or be willing to hold your camera pretty still for 20 or 30 minutes). So, just tap the shutter button to start your time lapse (a little clock animation appears where your shutter button was), tap it again to stop your time lapse, and your iPhone will do the rest (including all the math in the background). It's so much easier to capture, process, and compile it all on your phone, than it is to download a ton of images and compile them manually on your computer.

Shooting Panoramas Is So Much Easier

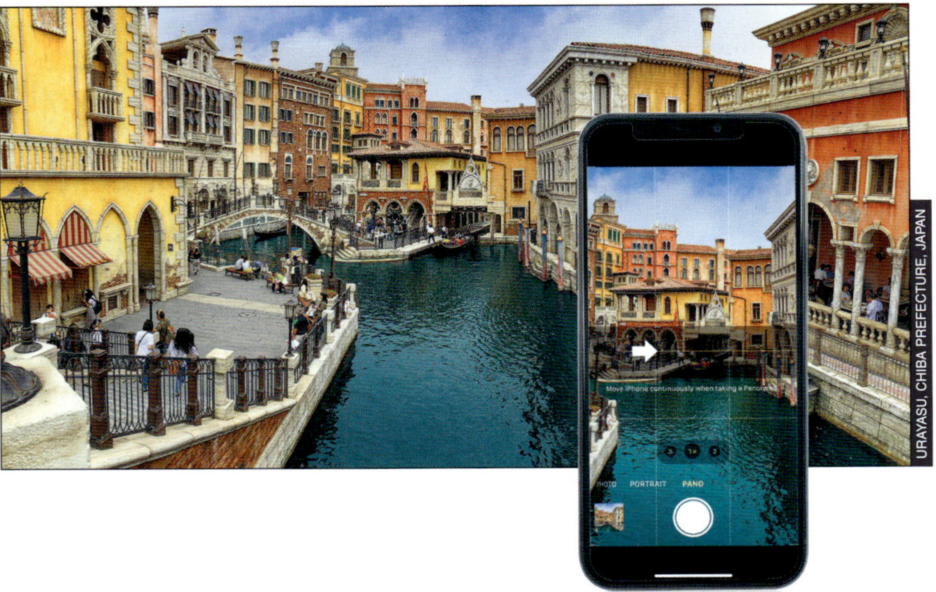

The nice thing about doing a panorama on your phone is that it compiles the images into a pano in just seconds, right there on your phone—you don't have to wait to get back to your computer, download the images, open Lightroom or Photoshop, and then stitch it all together. In fact, you don't even have to take multiple photos, like you do with your DSLR or mirrorless. You just take one image and that's your pano, which is pretty handy (no worrying about having to overlap frames, or your exposure or focus changing while you take the different frames—your phone handles all the math behind the scenes). Also, the pano feature on your phone is very forgiving. Your technique doesn't have to be right on the money, and in fact, you really don't have to do anything other than choose Pano in the Camera app and tap the shutter button to start shooting, slowly panning from left to right (although you can shoot reverse panos or tall panos, from bottom to top, too). When you get to the end of your pano, tap the shutter button again, and your pano is already done. (*Tip:* Shorter panos usually look better, and they look larger on social media.) I'd be willing to bet I've made more panos with my iPhone than I have with my DSLR and mirrorless combined. It's just too easy.

Super-Wide-Angle Shots

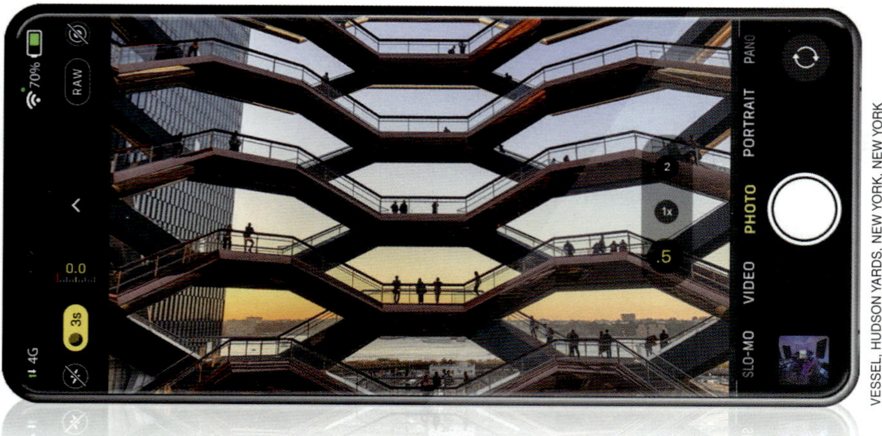

I've talked a lot about traveling light, and trying to get away with just one lens when you travel (like a 24–240mm or a 28–300mm), but if I need to shoot some super-wide scenes, like maybe a cathedral interior or a palace, or a cityscape where a super-wide-angle lens would rock, then I might bring my 14mm lens with me (but now I'd be carrying a camera bag or a lens bag and all that entails, so quite often I skip it, and I'm usually happy I did). Well, if you have an iPhone X Pro or later, you can leave that super-wide lens at home, as the iPhone not only has a super-wide-angle lens built in, but it's even wider than my 14mm (it's 13mm, which is awesome, and I'm already carrying it anyway, so…yeah!).

Shooting Video

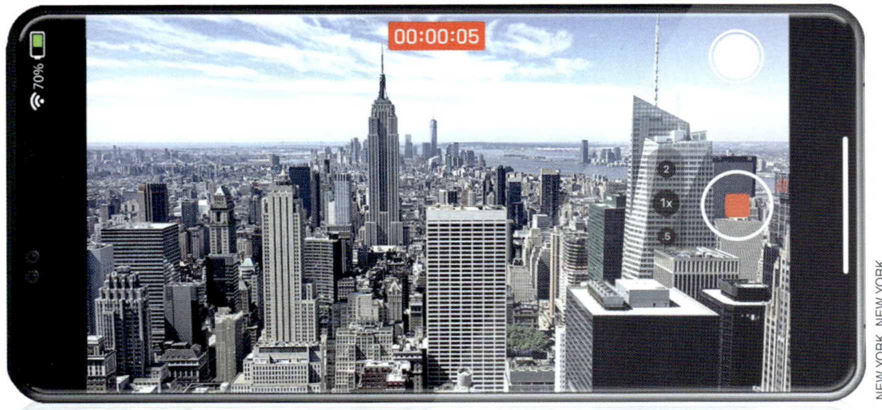

NEW YORK, NEW YORK

I've always said that the video features on a DSLR or mirrorless aren't there for photographers. They are there for serious video shooters, because there is a *lot* to getting good video from your camera. Not that it won't shoot great video—the quality is great—but there is a lot more to it than just pressing a button, including the fact that at some point you have to get those clips off your camera and into some kind of editing program on your computer. That's why I exclusively shoot video on my iPhone. For goodness' sake, it shoots in 4K!!! Plus, I can trim the video, edit it, add text and effects, and share it all right there on my phone. It has a built-in stabilizer for video that is pretty awesome, and it's all just so easy—you don't have to learn a whole new world of buttons and knobs. Think about it: you don't even have to learn how to shoot video on your phone because it works like your Camera app does, except you choose Video instead of Photo. Unless you're a working pro and need pro features to do your job, shooting video on your phone is the way to go.

Easy In-Camera HDR

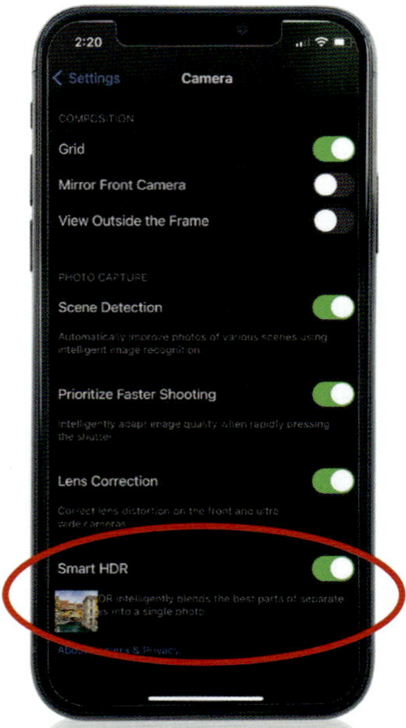

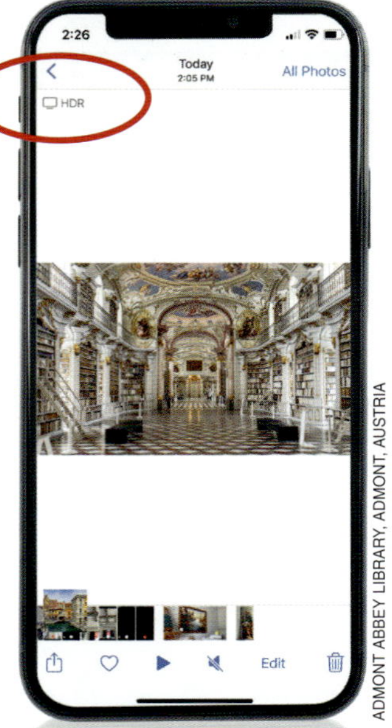

ADMONT ABBEY LIBRARY, ADMONT, AUSTRIA

Phones have had built-in HDR for years now—all you have to do is turn the HDR feature on (if it's not already turned on), and when you take a shot, your phone actually takes multiple shots behind the scenes, and then automatically (and pretty much instantly) compiles them into a single shot with a wider dynamic range than a single shot would have. You don't have to shoot multiple exposures, and then later compile them into a single frame in Lightroom or Photoshop. Your phone does all that for you. Now, there are some newer cameras today that do have a built-in HDR feature right in the camera, and they do a pretty good job (and of course, their resolution is higher so you can print a larger image), but if you're not going to be printing your images, it's hard to beat how easy shooting HDR is on your phone. By the way, if you have an iPhone, go to Settings, scroll down to Camera settings, and at the bottom, make sure Smart HDR is turned on (like you see above left). It will turn on automatically any time the scene has enough tonal variation that it would need to be an HDR image to capture it correctly. You'll know if HDR was used when you view the image after you take it—you'll see "HDR" up in the top-left corner (as seen above right).

When You Need Fully Silent Shooting

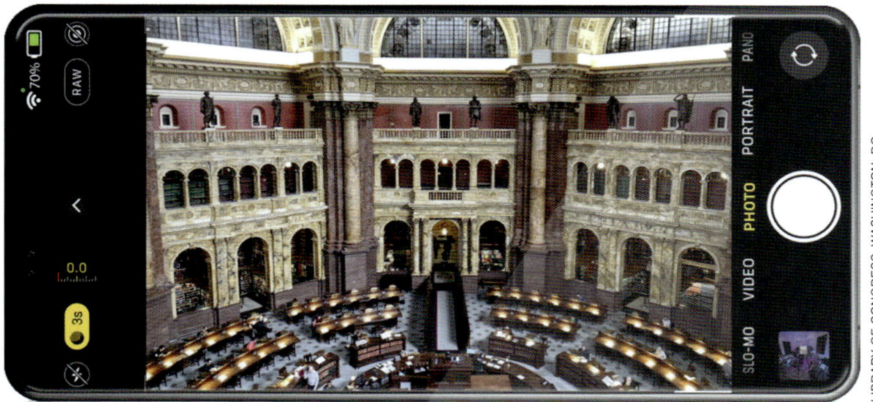

LIBRARY OF CONGRESS, WASHINGTON, DC

There are times when you need to be absolutely silent while you're shooting, like during a wedding, or in a library (that's the Library of Congress in Washington, DC, above), during a golfer's backswing, or photographing wildlife (where the sound of the shutter might send that squirrel scurrying away). Or, maybe you're shooting in a city where you're trying to blend in to get some great candid people shots. There are a dozen reasons why you don't want to hear that shutter sound (shooting a string quartet, photographing a tennis match, or you're in church, etc.), and even though some DSLRs have a "quiet" mode, they're not actually silent (they just don't make quite as loud of a shutter sound as usual, so while it is a bit better, you could still get in trouble, or at the very least get some serious stink-eye). That's why shooting with your phone is so great in these situations (the shutter sound is fake anyway because your phone is actually a mirrorless camera, and there is no mechanical shutter), because it can shoot in real, actual, honest-to-goodness silent mode just by setting your camera to silent mode (ringer off). That silences the shutter sound, so now you can fire away without distracting anyone. *Note:* Some mirrorless cameras also have the ability to shoot in completely silent mode like this, it just depends on your make and model.

Taking a Still While Shooting Video

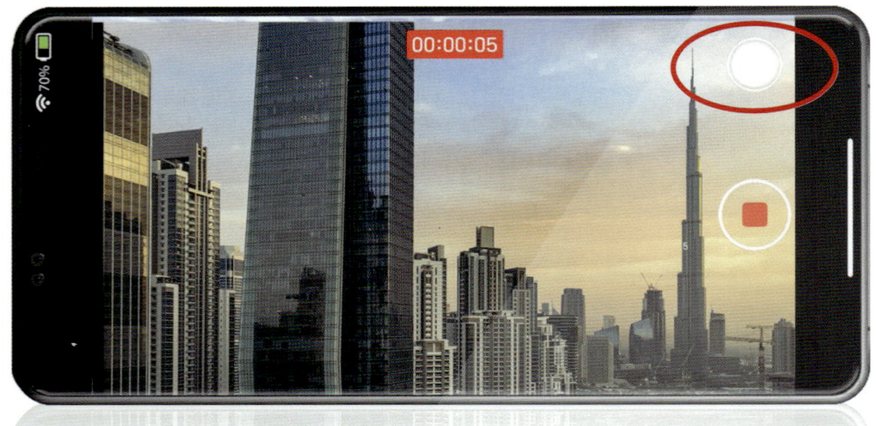

Another thing I love that we can do on our phones that we can't do on our video cameras is to take a still photo while we're in the middle of shooting video. Our regular cameras let us shoot in either video mode or in photo mode, but most can't do both. Your phone, however, lets you do this easily. For example, on the iPhone, when you're shooting video, there's a big, red Start/Stop button in the bottom center (or side center, if you're shooting in landscape orientation) of the screen. But, once you start recording video, just to the side of (or above) that red button, a white shutter button appears (shown circled above) and if you press it, it takes a still of whatever you're shooting in video mode. It also works vice versa: if you're shooting stills, you can instantly start shooting video by tapping-and-dragging the shutter button to the right (depending on which model you have and if you're on the latest phone operating system).

Shooting Straight Down on Food

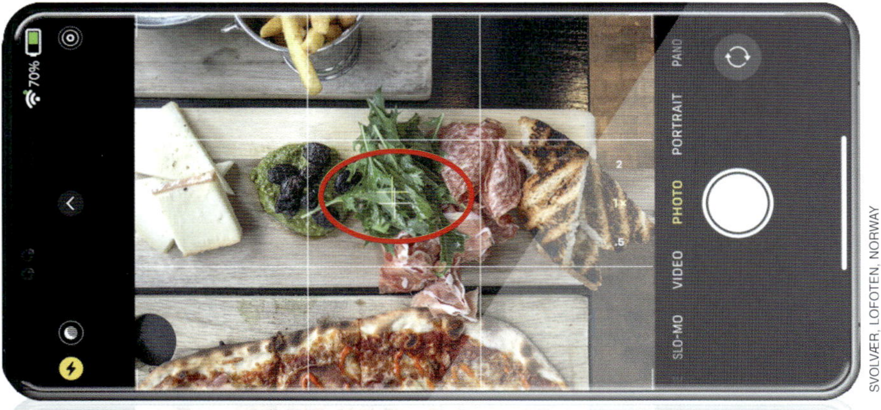

If you get served an amazing-looking meal on your trip, and you want to take one of those popular "my lunch from overhead" shots, if you have an iPhone, there's a built-in feature to help you get your phone's camera perfectly level (this feature only appears when you're shooting straight up/straight down). Here's how it works: When you're holding the phone over your meal, look in the center of the screen and you'll see two plus signs—one yellow and one white—and they'll be offset a bit from each other (as seen circled above in red). The goal is to get them to line up (so they look like just one plus sign), and to do that you just tilt your phone back and forth until they do (so, it's a feature that feels like you're playing a video game). Once they line up, you can take your shot knowing that there are no horizontal or vertical lens issues. Super-simple and so easy to use.

Shooting Where Cameras Aren't Allowed

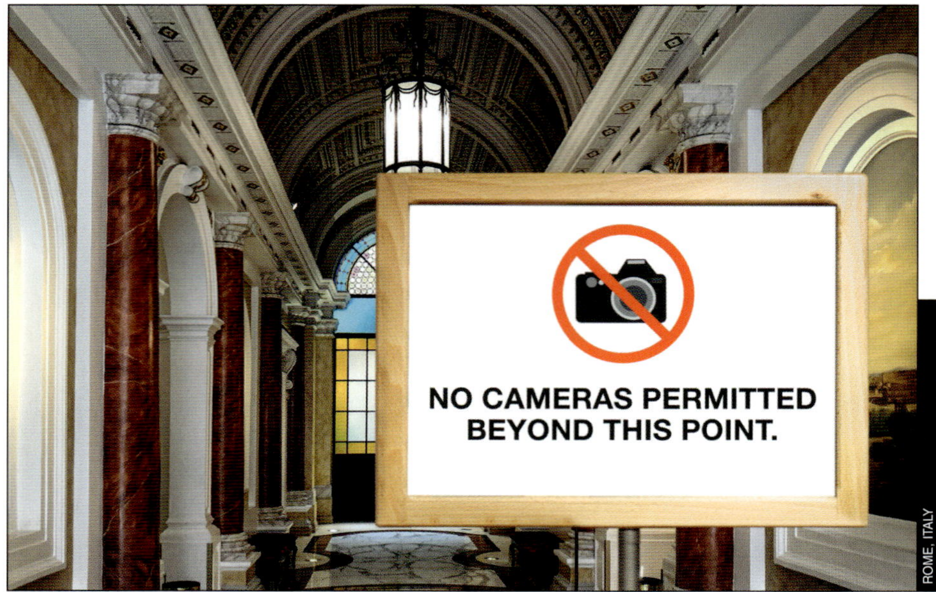

I remember being in Paris just a couple of years ago with my buddy Mimo, and we were taking photos inside a beautiful cathedral, when a guard and an administrator came up and told us we weren't allowed to shoot with "professional cameras" in the cathedral. These weren't some big pro-looking rigs with giant lenses and battery grips. I had a Canon EOS R at the time (a consumer camera) with a short 16–35mm lens, and Mimo had a Canon EOS 5D Mark IV and a 14mm (even shorter) lens. So, we pulled out our phones and started shooting, and they literally couldn't have cared less. This isn't the first time this has happened, and I've heard countless similar stories. I've been to places like St. Paul's Cathedral in London, where there are "No cameras!" signs posted all over, and if they see you shooting with a camera, they will come over to stop you, but they don't care one bit if your camera is also a phone, because everyone in there is taking phone pictures. Luckily, even though it's a low-light situation, you can still make great cathedral photos because of the camera's built-in HDR feature (see page 132) and stabilizer (and it's easier to hand-hold because it's so small and light). The next time you see a "No cameras!" sign, just remember: you're not holding a camera, it's a cell phone, right? ;-)

Slow-Motion Video

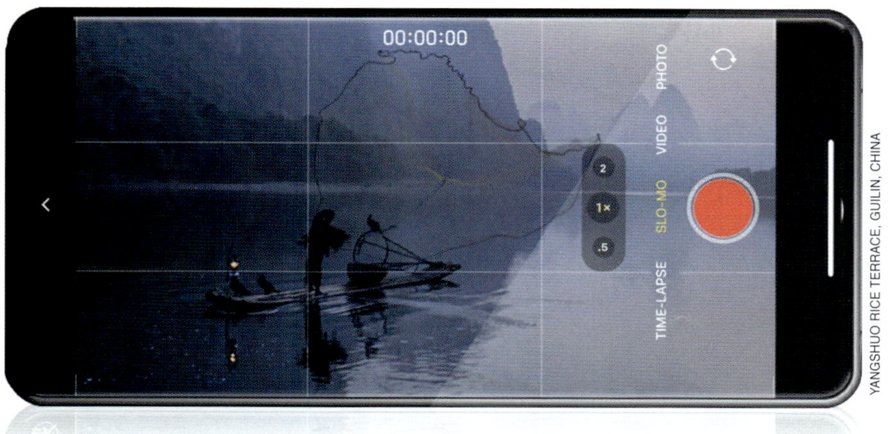

This is one of the most underrated features of the iPhone, and it's partially because of how Apple decided to implement the feature that makes it so great. When you choose to shoot using their Slo-Mo feature, it starts shooting regular video for a few seconds and then it goes to super-slow-motion, and the effect (because it started in real time) is just incredible. Every time I do one of these, I'm amazed that I don't do more of them because they are stunning, and they're so easy to share on social media. It works just like video: you choose Slo-Mo in the Camera app (instead of Photo) and press the red Record button, and it does the rest. You will be blown away once you try it. Again, it's one of the most underrated features, and to do something similar with a DSLR or mirrorless, you'd need to shoot regular video, and then edit it in an editing program, and apply a slo-mo effect to part of the clip there, and…yeah, that sounds like a lot of work. Or, you could just have your phone do it all for you right now while you shoot.

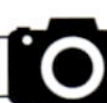

You Need to Edit and Post On-the-Go

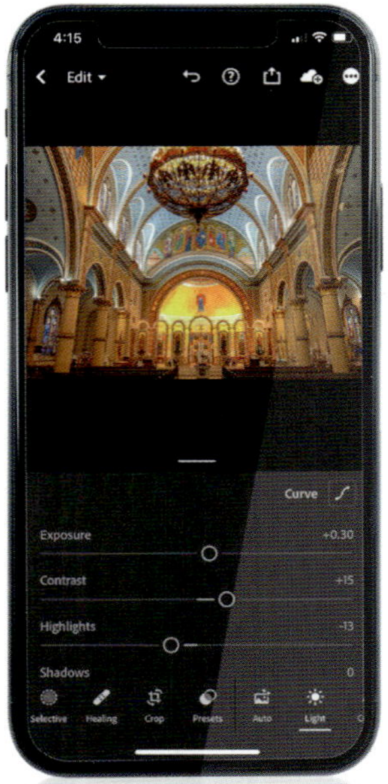
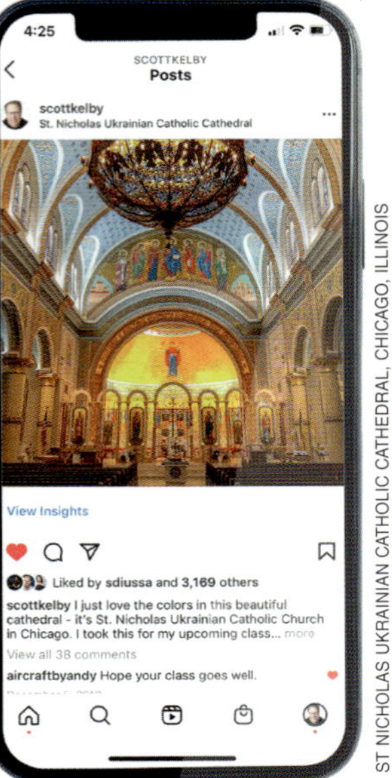

One of the big advantages to shooting with your phone is that you don't have to wait until you get back to your hotel room, get your memory card reader, download your images, import them into an editing app, and then edit your photos on your computer to get them ready to post to social media or to share with your friends or family. When you're shooting with your phone, you can start editing the image a moment after you take it, and share it a few seconds after that. I'll never forget being out in the middle of nowhere in China shooting, and my buddy's wife walks up to me, shows me her photo of the scene we were shooting, and it was already posted to her Instagram account. Imagine the look on my face when I knew I was literally hours away from being able to do that with my mirrorless camera (after going on a raft, then a long hike, and then two different buses to get back to the hotel), but there she was, showing me the image already posted to her Instagram account! It was cropped, edited, and already shared while we were still on the shoot, and it looked great! Ouch. That one stung, but it also reminded me that for some particular things, your phone can be a better option.

You Don't Have a Fast Enough Lens

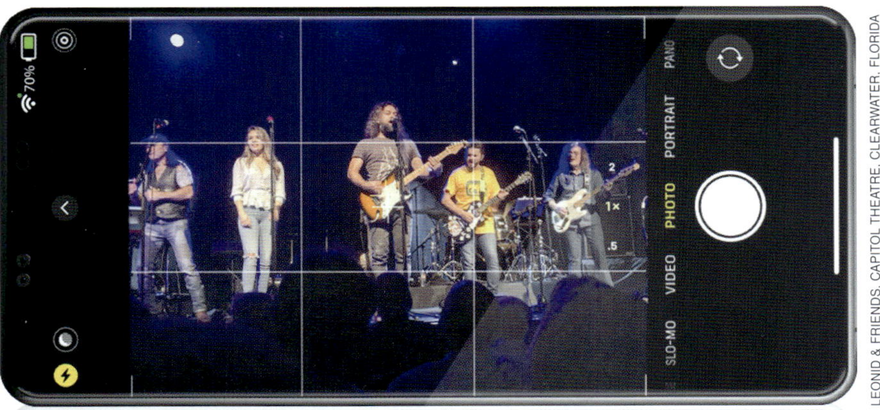

LEONID & FRIENDS, CAPITOL THEATRE, CLEARWATER, FLORIDA

If you wind up shooting in a low-light situation (like a concert) and you don't have a very fast lens (for example, your lens is maybe an f/4 to f/5.6), you might want to consider using your phone's lens, because it's probably a whole lot faster. In fact, I believe since the iPhone X (2017), you can shoot at f/1.8, which is really fast for a lens, and some newer phones shoot at f/1.6 or f/1.5. So, the next time you're in a low-light situation and you know you don't have a fast enough lens to pull it off without sending your ISO (and noise) to the moon, pull out your phone and give it a try.

Sharing Photos with Your Group

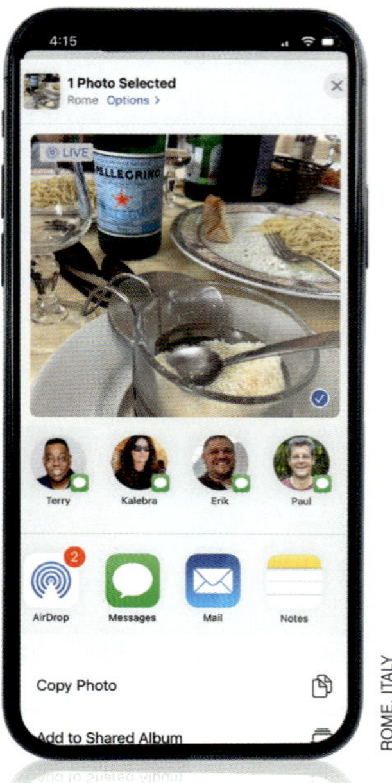

Another time you'll want to pull out your phone is when you want to share an image with the people you're traveling with. It might be a tour group, or your family, or the friends you're traveling with, and you want to share something you just photographed right now. You can (and should) shoot the shot with your DSLR or mirrorless, but then don't forget to pull out your phone and take a quick shot because you can share that phone shot immediately with everyone in the group. Then you can send the final hi-res from your DSLR or mirrorless later if you like, but at least you'll have the immediacy and impact of real-time sharing when you use your phone.

You Want to Take a Selfie

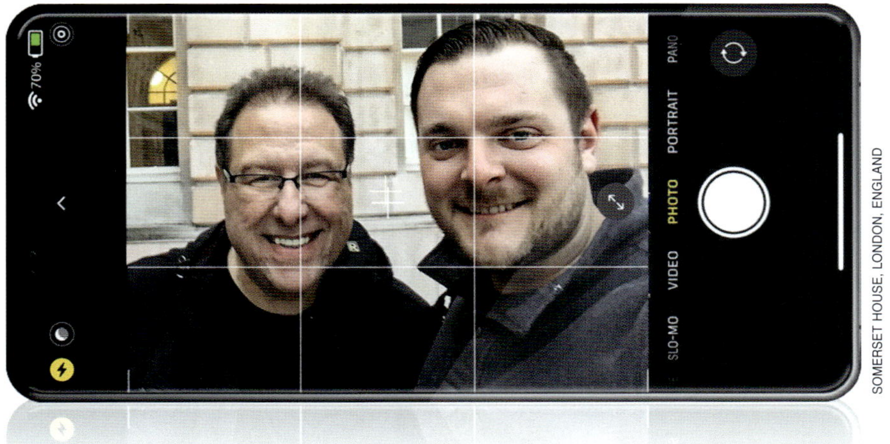

Can you take a selfie with your DSLR or mirrorless? I've seen it done, and I've even tried it myself (with little success), but why try to hold a heavy camera backward, shooting pretty much blind, while trying to reach the shutter button, when the camera phone in your pocket was born to do selfies. There's even a built-in self-timer that you can see onscreen in big numbers so you know when to smile, and of course, you can see and compose the shot right there on your phone's screen (the shot above was taken by my buddy, and pro selfie King of England, travel photographer Dave Williams. He's perfected the skill of making it look like he's not holding his camera way out in front of him). Anyway, skip the big camera and the whole "shooting backward and blind" thing, and reach for your phone anytime it's selfie time.

Much Bigger Monitor for Sharing

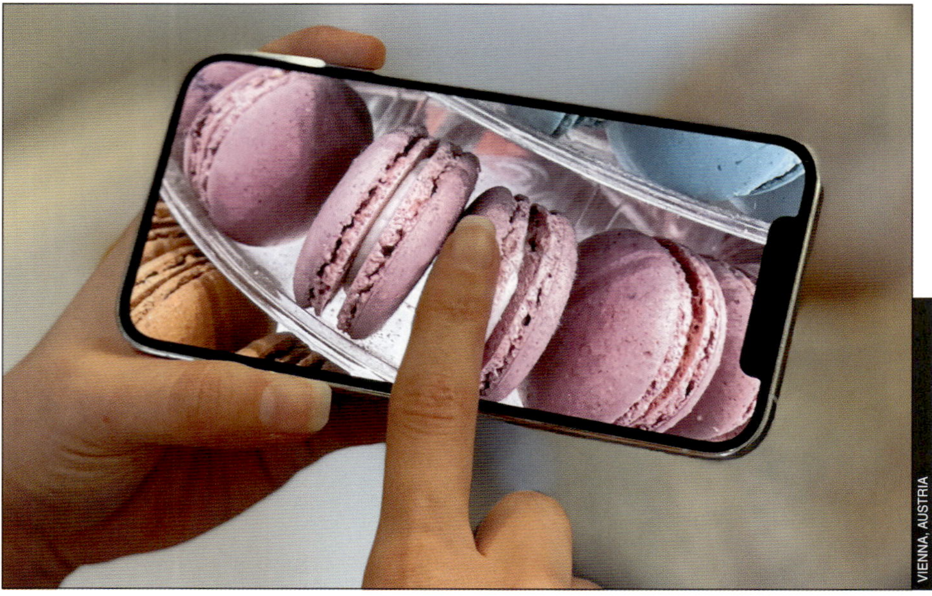

I'll bet you don't know anyone who has a screen on their phone that is nearly as small as the screen on the back of our expensive cameras. The screen on our camera's display is fine for a quick check of sharpness, or to see if a shot's in focus, or if the lighting's right, but that tiny 3-inch screen kinda stinks when it comes to sharing. You know what's great for sharing? Your phone, because even the smallest phones have way bigger screens than our cameras. Plus, you can pinch-to-zoom images on a phone, swipe to move to the next photo, and everybody you'd hand your camera to already knows how to do all these things. (*Note:* Some mirrorless cameras now have pinch-to-zoom and swipe, but still on a tiny 3-inch screen.) You'd be better off using your camera's built-in Bluetooth or Wi-Fi to send a photo you like from your camera to your phone before you show everybody at dinner, or the group in the lobby of your hotel, than you would to try to show it on the tiny screen on the back of your camera. Simply put, phones make great sharing devices for photography, and as a bonus, you don't have to worry about someone accidentally changing the dials on your camera while they're holding it as they peer into the teeny screen.

Shooting Really Close Up

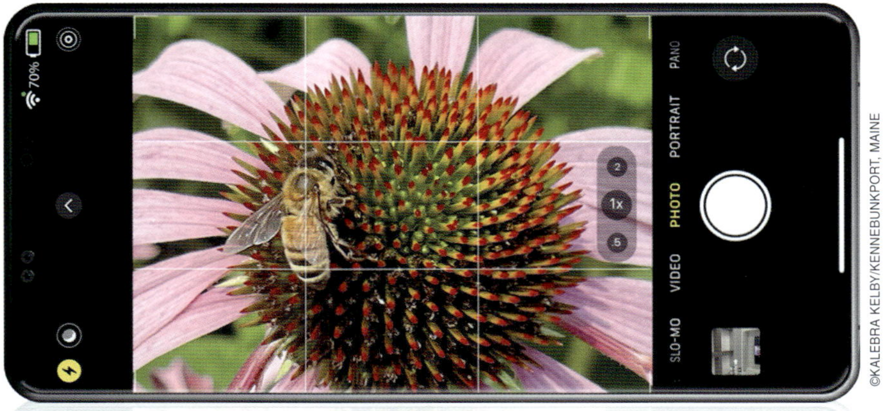

You don't have to drag around a separate macro lens if you want to shoot really close-up shots because your phone has a great built-in macro feature (you can focus as close as three inches). I love this because simple things you come across during your travels (like a bee landing on a flower, or a salt shaker, or a strawberry from room service) take on a whole new life when you photograph them super-close-up. There's nothing special to do: just get really close, tap on the screen to focus your image, and you're good to go!

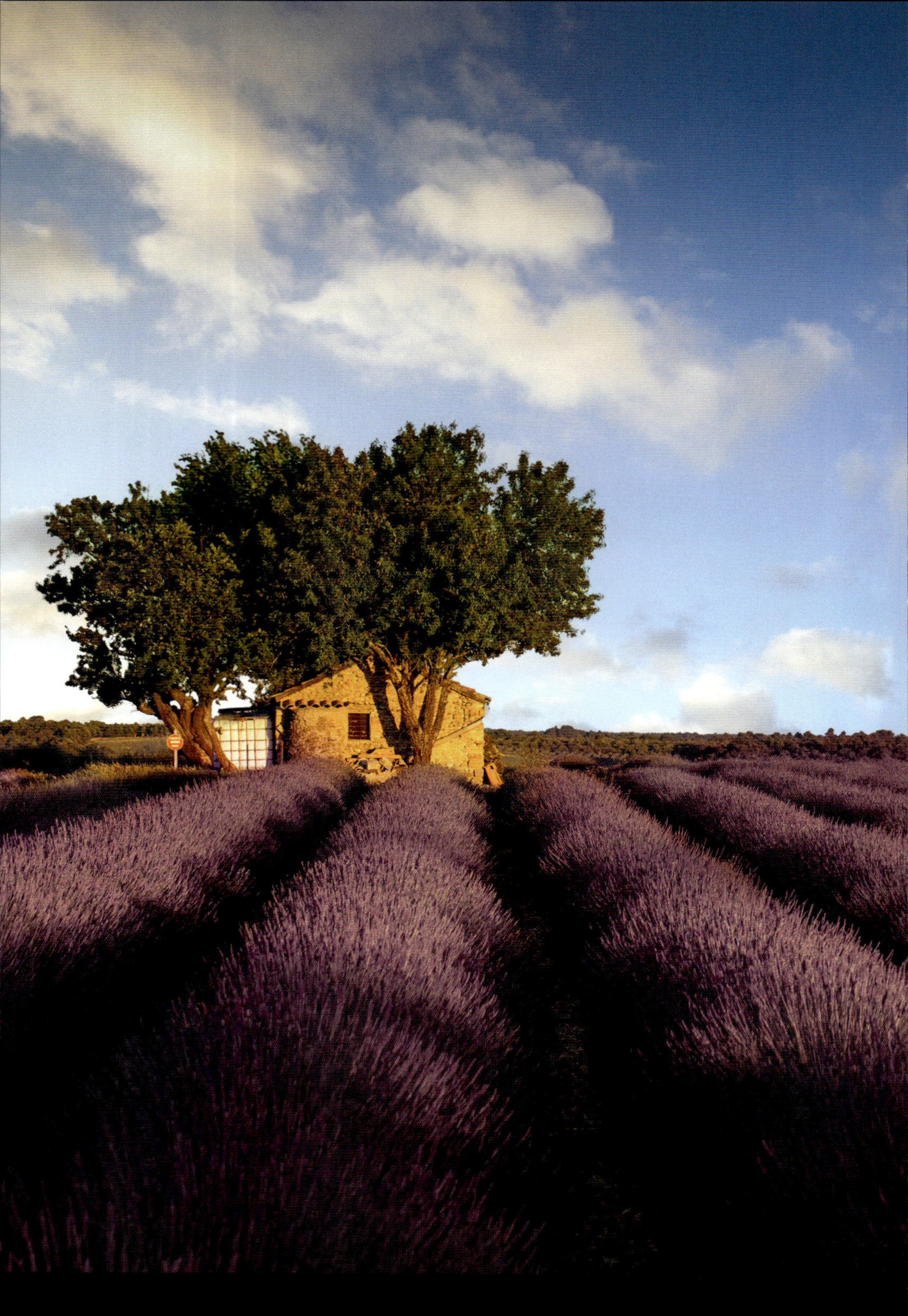

SHUTTER SPEED: 1/80 sec | F-STOP: F/7.1 | ISO: 100 | FOCAL LENGTH: 70mm
LOCATION: Valensole, France

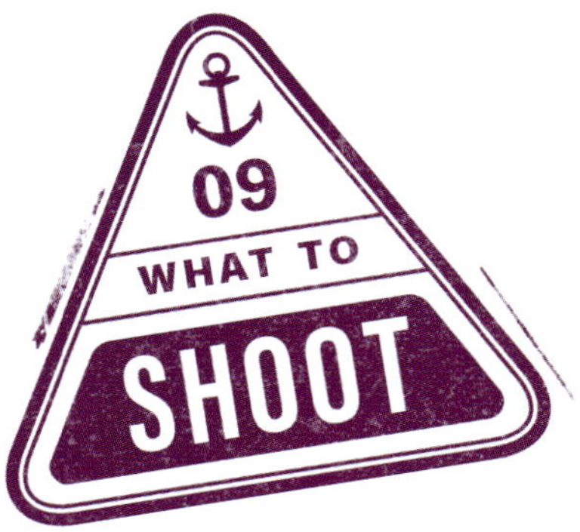

What to Shoot

And What You Can Skip

This seems like an easy decision: shoot the stuff that looks good, and avoid the stuff that looks bad. If only it were that easy. Then all I'd have to do is write this intro page and move on to the next chapter, with only a vast sea of nothingness in between. Unfortunately, you can't put blank pages between chapters because your publisher will murder you. I don't mean that as a euphemism—it's a well-known fact that publishers have hit squads trained by the Spetsnaz to take out authors who indiscriminately leave blank pages in books. The main reason is the cost of paper, which has risen to the point that it'd be cheaper to print your book on thin sheets of gold (well, that's what they told us at our six-week author training program and boot camp). Now, they would have to be very thin sheets because gold is still quite expensive (we learned that in boot camp, too), but paper costs are so high that the paper used to write photography books has become its own cryptocurrency called "ShutterCoin," traded exclusively on SDCard Global Exchange 3, which has ties to the Illuminati and a group of spiky-haired anarchists living in London who wear oversized white t-shirts with huge text that reads: "Frankie Says War!" (BTW: 15 points if you got that reference, and you're going to need those points to buy things like Metamucil and those poles with claws on the ends that let you pick up things you dropped, like tiny pills, because you're so old, you can't bend over anymore, and now you're more likely to buy a t-shirt that says: "Frankie Says Medicare!") Anyway, there was a day, long before Frankie could afford big t-shirts because he was in preschool, when publishers wanted you to write thick books with lots of pages because they thought people would see more value in a really thick book, but today, people don't like thick books and publishers cringe every time you add an extra page. The solution for authors is actually quite easy: You just start leaving out words, and it takes less space. You see what? You still meaning. It still sense.

Shoot: Old People and Kids

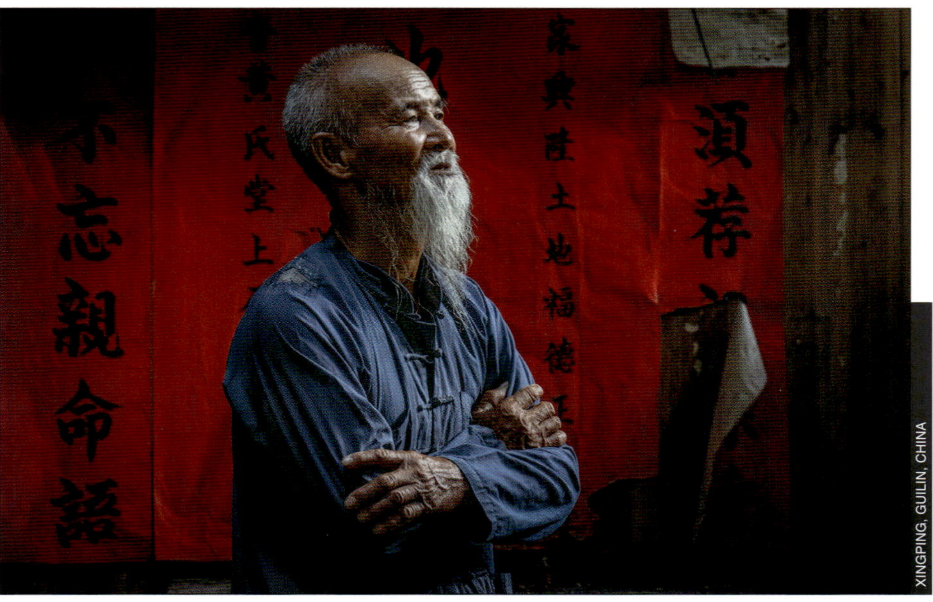

Okay, that title above gets the award for the "worst title of the year," but you know what I mean. When you look in travel magazines, you'll see a bunch of photos of little kids and really old people, probably because kids are adorable and old people give the place a sense of history. I'm surprised dogs and cats don't show up more often in travel, but I rarely see house pets wind up in the mags (but that's probably because they haven't seen my dogs, which are, by the way, the most beautiful and magical dogs on the planet. But, I digress). Anyway, add kids and old folks to your travel photo list if they're not already on there. By the way, when it comes to kids, I always ask the parent's permission before photographing a child. If you sneak around photographing kids, you're likely to run into trouble, so asking permission will help keep you out of trouble and get you some great shots of the locals.

Shoot: Color as Your Subject

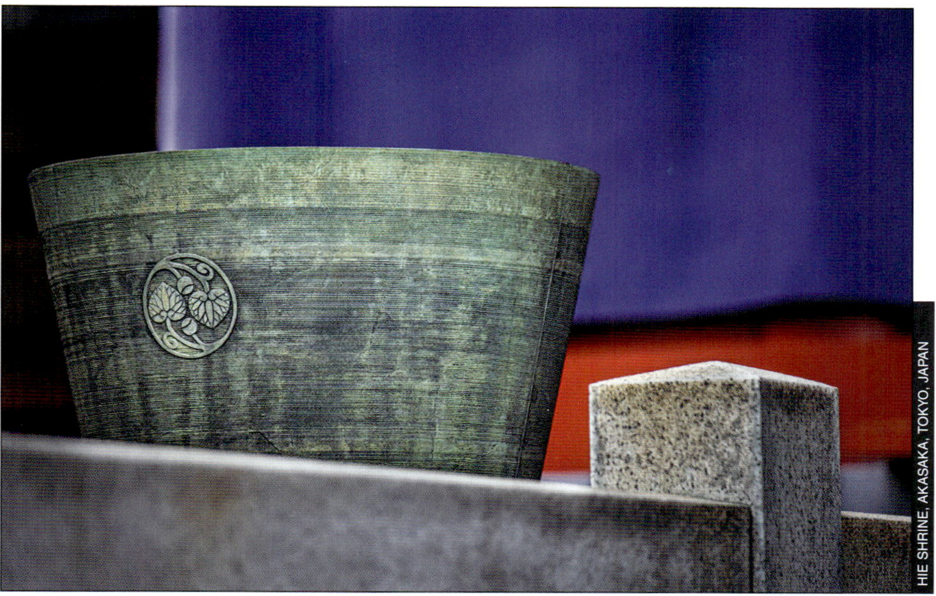

We are drawn to color, and you'll often see shots where the color is the subject, whether it's rows of brightly painted houses; or rows of soft, pastel shops; or just a red wall with a yellow door. You instantly know the reason why that shot is there is not because the subject is so interesting—it's because the colors are so intriguing. The thing to look for is contrast. Look for contrasting colors that look great together, and once you've found that, then it's time to start working the scene to find an interesting composition. Take a look at the shot above. It's just a vase (I think that's a vase of some kind, or maybe it's a planter without any plants. I'm not sure), but it really doesn't matter because the subject of this shot isn't the vase—it's the color. Keep an eye out for vibrant, contrasting, interesting colors in your travels, and you'll be surprised how many opportunities you'll run across.

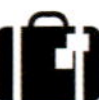
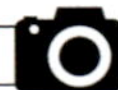

Shoot: What the Locals Are Wearing

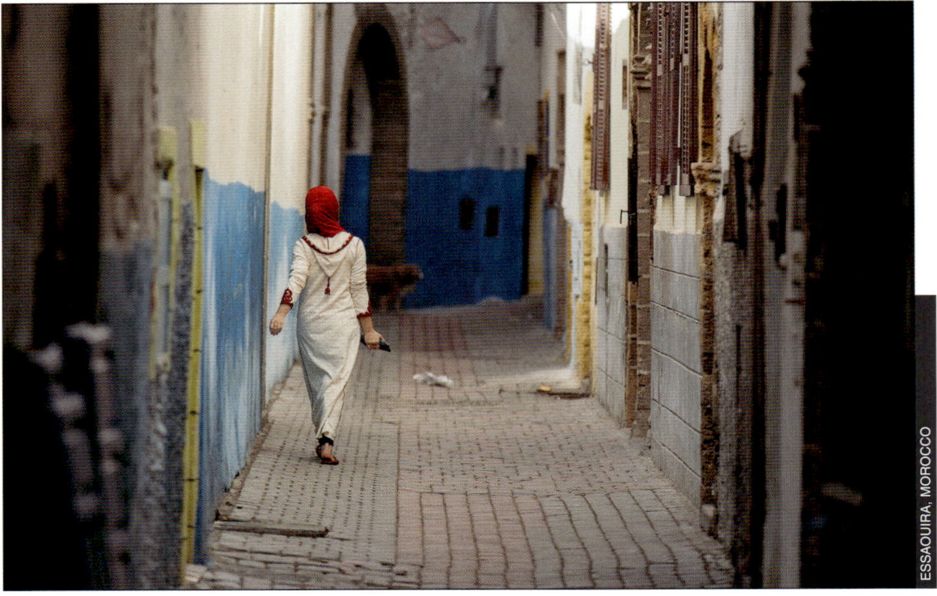

This is another one of those topics you want to capture to give people viewing your images a sense of the local culture, like with the image here, taken in Essaouira, Morocco. Now, it's very possible that they dress pretty much the same way where you're visiting as people do back where you live, so in that case, you might skip this topic. But, if they have a local flavor, or they just dress up to go out, add this to your shooting list (for example, I love the way the Parisians dress. Fashion is very important to them, and you'll see Parisians in stylish clothes, even if they're just going to the grocery store).

Shoot: Cityscapes from Up High

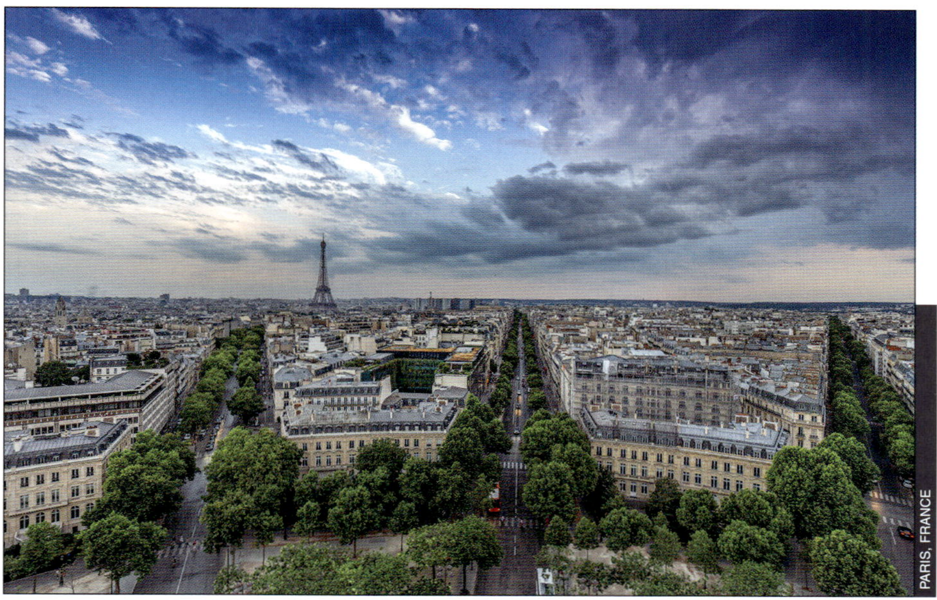

Here's another one of those shot topics that you see so often: a sprawling cityscape shot from up high, like this shot taken from the top of the Arc de Triomphe in Paris (though the best place for a Paris cityscape shot is probably the observatory at the top of Tour Montparnasse, the second tallest building in France, which gives you an even wider view of the city or the Eiffel Tower—plus they cut shooting holes out of the plexiglass that surrounds the top, and the last time I was there, they even let you set up a tripod). If there aren't tall towers or buildings you can shoot from, I've had great luck shooting from rooftop bars. They often have great vistas to shoot from, and they generally don't charge a fee (like rooftop observatories on top of office buildings do. For example, right now, the cheapest ticket you can get for New York's One World Observatory is $38 if you book online in advance, or $43 if you are a walk up. For two people that's $76, plus tax. By the way, from a photographic point of view in New York, you'll like the view from the Top of Rock much better, but that's $38 per person, as well. You'd be better off doing the research to find a great rooftop bar and put that $76 toward some appetizers and a drink). Find that awesome rooftop restaurant or bar, or book your room at the tallest hotel in town and ask for a room on as high a level as possible—and ask for one with a view. Also, if you wind up having to shoot through a window, gently put your lens flush up against the glass to cut the reflections you'll get if you're even an inch or two back from the glass.

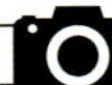

Shoot: Outdoor Cafes

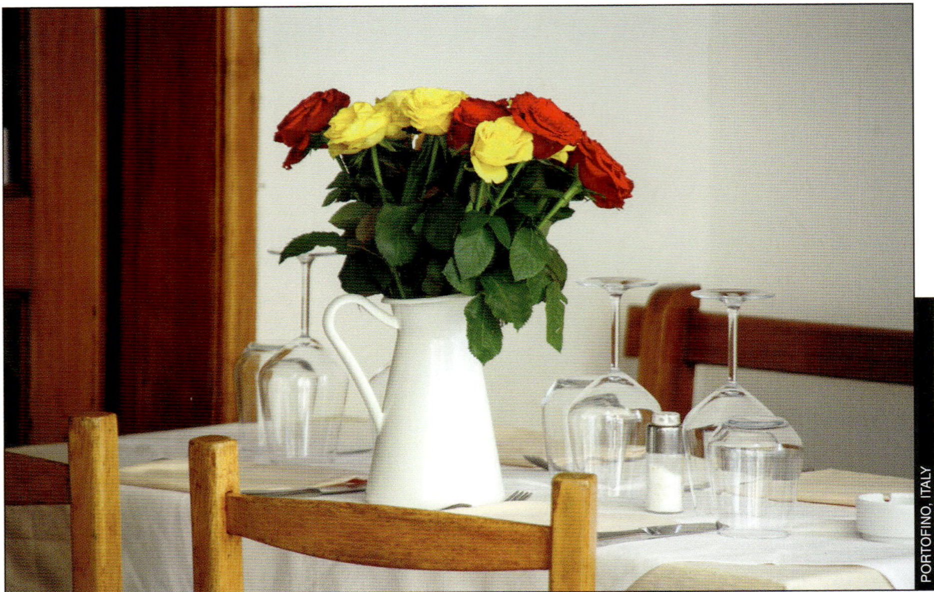

An easy way to show the charm of a city is to show one of its outdoor cafes. This is one of those things that people picture themselves doing when they visit a foreign country—sitting outside, enjoying a coffee or a meal, and just watching the world stroll by. So, when you show these quaint cafes, you're pulling at an emotional heart-string for viewers. I personally prefer to show these cafes without patrons, so it's like the table is waiting for them (and it keeps the shot from being about the people at the table and makes it more about the restaurant or cafe).

Shoot: Cathedrals, Palaces, and Theaters

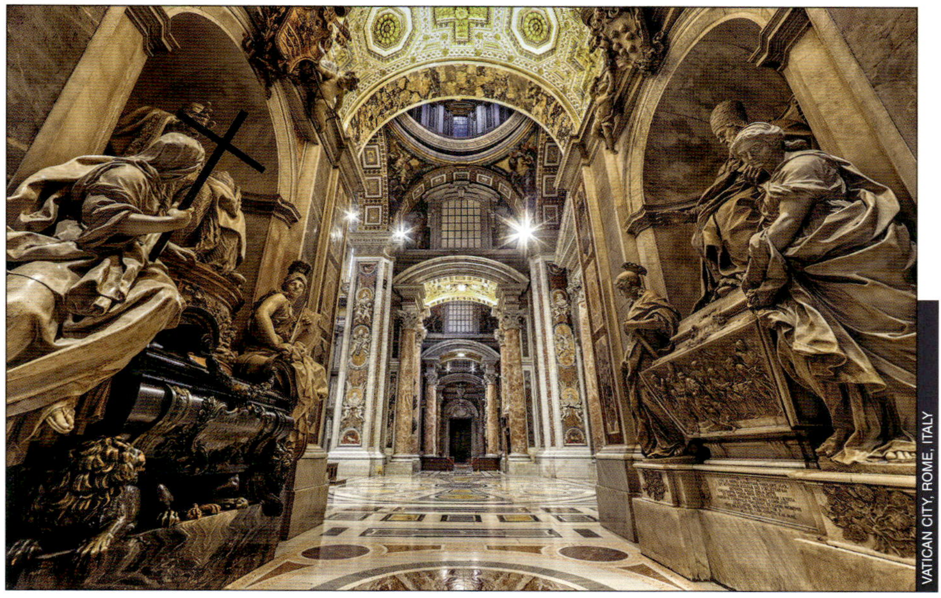

It doesn't seem like you can take a tour these days without visiting a cathedral, classic old museum, or palace, and I'm totally cool with that. I love photographing the old world craftsmanship and incredible detail some of these classic old buildings have (the shot above is from inside the Vatican, in Vatican City, Italy). The trick to these types of shots, which are generally low-light situations, is to keep your camera super-still, so you get sharp shots. The problem is that many of these places forbid tripods and the only way I was able to get this sharp a shot in low light was by mounting my camera on my Platypod Ultra (see page 66). The guards in the Vatican saw it, but as usual, since it doesn't have three legs, for some reason, they just didn't care. I was able to use it all over the Vatican (on the floor, along railings and barricades, etc.), as well as in cathedrals, libraries, and palaces all over the world, with no issues. If you're lucky enough to find a place that doesn't mind if you use a tripod, then great. Also, more and more places are now allowing you to shoot on a tripod if you buy a special "photo pass," which is more expensive than the normal entrance ticket, but then you get to shoot to your heart's content with a tripod, so I've always found it worth the small extra fee.

Shoot: Small Details to Help Tell Your Story

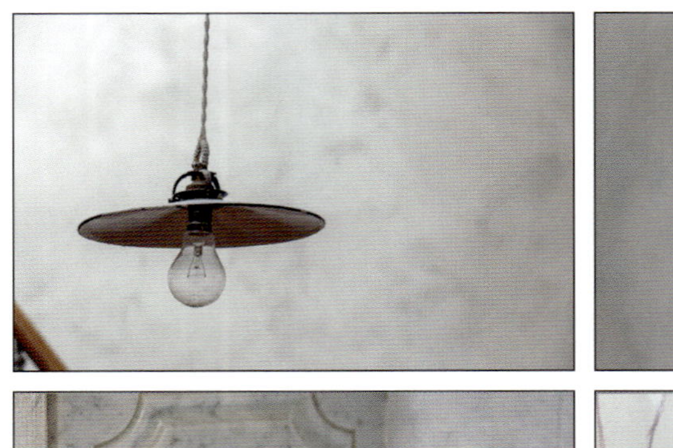

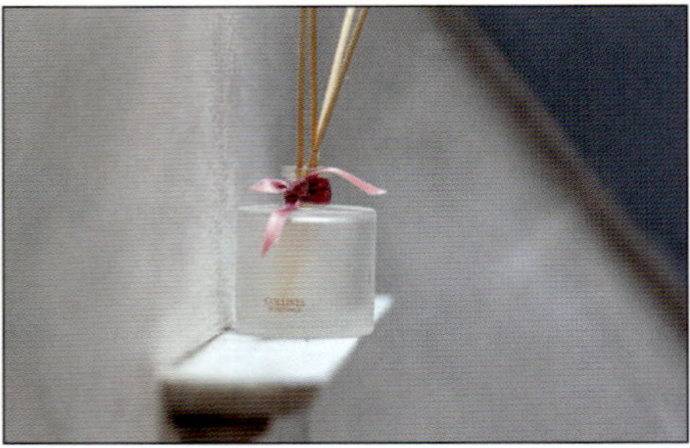

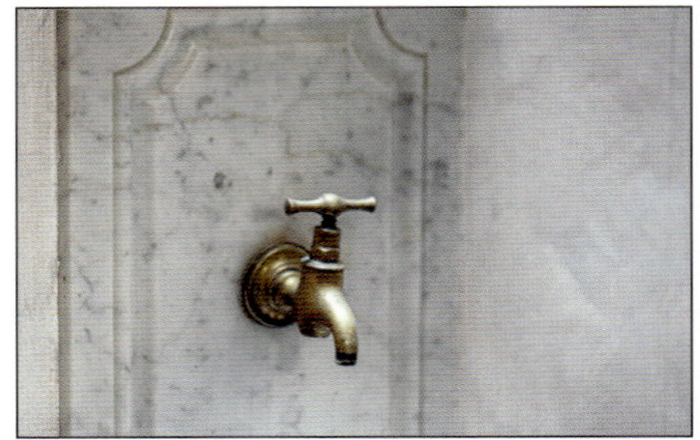

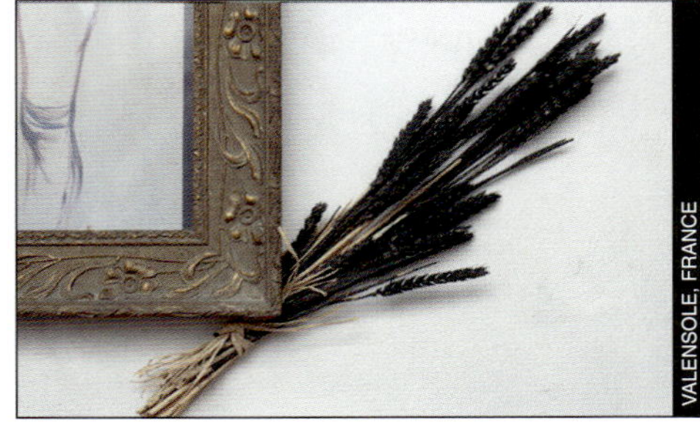

The four shots you see above were all taken in the same charming bed and breakfast in Valensole, France, and they help tell the story of my visit there. These are not "epic" shots, and one of them wouldn't really stand on its own. In fact, they're all just very regular, very simple shots, but they gain strength when they're put together in a series like this, where you're showing multiple shots together on the same page. By the way, the place to put multi-photo layouts like this together is in Lightroom Classic. Its Print module lets you easily put these together (it comes with a bunch of preset layouts, but they're easy to create your own), and then you can save the page as a JPEG to share on Instagram or Facebook, etc. You can also do all of this manually in Photoshop (but Lightroom makes it so easy). Put shooting the little details on your shot list—and not just of where you're staying, but any place where the little details make a difference—and they'll help tell the story of your visit.

Shoot: The Food!

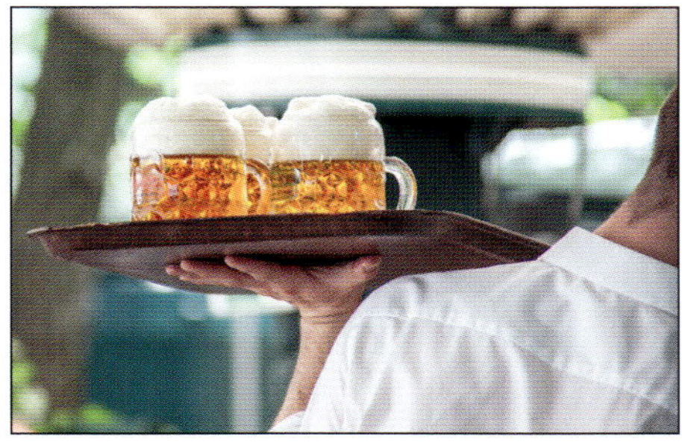

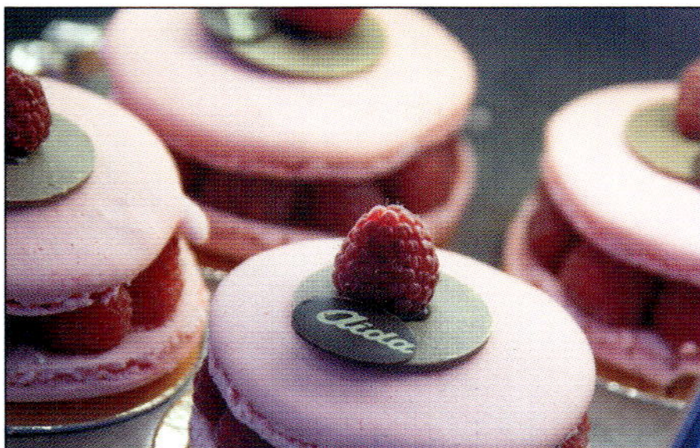

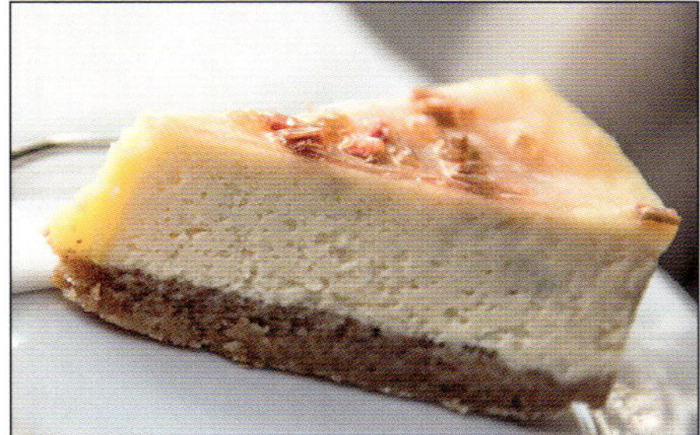

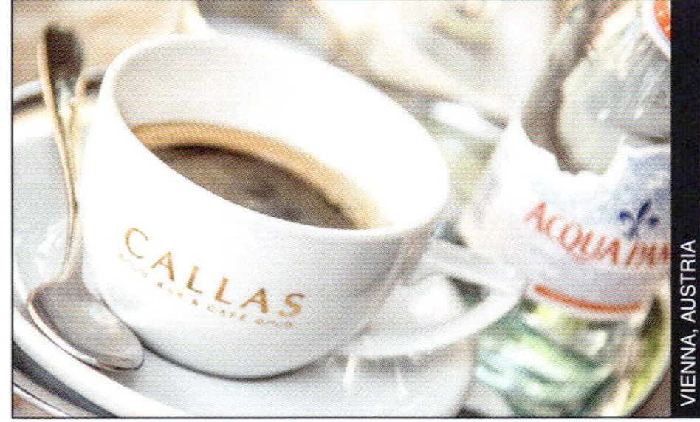

When they do research on why people love to travel, one of the top things on the list is that people love to sample foods from different regions. They love to try the local flavors, coffees, desserts, meals, and drinks, so when you photograph the food, you're taking pictures that people love to see (and you'll see lots of these types of shots in travel magazines. A very popular shot in them is one where you see the server bring the food, or a shot taken as they're setting down a coffee on the table, which brings a human element to your food shots—like the shot at the top left here, taken in Vienna, Austria, of the waiter delivering a round of beer). I have a recipe for shooting travel food shots that works really well (see page 244), but for now, put shooting the food that you're served (or you see on display) near the top of your "must shoot" travel shot list.

Shoot: Interesting Architecture

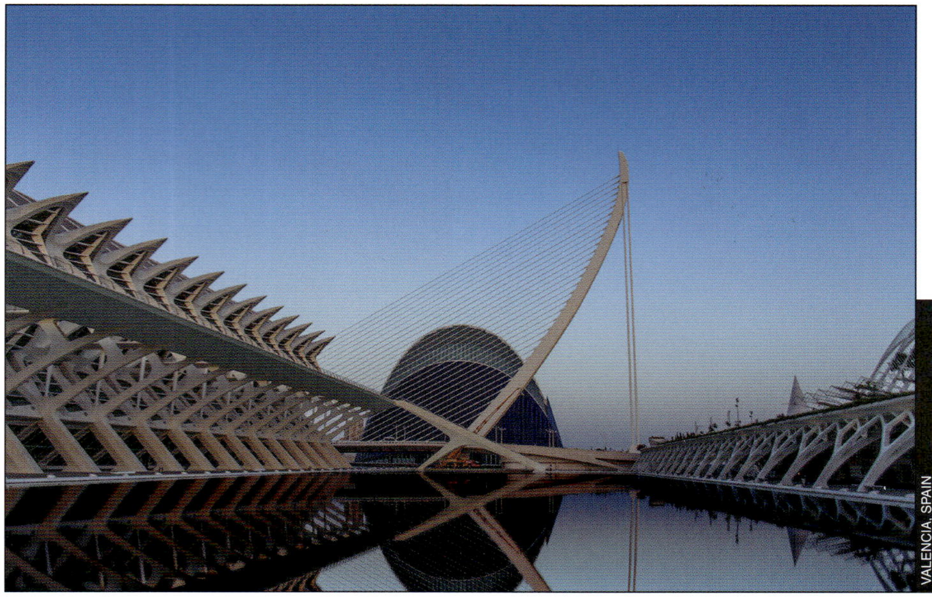

One of the most fascinating aspects of many cities is their architecture, and you can find a wonderful mix of old and new in many places, from China to Europe to the Middle East. The ultra-modern architecture you see above was designed by the world famous Spanish architect Santiago Calatrava (this complex of futuristic buildings is called "The City of Arts & Sciences" in Valencia, Spain). The rest of Valencia is what you'd expect in a wonderfully old Spanish town—beautiful old cathedrals, gorgeous classic buildings, and quaint winding streets lined with shops and cafes. But, in the middle of it all is this amazing architectural wonder, and you might want to capture it all because it reflects what Valencia is today. Paris has a section of ultra-modern architecture, called "La Défense," with towering skyscrapers that you seldom think of when you think of Paris, and the buildings are remarkable and totally worth the short taxi ride (technically, it's not in Paris proper, but yeah…it kinda is right there). Anyway, add interesting architecture to your travel shot list, and don't be afraid to shoot both the old and new (remember: when you're telling your photographic story online, you can group the modern shots together so they don't seem out of place. A lot of people will be surprised to see this modern aspect in cities they've seen many times before).

Shoot: At Blue Hour

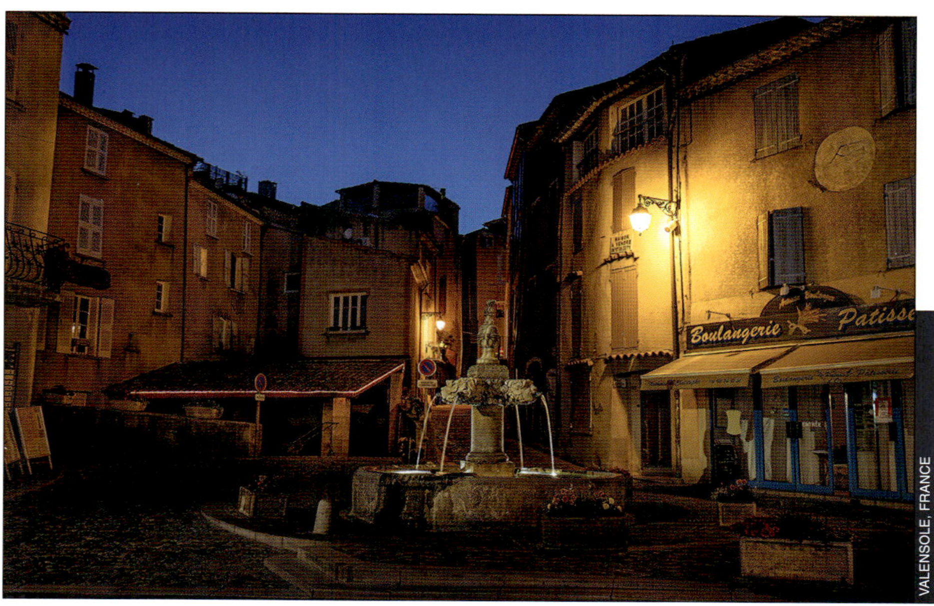

This is one of my favorite "after hours" times to shoot. Blue hour happens a bit after the sun goes down, and it's kind of a weird, but awesome phenomenon. After it gets dark, and the sky is almost solid black, for just a few minutes the sky turns an awesome rich blue color (like you see above—this shot was taken from an outdoor cafe in Valensole, France), and you've got this little window of time to make some wonderful shots because the warm lights of the city contrast beautifully with the blue night sky. Now, I will tell you this: the term "blue hour" is clearly a marketing term because this wonderful blue hour only lasts around 15 minutes max (if you're lucky), so be in place to capture the scene while the sky is still blue. One way to find out exactly when blue hour starts and ends on any given day is to use the PhotoPills app (see page 72), which shows that info for the location you're currently in (or for somewhere you'll be traveling to in the future).

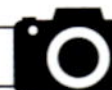

Shoot: Subway Stations

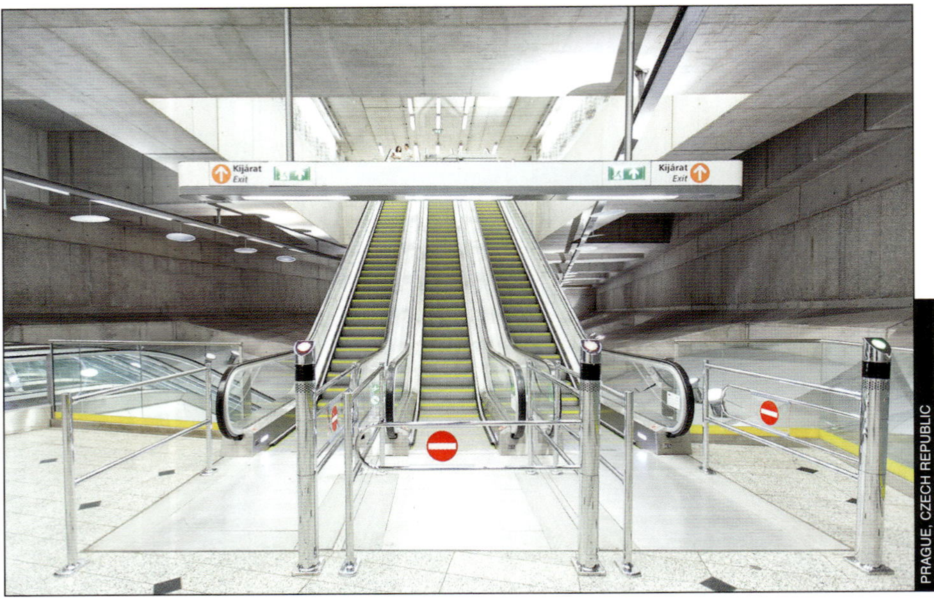

PRAGUE, CZECH REPUBLIC

Shooting subway stations has become really popular with travel photographers, and perhaps it's because subway stations around the world are becoming more and more interesting. From the ornate subway stations in Moscow, to the incredibly creative subway stations in Stockholm, Sweden, to the modern subway stations you see in Prague or Budapest (one from Prague is shown above). *Note:* I want to tip my hat to one of my all-time favorite travel photographers Elia Locardi, the photographer I feel started this subway photography craze with his stunning HDR shots of the Stockholm subway stations years ago. The stations are often a wonderful mix of chrome and glass, tile and bright lights, with nice bright areas of color that really bring it all together. You'll be surprised (well, I was anyway) at how much fun these can be to shoot, and the main skill you'll need is patience if you want to get shots without tons of locals and tourists in the scene. I've had to wait as long as 10 to 15 minutes to get a chance to take my shot of the station empty, but don't let that dissuade you. The key thing to keep in mind is: I don't need the station empty for three minutes; I just need it empty for 1/125 of a second.

Shoot: With a Foreground Object

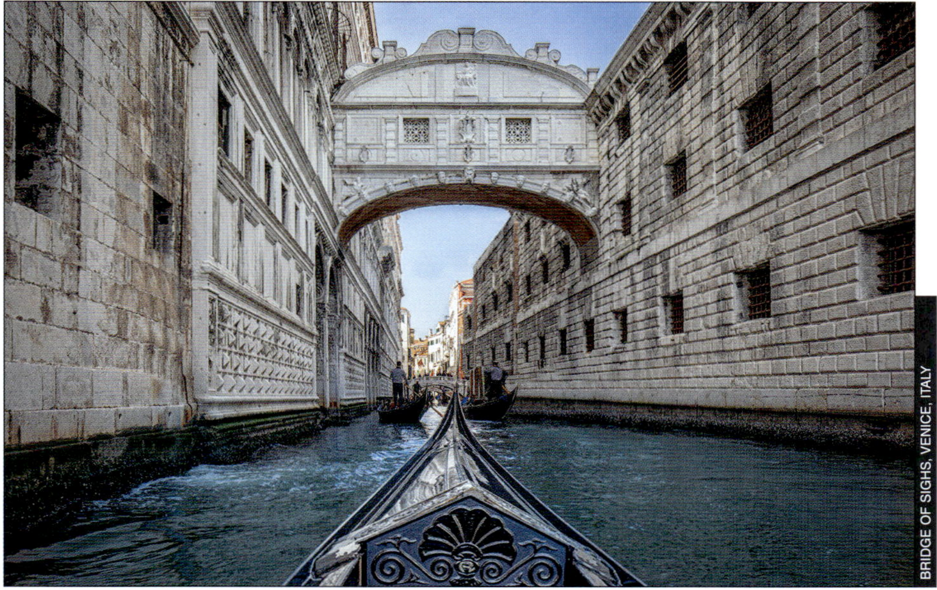

In the composition chapter, we talked about how having a foreground object helps add depth to your image by adding layers that draw the viewer into the scene. One popular thing you often see in travel photos is one where you include a foreground object like you see above—in this case, the front of a gondola—and you'll see lots of shots like this, with everything from rowboats to canoes, which do a wonderful job of making you feel like you're right there. One of the most popular Instagram foreground objects made travel photographer Murad Osmann famous, as his shots featured his wife in front of him, leading him by the hand, into these wonderful travel scenes. She made it feel like she was leading the viewer into the scene, and it's such a clever use of this foreground compositional idea. Keep an eye out for opportunities to use a foreground object (like a boat, or a bike, or a friend) to lead the viewer into the image and make them feel like they're right there with you.

Shoot: Where You Stayed

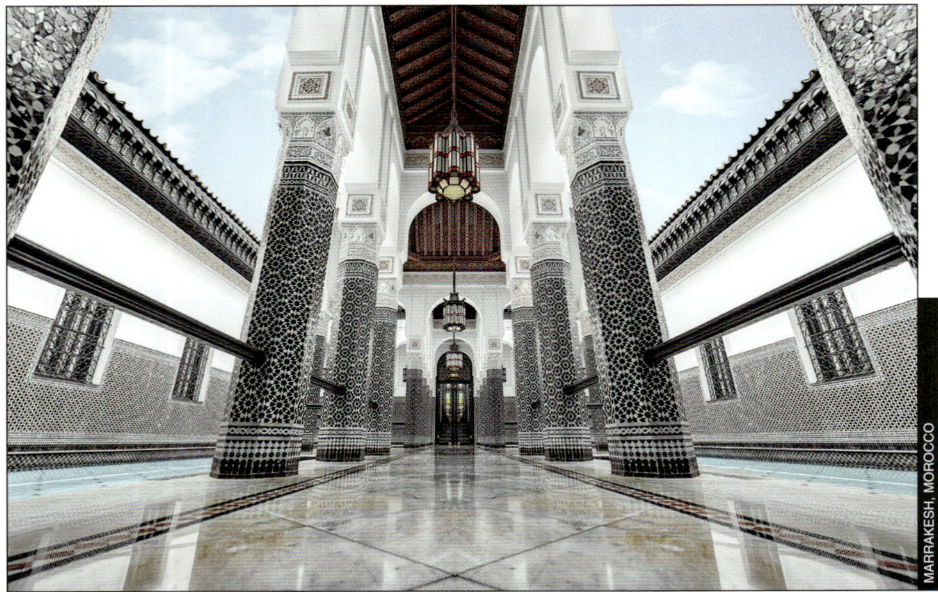

Of course, you want to take a few shots of everywhere you stay, just for your own memory book, but what I'm talking about here is taking the time to set up and make a beautiful shot—like the type of shot the hotel or inn would use on the their website to showcase the place (this is one of the connecting hallways in the La Mamounia hotel in Marrakesh, Morocco, shot with my camera way down low. Incredible hotel). When you show the hotel, inn, or Airbnb you stayed at, it brings another flavor and layer of interest to your travel photography. *Tip:* I often take a shot of my hotel room, with a wide-angle lens, when I first check in and the room is in tip-top shape. I roll my luggage into the bathroom, so it's out of the shot, set up my tripod, and take my shots while the room looks the best it's going to look during my stay.

Shoot: Markets

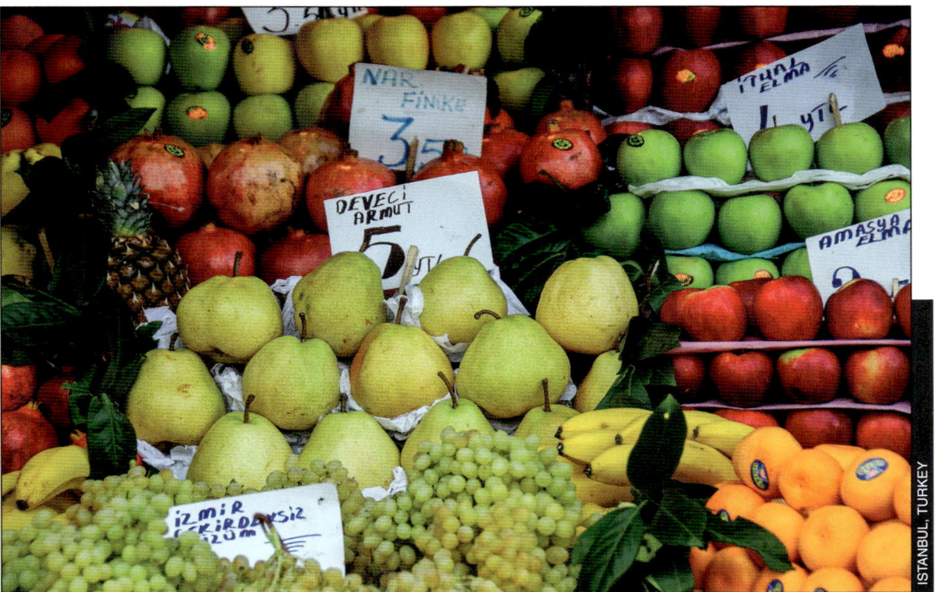

Besides seeing the local architecture, interacting with the locals, and sampling their yummy food, another thing we love to do in foreign lands is to shop. There are often wonderful open-air markets, many with food stands, that make wonderful images that add flavor to your overall story. For example, there are famous markets in Istanbul, Philadelphia, Valencia, and Germany (the street markets) that are a photographer's paradise (plus, I love when price and description cards are written in a different language, like you see above). While we're talking about this, another thing I always shoot are handwritten restaurant or drink menus on posters outside restaurants or on chalkboards. I find them so charming, and I often get great comments about them (even though it's something so simple). You're probably not going to get a shot of a drink menu that's going to be an epic showstopper that you'll print and hang on your wall, but they are wonderful pieces to help enrich and share the colorful story of your trip.

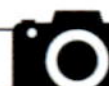

Skip: Animals

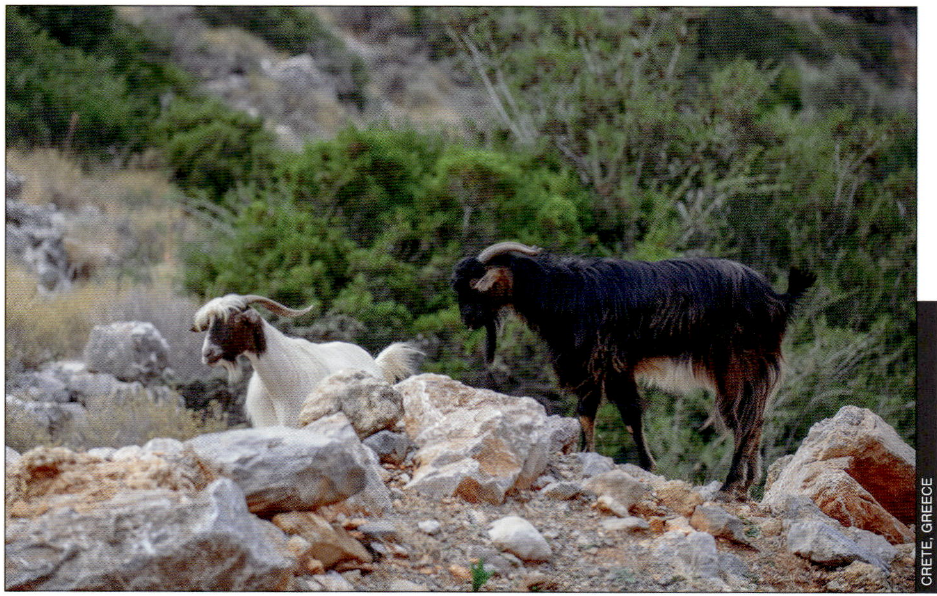

It would be great to get that epic shot of a herd of stallions, heading straight toward you as they race through a shallow pond with the water splashing and their manes blowing in the wind, but when we photograph animals on our vacation, that's probably not what we get. We get goats. Like these goats I shot on vacation in Greece many years ago. At the time, you're like, "Hey, honey—look at those goats!" and then you take a photo. Later, you look at that photo, and you're like, "Why did I think of taking this shot of these goats?" Your chances of getting an epic animal shot on vacation are slim, unless, of course, your vacation is based around photographing animals, like on a trip to Kenya or to Costa Rica. In a vacation city, what you get instead, are goats or donkeys or cows standing around eating grass, or sheep standing around eating grass, and...well, it's unlikely you're going to get anything you'd show anybody, so put this genre on your "skip" list.

Skip: Fountains with Frozen Water

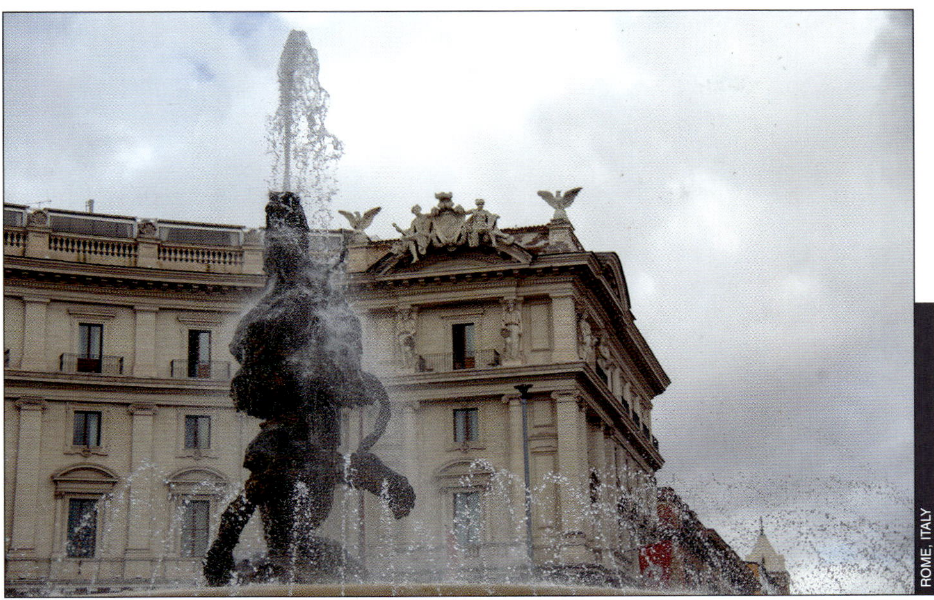

If you don't have an ND filter and a tripod with you, and you see a beautiful fountain, you're going to wind up with the dreaded "water frozen in midair" shot (as seen above). Here's what to do instead: Make note of the fountain's location, and then come back when (a) you have an ND filter and tripod, so you can get beautiful, silky water during the daytime (see page 115). Or, (b) if you have a tripod of some sort with you, when it's dusk, and it's dark enough outside for you to shoot at a high-numbered f-stop, like f/22 or f/32, which will keep your shutter open longer, so you can get nice, silky water. Or, (c) you have your tripod, and it's night, and the fountain lights are on, so you can get nice, silky water fountain shots (I love fountain shots at night—the colors can be really beautiful and getting that silky water is easy and almost automatic at night). You know what doesn't look good? That beautiful fountain with frozen water in harsh daylight. Skip it until you can go back either with the right gear, or at the right time to make a nice shot.

Skip: Messy Shots

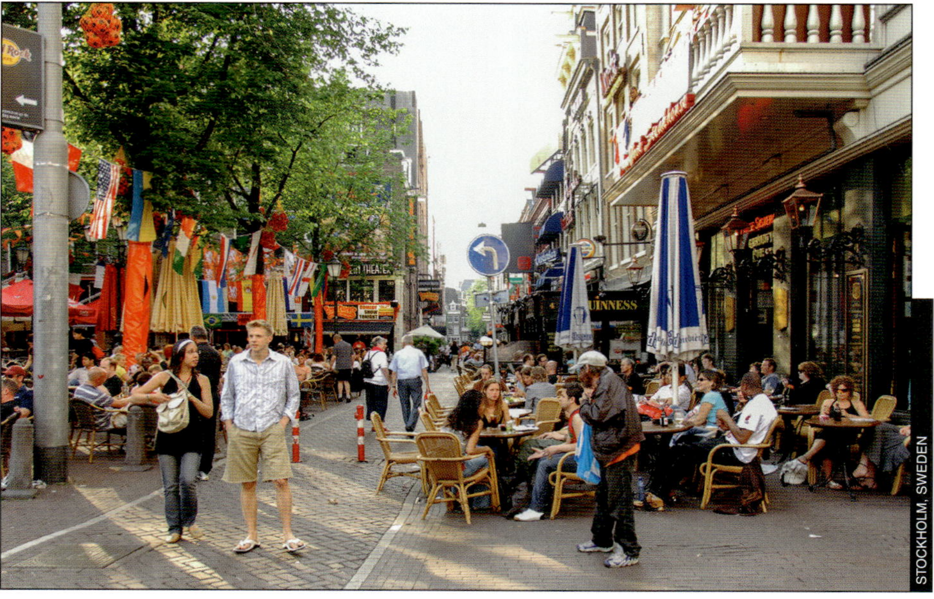

We talked about simplicity in our composition in an earlier chapter, but this is a great example of what not to shoot—messy scenes. These scenes are everywhere in a city. It's a mix of tourists and signs and people looking at their cell phones, and we're not even sure what we're supposed to be looking at—there's no clear focal point. It's not really a photograph; it's a snapshot. You don't want to come home with a bunch of snapshots, so when you see a really messy scene like the one above, either skip it or find something within the scene you want to highlight—zoom in tight on it, simplify the scene, and you might come up with something. But, in the meantime, you can save yourself a lot of time by just skipping messy scenes like this.

Skip: People Doing Everyday Things

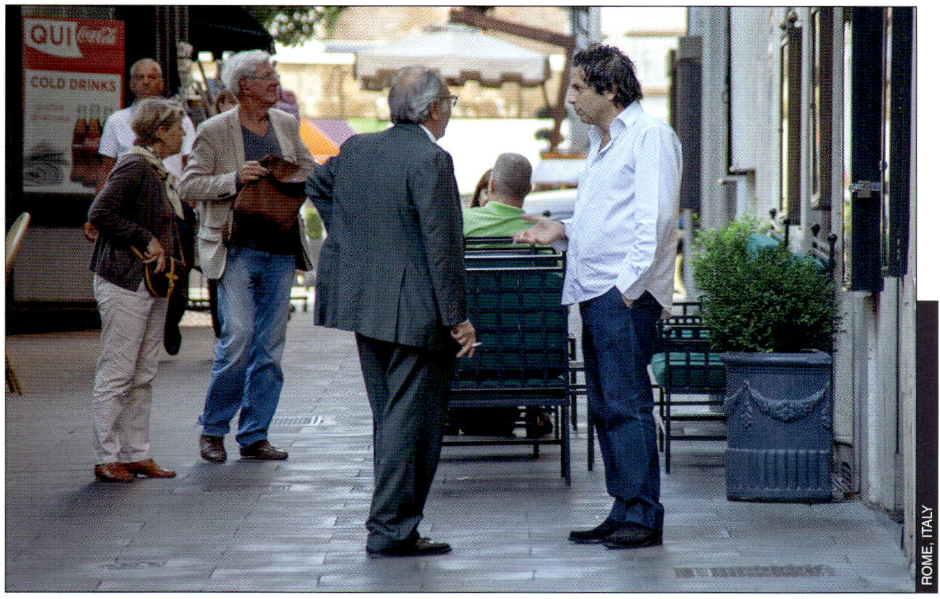

One of the living legends of photography is a man named Jay Maisel. He's brilliant, his work is celebrated around the world, and he's featured in an Amazon Prime documentary on his life. He wrote a landmark book (I feel it's his seminal work) called *Light, Gesture, and Color* (disclaimer: my company worked with Jay to produce this book), and in the book, Jay essentially says that for a photo to have that certain something, it needs to have either (a) amazing or interesting or dramatic light, (b) a person in the photo who is making an interesting gesture—something you wouldn't see your average person doing—or, (c) stunning color. Of course, if the photo has two of these, maybe great light and wonderful color, or a fascinating gesture in dramatic light, then it's even stronger, and if you get that rare image that has all three, then you're really onto something. His book is packed with great examples and wonderful storytelling. So, this is something you can ask yourself when you're shooting in the streets of a city, and you capture a shot: Does it have great light? An unusual gesture? Great color? Or, like the photo above, is it just another shot of people doing everyday regular things? This shot doesn't have great light (it has boring light). Their gestures aren't unusual or fascinating (they're regular), and the color is blah. It's a blah photo of people doing everyday things, which makes for some boring shots. Stay away from shots of people doing everyday things and search out the interesting, unusual, and colorful scenes bathed in beautiful light.

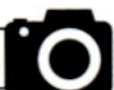

Skip: Instagram Clichés

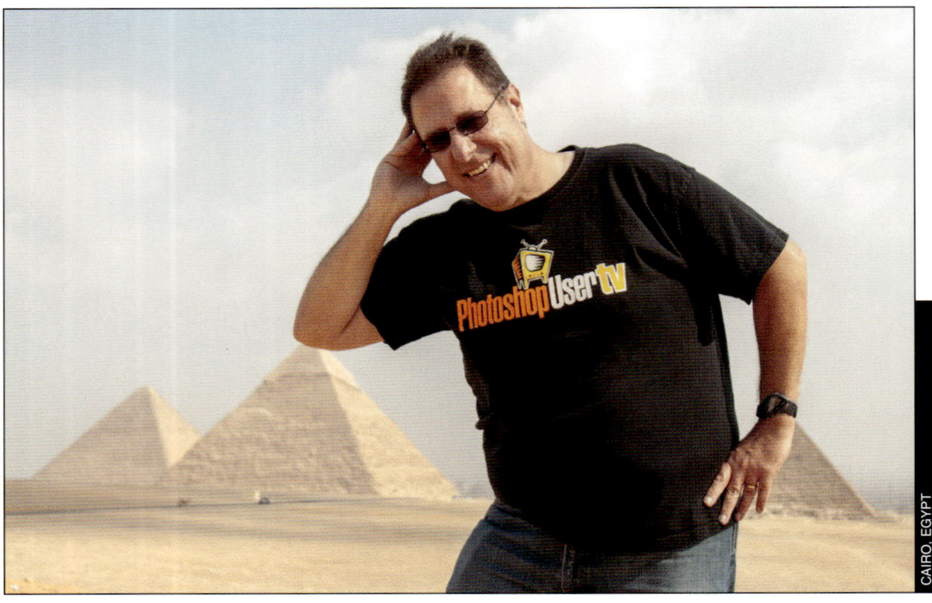

I'm pretty sure you've never seen this photo of me, leaning on the Great Pyramid of Giza, before and that's a good thing (I see a ton of similar type photos on Instagram every day). They're okay, just for fun, but ask yourself this: how do people react when they see one of these types of shots? They groan. They roll their eyes. They might chuckle a bit, but no one ever says, "Great shot!" So, how did I wind up taking this silly shot? I had no choice. I was at the pyramids, trying to make a shot, when two army guards with machine guns came up and told me to follow them because they wanted to show me where the great shot was. I reluctantly followed them to a spot not too far away, then one guard directed me to pose like you see here, and then again with me holding the pyramid in my outstretched hand, while the other guard took my camera and took the shot of me you see above. After a few shots, thankfully, we were done, but then the guard holding a machine gun told me I should tip the guard for taking my photos. I gave him the Egyptian equivalent of around $5, but the machine gun guard let me know that was not nearly enough, so I added another $5 to get us to $10, which still did not appease them. So, I finally got them to let me go once I gave him around $20. I was happy to still have my camera, and just get back to my wife and the tour bus. Well, at least you know why I have this shot I'm telling you to skip (and to watch yourself around the guards at Giza). Now, there are a whole bunch of clichés like this that have really fallen out of favor with folks on Instagram (they are tired of seeing them and happy to tell you so), so I'm giving you a heads-up to skip them altogether (like the shots at the beach where you show your feet in sandals from your beach chair, or you're holding the moon, or a shot with you looking out the window of the plane). Let these cliché shots die a peaceful death, and go shoot something people do want to see.

Skip: Other People's Art

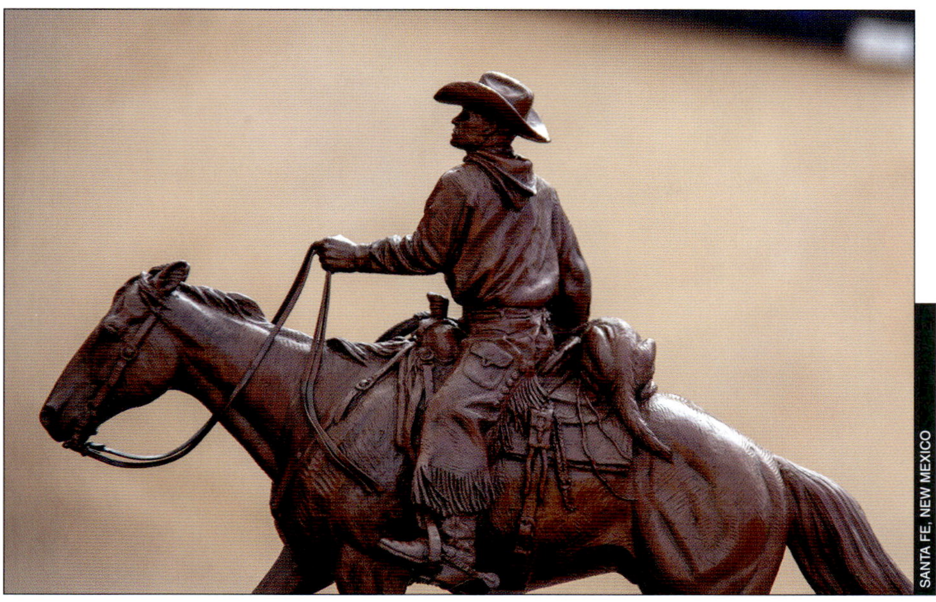

This is a wonderful sculpture I saw in Santa Fe, New Mexico, but me taking a photo of someone else's art doesn't make it art, and it certainly doesn't make it my art. This is a shot of somebody else's art, and while it's fine for me to take so I can remember it, it's not a shot I would share because (say it with me now) "It's somebody else's art." It's not like the art is in the background of the photo, or it's a statue in front of a building—their art is the photo, and that's why you should skip it.

Skip: Shots Filled with Tourists

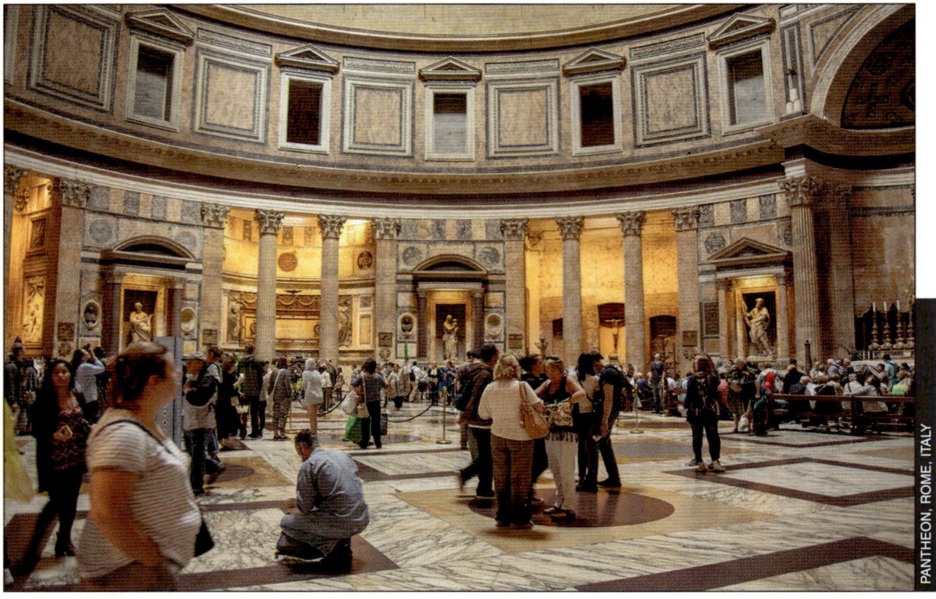

I think you'll find there's very little call for shots filled with tourists milling around, like this one taken in the Pantheon in Rome. It's another one of those boring, "people doing everyday things" shots. But, if there's anything worse than people doing everyday things, it's tourists doing everyday things. How do you get around this? Here are three ways: (1) Be the first one in, first thing in the morning. This has worked for me more times than I can count. You wind up with either a completely empty place for 10 or 15 minutes, or a place with just a handful of people, who you can usually shoot around, so it looks empty. (2) Be the last one out. This has worked out many times for me, too. Also, sometimes, if you book the last walking or guided tour of the day, it either ends right at or sometimes just after closing time. I've been on tours that when they ended, I was all alone in the place for a few minutes. So, end-of-the-day tours are big with me. I also tend to lag back, so that I'm the last one out of every room on the tour. Every once in a while, the tour guide will double-back and round you up, but they're usually leading the other 10 or 12 people, so they're up front, not in the back where you're straggling. Just make sure you listen when you're about to leave an area, so you hear the tour guide mention the next destination, like "Next, we'll head to the famous Hall of Mirrors," so at least if you lag way behind, you can catch up with the group. Lastly, (3) simply tip your camera up just a little bit, so you're shooting right above the heads of the tourists. You'll be surprised at how well this little tip works. No, you won't see the floor, but I've done this dozens of times, and I'll have people ask, "How did you get to shoot it with no people there?" If I had tipped my angle down a little flatter, they'd see the heads of hundreds of tourists. Give this one a try, and I'll bet you'll be surprised at how well it works. You'll avoid seeing a sea of tourists, which rarely makes even a decent shot.

Skip: Things under Construction/Renovation

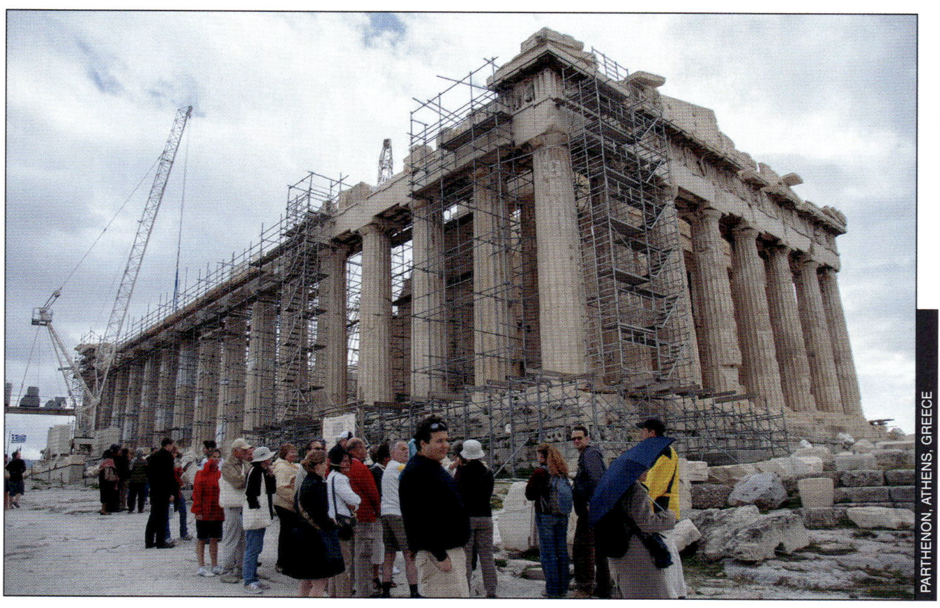

When you show someone a shot you've taken where something is under renovation or covered in scaffolding, they generally wind up saying, "Too bad all that scaffolding was there, right?" Right! So, don't shoot the scaffolding or areas under construction. Now, you might think this will mightily test your compositional skills, but in many cases, it's actually easier than you'd think. You just have to walk around the building, or monument, or castle, etc., until you find a viewpoint where you don't see the scaffolding (in the shot above, it was on the opposite side where most of the restoration work was complete and the scaffolding was down). Also, remember in the composition chapter, we talked about not having to show the entire structure because, like the photo you see here, you wind up seeing all sorts of other stuff, like the tour groups, or the big crane on the left, and so on? Remember, you're in charge of what gets in your frame, and what gets left out, so skip the shots of buildings under construction and find that angle where all that stuff is hidden from view (that way, people will ask, "How did you get this shot without all the scaffolding? When we were there, it was covered in it!").

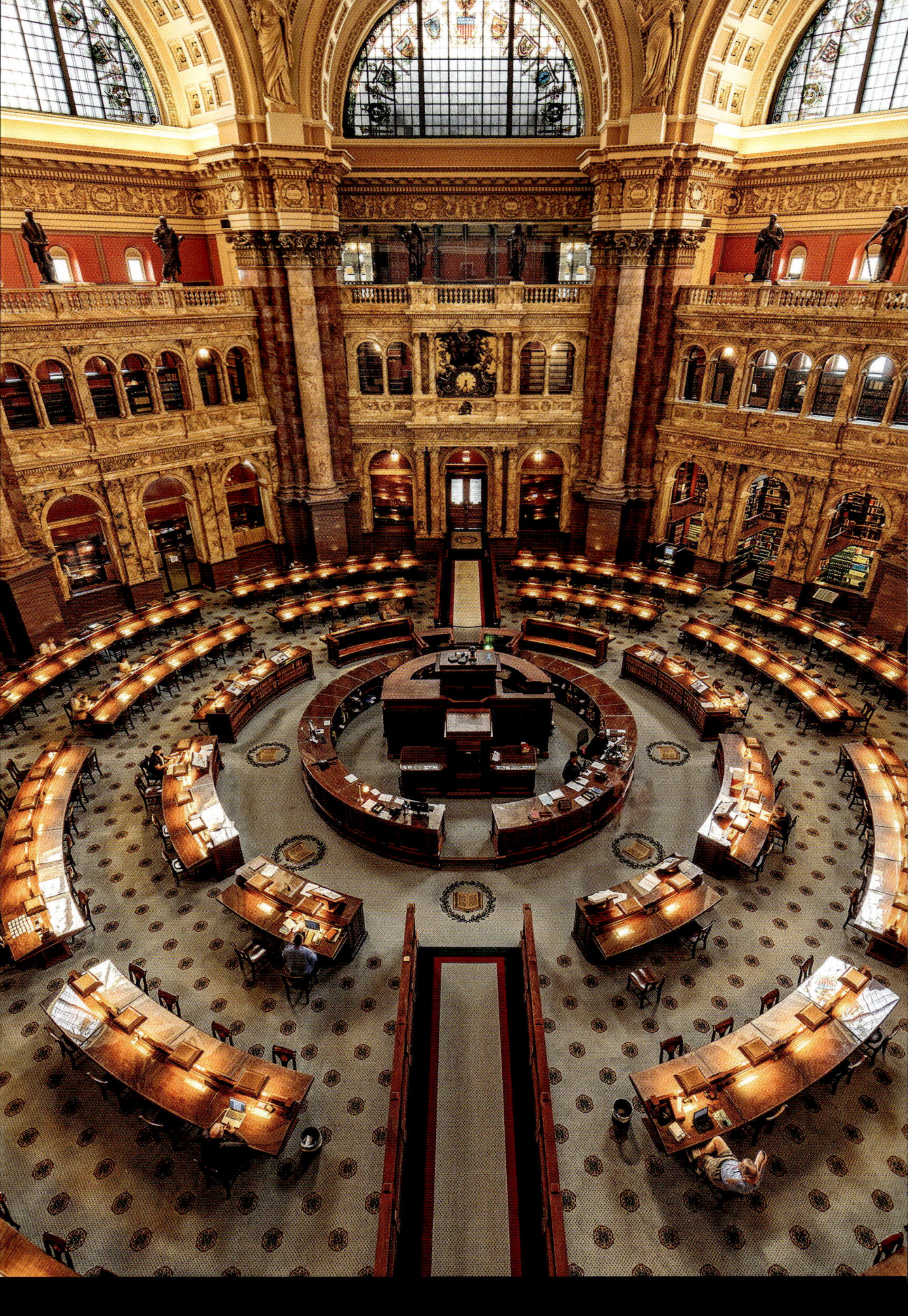

SHUTTER SPEED: 0.5 sec | F-STOP: F/11 | ISO: 100 | FOCAL LENGTH: 11mm
LOCATION: Library of Congress, Washington, DC

Sharing Images from Your Trip

Let's Get Those Awesome Images Out There!

This is what it's really all about: you come back from a trip to some exotic locale (or Indiana) and you want to share your images with people who you want to make insanely jealous. This is the glorious gift of travel photography. Sure, a great travel photo makes the viewer want to go there, but your job is to make them feel bad about them not having been there, and that, perhaps, something is wrong with them. You want them to feel the stench of failure because they didn't have the amazing experience you did. Crushing the spirit of others with your travel imagery is one of the greatest things you can experience, so don't let them steal one moment of your glorious trip. If they start with, "That reminds me of our trip to Cancun..." you shut that down on the spot. This isn't about them and their cruise to Mexico. This is about your trip of a lifetime and your spectacular images that will stay entrenched in their minds forever. Now, let me warn you about a possible scenario you may encounter when you share your shots from your trip: Let's say you're showing a friend images from your trip to Ibiza, and while looking through them, they casually drop, "Oh, I have a picture just like that from when we were there. We had the greatest paella on that trip!" That. Right. There. That's some bull! They turned the tables on you. You gotta call 'em on it right there. "Oh really, Mildred? You got the same shot? I'd like to see that. In fact, I'd like to see that right now." Well, you know, and I know, Mildred was shooting with a disposable film camera and her shot probably looks like trash, so you have to make her dig it up—I don't care how long it takes, or how long you have to wait. And when she finds it, and it looks nothing like the amazing, artistic, Michelangelo-quality image you crafted, you can tell her, "Really, I found the paella a bit fishy," and just let it hang there. That, my friends, is sticking it to the man! (In this case, the role of "The Man" was played by Mildred, but you knew what I meant, right?)

Adobe Spark Page: Best Way to Share Online

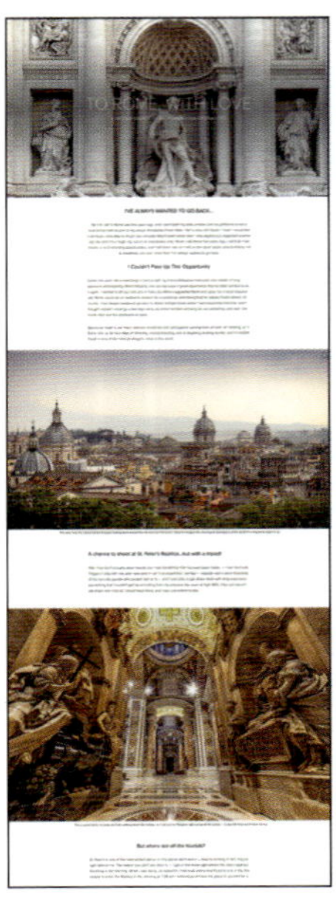

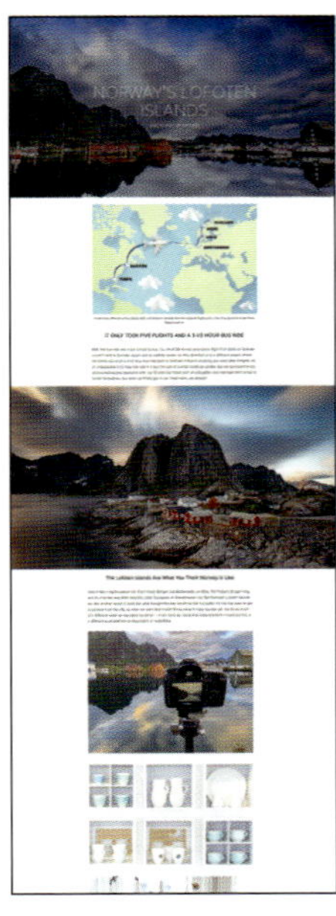

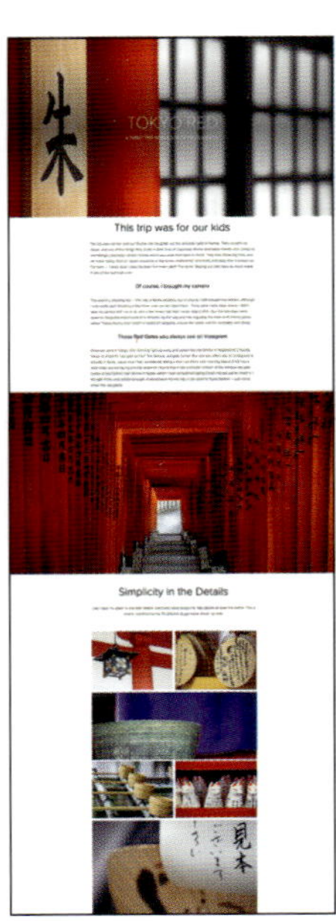

The best way I've found to share the visual and written story of a trip online, and the one that I hands-down get the greatest response from, is using Adobe Spark Page. If you have any one of Adobe's subscription plans, like their Photography plan, this service is included for free. Essentially, it's a webpage that looks and reads like a magazine article. Big, beautiful photos (you pick the size and style, and it's all just drag-and-drop), and if you want to add a headline or some text to tell your story, you just click and start typing. It's all predesigned for you. You just choose a template you like and start making your Spark page. There's no coding. No HTML. No experience necessary, and you can have yours up and running in no time (a perfect Saturday morning project). The images can appear edge-to-edge in your browser (so great for panos), and once you add an image, you can simply type your story below it, or just add captions to your images instead, and wow—it just shows your images online in the best way I've ever seen. When you're done, it looks like an online magazine article in a high-end travel magazine, and you're going to get reactions from it you'll never get from just sharing your images on social media (though I do lead people to my Spark page by posting about it on Twitter, Facebook, Instagram, etc.). You start your story at spark.adobe.com (you'll log in with your Adobe ID and password and choose your template). When I teach in-person travel photography workshops, I teach my class how to create these (well, we all build our pages together in class), and it's so much fun, and so easy, and everybody winds up with these beautiful stories. I just can't recommend this enough, and that's why it's the first thing in this chapter on sharing.

Getting Big, Beautiful Prints from a Photo Lab

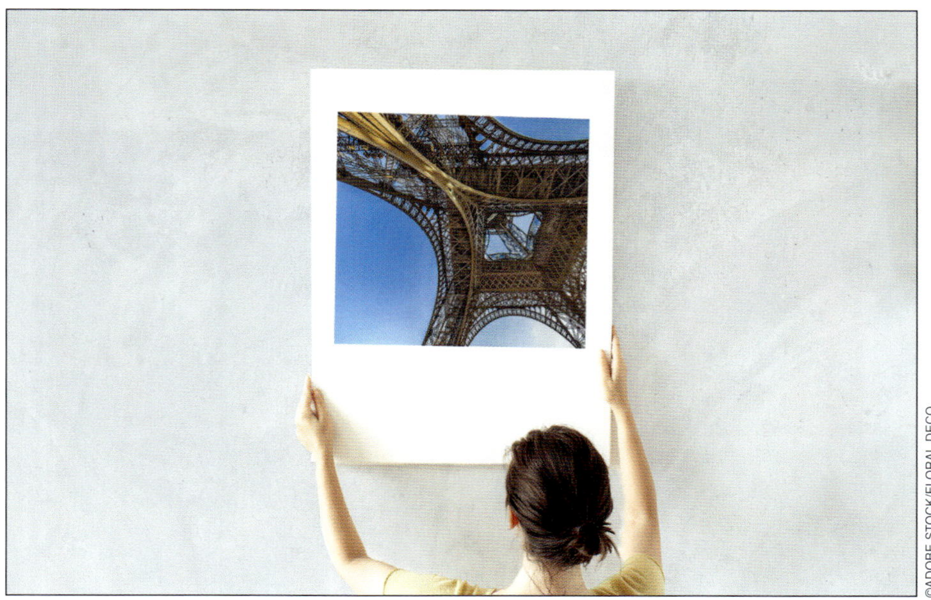

You don't have to buy a printer and learn the craft of photographic printing to enjoy big, beautiful prints of your images because using an online photo lab today is so easy and affordable. Just upload your image, choose the size you want, hit upload, and in a couple of days, your print arrives and you'll fall in love with your photo lab. I have my own printers (a number of them, in fact), but it's just so easy to use a photo lab that I wind up using them more and more. I'm always delighted with the results because they handle everything (they'll even color correct your photo if they notice something wrong—unless, of course, you choose "don't color correct my photo"). I use BayPhoto.com and MPIX.com as my go-to online labs. Both deliver great quality prints—they'll even frame them (with your choice of glass and the whole nine yards) if you like—and have impeccable customer service. They're legends in the industry. You'll be hooked! Two tips: (1) Get your print mounted on foam core or double-weight matboard or masonite—some kind of mounting to keep it from getting warped or wrinkled (plus, they'll last longer). Another bonus of mounting is that you can just hang it on the wall like that with no frame (though, if I'm going to do that, I get the mounting in black instead of white), or you can lean it against a wall or a dresser, so it's kind of ready to go when you get it. It costs a little more, but it's worth it. (2) Go big. The bigger the print, the more the impact. If a friend asked me what size to go with, I'd tell them to go with a 16x24" print or larger. That size perfectly fits the physical dimensions of images from today's DSLR and mirrorless cameras without having to crop the image, and the print size is big enough to really have that "wow" factor. Start making prints—big prints—and it will open up a whole new world of appreciation for your photography. Plus, if you want to blow somebody's mind, send them a large print as a gift. Seriously, the reaction you'll get will astound you!

Printing a Photo Book

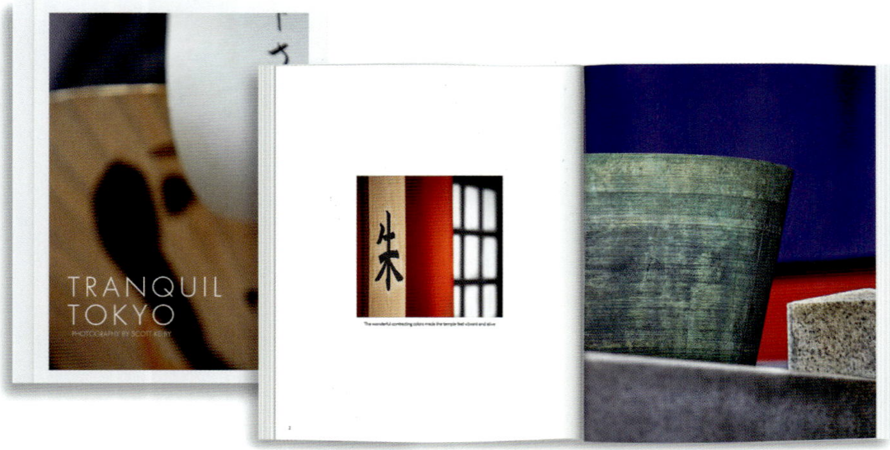

Not only will you love having a coffee-table-quality photo book of your trip, you will absolutely fall in love with the process of putting it together. You become the "photo editor" of your book as you decide which images make the cut, which images go on which page, how many images go on a particular page, and what size and orientation to make them. It's such a fun, creative experience, and I can't recommend it enough. The nice thing is: Lightroom Classic has its own photo book feature built right in with its Book module. You do all the layout there, putting your photos in the order and size you want them, and when you're done, you hit Send Book to Blurb, and it packages everything up and uploads it to Blurb.com for printing. Then, within just a few days, you're holding a beautiful book of your trip, and it's a very powerful way to share your trip with other people (you can see part of the photo book I put together from my family's trip to Tokyo above). You can make it a simple softcover photo book (most of the books I make are softcover—the prices are great and they look fantastic), or you can literally go for a bookstore-quality, large, coffee-table-style book, complete with a dust jacket wrap. You have a choice of styles and layouts right there in Lightroom, and the whole process is really easy and surprisingly fun (shameless plug: I have an online course on how to build photo books in Lightroom at kelbyone .com, ya know, just in case). This is one of the best and most fun ways to share your trip, and you'll get incredible reactions from it. Two tips: (1) You don't have to print your book. You can lay it all out in Lightroom, then save the book as a PDF and email it to friends or post it for downloading. (2) When you print a book through Blurb .com, you have the option of making it for sale through their online store. You get to choose your price, your markup, etc., and then you can lead people to where they can buy a copy of your book. Come on now, that is pretty darn cool!

Sharing on Instagram

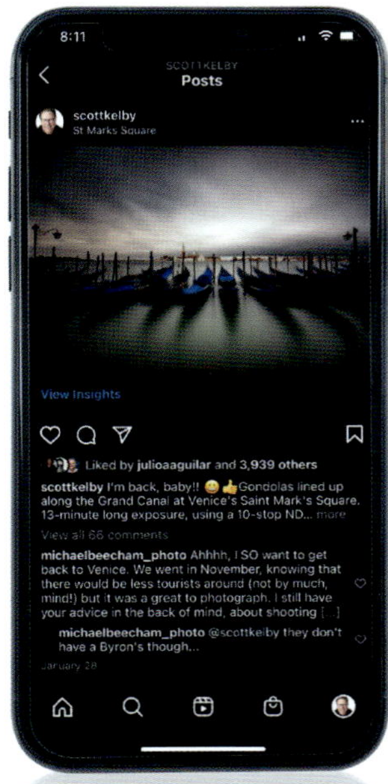

It's the most popular place in the world to share travel photos, and each day, a whopping 95 million+ photos get uploaded to Instagram, which is just staggering (I didn't make that number up—I looked it up—but if I had made a number up, I wouldn't have been so bold as to choose a number as high as 95 million. That's just crazy, right? I'd hate to have to pay their online storage bill). Anyway, Instagram is free to use, free to view, and…well, it's just free. The tricky part about Instagram is getting the photos from your camera onto your phone to post them using the Instagram app (and yes, there's a way around this using your desktop computer and a bit of configuration, but it's a limited version of posting and editing—not the full Instagram experience). On my Mac, I add photos to my Apple Photos app, which sync over to my iPhone, and then I upload them to the Instagram app. It's a bit of an "instapain," but it is what it is, and we do it, but we grumble the whole time that it should be easier. Anyway, pain that it might be, it's one of the best ways to not only share your images with friends online, it's also the best way for your images to reach a broader audience. When you include popular travel hashtags in your caption (hashtags are simply search terms), your image has a chance to reach lots of people. The better your image looks at a small size, the more likely people will be to tap on it, see it at a larger size, and then want to follow you to see more great travel photos (travel photos are all I share on my personal Instagram page: @scottkelby). If you want to resize your images for posting on Instagram, set your width to 1080 pixels. You can post larger sizes, and Instagram will automatically resize them for you, but I'd rather do that part in Photoshop, which I feel does a much better job quality-wise. One more thing: the community, in general, on Instagram is very kind and support-ive of you sharing images, so start posting and get ready for lots of "likes."

Sharing on Facebook

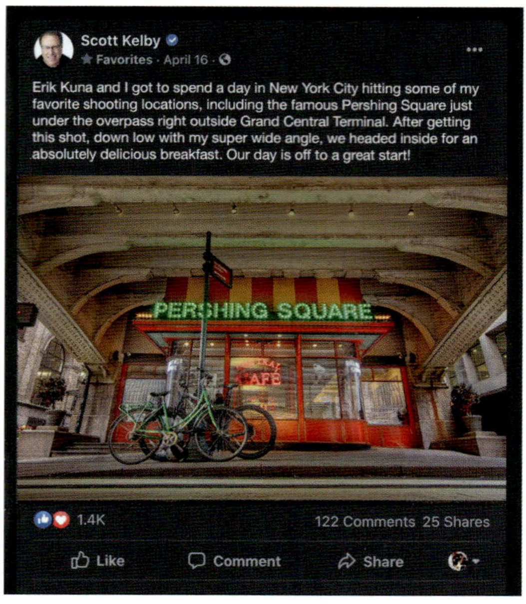

If you want to share the images from your trip with just your family and friends (and not the general public, like it does if you share on Instagram from a public account), Facebook is the place. Like with Instagram, I prefer not to let Facebook resize my images (so I get the best quality results and the photos still look nice and sharp after posting), so I go to Photoshop and resize them down so the width is 1200-pixels wide by whatever that winds up being for your image. Now, Facebook (and Instagram) could change these ideal settings at any time, so it wouldn't hurt to do a quick Google search to see what today's ideal dimensions are (and be prepared to find conflicting info on exactly what the right size is for Facebook, as it seems there's little agreement on this topic online). But, of course, you could just let Facebook resize your images for you. It won't trash them—they just might not be quite as sharp as they would be if you resized them yourself in Photoshop or Lightroom.

Group Sharing with Download Privileges

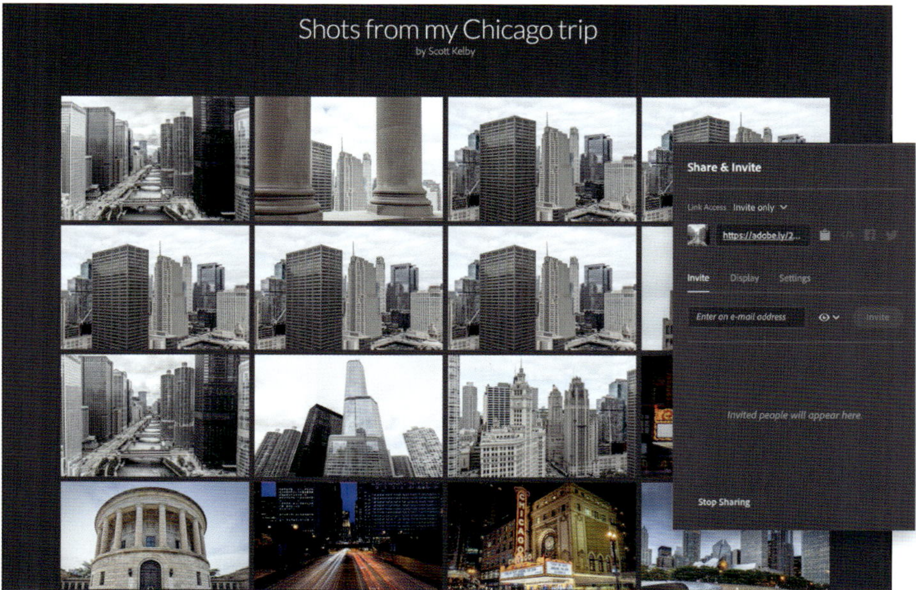

This is one of those kinda hidden features of Lightroom that a lot of folks miss. Lightroom will let you not only create an online collection of your photos, but it allows you the option of letting people download your photos (maybe you want people that were on your tour group to download some of your images), mark their favorites, and even leave comments. This feature is already enabled if you're using the cloud version of Lightroom, but if you're using Lightroom Classic (like me), then all you have to do is turn on Sync, then make a collection of the photos you want to share and sync that collection. Once you do that, go to your web browser, head to lightroom.adobe.com, enter your Adobe ID and password, and you'll find your collection already online. To share it with other people, click on it, then click the Share button, and now you can choose the options (seen above in the inset), including whether this page is private or available to anyone with the link to see, if you want them to be able to download the high-resolution images, and so on. Plus, it will give you a web address (URL) that you can email or text to anyone, so they can view and download images from this webpage. It's all much easier and more intuitive than it sounds, and it offers you lots of sharing options.

Create a Portfolio of Your Travel Work

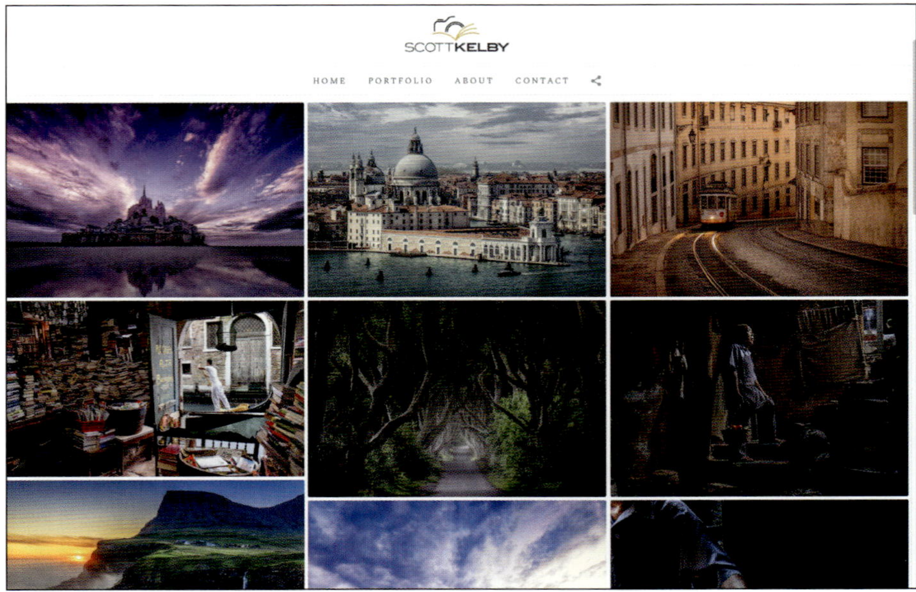

It's one thing to share the images from your most recent trip, but wouldn't it be great if there was a place you could send your friends, family, and other folks where they could see all your best travel images from all your favorite destinations all in one place? That's when a portfolio is really handy. I'm a big proponent of having a portfolio in the first place, and one of the main reasons is: putting one together helps you to know where you are in your journey as a photographer. If you take the time and careful thought process to put together 24 of your best travel images (I think 24 is about the right number for a photography portfolio), when you put them into a portfolio, one way or another, you'll know exactly where you stand on your journey. You might look at the 24 images as a group and think, "Ya know, these are pretty good!" and that can propel you forward to continue on your journey to make even better images. You might also compile these 24 images and think, "Ya know, these are okay, but I can do even better," which is actually good, too. It still propels you forward to learning more about capturing the type of images you'd be proud to share in your portfolio. Now, if you look at your portfolio and think, "Man, these images are trash," then you really have some work to do. But, at least you'll know, and now you can get to work. I use SlickPic.com for my portfolio—they create portfolios just for photographers and they have great templates. You just upload your images, arrange them in order, and customize the site easily without any experience necessary. They also have an option where a designer can work with you one-on-one to custom design your site (it's cheaper than you'd think). Another route, if you have an Adobe subscription plan, is to use Adobe Portfolio (myportfolio.com. It's included in your subscription). It uses templates, too, but it's a bit trickier to set up than SlickPic, but then again, it is free for Adobe subscribers.

Take a Portable Hand-Held Printer

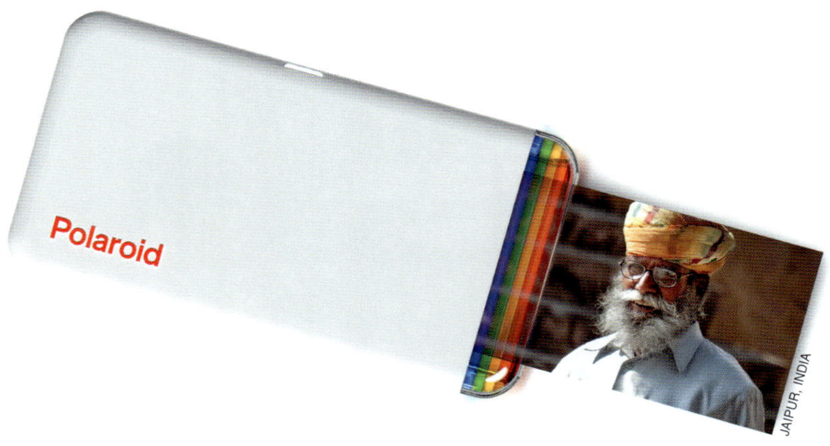

When you carry a tiny battery-powered printer that fits in the palm of your hand with you on your trip, it has the power to do something very special. Imagine taking the portrait of someone you've met on your travels, someone who agreed to pose for a portrait, or maybe a photo of a mother and child, and in 46 seconds, you hand them the print. It's something they will treasure. Something they'll keep forever. Something with real value to them, and something they may not have any other way if you didn't gift it to them. I know friends who have taken a hand-held printer, like this $99 Polaroid Hi-Print 2x3 Pocket Photo Printer, on trips with them and the stories they tell would bring a tear to your eye (well, they did to mine). Consider taking one of these on your next trip. You never know the doors it might open, and the hearts you might touch forever from something so simple, yet so powerful.

Sharing on the Big Screen

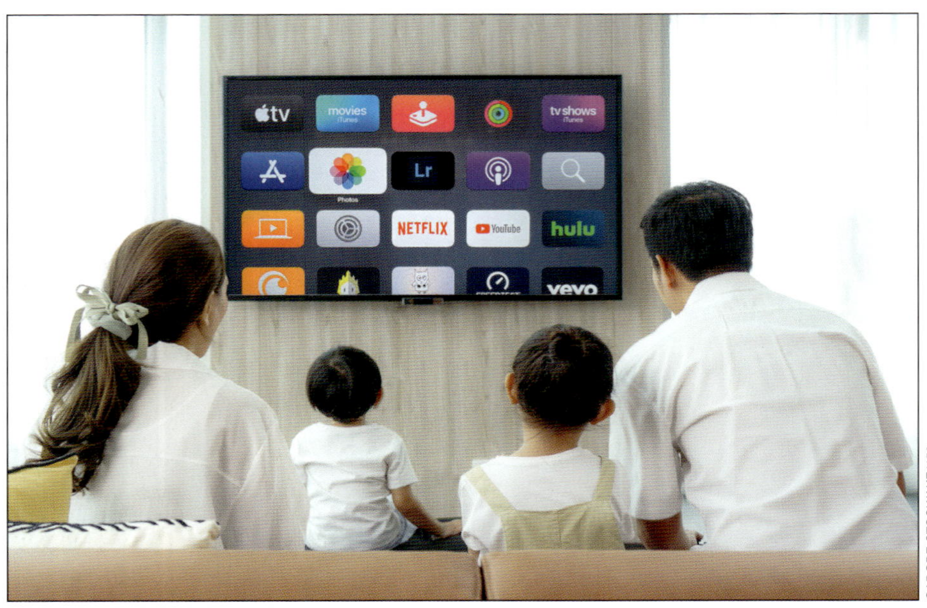

This is one way of sharing travel shots from your trip that a lot of people overlook, but with today's technology, you can easily share your images from your phone, or straight from your computer, right on your TV. If you have an Apple TV, there's even a Lightroom app that you can share from. If you're a Lightroom Classic user, any collections of images you've synced (if you're a Lightroom cloud user, there's no need to sync) are available to view on the big screen, right there from within the app. If you're a Mac user, you can share your images to an Apple TV through Apple's Photos app and see them full screen, or if you're an iPhone user, you can share any photos you've imported into your phone's Photos app. *Tip:* This is the modern day equivalent of having friends over to see the "slides" from your trip, but don't do what we did back in the '70s and '80s, which was to show *every* photo from our trip. Keep it short and narrate as you bring up each picture. I would also split the presentation into two parts: (1) start with your beautiful photographic shots that really show the charm and wonder and fascinating side of the place you visited, and then (2) show the "family" style shots with you and your spouse posing with a camel, or having a gelato, and stuff like that. Otherwise, you go from a few "wow" shots to a shot that's kind of "meh" (look, it's a photo of their appetizer), then back to a great shot, then a family shot, and it's kind of all over the place. Make it two parts: great shots, and then the family shots last. And, close out with a killer shot or two from the trip. Open strong, end strong. It works like magic.

Sharing an HD Slide Show Complete with Music

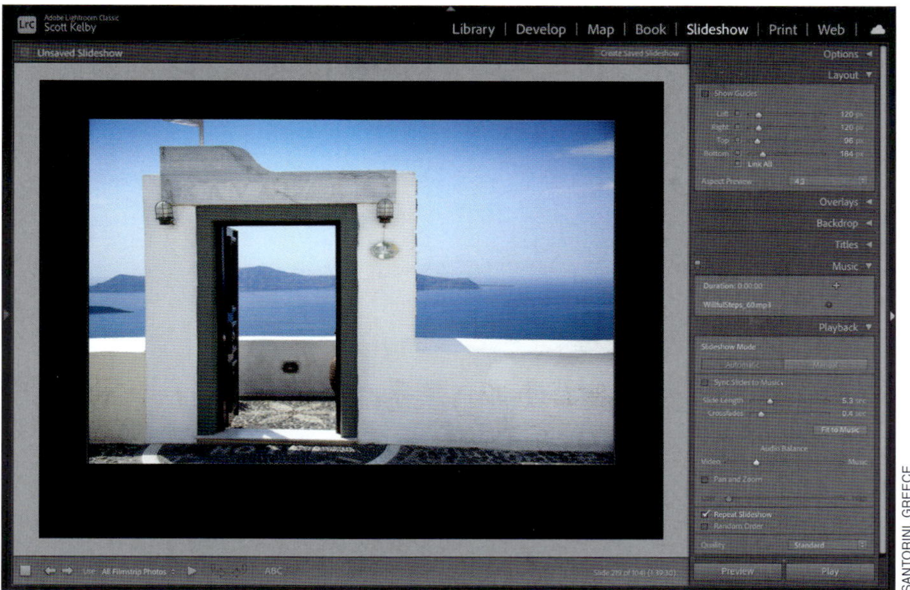

I'll be the first one to tell you that Lightroom Classic's Slideshow feature is not the best one out there—it's not even in the top 20. But, here's what it does let you do: you can take a collection of the best images from your trip, add background music, have it do nice, smooth dissolves between each image, and even have it add the Ken Burns effect (called Pan & Zoom in Lightroom), which adds a subtle movement to your images, giving the whole slide show a nice feeling of movement. You can control how much time each slide stays onscreen, and even the speed of the dissolves (cross fades), and it has a few other features, too. Best of all, when you're done, you can save it as a full HD 1080p movie to email to friends, post online to social media, whatever, and it will have all those features (and music is just so important for slide shows). It's another way to share the images from your trip, but the background music adds that emotion and mood, which can really take it over the top.

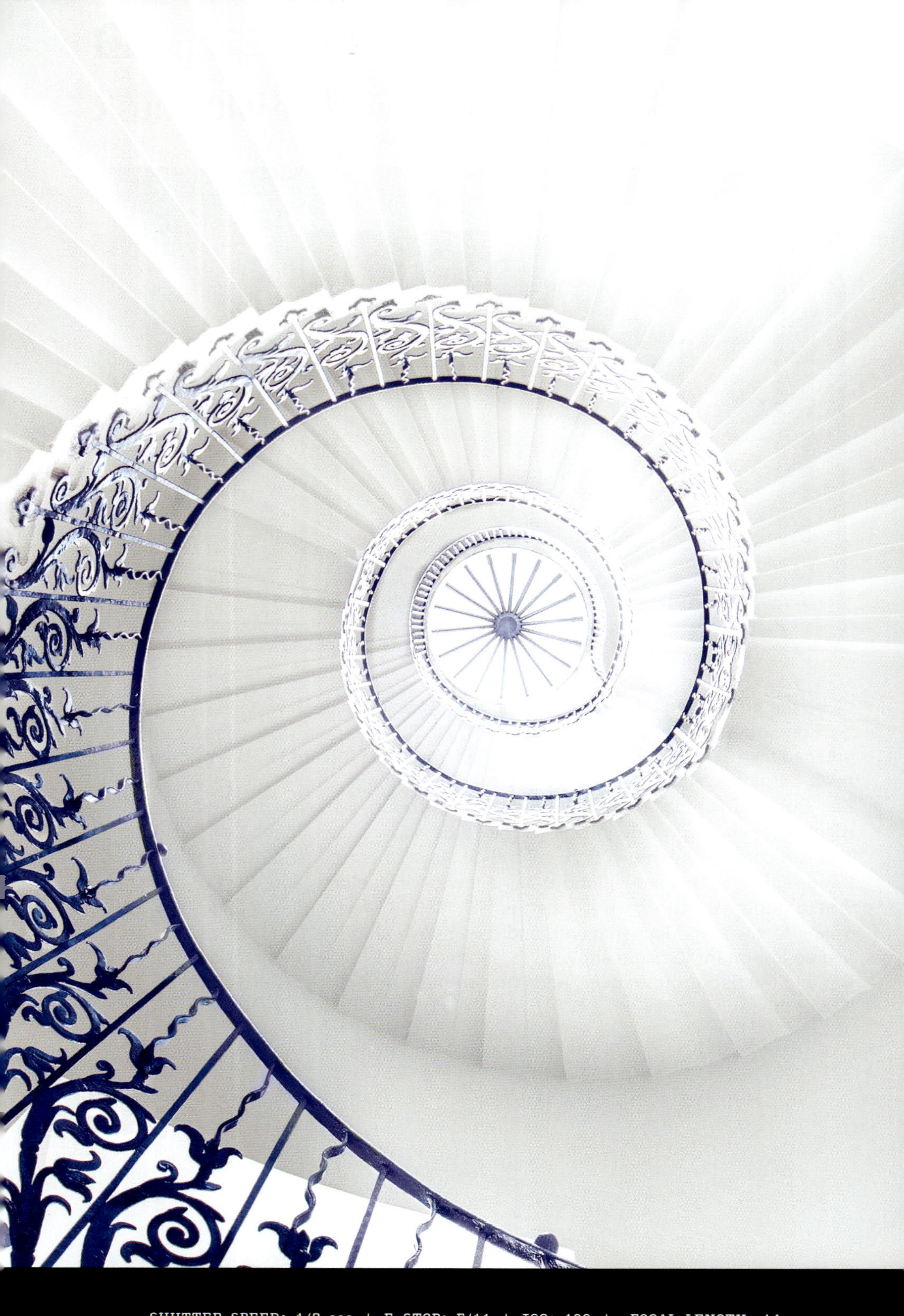

SHUTTER SPEED: 1/8 sec | F-STOP: F/11 | ISO: 100 | FOCAL LENGTH: 14mm
LOCATION: Tulip Stairs, Queen's House, Greenwich, London, England

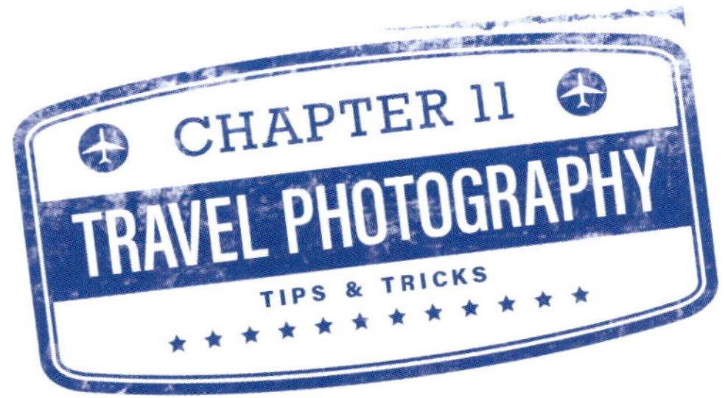

Travel Photography Tips & Tricks

Tips for Working Smarter, Faster, and Better, and Keeping Your Gear Safe

Okay, pop quiz: Would you walk around Chicago with a brown paper bag with "This bag is packed with $20 bills" written on the outside in big letters? Probably not, right? But when you walk around a big city with a camera bag, it might as well say, "This bag is packed with $100 bills" because if that camera bag gets snatched (hey, it happens. I could tell you story after story), you're probably going to lose thousands of dollars worth of gear, and probably some irreplaceable photos you took that day, and it's just a bad scene all the way around. Now, there are certain cities around the world that have earned a reputation for being a bit sketchy when it comes to pickpockets and purse snatchers and camera bag grabbers. If you go to Google and do a search for "pickpocket hot spots in Europe," there's a reasonable chance the tourist board of Barcelona won't be happy with the top result. (*Side Note:* I warned a buddy who was traveling there about this, so he and his wife were extra careful with their belongings out in public, and yet her purse was swiped right out from under her in the blink of an eye.) Now, since this is a possibility, albeit a small one (unless you're on a street named La Rambla, in which case, hide your stuff!), there is something very effective you can try that I've done for years. Instead of carrying a bunch of gear in your camera bag, get an extra-large ziplock bag, but make sure you get one that's leakproof. This is important because you're going to line your camera bag with this leakproof ziplock bag, and then you're going to fill your camera bag with red-bellied piranha (the only man-eating ones). You should see the look on their face when a dozen or so really agitated piranha (they hate being in a ziplock bag) come shooting out of that bag like a Japanese bullet train—they don't waste any time chowing down on the crooks. All the while, your expensive gear is secure back in your hotel room safe, along with some fish food. Good times. Good times.

Safety Tip: Blacking Out Your Camera's Name

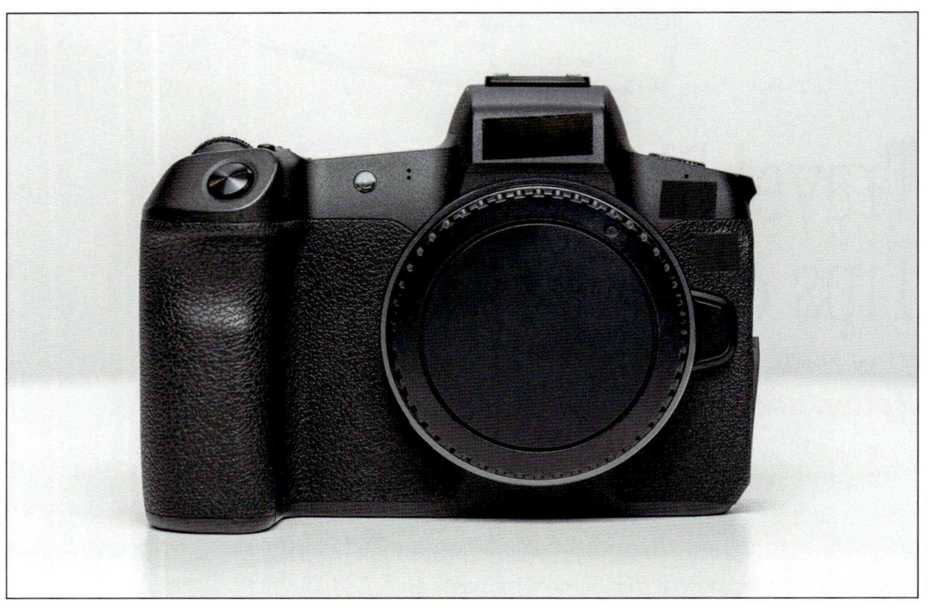

Thieves that target tourists' cameras know which makes and models are the most expensive and worth the risk, versus older, inexpensive cameras. For example, they know a Sony Alpha 1 is a very expensive body, and they also know an Alpha a6000 is not (the Alpha 1 is worth 10 times as much). But, if they don't know which camera you have, it's easier for them to not take a chance and move on to somebody else. That's why pro photographers who travel, especially to areas where street theft is more of an issue, put black gaffer's tape over the name and model of their camera, so it looks just like a generic camera (I recommend using gaffer's tape because it comes right off without doing any harm to the camera or leaving a bad sticky residue. You can get a small roll at B&H Photo for around 7 bucks). It's a little thing, but it might save your gear.

What to Do When It's Been Shot to Death

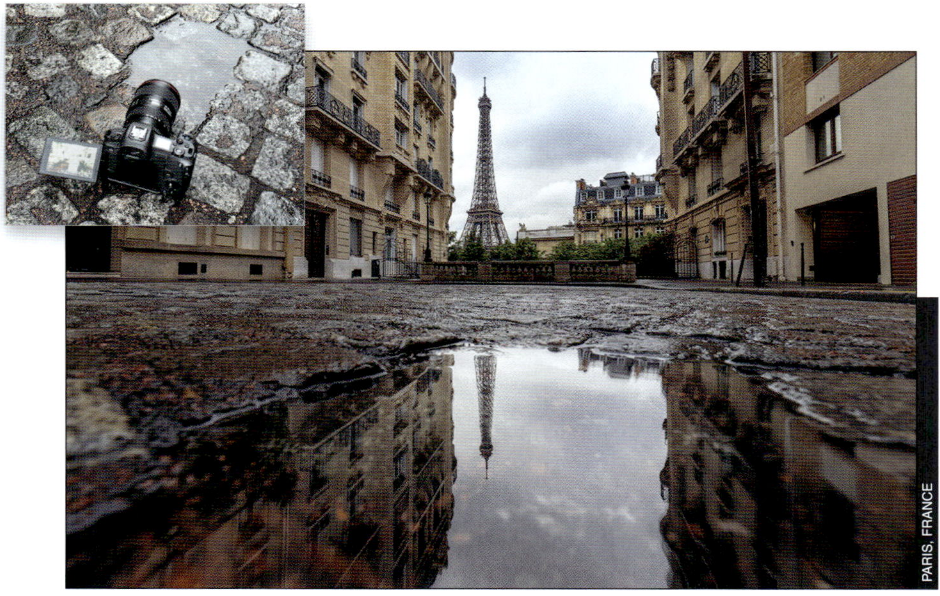

There are so many wonderful monuments and scenes that have just been shot to death, like the Eiffel Tower, the Leaning Tower of Pisa, the Colosseum in Rome, Niagara Falls, the Temple of Heaven in China, the Statue of Liberty, Big Ben, and on and on. Our first inclination might be to stand right in front of it, where everybody has shot it, and get the same shot. There's nothing wrong with that (see page 192 on shooting the classic shot). It's what we call a "Wikipedia" shot—it's a reference shot that, if nothing else, proves you were there. "Yup, that's the Eiffel Tower" (we already know what it looks like—a quick search on Google brings up over 93 million results). But, you know what's harder (and a lot more fun)? Finding a different way to show the Eiffel Tower, or whatever famous landmark or monument you're standing in front of. Here, I set my camera down at the edge of a tiny puddle (as seen in the inset above), but getting that close to the puddle makes it appear much larger, and I get part of the Eiffel Tower in the reflection. It's not your standard shot of the Eiffel Tower (I found that neighborhood searching on 500px, and then Google Earth), which is why I like it. Finding a new way to show something that has been "shot to death" is definitely a challenge, but it's a fun one, and one that stretches your skills as a travel photographer, which is a great thing.

Tourist-Free Shots, #1

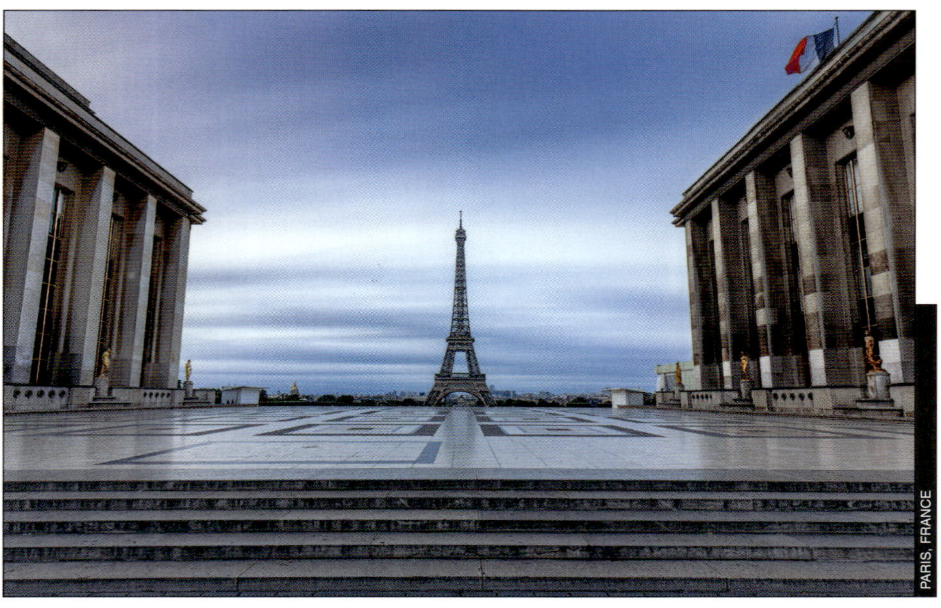

If you're wondering how I got this tourist-free shot of one of the most popular viewpoints of the Eiffel Tower (the Trocadéro), it was easy. I just got up really early and took a taxi out there while it was still dark (right before sunrise). The great thing about tourists is: they don't like getting up early while they're on vacation, and if they do get up early, they're still at breakfast at sunrise (and for around 30 minutes or so afterward). I've been to places that would normally be packed (an hour later, there were about 800 tourists in this same spot), but around sunrise, when the light is perfect, they're empty. When I say "empty" I mean I'm the only one there, and I'm talking in front of the Colosseum in Rome, or in front of the Vatican, or the Leaning Tower of Pisa—you are usually, literally, the only person there, or maybe there's one other person. The most photographers I've ever encountered at dawn was at the Taj Mahal. There were eight of us, but the area there is absolutely huge, so once we got in, I didn't even see them again, but an hour later, there were literally thousands of tourists everywhere. Plus, if you've booked a tour, it won't be leaving that early, so you can have this glorious tourist-free morning shoot, and still catch your tour bus and probably be back at a great location for sunset, which will give you great light, but probably lots and lots of tourists, as well. That's why the tourist-free #1 choice is getting up early. The bonus? When you're done shooting, it's still breakfast time! (*Note:* This smooth, streaky sky was created using an ND filter. See page 71.)

Let Photoshop Remove Tourists for You

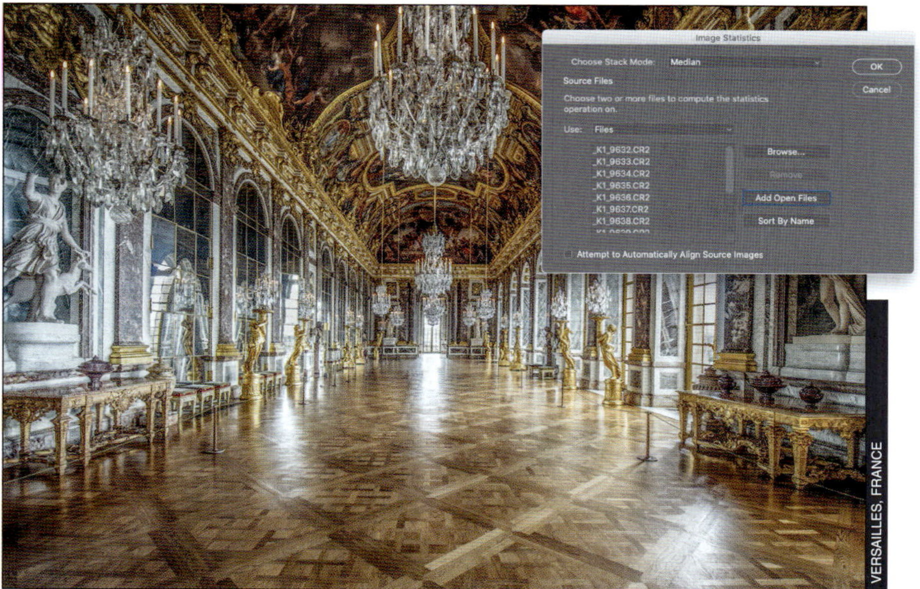

This is another way to get a tourist-free shot, and it's part camera technique, part Photoshop magic (but Photoshop does all the work for you—you just have to turn on a feature and it does the rest. It's pretty brilliant and super-easy). Take a look at this shot of the Palace of Versailles's famous Hall of Mirrors. Well, it was absolutely packed full of tourists. Packed! But, I was able to get this tourist-free shot using this trick: First, pick a spot (here, I stood in the center of the hallway with people moving around me on both sides). Then, put your camera up to your eye and take a photo about every 15 seconds or so until you've taken around 15 or 20 photos. *Do not* take the camera away from your eye the whole time—hold it up and hold it as steady as you can while you're taking this series of shots (I count out loud while I'm doing this, which is probably annoying to everybody around me). Now, of course, if you can shoot on a tripod, this is even easier, but again, it's still 15 or 20 seconds between shots for 15 or 20 shots. When you're done, open all 15 or 20 shots in Photoshop, go under the File menu, under Scripts, and choose Statistics (I know, it's so obvious, right?). When the Statistics dialog appears (shown above), choose Median for the Stack Mode, and then click Add Open Files. If you shot on a tripod, you're done, but if you hand-held, turn on the Attempt to Automatically Align Source Images checkbox (which works really well *if* you kept the camera to your eye the whole time). Click OK and Photoshop will analyze the images, looking for anything that changes between frames, like people walking, and it removes them. It's like magic! Now, the one time you'll get burned in this process is when somebody just stands there in your scene while you're shooting. If they're standing in front of a painting or a statue and don't move, they'll still be in your final shot. So, I would have a friend nicely ask them to move (which is what I actually had to do here). Magnifique!

Yet Another Tip for Tourist-Free Shots

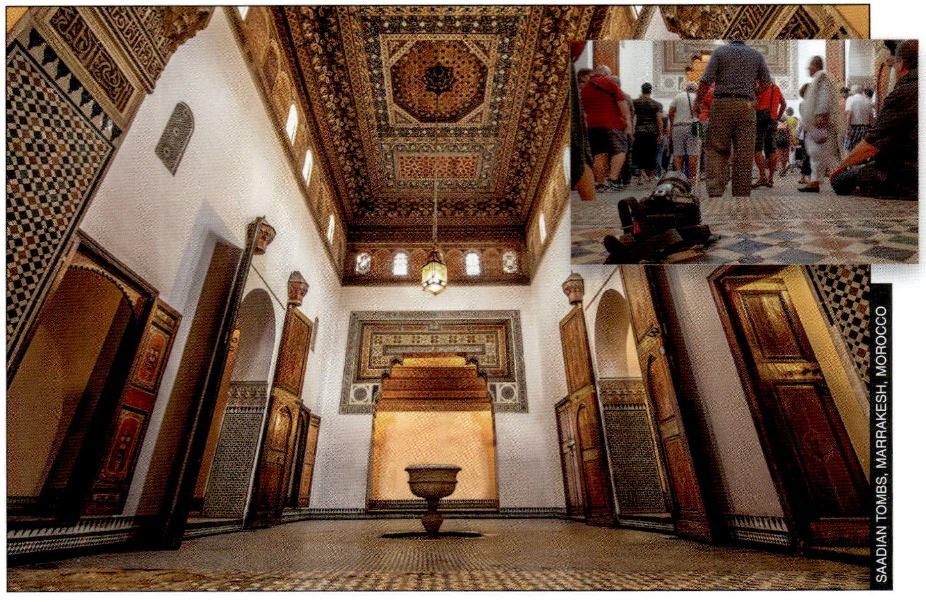

For some folks (me included), this will be among one of the hardest tips in the book. You see the crowd of people in the shot in the inset above? Yup—it was packed like that non-stop, with tour group after tour group flooding into the room, and at one point, I thought to myself, "I'm never going to get a shot of this place without it being packed with tourists." But, then I made up my mind to try one of the hardest techniques in all of photography: patience. I sat down, put my camera on the floor, tilted up a bit with a 16–35mm lens set at 16mm (super-wide-angle), and I just waited. And I waited, and I waited. But, like I said earlier in the book, I don't need the room to be empty for five minutes—I only need 1/125 of a second when there's nobody in the room to grab the shot. Just a super-short gap between tour groups is all it takes. So, I sat there and sat there until I finally got my opportunity. That patience thing, it's a killer, but it gets results (by the way, I tried this patience thing at night in front of Sleeping Beauty's castle at Disneyland California once. You know how many people stream through the front of that castle on a busy night? I do. It's a bunch. But, I just stood there waiting and sure enough, I got that 1/125 of a second gap, and I finally got the shot).

Getting Rid of Tourists, Method #4

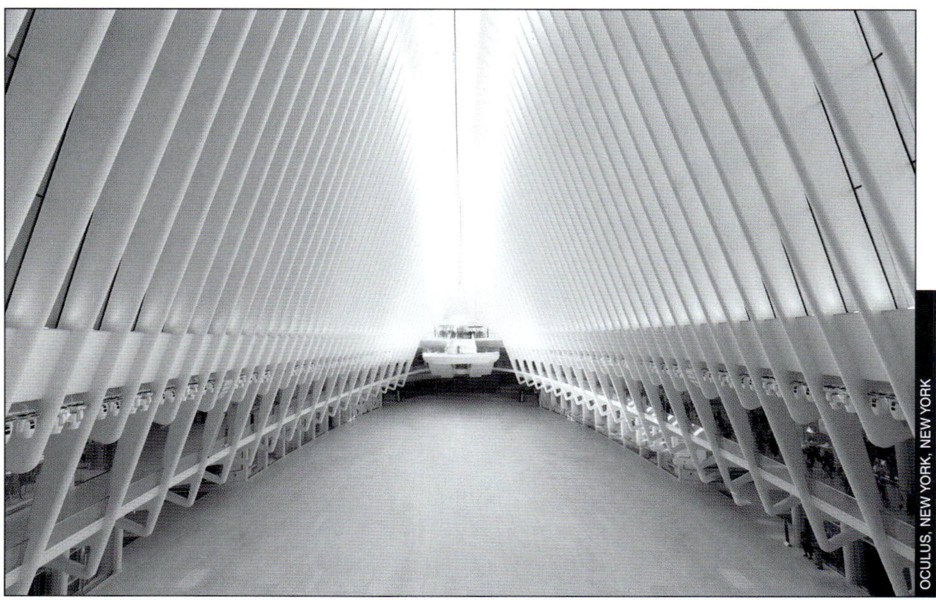

This is one that sounds like it wouldn't work, but most of the time it works brilliantly (with one caveat I'll talk about in a moment), and you don't have to do anything special in Lightroom or Photoshop to make it happen—it all happens in-camera. I use this technique at monuments and attractions that are packed with people and it works really well. What you do is you create a super-long exposure, and while your shutter is open, anyone who walks in front of your camera disappears. This might take a 5- or 6-minute exposure, so everybody has a chance to walk by, so you'll need a 10-stop ND filter (see page 71) to get it dark enough during the day (maybe even add a 3-stop ND filter on top of that 10-stop), and then just follow the regular steps for shooting a long exposure (see page 115). That's all there is to it. Now, remember that caveat I mentioned? Where this can get messed up is, like with an earlier tourist technique, if somebody in the scene just stands still and doesn't move. Everybody has to move. If somebody stands still, when your exposure is done, everybody will be gone but that one person who will still be in your photo. When this has happened to me, again, I have a friend walk over to let them know we're shooting a photo and kindly ask if they would mind moving for just a minute, and in every case, they've been very accommodating—no issues whatsoever. So, making a really long exposure is the secret (well, that and making sure everybody keeps moving). *Tip:* My friend Andy has a trick he uses to clear a scene. He just casually walks up to people and kind of "herds them" out of the way, like he's herding sheep, and it actually works. He just kind of gets close to them and people move right out of the way (plus, it's fun to watch, mostly because it works so well).

Get Down Low with a Wide-Angle Lens

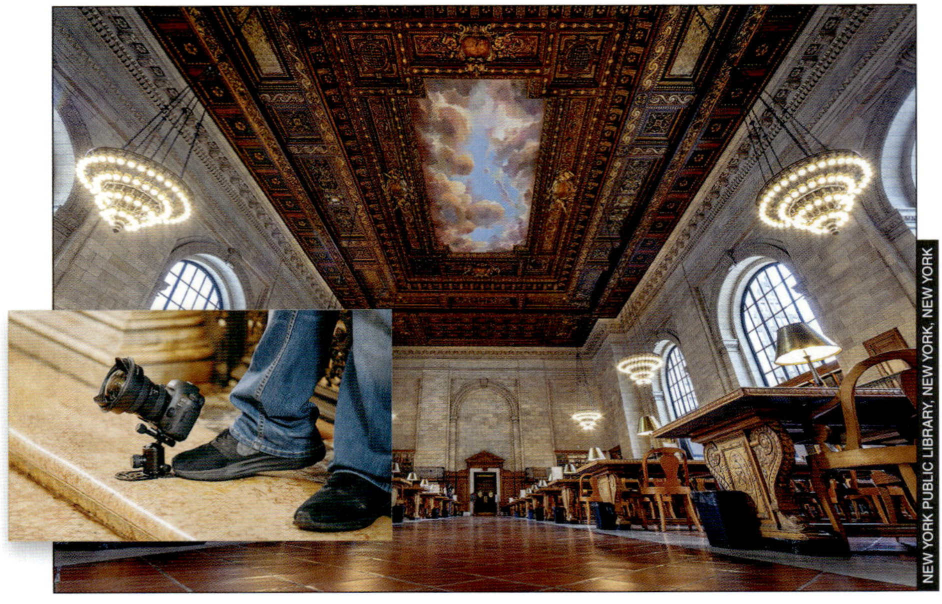

This is my most-used technique for shooting indoors in iconic buildings, museums, cathedrals, etc., and it's to get my camera really, really low (just inches from the ground) with a super-wide-angle lens (ideally, a 16mm on a full-frame or around a 12mm on a crop-sensor body), tilted up to capture the whole scene, from the floor to the ceiling. To get down really low, you can splay your tripod's legs (unlock them where they connect to the top plate, so you can swing them out really wide), or use a Platypod (see page 66), or even lay your camera on the ground if you have to—but you'll have to prop something up under the lens, so it tilts up a bit. One thing that'll make this easier is if your camera has a pop-out, articulating screen on the back, which you can swivel out to easily see what the scene looks like without having to get down on your knees. Of course, you can do what I've often done, which is guesstimate how much angle is needed, and the overall framing, and then take a test shot to see what that looks like. Another way is to use the free phone app that connects to your camera (see page 69). Now, I'm going to admit to doing something that's fairly effective while using the app, but I'm not proud of it. With those apps, you can see your camera's view, so you're holding your phone and you can see your composition. What I do is (cringe) reposition my camera using my foot (as seen in the inset above). I know, it's lame, but it beats the heck out of getting down on your knees, which shouldn't bother me because I'm super-young and youthful and youngish, but…well, I'm not digging it, so I use the app, and my foot, and I still get some good shots here and there. So, that's the formula: a wide-angle lens, down really low on the ground, tilted up, and then use either an app or your pop-out screen to see the framing as you position the camera. And, oh yeah, move it around with your foot…like a boss!

F/22 Starburst Effect

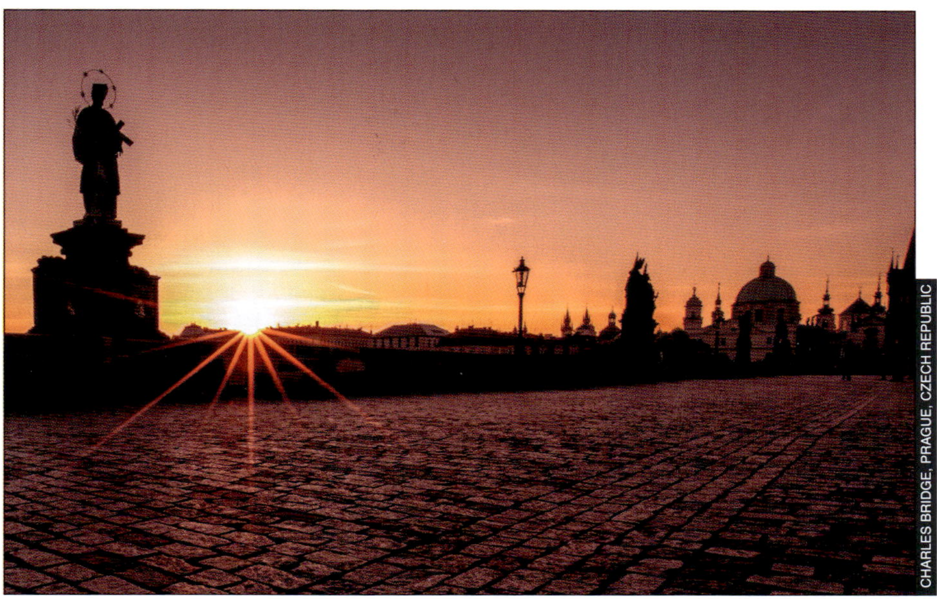

Back when I used to shoot film (in the late 1800s), to get a starburst effect I'd put a special filter on my lens that had a pattern of super-thin wires running through it, and when light intersected those wires it created a starburst on the light. Today, life is much easier (I no longer have to spend my days churning butter) because you can get a starburst effect by simply (1) setting your f-stop to f/22, and (2) framing up your shot so the sun is touching something physical in it (like a rooftop, or a mountain, or the edge of a railing on a bridge, like you see here, or any object where part of the sun is visible and part is touching that edge). That's all there is to it.

An Ideal Way to Photograph a City

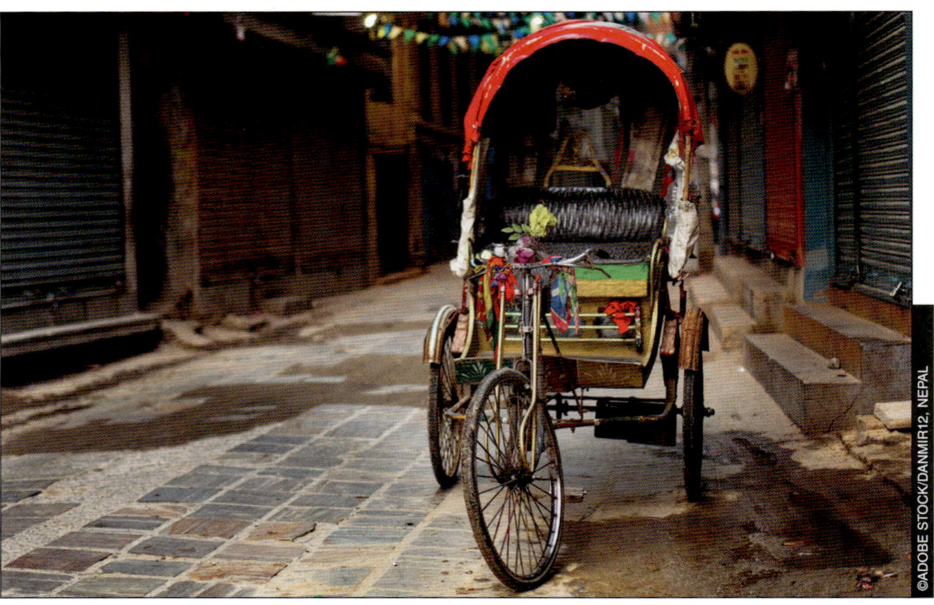

I love taking a taxi or a Lyft to get me from one side of a city to the other, but my favorite way to photograph a city is by a bicycle-powered rickshaw, like you see above. The problem with taxis is finding a parking space, so they have to circle and they're charging you while they circle, and then you're waiting for them to come back around. You lose a lot of time, and you miss a lot of shots, because they often can't just stop to let you out to grab a shot. But, with a rickshaw, they can stop on a dime, parking is never an issue, you can shoot from right within it without having to shoot through glass or other obstructions, and you'll wind up shooting more, getting more great shots in less time. If you're in a city where they have these, ask how much it'd be for an hour or two, or the afternoon. I'm always surprised at how little it winds up being (especially compared to three or four taxi rides). A rickshaw might be your travel photography secret weapon, so it's super-worth giving it a try.

Hire a Model

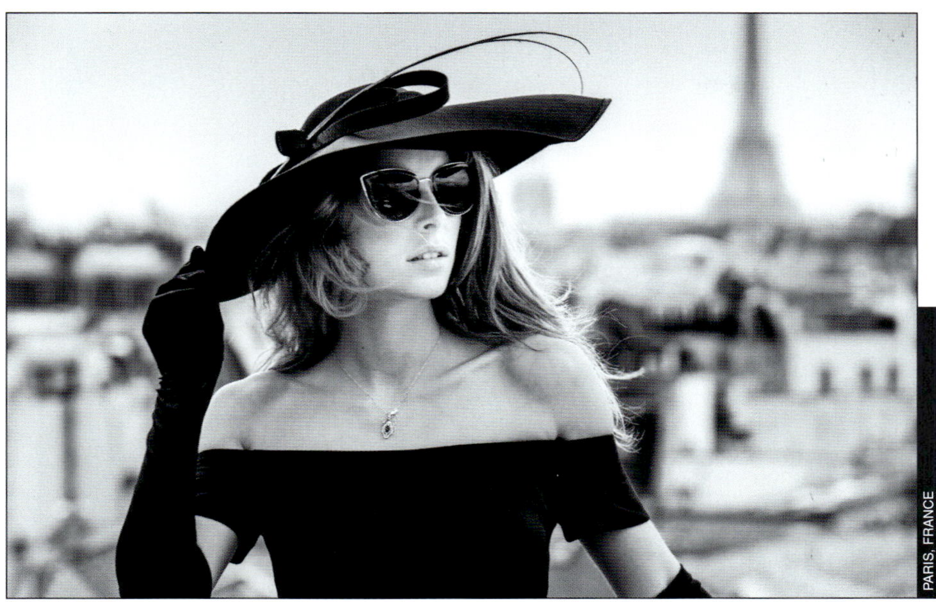

If you're a bit squeamish about photographing strangers on the street (I sure am), then consider hiring a model in the city you're visiting. They'll gladly pose right where you want, so you can get the perfect light and angle, plus they're super-patient, can have multiple outfit changes, and you can set up the travel portrait you'd love to get that might be almost impossible by just talking to someone on the street. To find models, start your search before you arrive in the city, and the first place I look is Facebook. I've hired a number of models for my workshops, or just for my portfolio, and I've had great luck there. Also, reach out on social media to photographers in that city, asking if they know any local models. I've paid anywhere from $50 to $100 for a couple of hours, and it's always worth it. I hired this model in Paris. We shot at our hotel's rooftop bar with the Eiffel Tower in the background, which was awesome. The bar was closed during the day, but I asked the concierge if I could shoot up there and he was happy to oblige (see page 8). The models I've hired spoke enough English that communication was never a problem (I ask if they speak English before I book them), and you wind up meeting some very nice people. They often share their favorite local restaurants and shops, so you get great shots and you get some tips from locals. Also, besides hiring male and female models, another thing I do is rent a cool car. I've rented everything from a classic 1960s Renault in France, to a red Cadillac convertible in Savannah, Georgia. I just rent them for an hour, so it's not too expensive, and having a prop like an awesome car can really make the shot! Where do you find these? In the tour brochure in your hotel's lobby or search online. These are usually tours where you ride around with a driver, seeing the sights. But, I tell them I want to just photograph the car (I offer to give them my best shots), and they usually cut me a great deal for just an hour.

Why You Need to Shoot the Classic Shots

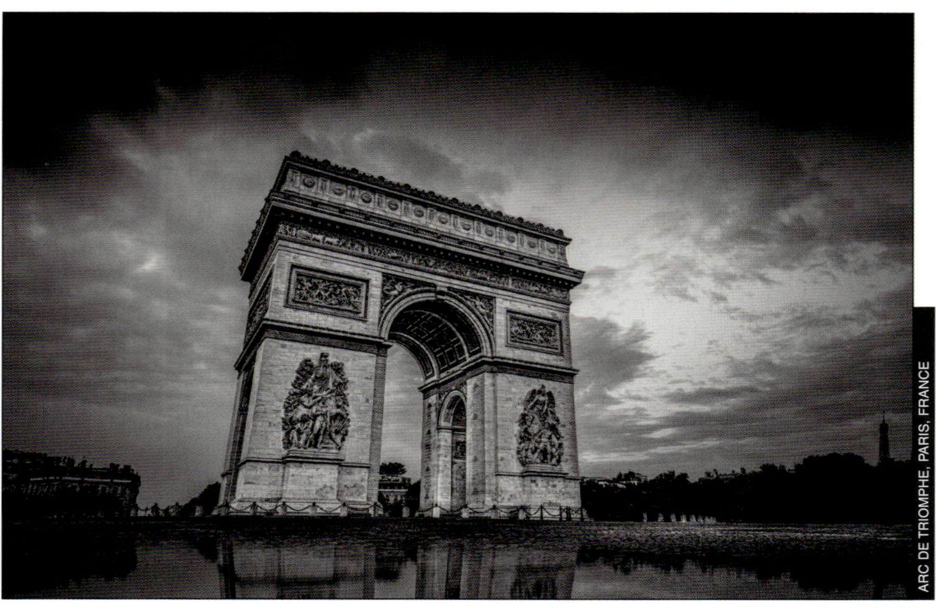

I learned this lesson the hard way many years ago, and I'm passing this on to you to help keep you from a similar fate. What I learned is this: when you mention a particular city or country to people, an image pops into their minds. If you mention Paris, it's the Eiffel Tower. If you mention China, it's the Great Wall. If you mention London, they picture Big Ben. New York, and it's either the Empire State Building or the Statue of Liberty, and so on. So, when you show people your photos from your trip, whether it's in a photo book you made, or a slide show, or just flipping through images on your phone, if you don't show them the image they're expecting to see (like the Eiffel Tower) right up front, they get anxious waiting to see that classic photo. So, they're not really paying attention to your beautiful, artistic photos of Paris because they're waiting and getting anxious to see that Eiffel Tower photo. So…show that classic "shot to death" shot right up front. Play to the crowd and give them the shot they want right away, so they don't get anxious and uptight waiting for it. That way, they can then enjoy your beautiful, artistic shots and appreciate how you saw that city, instead of impatiently waiting and finally asking, "Did you get any shots of the Eiffel Tower?"

Putting Your Camera's GPS to Work

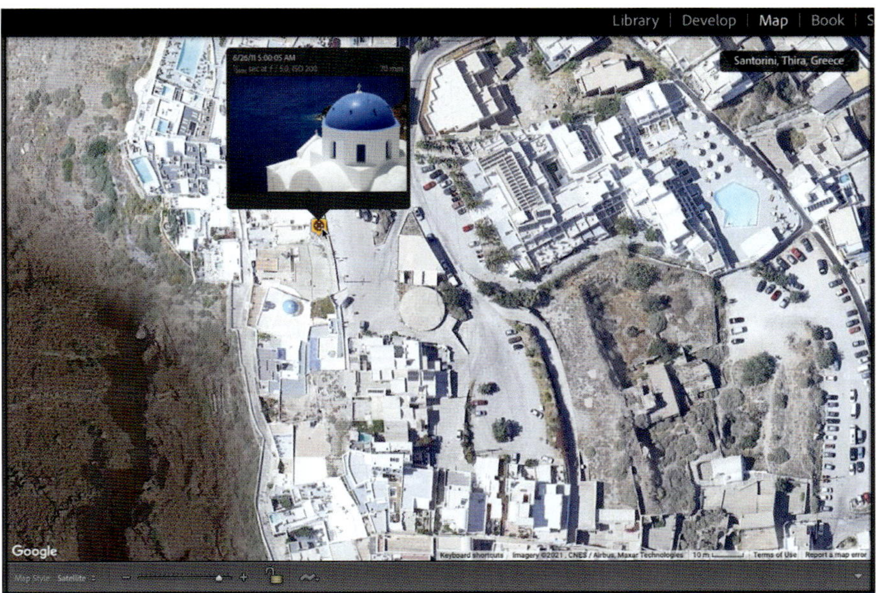

Most cameras these days have built-in GPS (heck, even your smartphone has built-in GPS), and if you use Lightroom Classic, you can really make the most of this. When you have GPS turned on in your camera, it automatically embeds the exact GPS coordinates of where you took a shot right in the shot. That itself is fairly cool, but where it gets really cool is: once you import these images into Lightroom, behind the scenes, Lightroom automatically organizes them by location on a world map. It literally puts a "pin" on every location and to see the images you took at a particular location, all you have to do is go to Lightroom's Map module, click on the map, and there are all those images. Best of all, you can choose a satellite image view of the map (like you see above). It's so awesome to see it doing this organization for you, automatically, without you having to do anything. Now, what if your camera doesn't have built-in GPS? Well, you can still use this Map feature, but you'll have to do the organizing manually (it's not as bad as it sounds). You start by doing a search on the map by city, or attraction, or monument, or even address, and it takes you to that point on the map. Now all you have to do is select the photos you took at that location (down in Lightroom's Filmstrip, along the bottom), drag-and-drop them onto the map, and it adds a pin with those images. Now they're "on the map."

What to Shoot in Bad Weather

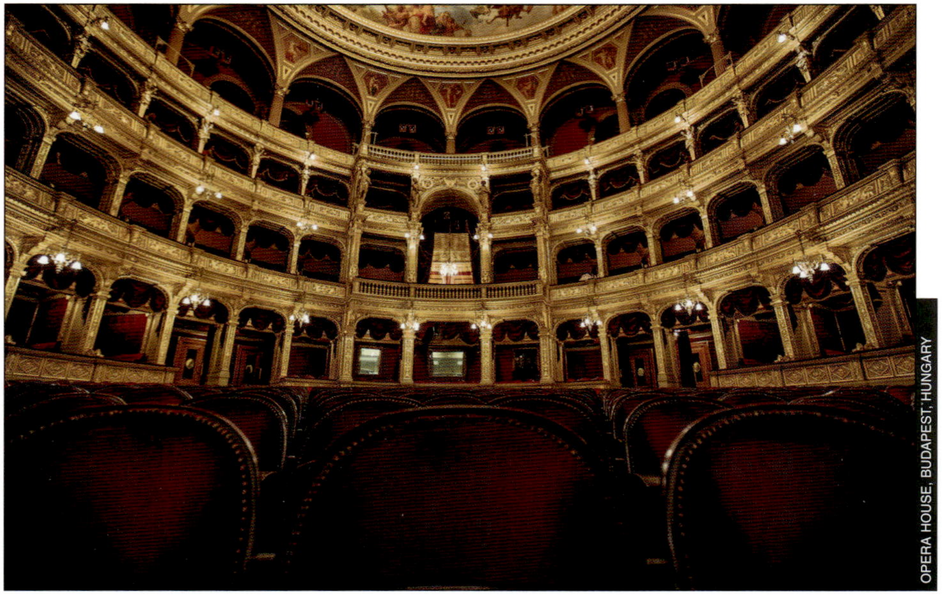

It's hard to visit just about anywhere (well, except maybe the desert) without having at least a day or two of rain. So, I don't plan any indoor shoots at palaces or cathedrals or theaters—I save them for that morning when I wake up and it's pouring rain and gray and awful outside. That's when I hit the museums, Gothic churches, halls of government, and stuff. Don't waste sunny days shooting these indoor locations, and if you get through your stay in a city without having a rainy day (lucky you), then put shooting indoors on your "last day in town" shot list.

Getting a Sharp Shot Under Bad Conditions

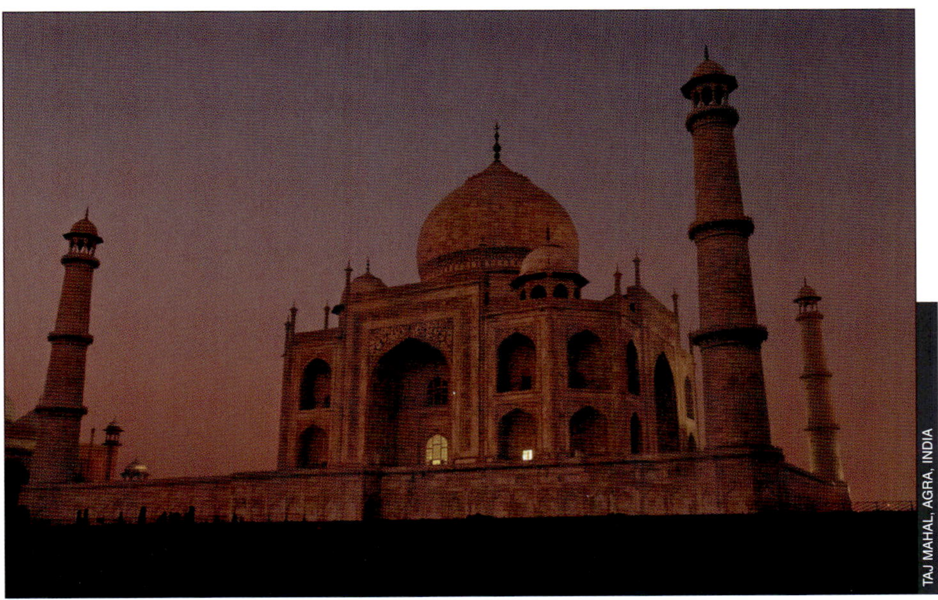

There will be times when you want to take a shot, but the conditions are horrible for getting even a reasonably sharp shot. It's a low-light situation, you don't have a tripod, or worse yet, you're on something moving (a tuk-tuk, a boat or ferry, a double-decker bus, etc.), or you're indoors where you know it's so dark there's no way to get a decently sharp shot. Well, I'm going to turn you on to a trick which has worked for me more often than not, but there's a bad part and a good part: Step one is to try to brace your body up against something. A doorway, a column, a wall—doesn't matter, just something to keep you from moving to give you a better shot at keeping your camera from moving. Step two is to switch your camera to Burst mode, so it keeps taking pictures until you stop pressing the shutter button (or your camera's memory buffer gets full). Step three: use the lowest-numbered f-stop your lens will allow (so, f/2.8, f/3.5, f/4) and maybe raise your ISO to 800 (or even higher if your camera is pretty good at controlling low-light noise). Okay, now you're set up and ready to fire a long burst of shots. We're talking 30, 40, or more in a row in Burst mode. First, the bad part: When you're going through those 30 or 40 shots on your computer, you're going to see out-of-focus, blurry shot after out-of-focus, blurry shot. It's going to be a demoralizing mess, until the good part: inside that group of horribly out-of-focus, blurry shots, for some inexplicable reason, there will be one really sharp shot. I know it sounds crazy, but even a blind squirrel finds a nut every once in a while, and I cannot tell you how many times this has paid off for me. If you just need one nice, sharp shot in the worst possible conditions, this will probably pay off. Notice I said, "probably"—it doesn't work every time, but once it does, it pays off big. Remember: no risk it, no biscuit. Insert your own motivational phrase here, but in the meantime, give this one a try—I'll bet you come out with a winner.

Consider Emergency Evacuation Insurance

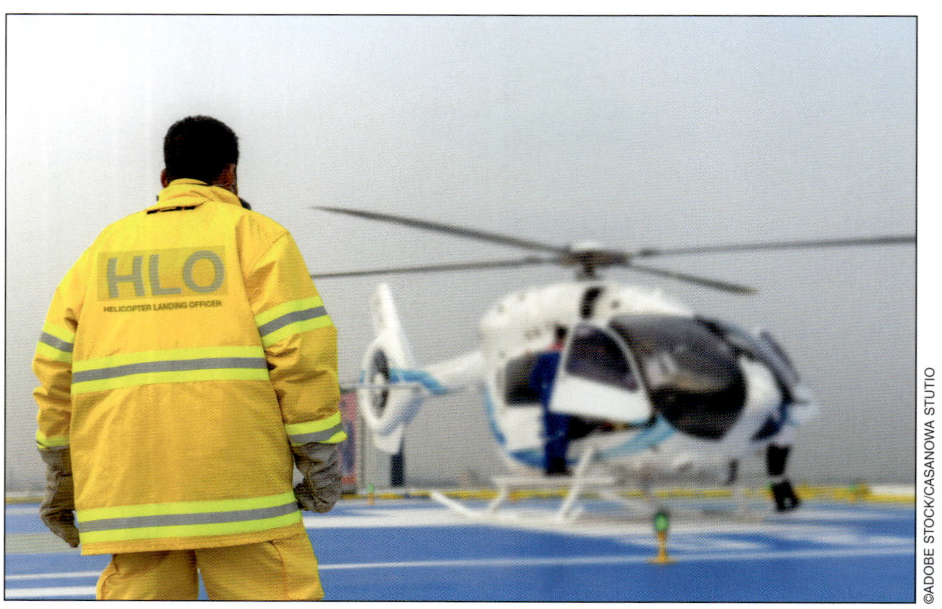

©ADOBE STOCK/CASANOWA STUTIO

I took out this temporary insurance on my last trip, and thankfully, I didn't need it, but a buddy of mine did—he slipped while crossing a creek and got a simple cut on his leg. But, something in that water was funky and within a day, he got an infection so bad he was totally incapacitated and had to be airlifted to a hospital. Luckily, he had taken out one of these short-term medical rescue policies (he always takes them), and it paid for his extraction, which would have been many thousands of dollars, not to mention the fact that you'd have to find a way to arrange it wherever you are. Insurance like this sounds expensive, but I just got an online quote, and for a seven-day trip it's around $120, which would save you many, many times that if you ever need it. Make sure you get the kind that includes a medical air ambulance because you just never know (it's why they call them "accidents," and they can happen when you least expect it, in places where a regular ambulance may not be able to go). Essentially, what you're paying for is peace of mind—that "just in case" type of scenario—but in the past year or so, that type of thing has now happened to two of my friends. So, if I take a trip, I'm taking that insurance along with me.

Safety Tip: Get Gear Insurance

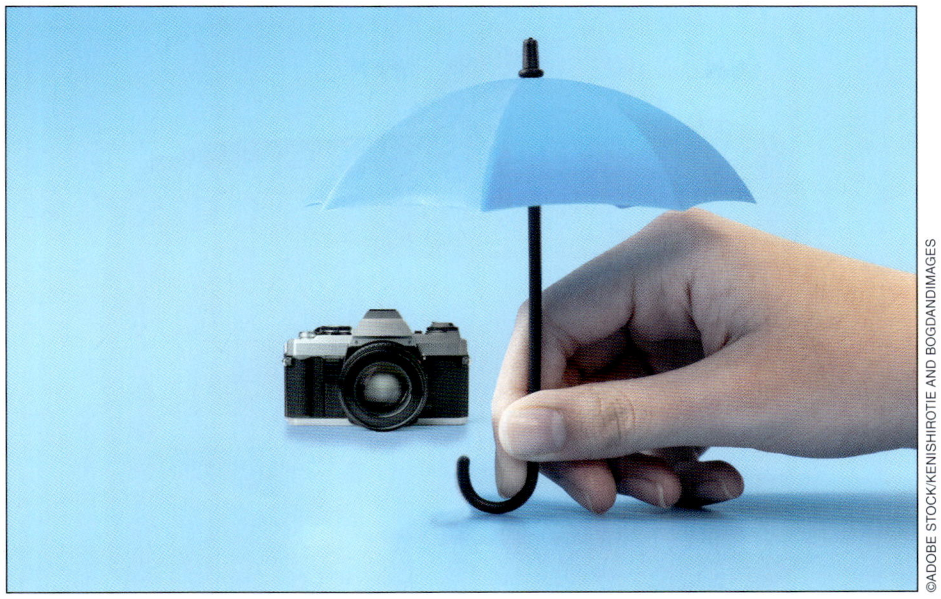

It's quite possible that your homeowner's insurance policy includes a provision for you losing your camera while on vacation or for having it stolen, but it's just as possible that it does not (or maybe you don't have a homeowner's policy at all—maybe you're a renter), or it covers theft, but doesn't cover accidental loss, or if you drop a lens and it cracks. So, first, it's worth checking with your insurance company before your trip to see if you're covered, and what exactly is covered if your gear gets lost or stolen. If you're not covered, I would definitely recommend getting an insurance policy that's designed for camera gear. There are a number of companies out there that specialize in just that, and the prices are surprisingly reasonable. This is worth checking into.

This Might Save You If You Lose Your Camera

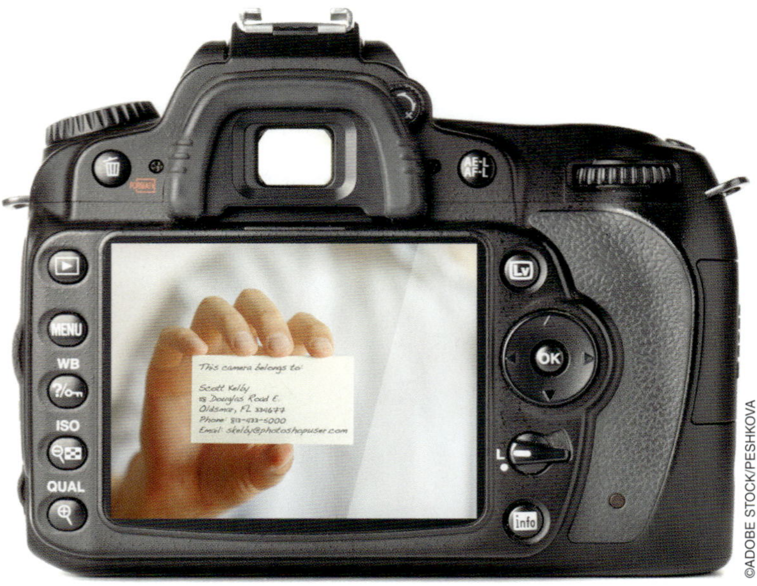

©ADOBE STOCK/PESHKOVA

If you're traveling and you lose your camera (you leave it in a taxi, on a tour bus, in a restaurant—I've heard so many stories of travelers walking off and leaving their camera), what are your chances of getting it back? Even if the person who finds it has the best intentions, if they have no idea who owns the camera, there's no way for them to get it back to you. It's gone forever. For this very reason, some folks put a sticker with their contact info on the bottom of their camera, and that increases their chances of getting it returned big time. You could also use a temporary sticker with the info of the hotel you're staying at in that city, so if someone finds your camera, you could potentially get it back the same day. Another simple method is to write your contact info on a business card, and take a shot of that card, so on the camera is a shot of your name and contact info. They say when people find a lost camera, the first thing they do (well, if they're a nice person) is to search through its shots to see if they can determine who the owner is. Well, if there's a shot with your name and contact info on it, your chances go way, way up (if I found your camera, and saw your address in the camera roll, I would absolutely return it to you, and I bet you would, too). This is such a quick and easy thing to do, and what could it hurt? So, grab a business card or write your info, and at the beginning of each fresh memory card, take a shot of it, and off you go. Hey, it might save your camera one day.

Shoot the Sign While You're Still There

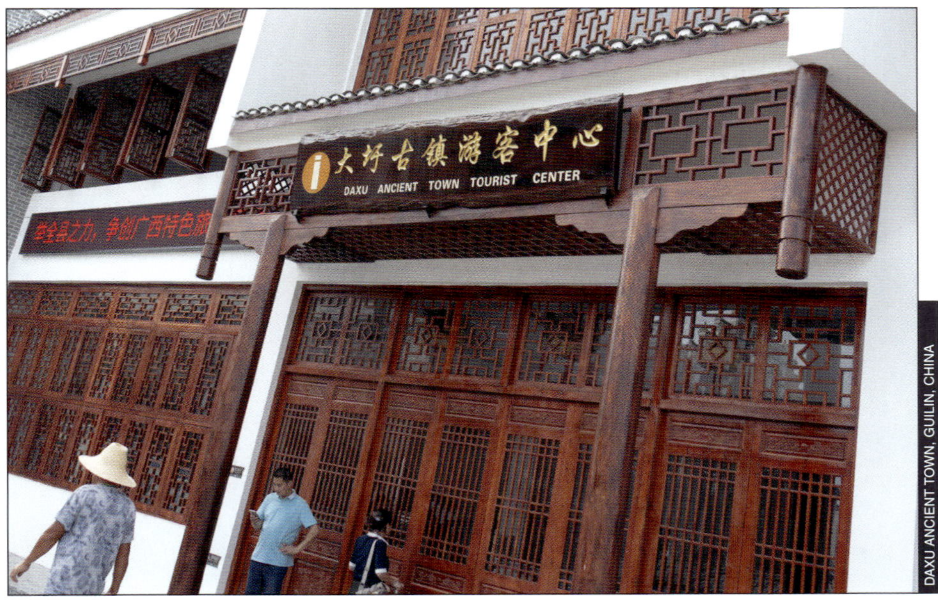

DAXU ANCIENT TOWN, GUILIN, CHINA

This is another tip I learned years ago (the hard way) when I got home from a trip and had a shot of a temple I visited, but had no idea what the name of the temple was (it was like my 10th temple visit that day). People were asking me about it, and I was like, "I dunno. It was somewhere in Japan." Well, that narrows things down now, doesn't it? I spent so long searching online, trying to find it again, but no luck. If I had just snapped a quick shot of the name of the temple as I was walking in or out, I could have sidestepped all the research (and the embarrassment of not knowing where I shot it). It's such an easy thing to do. That's why, when I was in a small village in China, I stopped to take this snapshot of the name of the city posted above a doorway. It was the only way I knew I had been shooting in "Daxu Ancient Town," and when I typed that into Google, there was all kinds of information on the city, it's history, etc. I was also able to include its name when I was sharing my story online. Take a shot of that sign as you arrive, or as you're leaving. It's just a snapshot, a reference photo that takes two seconds, but it can save you a ton of time later when it's time to tell the story of your trip.

Invest in Travel, Not in More Gear

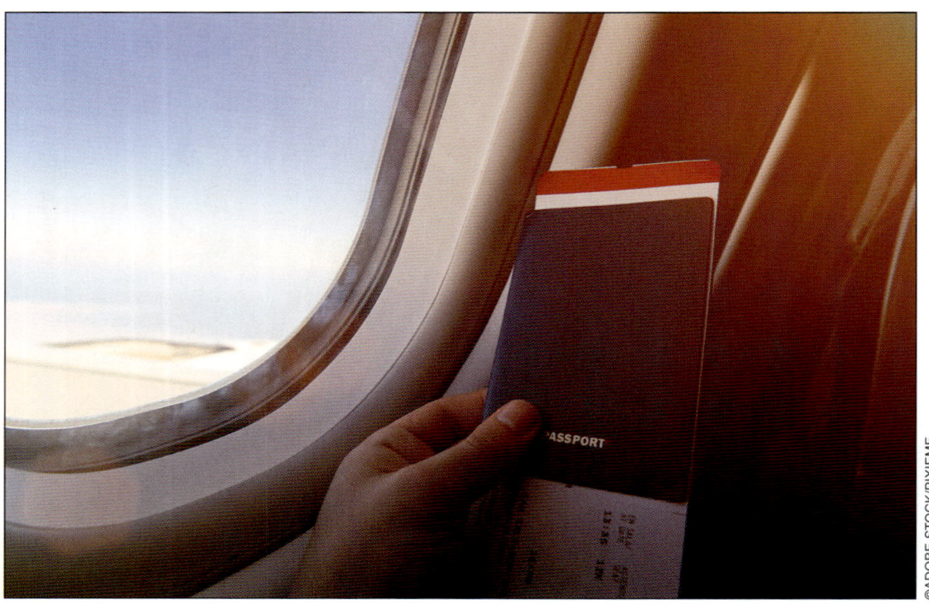

©ADOBE STOCK/PIXIEME

If you're serious about making great travel photos (and if you bought this book, I imagine that you are), the gear you already own will make great images. Heck, your cell phone camera can make great images, right? Instead of buying more gear thinking it will bring you better images, invest in something that will actually bring you better images—invest in a trip. Invest in a flight to somewhere amazing, somewhere you've always wanted to photograph, somewhere that you'll come back from with the type of images you've always dreamed of. If you want to invest in your photography, don't buy more expensive gear, buy an inexpensive ticket to someplace awesome. Great travel photos aren't waiting in a box at the camera store. They're out there waiting for you to arrive. So, instead of investing in more gear, invest in yourself. Invest in making great travel images by traveling. It's like the old saying goes, "Travel is the only thing you buy that makes you richer." Go get richer!

Where to Shoot in Paris, Venice, London, or…

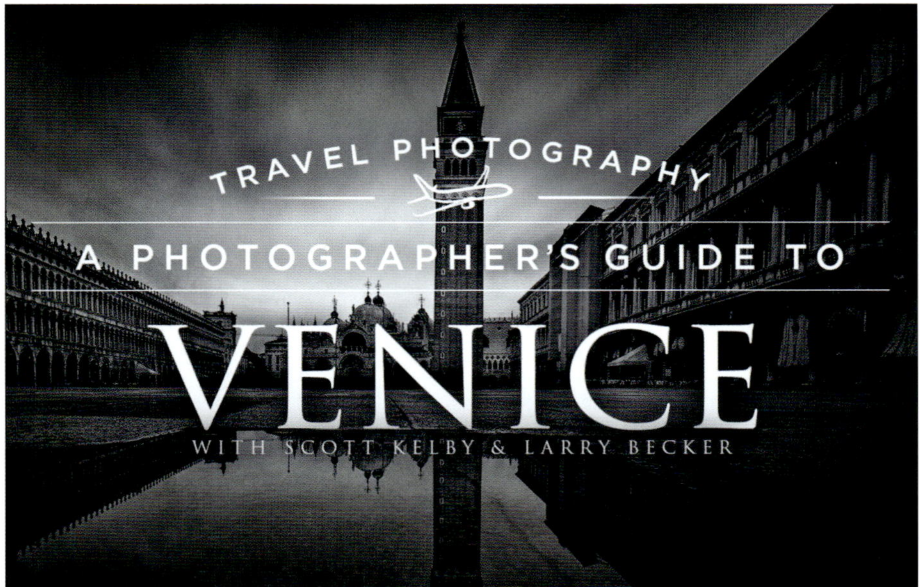

If you're looking for ideas on where to shoot in a particular city, like Rome, or Chicago, or New York City, or London, I've done a series of online courses, co-hosted by my good friend and photographer Larry Becker, where I share my favorite places to shoot in cities around the world. I show the shots, behind-the-scenes images, ticket prices for entrance (if necessary), along with as many insider tips as I can, so you come home with some great images. The classes are titled, "Travel Photography: A Photographer's Guide to [the name of the city]," like you see above. If you're a KelbyOne subscriber, of course, you can watch them all as part of your subscription. If you're not, you can buy any one of them and download it to keep if you'd like, or just get a one-month membership. Anyway, I've gotten so many wonderful letters and images from people around the world who've watched these courses, and they've told me how helpful they are (I even give you a downloadable PDF with addresses and GPS coordinates). Quick story: I'm revisiting one of the locations in my where to shoot in Paris video with some of my students in a workshop, and there are two photographers already set up shooting there. One of my students starts chatting with one of the photographers who told him, "I saw this location in Scott Kelby's class on Paris," and the other photographer shouts over to them, "That's how I got here, too," and of course, he brought them over to meet me. That was such a thrill for me as an educator to see people taking what they've learned from me and applying it in such a cool way. What a kick! Anyway, if you decide to check them out, I hope you find those courses helpful (and thanks for letting me share them with you here in the book).

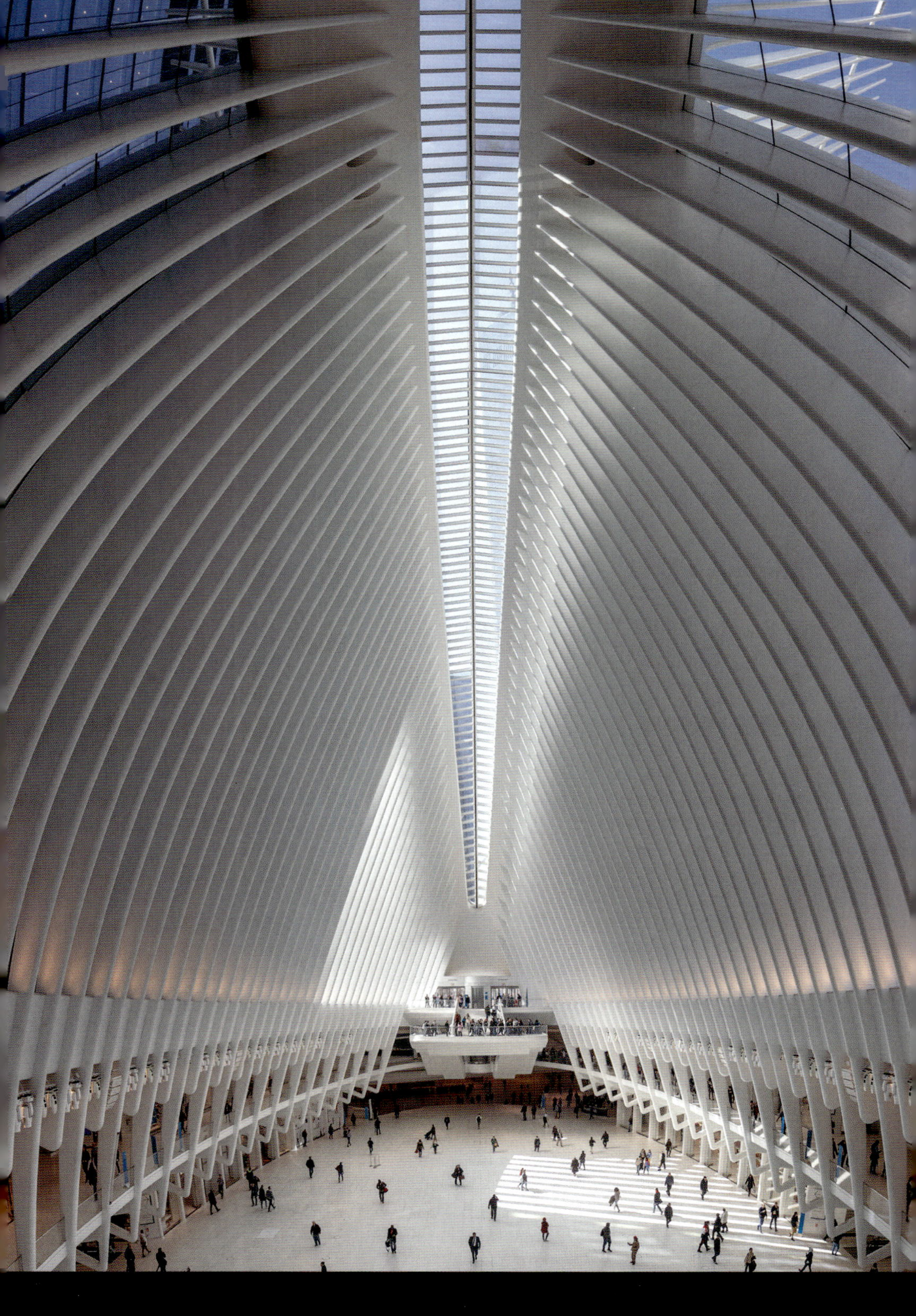

SHUTTER SPEED: 1/125 sec | F-STOP: F/8 | ISO: 160 | FOCAL LENGTH: 14mm
LOCATION: Oculus Transportation Hub, World Trade Center, New York, New York

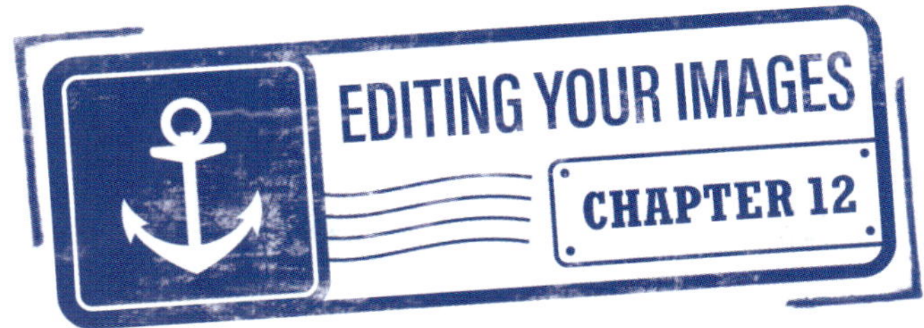

Editing Your Images

How to Post-Process Your Travel Images Using Lightroom and/or Photoshop

You know when you see spectacular travel images on Instagram? They don't look like that straight out of the camera. They've had major post-processing. It would be great if all our shots came out post-processed, but sadly, that extra pizazz happens after the fact. Remember the incredible landscape photographer Ansel Adams? He wasn't only a master photographer, he was a magician in the darkroom, and he made his creative vision come alive with the edits he made. We're lucky that today we have the tools to create our own masterpieces without being exposed to harsh darkroom chemicals. Instead, we get our daily intake of harmful chemicals from fast food, so you don't have to worry about missing out. Anyway, what I love about post-processing is that it adds another creative layer to your photography. Of course, taking the images can be a lot of fun (unless it's raining, or a giant elk charges you, or you open your camera bag and it's full of man-eating piranhas), but being able to change the tone, the feel, the arrangement, the crop, the light, and the color is also a lot fun. There's another aspect of post-processing (well, of Photoshop in particular) that makes it even more fun, and that is the ability to cheat. Normally, in every other aspect of life, cheating is frowned upon, but if you learn how to cheat in Photoshop, you'll get respect from photographers who would love to be good at Photoshop, and be able to cheat and do wild things to make their images look more amazing. At the same time, there will be a group of photographers who will discount your work because it's not all "out of camera," and it somehow crosses over to real-life cheating, even though the most famous, most celebrated, and most brilliant photographers on the planet all use Photoshop. So, who are these angry folks who decry the use of Photoshop on our images? People who aren't any good at Photoshop. I'll put it this way: I've never met anyone really good at Photoshop that thought using it was bad.

The "Standard Stuff"

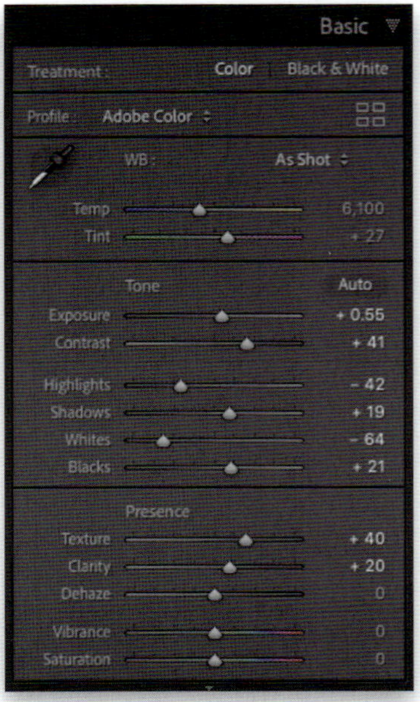

There's a standard set of things I do in Lightroom (or Photoshop's Camera Raw—they're the same thing) to all my travel images. I usually don't have to jump through a bunch of hoops and do crazy post-processing tricks for travel shots—it's a pretty standard set of edits, which start with getting your color right and the exposure where you want it. Next, you're dealing with any problems (like an image where your subject is backlit, or maybe clouds in the sky are too bright and blown out). Then, we add a lot of contrast. It's kind of my "thing," and there are a number of ways to add contrast. If you can see the sky in an image, you want it to look great, so there are a few things you can do to make that happen. We can enhance the detail in an image (which I always do) using either the Texture slider, the Clarity slider, or both. Then, as a finishing move, we very subtly darken the edges of the image all the way around to draw the viewer's attention toward the subject (this is optional, but I nearly always do it to my images). Lastly, we sharpen every single image. Always. 100% of the time. No image slips by without getting sharpened. That's the "standard stuff," so in the next chapter (Photo Recipes), when it comes to the part where I talk about the post-processing I applied to the image, if you read, "I applied the standard stuff" (or something like that), it's the stuff I just mentioned (which you'll learn more about in the rest of this chapter), but at least now you know what the "standard stuff" is.

Getting a Better Starting Place

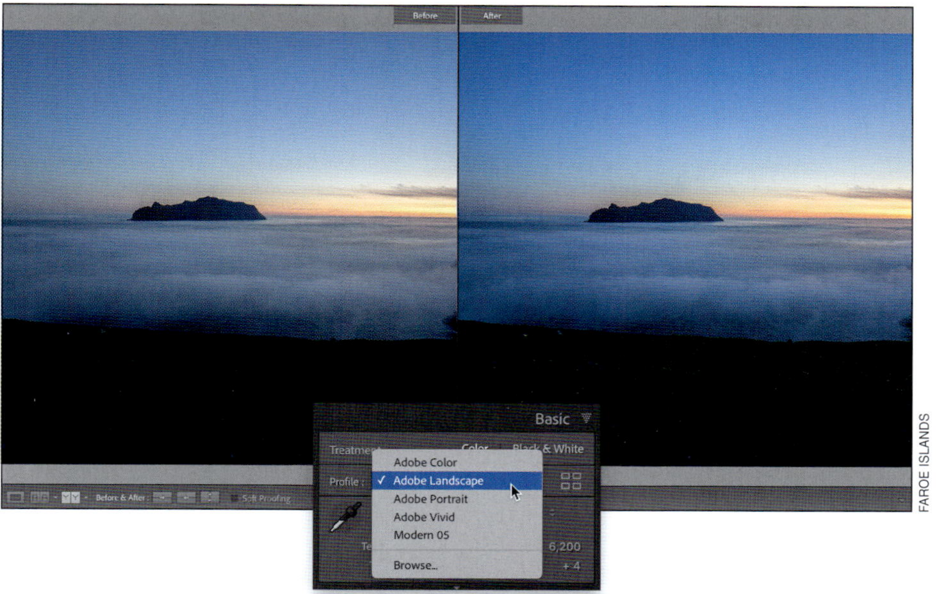

If you shoot in RAW, doing this one simple thing can give you a better, more vibrant, more contrasty starting point for your edits (I do this before I do anything else). I'll cut straight to what I do, and then I'll explain why it works (it's a tad nerdy, so you can skip that part, if you want). I go to the Profile pop-up menu at the top of the Basic panel, and for travel images, I choose Adobe Landscape. That's it. Done. Your image either looks a little better or a lot better (just depends on the image), but it's almost always worth doing. Okay, now for the nerdy stuff: In short, when you shoot in RAW, you're telling your camera to turn off all the stuff it would normally do to a JPEG image, like adding sharpening and contrast, boosting the color vibrance, adding noise reduction, and all that stuff. You're asking for the flat-looking, untouched RAW photo. Well, Lightroom has to interpret that RAW image and the math it uses is called "Adobe Color," which is a slightly better version of the super-flat RAW photo your camera captured (in fact, it applies +40 of sharpening to RAW photos), but it also has its own look, subtle though it may be. I feel it's way too subtle, which is why I choose Adobe Landscape for all my travel photos—it usually just looks better. It's not a "knock your socks off" type of better for most images, but still, if I can get a little head start on my editing by just choosing Adobe Landscape, I'm going to do it (and I always do). You can also try Adobe Vivid, which can also look good, depending on the image (but about 95% of the time I wind up going with Adobe Landscape). *Note:* These RAW profiles were designed to mimic the picture styles you could have chosen in-camera if you were shooting in JPEG, which is why seeing Landscape and Vivid and Portrait might seem familiar from those settings in your camera. Anyway, give it a shot and see what you think (I think you'll dig it).

Doing an "Auto" Correction

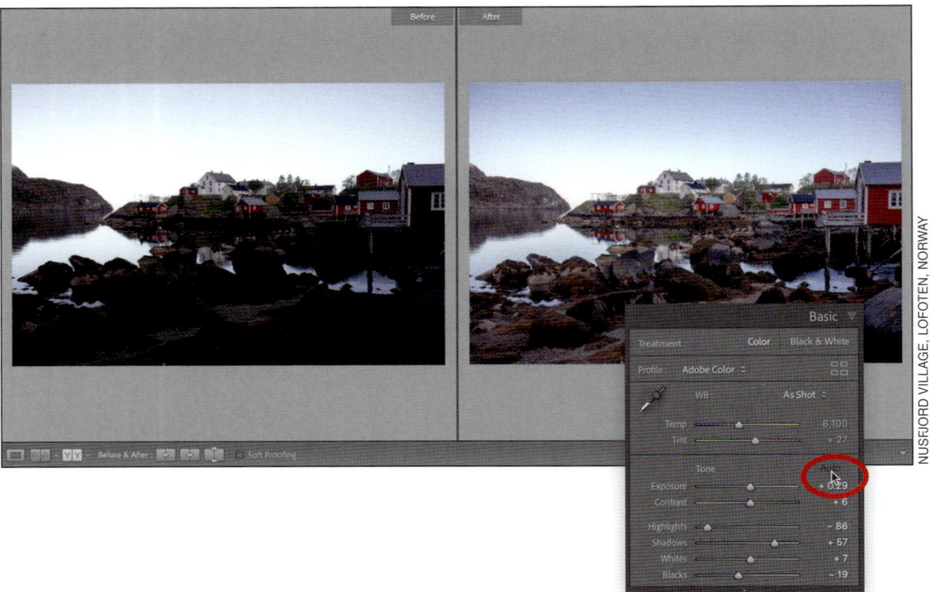

For many years, I warned photographers to stay away from Lightroom's Auto button (circled in red above) in the Basic panel because it did such a crummy job (and I didn't want to use the word "crummy"). We used to joke that it was the "Overexpose my image" button because clicking it pretty much ensured your image was way too bright and awful. However, over the past few years, Adobe has majorly improved the Auto correction feature (adding AI, machine learning, killer robots, etc.) to where it's now actually pretty decent—decent enough so that if you're not sure where to start on editing an image, you could give it a click and see how it works. Sometimes it actually does a pretty darn decent job, and other times it certainly doesn't (and you'll know instantly), but the good news is that if you don't like the results, you can just press Command-Z (PC: Ctrl-Z) to Undo the Auto correction, and then you can edit your image like usual. This is worth trying, and I'll bet you'll be surprised sometimes at what a good job it does. Even if it doesn't get you all the way there, at least it can give you a decent starting point.

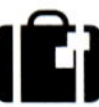
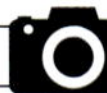

Getting Your Color Right

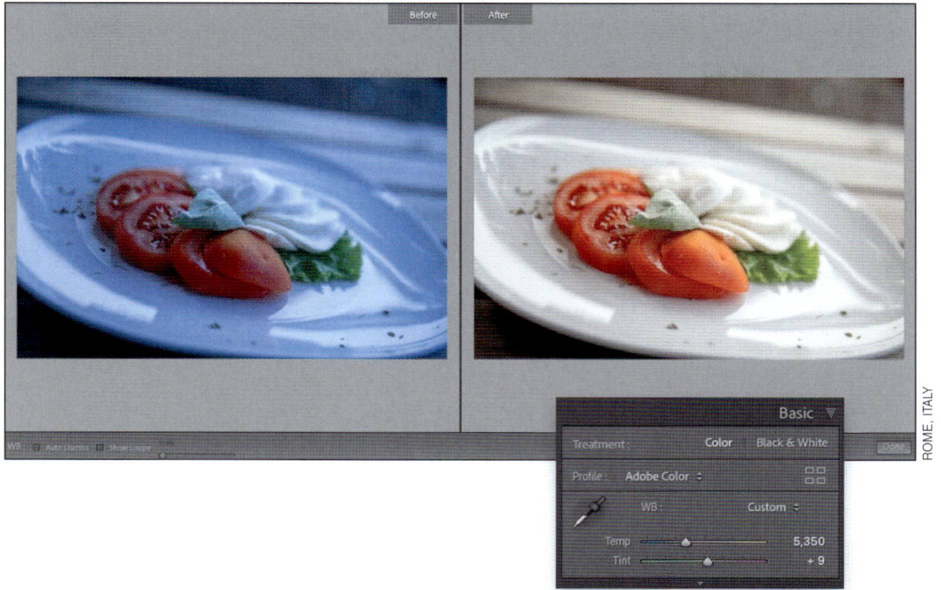

If you've watched any of my videos, or have seen me present live, you've probably heard me talk about why getting your color looking right on the money is so important. I explain it this way: "If your color's not right…it's wrong," and we get our color looking right by adjusting the image's white balance. If you didn't choose the proper white balance setting in-camera, it's easy enough to fix in Lightroom or Photoshop's Camera Raw. First, if you shoot in RAW, at the top of the Basic panel, you'll see a WB (White Balance) pop-up menu of presets (the same ones you could've chosen in-camera, but here, you can choose them after the fact). Click on this pop-up menu, and you'll see the standard white balance settings: Daylight, Shade, Tungsten, and so on. Try each one to see which one looks best for your image. Again, these choices only appear if you shot in RAW. If you shot in JPEG or TIFF, you'll only see As Shot and Auto. Another method for getting your white balance looking good is to use the Temp (Temperature) and Tint sliders. If you look behind the sliders, you can see the color it would bring by moving the slider left or right (for example, if your image looks too blue, drag the Temp slider to the right, toward yellow, which makes it warmer and more yellow. If your image looks too yellow, drag the Temp slider the opposite way, to the left toward blue). A third method for getting your white balance looking good (and my favorite of the three) is to use the White Balance Selector tool (the eyedropper) at the top left of the Basic panel. Click it on something in your image that's supposed to be light gray and it sets the white balance based on that color (light gray is the ideal color for setting white balance). If you can't find a light gray, try something neutral, like beige or tan. The nice thing is, if you click somewhere and it doesn't look right, just click it somewhere else until you find that perfect sweet spot.

Nailing Your Exposure

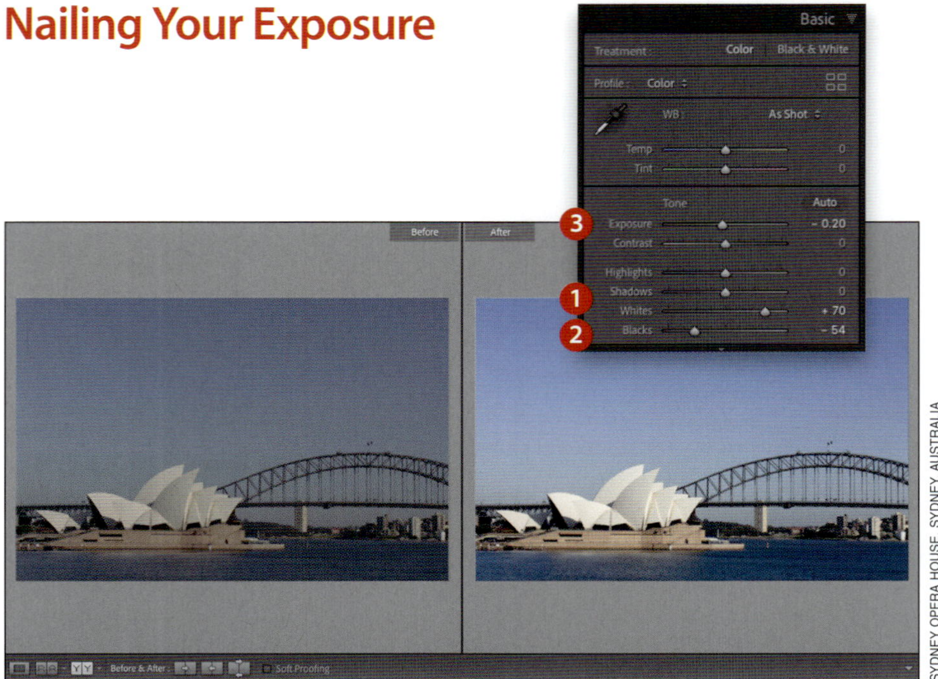

This is a very simple three-step process in Lightroom (or Photoshop's Camera Raw) to get the overall exposure (brightness) of your photo where you want it. You start by setting what is the darkest part of your photo and what will be the brightest part. This is called "setting your white and black points," and doing this (actually, we're going to let Lightroom do it for us) expands your tonal range, and it sets you up to move just one simple slider to get your exposure right on the money. The way to have Lightroom (or Camera Raw) set your white and black points for you is to press-and-hold the Shift key, then double-click directly on the little "nub" on the Whites slider (the thing you click-and-drag to move the slider), and then do the same Shift-double-click on the Blacks slider. That's it. It automatically sets your white point and black point for you, expanding the tonal range. A nice thing to note: the worse your photo looks, the better this technique works. Also worth noting: if you Shift-double-click these two sliders and it moves very little, or one doesn't move at all, it means your tonal range is already good so there wasn't much for Lightroom to do. Once you've set the white and black points, take a look at your image and see if you think it's too bright or too dark overall. Let's say you think it's a little too dark (underexposed). All you have to do is drag the Exposure slider a little bit to the right. That's it. Once you set the Whites and Blacks, the amount you have to drag the Exposure slider will probably be very small. So, that's the process: you auto-set the white and black points, then you evaluate whether the image is too dark or too light, and move the Exposure slider to the right to make the overall image brighter, or to the left to make it darker. Boom. Done.

Dealing with Backlit Photos

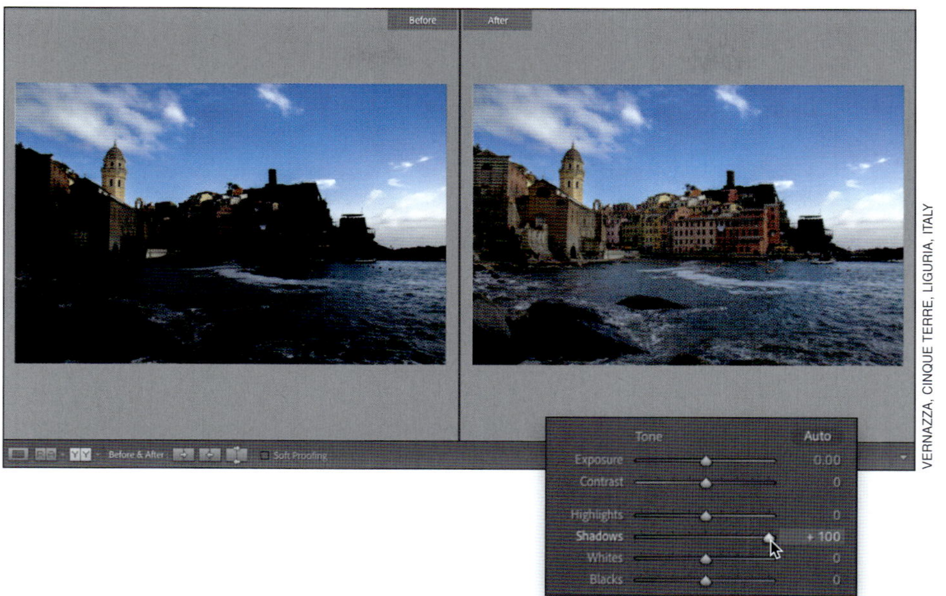

VERNAZZA, CINQUE TERRE, LIGURIA, ITALY

On page 215, I talk about the difference between the range of tones the human eye can capture versus what your camera's sensor can capture. Well, this is another casualty of that thin range of what our camera's sensor can take in. We're standing there in a city, and we're looking at a row of backlit buildings, and we don't even really notice that they're backlit because our eyes instantly balance the light for us. But then we take the picture and see the buildings (or our subject—could be a person, right?) wind up pretty much looking like a silhouette. There's an easy fix for this (thankfully): just drag the Shadows slider to the right to open up the shadow areas that our subject is in. The farther you drag the Shadows slider to the right, the more it opens up those shadow areas, but our goal is to get the scene looking more like it did when we took the shot. So, look for that sweet spot where there's a nice balance between the subject being brightly lit and being in the shadows, and you're done. Problem solved.

Fixing Clipped Highlight Problems

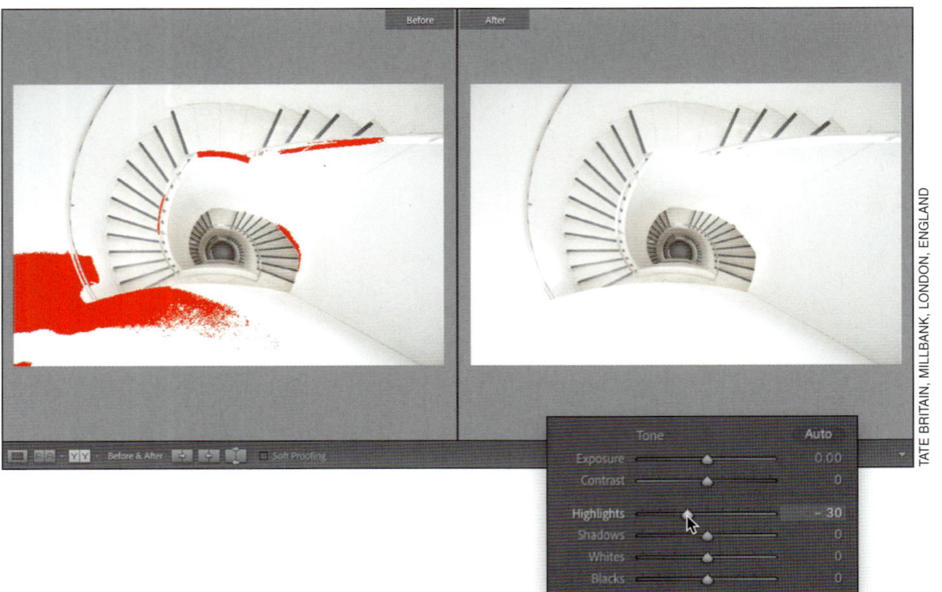

TATE BRITAIN, MILLBANK, LONDON, ENGLAND

Every digital camera these days (well, since as long as I can remember) has a built-in warning feature to let you know if something in your scene has gotten so bright that it's clipped the highlights (we call it a clipping warning, but on your camera it probably uses the term "Highlight"). If something gets that bright, you won't have any detail there—no pixels, no nuthin'—and if you printed the image, in those areas there wouldn't be any ink at all. That's why cameras have those built-in warning features, but we miss them sometimes (okay, fairly often). If that happens to you, you can usually fix the issue in Lightroom (or Photoshop's Camera Raw) by simply dragging the Highlights slider to the left to recover those lost highlights. First, to see if you have a clipped highlight issue, go up to the Histogram (that graph at the top of the right-side panels) and click on the triangle in its top-right corner. Any parts of your image that are clipping in the highlights will appear as solid red on your screen (as seen above left). If those areas should have detail (if you see the sun in your image, it's going to clip, but you can ignore that since we don't think the surface of the sun has a bunch of detail), then drag the Highlights slider to the left until those red areas disappear. It's as easy as that.

Fixing Sunny, Washed-Out Photos

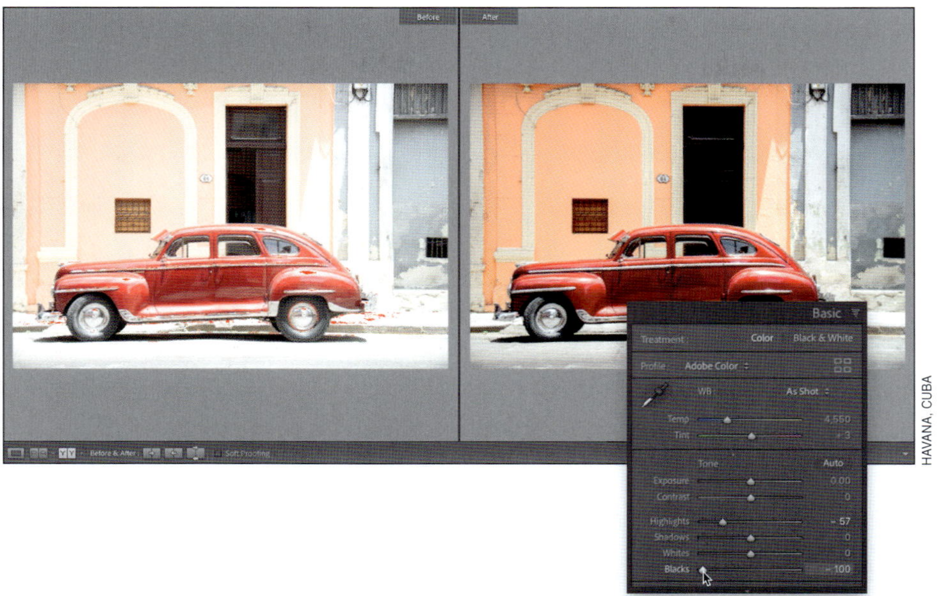

One of the worst things about shooting outside on a sunny day is that beautiful, vibrant colors get totally washed out. Direct midday sun is a color killer, but you can usually counteract that with two easy moves: First, pull the highlights back quite a bit (drag the Highlights slider to the left). That only lowers the highlights in the brightest areas of the photo; it doesn't give you back that nice color saturation that you lost in the daylight. To get that back—and bring back a lot of the rich, vibrant color—drag Lightroom's Blacks slider way over to the left, until the color looks good overall (as seen above right, where the pink wall behind the car—and the car itself, of course—looks more colorful and saturated). When you crank the Blacks way over, it makes all the black areas darker, so if it causes an issue with the rest of your image, you can apply the Blacks "on a brush," using the Brush tool, instead. Once you've chosen the Brush tool (K), drag the Blacks slider way over to the left and just paint over vibrant walls, or in this case, the car too, and watch those washed-out areas disappear while the rich, vibrant color comes roaring back.

Five Ways to Add Contrast to Your Images

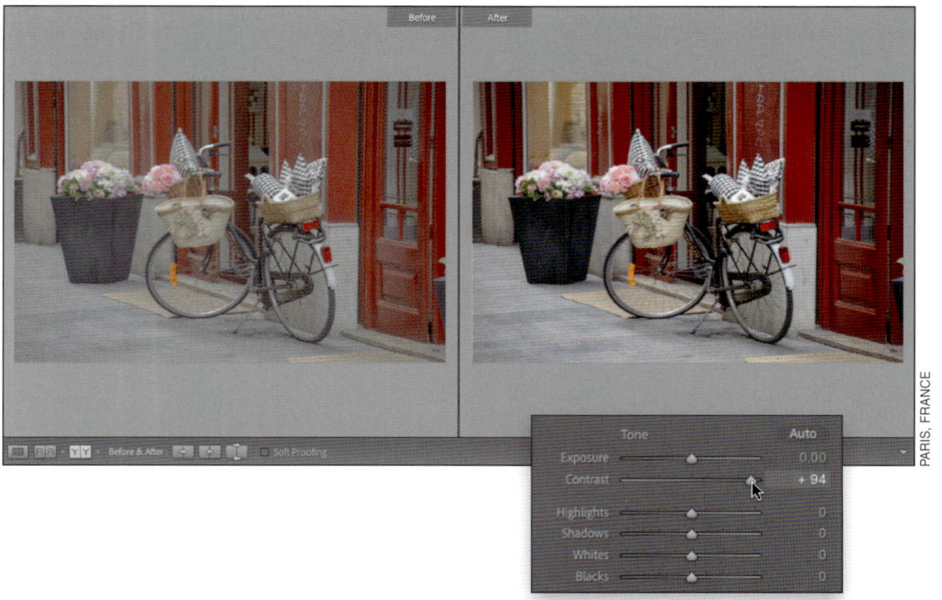

I'm a big fan of contrast—it makes the brightest parts of your image brighter and the darkest parts darker, it makes your colors more saturated and vivid, and it's just a lot of awesomeness for one adjustment. There are five different ways to apply contrast, but the one I use most is (1) the Contrast slider in the Basic panel. The farther you drag it to the right, the more contrast it adds (and I'm not shy about dragging it way over to the right). Let's say you've dragged it all the way over and you don't think that's enough contrast (hey, it happens), you can add more contrast on top of what you've already added by (2) going to the Tone Curve panel, and from the pop-up menu at the bottom, where it says "Linear," choose either Medium Contrast or Strong Contrast. Remember, this doesn't replace the contrast you added in the Basic panel; it adds contrast on top by adding an S-curve to the graph. The steeper the curve, the more contrast it adds, so you can click on the points on that S-curve and drag them to create even more contrast. Another way to add contrast (3) is to increase the Dehaze slider amount by dragging it to the right. This form of contrast does an amazing job of cutting through haze (it's well-named), but it also works well as a form of contrast with a different look. Some folks love the Dehaze look, so give it a try and see what you think. (*Note:* If you drag it too far to the right, it starts adding a blue tint to your image, so don't drag it too far.) (4) The Clarity slider adds midtone contrast (and enhances detail), and you'll notice when adding a lot of clarity, your image starts to get a gritty feel, so be careful not to overdo it. Lastly, if you need even more contrast, you can (5) get the Brush tool (K), drag its Contrast slider over to the right, and paint over any individual areas (or even the whole image) to add yet another layer of contrast. There ya have it: five ways to have a contrast lovefest!

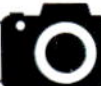

Enhancing Detail

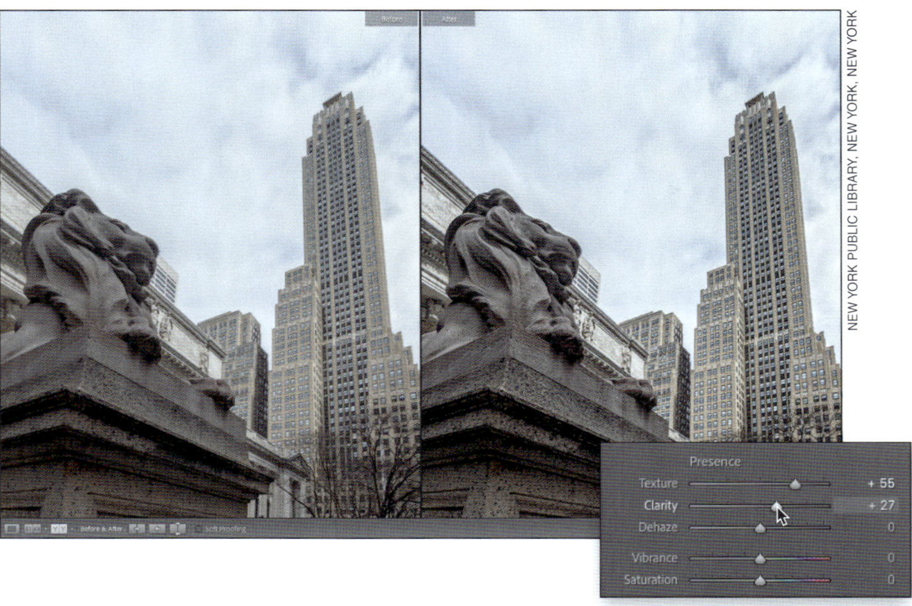

NEW YORK PUBLIC LIBRARY, NEW YORK, NEW YORK

There are two main sliders I use to enhance the detail in my image (well, three if you count the Sharpening Amount slider, but we cover that on page 227). The first is the Texture slider, which does just what its name implies—it brings out the texture in the image. It really does an amazing job, and I use this on pretty much every photo, unless I want the image to have a softer nature (for example, in a photo of a baby or a portrait of a woman, I don't want their skin to look all "texturey," so I generally skip it). You can usually apply quite a bit of texture and it still looks good. The other slider, Clarity, actually enhances midtone contrast (that's the nerdy explanation, in case you care), but it has the effect of bringing out detail, with the added bonus that it makes water, metal, and glass look shiny—it's just great for bringing out that shine. However, it has its downsides: One is that it changes the tone of your image (the Texture slider doesn't do that). It often makes the image look darker and more gritty, which is why you have to be careful to not apply too much of it. Also, clarity can look great on men, accentuating the character and cragginess of their skin, but I rarely use the Clarity slider on photos of women and children because it tends to make their skin look bruised. However, I often wind up using these two sliders together, so I add a lot of texture, but then only half as much (or less) of clarity (so, if I set my Texture slider at 40, I would use 20 or less for my Clarity amount). These are great tools for bringing out detail, but like any great tool, you can overdo it and then things start to look funky, so just keep an eye on your amounts. They're like seasoning in food—you can definitely overdo it (but interestingly enough, you cannot overdo the application of grated cheese to pasta. It's a magical topping).

Sky Replacement

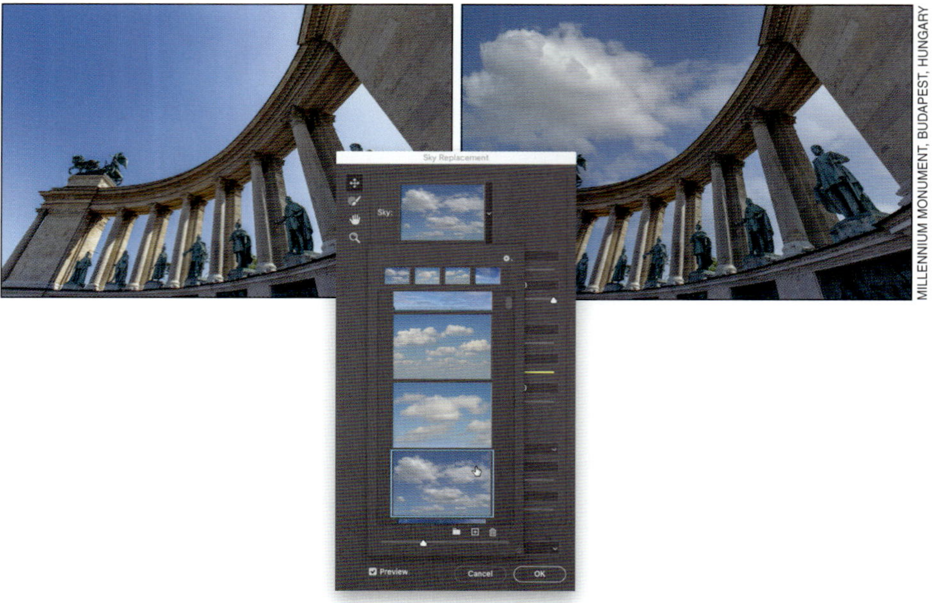

I used to really struggle with the idea of putting a better sky into my image than was actually there (so, using a sky from a different photo), until I learned that nearly all of my colleagues, including the biggest and best-known names in the photographic industry, routinely replace the sky if it's less than awesome. Apparently, I was the last one not doing it, and recently Photoshop added a Sky Replacement feature that makes the process absolutely simple, so I expect we'll see even more photographers replacing skies than ever. *Note:* If you don't use Photoshop, there is a plug-in for Lightroom you can get called "Luminar" (from Skylum software) that does a wonderful job with sky replacements. In Photoshop, here's how it works: You open the image, go under the Edit menu and choose Sky Replacement, and a floating window appears that automatically detects the sky in your image and replaces it with one of Photoshop's built-in collection of skies. There's a sky picker at the top, and if you click on it, a pop-up menu of different skies appears. Those are really just sample photos for you to try to see if a sky replacement would look good on your particular image. If it does look good, you should upload your own skies and use one of yours instead (or someone will recognize those sample skies and call you out on it in public, and…well, do you really need that kind of humiliation in your life?). To add your own clouds, click the + (plus sign) icon at the bottom of that sky picker. What's really clever about this sky replacement is how it blends the colors of the sky you choose over the rest of the image, so the colors overall look correct. Very slick, and all of this is just a click away.

Better Skies Using the Linear Gradient

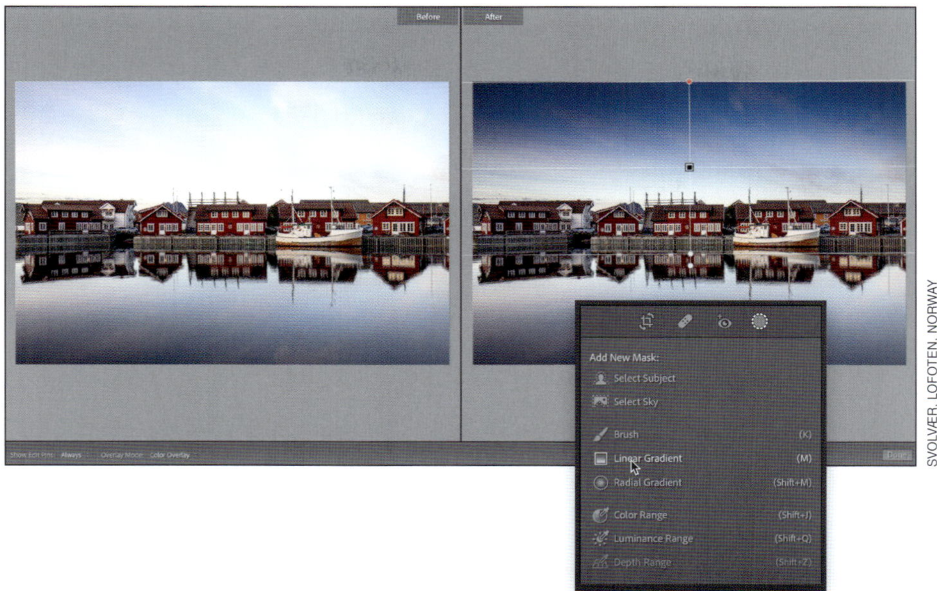

One reason our skies often look washed out is because of a limitation of our sensors, which causes our skies to look too bright when we expose for the foreground. We adjust for that by putting a neutral density (ND) gradient filter in front of our lens (see page 71), which is dark at the top (to darken the sky), but then gradually goes down to transparent so it doesn't darken our foreground. If you didn't use one of these filters when you took the shot, you can add one in Lightroom. You do this using a Linear Gradient mask. Click on the Masking icon (the gray circle with white dashes around it) in the toolbox below the histogram in Lightroom Classic (or in the toolbox on the right in Camera Raw or Lightroom cloud), then click on Linear Gradient in the Add New Mask panel that appears. Now, drag the Exposure slider over to the left to –2.00, then click-and-drag the tool from the very top of your image straight down until you reach the horizon line (or the tops of buildings, or mountains, etc.), or even a little farther. This darkens the top of the sky, and gradually becomes transparent at the point where you stopped dragging. If you think your sky needs to be even darker, drag the Exposure slider farther to the left, or if it's too dark, drag it back to the right until it looks good. Also, another nice thing is: once this gradient is in place, you can actually make your sky bluer by simply dragging the Temp slider to the left to apply a blue tint to your gradient.

If Your Sky Gradient Covers Something

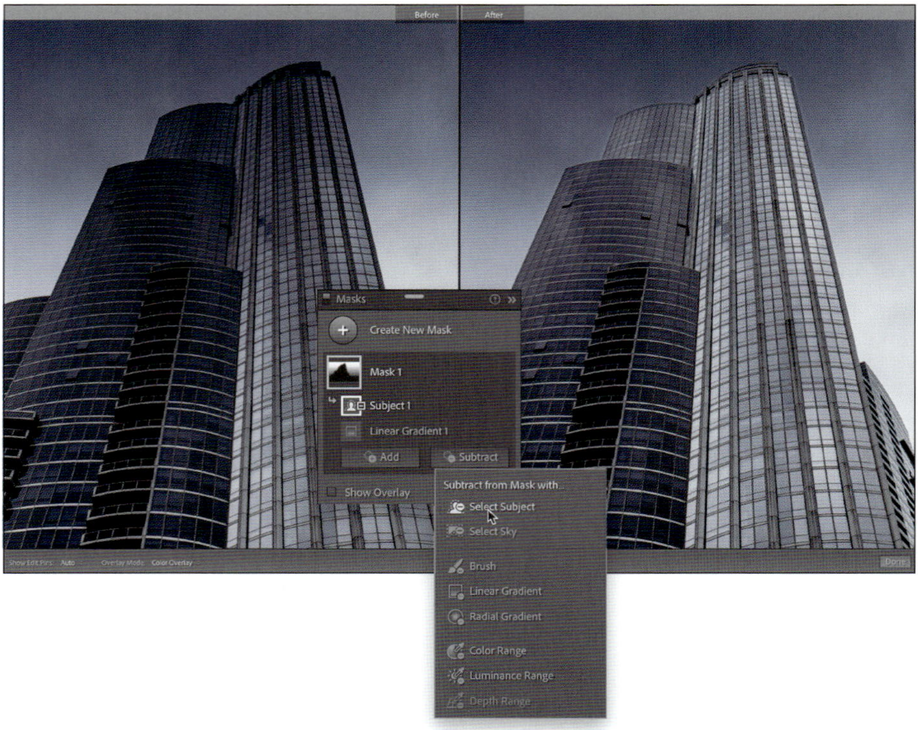

CHICAGO, ILLINOIS

Okay, so what if you apply a Linear Gradient mask to darken the sky (like we talked about on the previous page), but it covers something in the foreground you don't want darkened, like a building, or a mountain, or a monument? For example, look at the Before image above on the left. See how the Linear Gradient is covering the top of this skyscraper in Chicago? That's the problem I'm talking about, but luckily, there's a simple fix to remove the building from the gradient, so we're only darkening the sky behind it. Once you have your Linear Gradient mask in place and have darkened the sky (I added a little blue white balance here, too, using the Temp slider), in the Masks panel, click the Subtract button (to let Lightroom know you want to remove something from this Linear Gradient. Click on the mask in the Masks panel if you don't see it), and then click on Select Subject in the pop-up menu that appears (as shown above). This uses Lightroom's AI to recognize the building and it quickly removes it from your Linear Gradient mask, and it does it surprisingly well most of the time (as seen above right, where the top of the building is no longer affected by the Linear Gradient mask). It's like magic. If, for some reason, it was less than magic in how it worked, just click the Subtract button again, but this time, click on the Brush tool in the pop-up menu. Now you can paint over any areas of the building that the mask might have missed, and as you paint, it paints away that part of the Linear Gradient. So, it's an easy cleanup with the Brush tool.

Another Bluer Sky Method: The Color Mixer

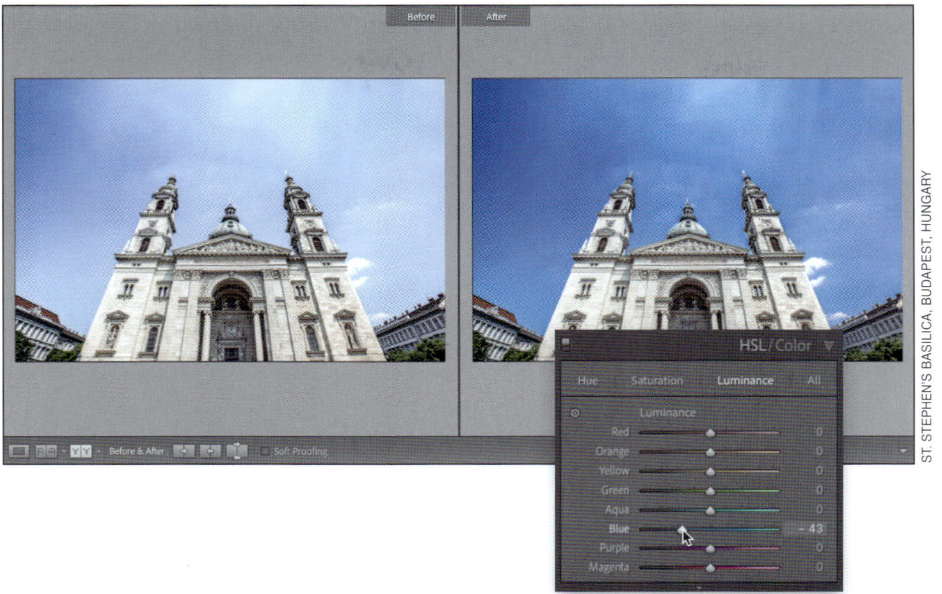

This one is so simple, but can work wonders for making your sky bluer (well, provided your photo has some blue in the sky already, so it's a "blue enhancer"— it won't take a gray, overcast sky and make it nice and blue). So, if you have some blue in your sky, especially if your blue sky is washed out or too light, try this: click on HSL in the panel header of the HSL/Color panel in Lightroom Classic (set the Adjust menu to Hue in the Color Mixer panel in Camera Raw and Lightroom cloud), click on the Luminance tab up top, and then drag the Blue slider to the left. Now, keep an eye on your sky because it's about to get a whole lot better.

Better Skies: Technique #3 (Select Sky)

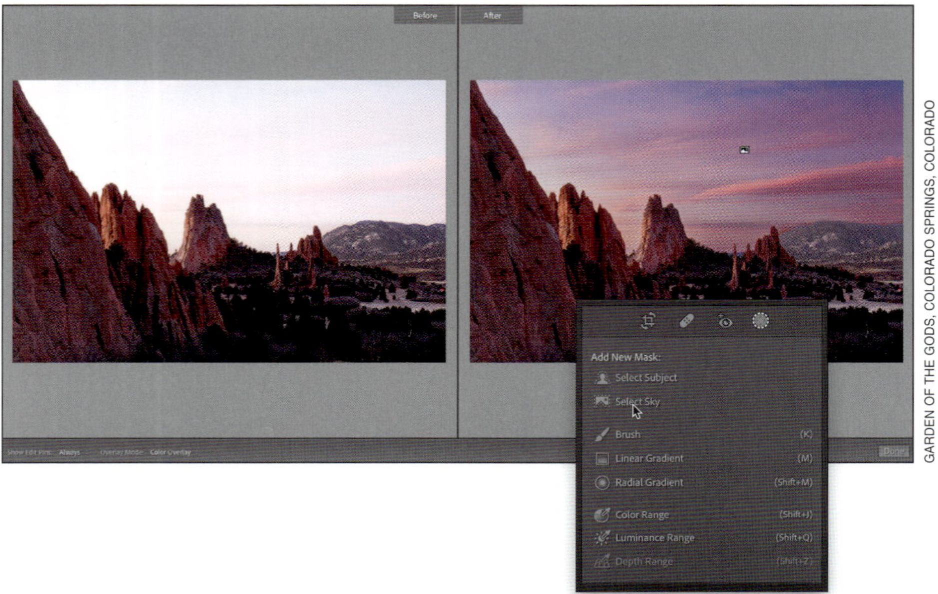

GARDEN OF THE GODS, COLORADO SPRINGS, COLORADO

If you want your sky brighter or darker, or more colorful, or whatever, then you will love this technique (yet another in a long line of "fix that sky" techniques). With this one, you start by clicking on the Masking icon (the gray circle with white dashes around it) in the toolbox below the histogram in Lightroom Classic (or in the toolbox on the right in Camera Raw or Lightroom cloud), then in the Add New Mask panel that appears, click on Select Sky (as shown in the inset above). That's it—it uses machine learning, some crazy AI, and death robots from Mars to make a perfect selection of your sky for you, and now you can use the sliders to adjust the sky without messing with the rest of your image. For example, one trick I use a lot is to lower the Exposure of just the sky—that usually has the effect of making it look great, and it doesn't darken or mess up the rest of the image because the mask only affects the sky (how cool is that?). So, try dragging the Exposure slider to the left to darken the sky and bring back some color and depth, and then increase the Contrast and the Whites sliders to help make them pop. You can try the Highlights slider, as well, to bring out the brightest parts of the sky. The best way to see what works for your particular sky is after you lower the Exposure, drag those sliders (Contrast, Whites, and Highlights) over to the right, and then back a few times to see which ones work best (and which ones you should leave alone).

Better Skies without Messing Up the Clouds

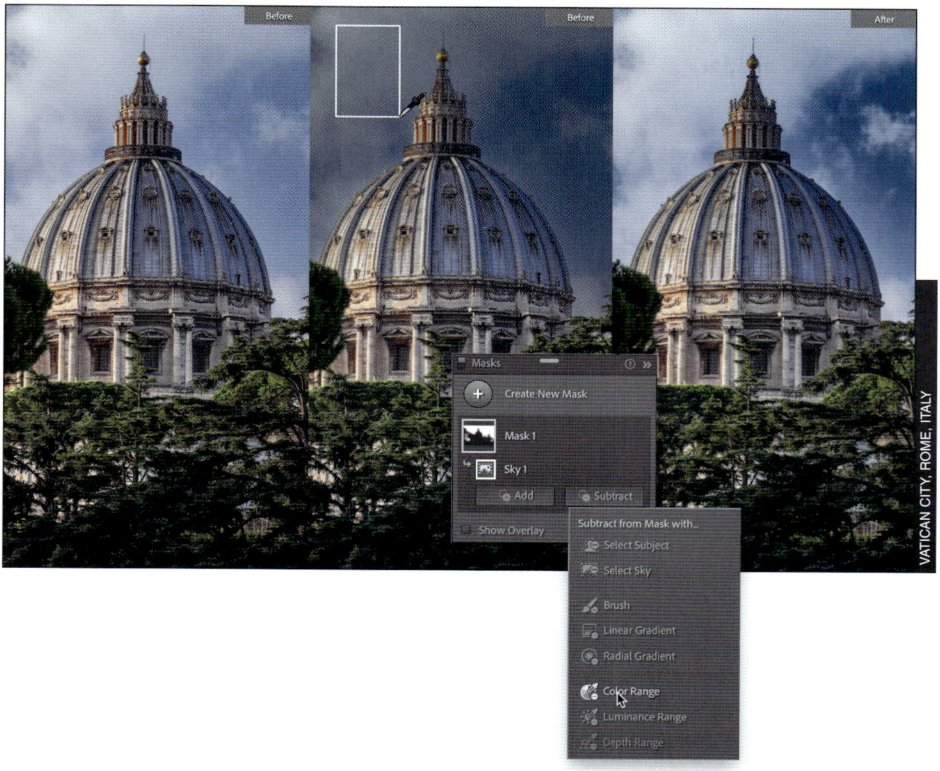

Okay, one last sky technique, but it's a handy one. On the previous page, we made the sky look better by darkening it and adding lots of contrast, but because that shot was taken at dawn, making the clouds darker looked really good. Now, what if it's a sunny day with nice, puffy white clouds? You may not want those nice, puffy white clouds looking dingy (like the ones you see in the center above, where I added a Select Sky mask and darkened the sky by dragging the Exposure slider to the left). Here's how to do that: First, you start the same way—click on the Masking icon and choose Select Sky from the Add New Mask panel to get your sky selected, but of course, it selects the entire sky, clouds and all, so when you darken the exposure, it darkens the clouds. To get our clouds out of that Select Sky mask, first go to the Masks panel and click on Mask 1 to reveal two buttons beneath it. Click on the Subtract button, because we want to subtract something from our sky mask (the clouds), then from the pop-up menu of tools we can use to subtract from that mask that appears, click on Color Range (as shown in the inset above). Now, take that tool, click-and-drag out a rectangle over part of the clouds (as seen above center), and it samples the colors in that cloud and removes them from the mask (as seen above right). Now, you can mess with the sky's exposure or even add some blue white balance using the Temp slider, and it no longer affects the clouds.

Making Your Colors More Vibrant

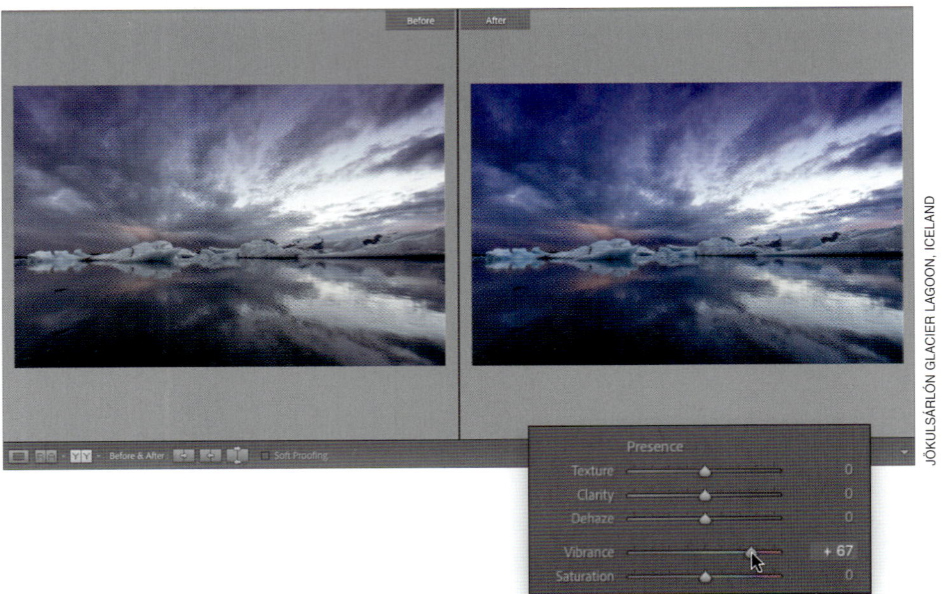

If the colors in your image seem like they need a boost (wait to determine this until after you've applied your contrast, because applying contrast makes your colors more vibrant), you can use the Vibrance slider near the bottom of Lightroom's (and Camera Raw's) Basic panel. Stay away from the Saturation slider, as it's only good for removing color (desaturating the image), not adding color—it's too coarse. The Vibrance slider is kind of a "Smart Saturation" (if I had to give it a name), and you add vibrance by dragging the slider to the right. It has the greatest effect on dull colors, much less effect on colors in your image that are already vibrant, and it has a special mathematical algorithm that avoids adding too much color to skin tones, so people don't wind up looking sunburned in your image. That's a lot of smarts for just a single slider. Again, I don't have to use this slider very much because of how much contrast I add, but I do use it now and again, so it's worth knowing.

Making Your Light More Interesting

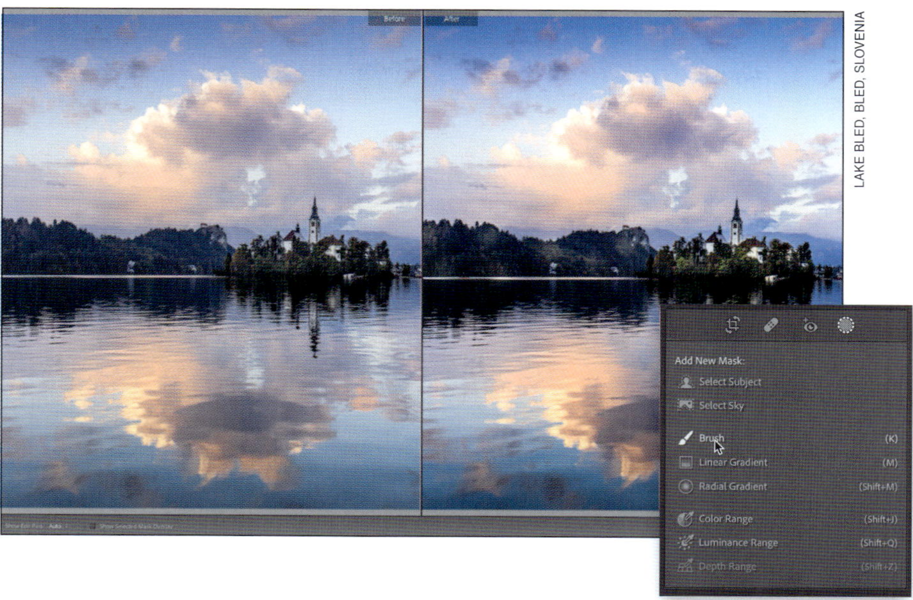

This is another technique I've been using on my travel photos for many years. I even get comments about how lucky I was to have such interesting light, but in reality, it was added in Lightroom (or Photoshop's Camera Raw). You're going to add "light hits" to your image using the Brush tool, and what I'm about to explain is going to sound really simplistic, but it's incredibly effective. You get the Brush tool (K) by clicking on the Mask icon in the toolbox below the Histogram in Lightroom Classic (or on the right in Camera Raw or Lightroom cloud), and then clicking on it in the Add New Mask panel. Drag the Exposure slider to the right to 2.00, make your Brush Size really big (you can change your brush size using the Left and Right Bracket keys on your keyboard. They look like this: [ ], and they're found to the right of the letter "P"). Now, just click one time (don't paint with it, just click once) over places in your photo that either already have a little bit of a highlight (a bright spot), or where you wish one was, and it adds a big pool of light there. At 2.00, it's probably going to look way too bright, but we'll fix that in just a sec. For now, go through, and like a magical light fairy, drop little pools of light in different places in your image. Once you're done, drag the Exposure slider back toward the right a bit until the light hits look natural and more subtle. A lot of top travel and landscape photographers use this technique to add a bit more interesting light to their images, and now you can too.

Darkening or Brightening Individual Areas

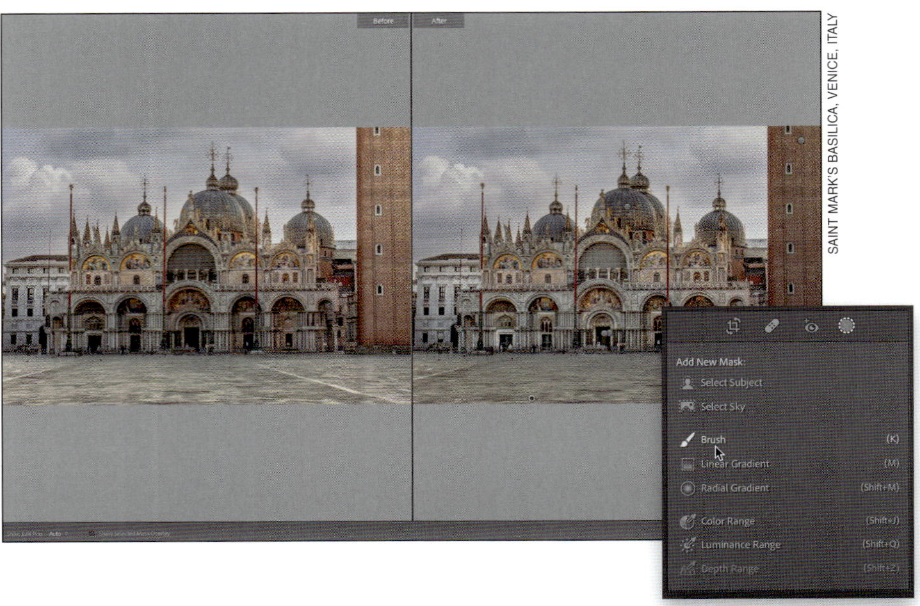

If you go to Lightroom (or Camera Raw's) Basic panel and move any slider, those changes affect the entire image, but there are times when you might want to adjust only a particular area of your photo (called "dodging and burning" in traditional film darkroom days). That's when we reach for the Brush tool (K). It's the same sliders, in the same order, that do the same thing, but now those adjustments aren't added to your whole image; instead, you paint them on. So, for example, if you want to brighten an area, you'd increase your Exposure to 1.00, paint over that area, and it gets brighter as you paint. Once you're done painting, you can adjust the Exposure slider so it's exactly the right amount. That's the process, but you don't have to adjust one slider at a time. Instead, you could paint over an area to darken it (dragging the Exposure slider to the left), but then warm up its white balance at the same time by dragging the Temp slider to the right, and then add some Texture with the Texture slider. Now, if you've painted over an area and want to keep those changes intact, but want to adjust a different area, click on Create New Mask at the top of the Masks panel, and then click on Brush. This adds a new Edit pin, leaving your previous changes untouched (a little brush icon appears where you started painting), and now you can adjust this new area separately. If you want to return to that original area to paint more or adjust the sliders, in the Masks panel, click on its mask (you can rename these masks by double-clicking on them). To reset all the sliders to zero, in Lightroom Classic, double-click on the word "Effect." In Camera Raw or Lightroom cloud, click on Preset in the top-right corner of the panel and choose Reset Sliders. Lastly, if you make a mistake and paint over something you didn't mean to, press-and-hold the Option (PC: Alt) key, and it changes to the Erase brush so you can paint away those mistakes.

Adding a "Look" to Your Image

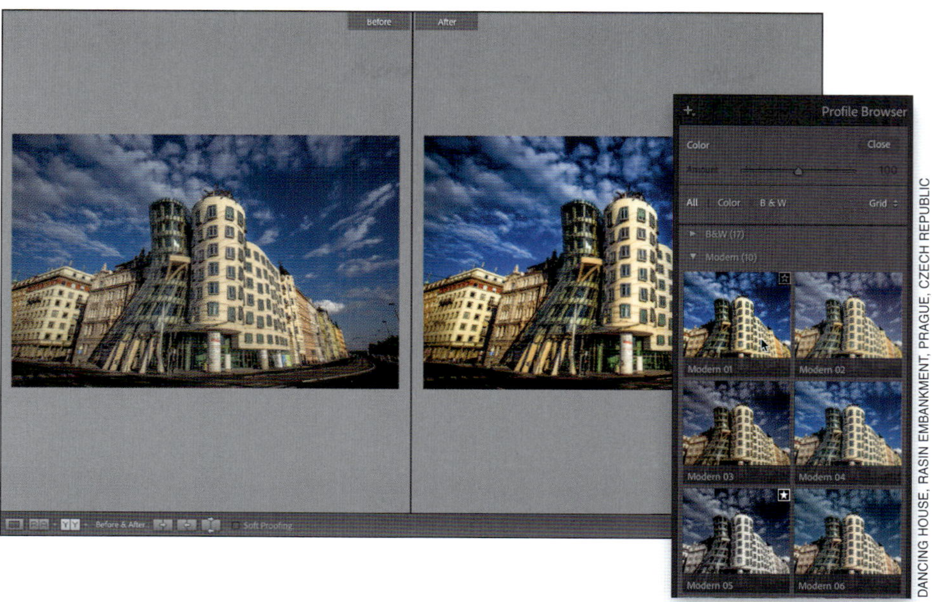

In Lightroom (or Camera Raw) you can apply a "look," which is a combination of color tweaks and contrast tweaks (sometimes adding more or less contrast to an image) that are kinda like the "looks" you can apply to an image in Instagram using its built-in filters. What's nice about applying any one of these looks is that it doesn't move your Lightroom sliders (like using a preset does—presets just move your sliders to a preset location, and if you move those sliders afterward, then it changes the look of the preset. Not so with creative profiles—you can apply a look and all your Lightroom adjustments are still set to zero, so you can tweak to your heart's content without losing the look. Sweet!). Anyway, there are a bunch of these "looks," and here's how to apply them: In the Basic panel, near the top-right corner of the panel, you'll find an icon with four small rectangles. Click on that and it brings up the Profile Browser (seen above), and you can look through different sets of profiles right there. To see how a profile would look on your image, just hover your cursor over one of the thumbnails and it temporarily applies that look to your image. If you like the look, just click on it and click the Close button to close the Profile Browser. One more thing: if you apply a look and wish that the effect was either more or less intense, there's an Amount slider right above it that you can drag to add more or less of it.

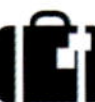
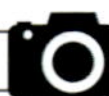

Converting to Black and White

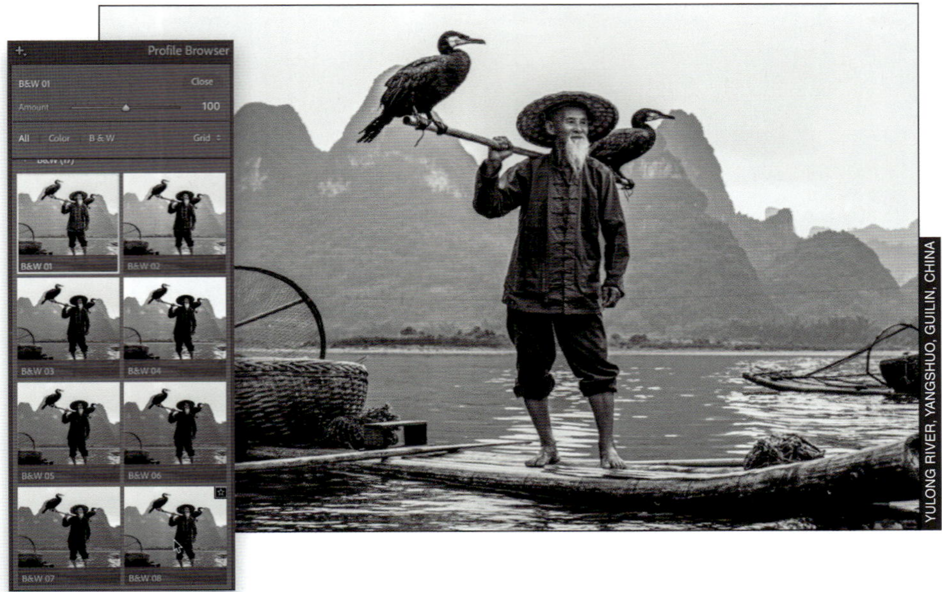

Lightroom (and of course, Camera Raw) has 17 different creative profiles for converting your image to black and white, and many are based on popular traditional darkroom techniques for creating black-and-white images. You access these the same way you do the color creative profiles: in the Basic panel, click on the icon with four small rectangles to bring up the Profile Browser, and scroll down to the B&W folder. That's where you'll find the 17 black-and-white conversions. Just hover your cursor over each of the thumbnails to see the conversion applied to your image, until you find one that looks good for your particular image. When you find it, click on it, and Lightroom applies that black-and-white look. Now, after I do a conversion like this, to make it look more "old school film-like," I add a little bit of film Grain to help really give it that traditional darkroom film look. You'll find this at the bottom of the Effects panel (I just increase the Amount until I start to see the grain; I leave the Size and Roughness sliders at their default settings). Also, I think what generally makes a great black-and-white image is lots of contrast, so when it comes to black and white, I add lots of contrast (see page 212), and I bring out the detail a lot with the Texture and Clarity sliders (see page 213), and of course, I sharpen it to death (see page 227). One more thing: Just like with the color creative profiles, once you choose your black-and-white profile, you can control the intensity of the effect using the Amount slider at the top of the Profile Browser.

Fixing Lens Problems

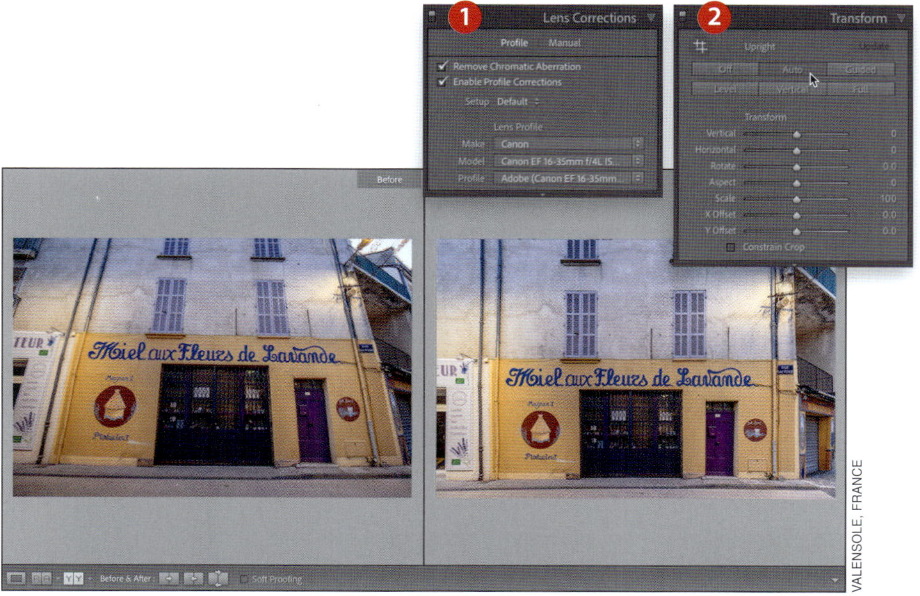

There are a number of issues caused by our camera lenses (everything from distortion, where our image looks like it's bowing outward, making doors or walls look like they're bulging, to buildings and walls that look like they're leaning backward, to an annoying darkening in all four corners of your image). Luckily, fixing most of these issues is simply a matter of two clicks. These lens problems are so common that Lightroom (and Camera Raw) has a huge built-in database of lens correction profiles that it can apply to fix many of them—all you have to do is turn it on. In the Lens Corrections panel in Lightroom Classic (the Optics panel in Camera Raw or Lightroom cloud), simply turn on the Enable Profile Corrections checkbox. When you do this, Lightroom looks at the camera data embedded in your image to see the make and model of your lens, and then it applies the proper lens correction. It has a huge database of lenses, but if for some reason it doesn't find yours, from the Make pop-up menu, choose your lens brand (Sony, Tamron, Nikon, Canon, etc.), and it will usually find a profile. If, for some reason, it doesn't find your exact lens, then choose the next closest one from the menu, and that will usually do the trick to get rid of the distortion and corner darkening (the bad type of lens vignetting). If you have buildings leaning backward in your image and want to correct that, go to the Transform panel in Lightroom Classic (the Geometry panel in Camera Raw or Lightroom cloud), and in the Upright section, click the Auto button. If it leaves white gaps in the corners, turn on the Constrain Crop checkbox to have it crop those corners away, or you can manually crop them away using the Crop Overlay tool. That sounds like a lot, but it's really just two clicks: Turn on the Enable Profile Corrections checkbox, then go to Upright and click the Auto button. That'll do the trick.

Darkening the Outside Edges

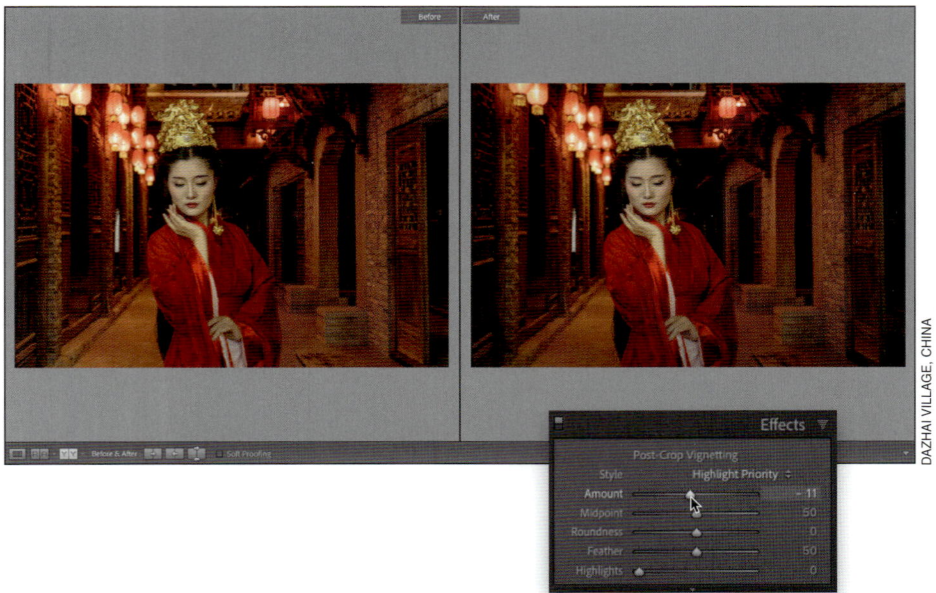

For the most part, we're not putting really interesting or important things right at the outside edges of our image, especially when we're shooting with wide-angle lenses where the edges have a bit of distortion. So, a finishing move I do to nearly all my travel shots is to use the Post-Crop Vignetting effect to darken the edges all the way around the image evenly. This takes the heat off those meaningless outside edges, and helps to focus the viewer's eye on your subject. It works really well, especially if you use a subtle amount—so subtle that even another photographer wouldn't know you added an edge vignette, but if you toggle the effect on/off, you'll immediately see the difference. The amount I use is –11 (so, in the Effects panel, in the Post-Crop Vignetting section, I drag the Amount slider to the left to –11). That's all there is to it, but it really makes a difference.

Sharpening Your Image

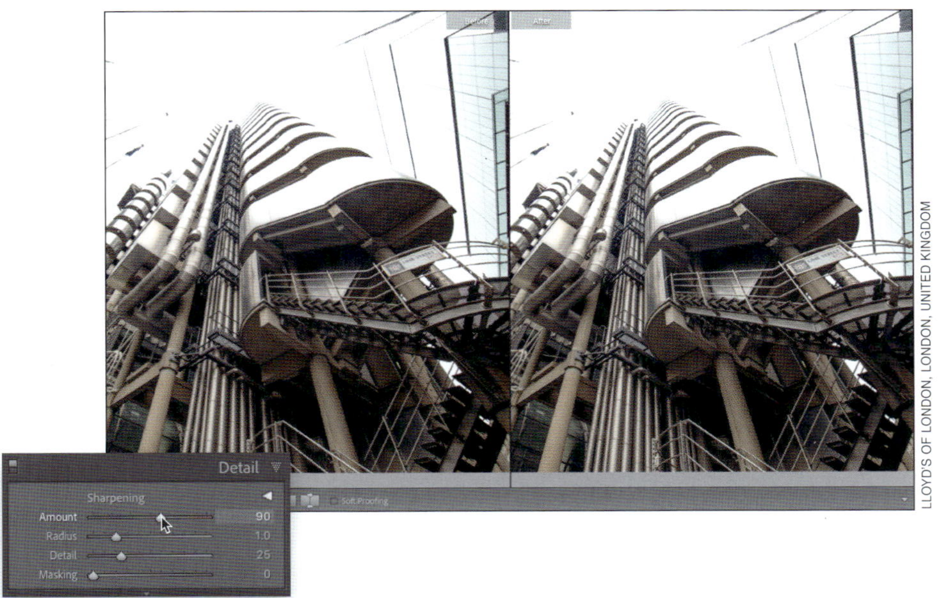

Like I mentioned on the first page of this chapter, every single photo gets sharpened (it's a must), and we do that in the Detail panel in Lightroom (or Photoshop's Camera Raw). We can keep this simple (and avoid digging into the nerdy stuff) by simply going to the Detail panel and increasing the Amount slider to add more sharpening. If you shot in RAW on your camera, a Sharpening Amount of 40 is automatically applied (to replace the capture sharpening that gets turned off in your camera when you shoot in RAW). But, I think an Amount of 40 is a bit too low, so if the image is of a softer nature, like a portrait, you can increase the amount to 50 or 60. If your subject is a cityscape or typical travel city shot, you can go higher, to 70 or 80, or even slightly higher (depending, of course, on how it looks in your photo). If you have a really high-megapixel camera, like a 45- or 50-megapixel camera, you can increase the Radius amount as well, bumping it up to 1.1 or 1.2, if moving the Amount slider doesn't seem like it's doing enough to your image. *Note:* The only way to really see how much sharpening you're applying to your image, and how it's affecting your photo, is to zoom in to a 100% (1:1) view, and then it will be easier to see the effect. However, if you're sharing this photo on Instagram or on social media, your image will wind up being much smaller, so don't let it freak you out if you see some noise from the sharpening when you view the image at full size—you won't see that noise at Instagram- or social media-sharing sizes.

Stitching Panos Together

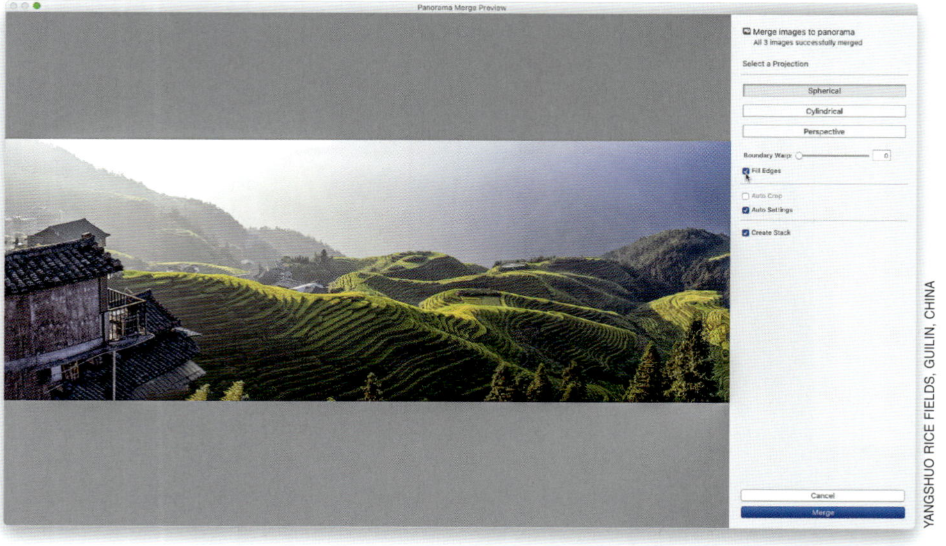

If you followed the steps for shooting a panorama (on page 116), then putting those individual frames into one big, beautiful pano will be a breeze. In Lightroom, select all the images in your pano, then Right-click on any one of them and in the pop-up menu that appears, under Photo Merge, choose Panorama. In Photoshop's Camera Raw, when you Right-click on one of those selected photos, you'll see a Merge to Panorama menu command. (*Note:* If you shot an HDR pano [see page 118], choose HDR Panorama. I created a video showing you how to do this, which you can find on the book's companion website mentioned on page xiii). Both bring up the Panorama Merge Preview window, with a preview of your images stitched together into a single pano (well, as long as you overlapped the images by 20%–30%. That's the key). You'll see either small or large white gaps at the top, bottom, or corners of your image in this preview window. That's normal, but it's also normal to fix 'em. You have three choices: (1) You can turn on the Auto Crop checkbox and it will crop those white gaps away. The downside is it makes your pano thinner and smaller, and you might clip off important parts of your pano, so this is my least favorite choice. (2) You can drag the Boundary Warp slider to the right, and it somehow magically extends your image so it fills the frame. This works astoundingly well, so it's worth trying (drag it all the way to the right in most cases). (3) You can turn on Fill Edges, which is also often amazing and uses Photoshop's Content-Aware Fill technology to fill those white gaps with information from areas right around the gaps. It often gives you mind-blowing results (occasionally it does a stinky job, but for the most part, it rocks). Try out all three options, see which you think looks best, and go with that one. When you're done, click the Merge button, and it creates your pano as a RAW image, as if you shot it that way in-camera, which is pretty mind-blowing in and of itself.

Creating an HDR Image

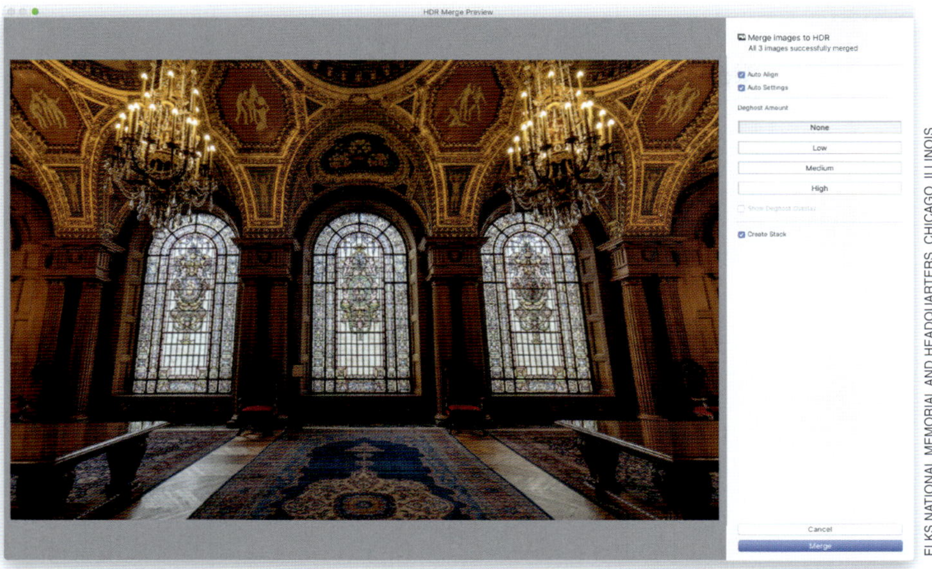

We talked about the advantages of HDR images (made from exposure bracketed photos), and how to shoot them, back on page 117, so here we're going to look at combining your bracketed shots into a single exposure. You do that in Lightroom in much the same way that you combine multiple frames into a panorama (see the previous page): select the images, Right-click on one of them, and from the pop-up menu that appears, go under Photo Merge, and this time, choose HDR (in Camera Raw, after you Right-click on your bracketed images, choose Merge to HDR). This brings up the HDR Merge Preview window (seen above), which combines those bracketed exposures into a single image that doesn't look that different than the normal exposure, because outside of its default function of applying Auto Settings (the same as the Auto button in the Basic panel), it is pretty much the same (the magic happens when you start editing it in the Develop module). There's an Auto Align checkbox at the top, and if you hand-held your HDR shot, leave this turned on—it will attempt to perfectly align your bracketed images. If you shot your pano on a tripod, turn that checkbox off, and it will combine the images faster. You'll only use the Deghost feature if something was moving in your image (if people were walking through your image while you were taking your bracketed exposures, they will probably appear either a lot or a little bit transparent, hence the "Deghost" name). This feature lets you choose from three different levels of fixes for it, and in many cases it works out pretty well, but only turn this on if you see ghosting. When you're done (if you had to do anything at all in this preview window), click the Merge button and it creates a new RAW image with "-HDR" added to its name, so it's easy to see which of the images is the HDR image.

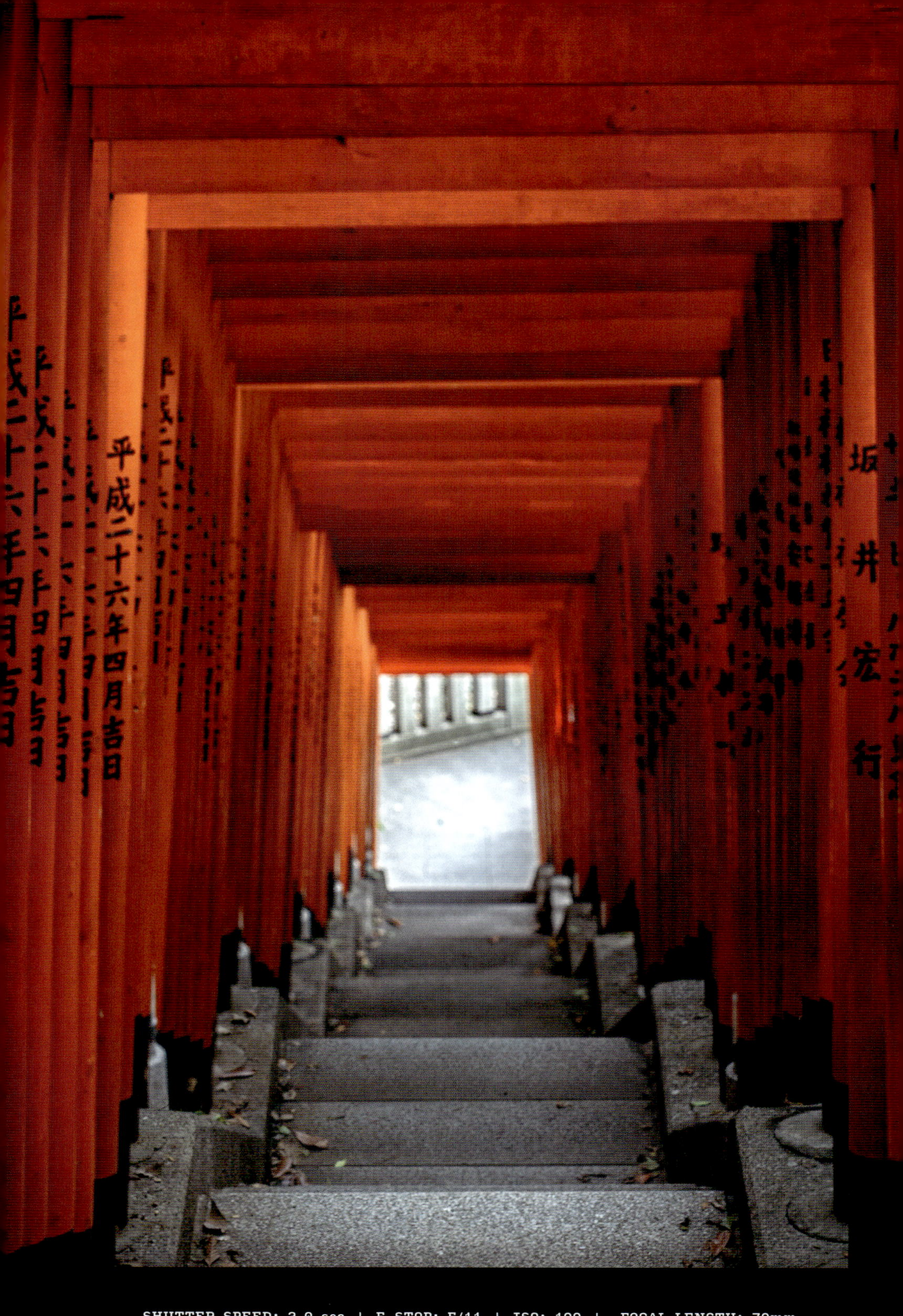

SHUTTER SPEED: 2.0 sec | F-STOP: F/11 | ISO: 100 | FOCAL LENGTH: 70mm

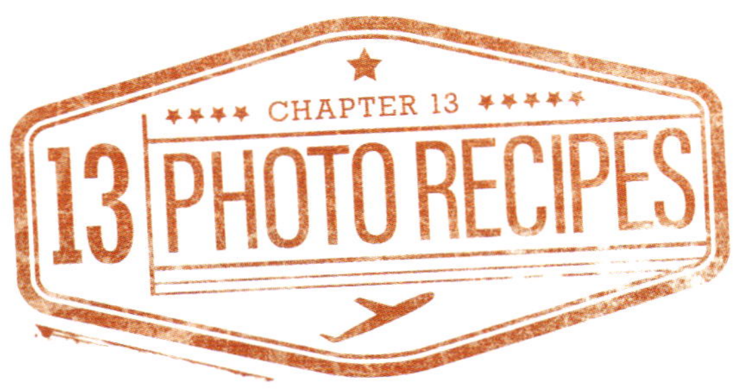

Photo Recipes to Help You Get the Shot

The Simple Ingredients That Make It All Come Together

When you're in the kitchen, and you've got all the right ingredients to make a wonderful meal, I've learned that you can still totally destroy dinner. I've had situations where the only viable option, after carefully following the directions, was to throw the entire thing out and call Domino's. (*Tip:* Get the Ultimate Pepperoni specialty pizza and get it Brooklyn Style. Make sure you look under Specialty Pizza. Don't just get a regular pepperoni pizza Brooklyn Style—it's not the same. No charge for the awesome tip. It's on the house.) Anyway, before we get to how this all relates to photography, there is something I need to address, because I think a lot of folks misread this chapter as "Photo Recipes," like you're making a dish, but it's actually pronounced "Photo Re-Cipes," and RECIPES is actually an acronym that is used quite a bit in professional commercial photography. It stands for "Rectilinear Exposure Compensation In Photographic Effects Situations," which is a nerdy term for something that generally happens when you mix certain camera settings that don't belong together. For example, if you have a mirrorless camera made within the last couple of years, it most likely has a built-in high dynamic range (HDR) feature, but if you were to couple that feature with exposure bracketing, with your exposure set to more than –1, it creates an effect that is similar to "crossing streams." You should also be aware that, by now, after reading 12 other of these meandering, semi-conscious chapter intros, there's a pretty good chance (a better than good chance. Okay, it's a lock) that this is all made up, that there is no RECIPES acronym and it's not called Re-Cipes, and that we're all actually living in a simulation run by whomever the bad guys were in *The Matrix*. I never could make heads or tails of that part, but I know this: I hate those little Sentinel robots with the insect-like legs. If I saw them coming at me, you know what I'd do? I'd yell, "Hey, look! Is that Beyoncé?" Works every time. Boom. Drops the mic.

The Recipe for Getting This Type of Shot

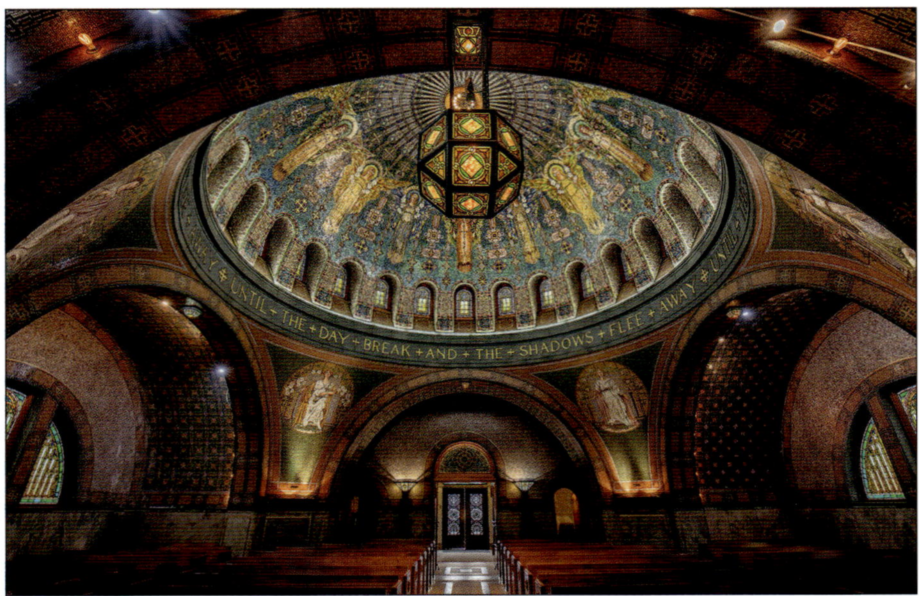

Characteristics of this type of shot: A dark, dramatic interior shot with a wide range of tones (from dark to light), a sweeping floor-to-ceiling view, and vibrant color.

Location: Lakewood Cemetery Memorial Chapel, Minneapolis, Minnesota

GEAR: This was taken on a full-frame mirrorless camera body. To capture both the floor and the ceiling like you see here, you'll need a super-wide-angle lens, and I used a 16–35mm lens zoomed all the way out to 16mm (that would be around 12mm on a crop-sensor). In a low-light setting like this, you'll need to be on a tripod (or, in this case, I used a Platypod Ultra). I positioned my camera on top of the lectern, so it would align perfectly with the center aisle.

SETTINGS: Shot in aperture priority mode, at f/9, which puts everything in focus (I normally would've shot this at f/11, but at some point, I probably moved the aperture dial by accident), and 100 ISO (or your lowest, cleanest setting). This was taken using Exposure Bracketing (see page 117) to capture the dark interior detail without blowing out the stained glass windows above.

KEY TECHNIQUE: It's the point of view. It's different because it was taken from the altar looking back at the front door, where the congregation sits. We usually see the view from the pews looking toward the altar. Also, the super-wide-angle lens lets you include so much in one shot, including the beautiful ceiling, which is key.

POST-PROCESSING: The first step was to combine the multiple exposures into a single HDR image in Lightroom (see page 229), then I dropped the Highlights slider to –100 to lessen the light hitting the stained glass windows. I increased the Contrast a lot, which made the image more colorful, and I also increased the Texture slider a lot, and Clarity a little bit. I also added sharpening to give it a crisp look.

The Recipe for Getting This Type of Shot

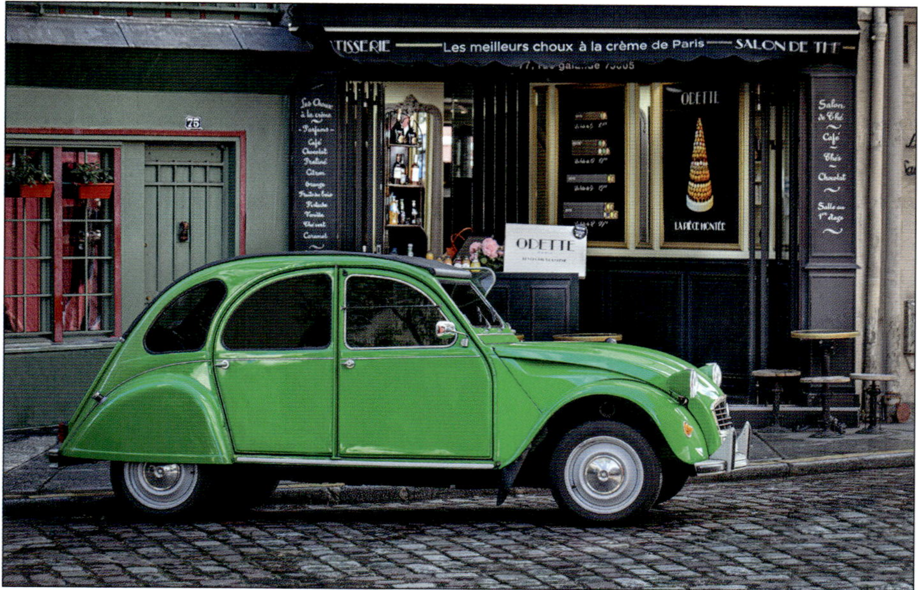

Characteristics of this type of shot: A romantic, timeless street scene of Paris with a charming pastry shop as our background.

Location: La Maison Odette Pastry Shop, 77 Rue Galande, Paris, France

GEAR: Taken on a full-frame body, with a 70–200mm f/2.8 lens at 100mm. This was taken hand-held while standing in the street with a friend watching for cars.

SETTINGS: Shot at f/5.6, ISO 100, and 1/80 of a second shutter speed.

KEY TECHNIQUE: What makes this scene is its timelessness. I found this great location researching on 500px.com, and then to give the shot something special, I hired an old French classic car from a tour operator (they drove the car out to the location and positioned it where I wanted. They were very helpful). The lucky part of all this was getting the parking space right in front of the pastry shop, so we could shoot without seeing any other new cars that would take away from the romance of the shot. I zoomed in tight to keep from seeing any modern signs or other distractions, and I intentionally included a good amount of the cobblestone street, which adds to the timelessness. I put the car near the bottom of the shot because it's not about the car; it's about the scene (the car is a prop in the scene).

POST-PROCESSING: Nothing too special with the post-processing for this shot, just mostly adding a lot of Contrast (which I commonly do—contrast is my "thing") in Lightroom, then using the Texture slider to bring out detail, and a little bit of Clarity to make the car look more shiny and darken the street. I also used Photoshop's Healing Brush tool to remove any little distractions on the car body, the building, etc., to simplify the image. I darkened the edges all the way around by adding a –11 vignette (see page 226), and of course, I finished it off by adding sharpening.

The Recipe for Getting This Type of Shot

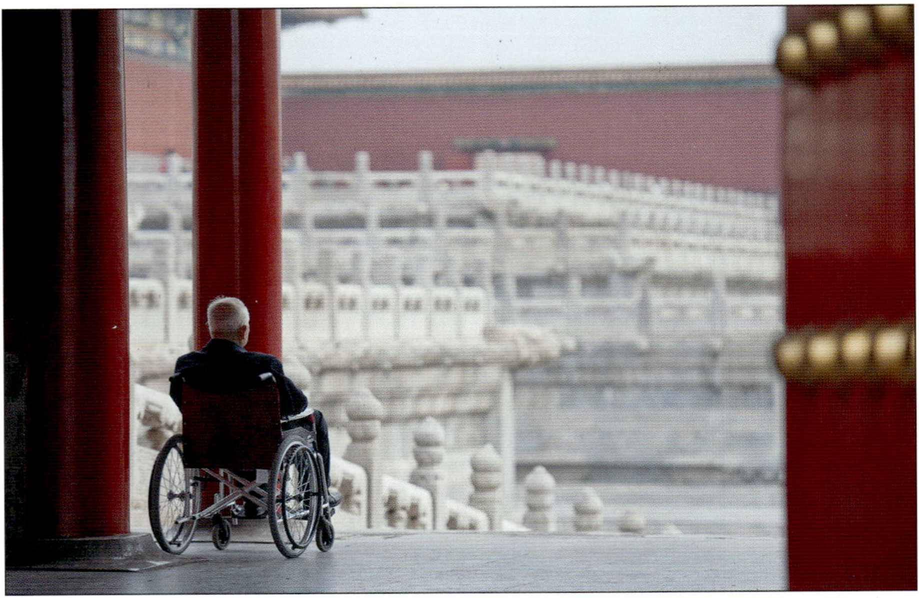

Characteristics of this type of shot: An environmental, storytelling-type of candid portrait with great simplicity and minimum distractions.

Location: The Forbidden City, Beijing, China

GEAR: Taken on a full-frame body, hand-held, with a 70–200mm lens.

SETTINGS: I zoomed in to 140mm and set my aperture to f/2.8 to help get the background out of focus, which separates it from the subject. ISO 200 and shutter speed 1/1600 of a second, so I didn't have to worry too much about camera shake.

KEY TECHNIQUE: Hands-down, the key technique here is patience. As you might imagine, The Forbidden City is packed wall-to-wall with tourists, so framing this up without seeing any was the start because the gentleman in the wheelchair was also surrounded by his family, including very young children. I'm positioned on the far edge of the large door you see on the right, and I just stood there, leaning against that door, hoping to get a shot where the family wasn't in the frame because then it just looked like a shot with some tourists. Some family members kept walking over to the left, out of the frame, so I just stuck with it (doing that whole patience thing, which is so hard for us photographers), and son-of-a-gun, for a moment or two they were all out of the frame to the left, and I was already aimed and ready to take the shot, which you see here.

POST-PROCESSING: Just the standard Lightroom stuff, like adding Contrast. I post-processed this shot before Lightroom had added the Texture slider, but I can see that I used the Brush tool to apply Clarity to him and his wheelchair (Clarity makes metal shiny, but I would avoid using it on the out-of-focus areas because it looks weird and processed). And, of course, sharpening to finish.

The Recipe for Getting This Type of Shot

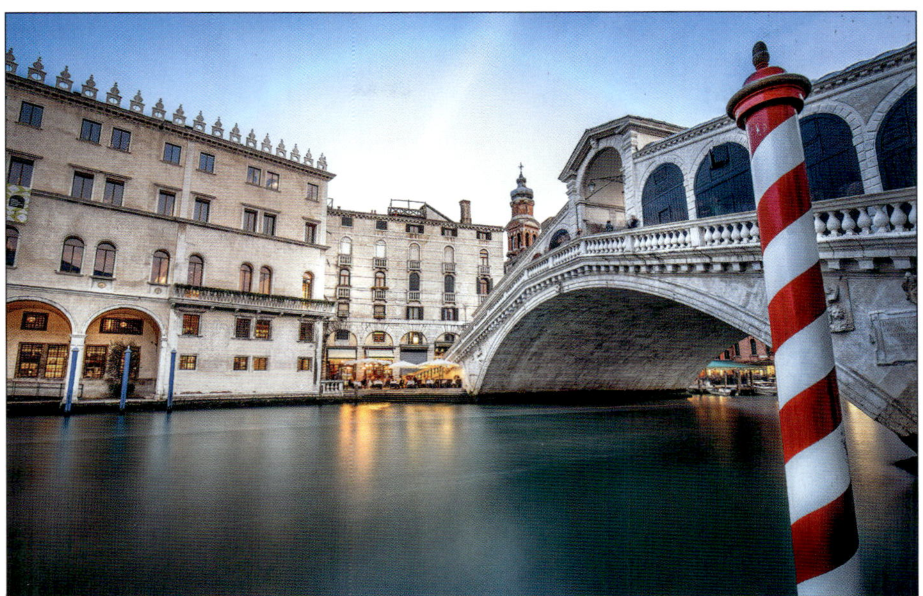

Characteristics of this type of shot: A classic travel-style shot with smooth water in the canal, vibrant colors, and lots of texture. An overall simplified image.

Location: Rialto Bridge, Venice, Italy

GEAR: Taken on a full-frame body, with a 16–35mm f/4 lens, and mounted on a tripod with a shutter release.

SETTINGS: The aperture was f/9, ISO 100, and my shutter speed was 89 seconds (you read that right—89 seconds). It's a super-wide-angle shot at 16mm.

KEY TECHNIQUE: I think what makes the shot is the smooth, silky water in the canal, which is created by using a 10-stop ND filter to get a really long exposure (see page 115) to make my shutter stay open 89 seconds even during the day (though this was late in the day, which helps. At high noon, I would have needed to stack ND filters—like a 10-stop and a 3-stop—to get that long of an exposure). Because the shutter was open so long, traffic going by on the canal (it's not just charming gondolas, there are also garbage boats and ferries and other random boats) disappears. Compositionally, including the "barber pole" on the right side not only acts as a foreground object to help lead you into the image, but it also adds a nice pop of color, which contrasts nicely with the other colors in the scene. The leading lines in the image lead the viewer's eye to the outdoor cafe in the center of the image, but the bridge itself is such a large part of the image that it becomes the subject.

POST-PROCESSING: The colors are really vibrant in this image, so to bring them out, not only did I add lots of Contrast in Lightroom, but I also increased the Vibrance slider a bit. I added both the Texture slider and some Clarity to add shine to the water, and sharpening to finish.

The Recipe for Getting This Type of Shot

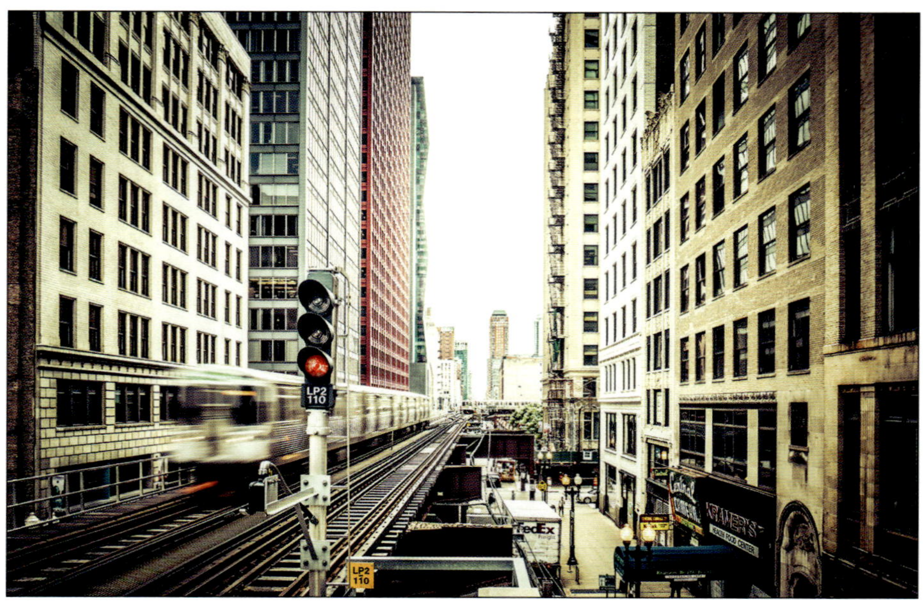

Characteristics of this type of shot: A gritty-style city shot with a sense of movement and a color effect added in post-processing.

Location: Adams/Wabash "The L" station platform, Chicago, Illinois

GEAR: Taken on a full-frame body, with a 24–240mm lens at 62mm, and mounted on a travel tripod with a cable release.

SETTINGS: Aperture was set at f/22, ISO 100, and shutter speed at 1/3 of a second.

KEY TECHNIQUES: The motion of the train and the post-processing. The motion is created by using an f-stop that would keep my shutter open longer (f/22), so it would show the movement of the train. It was kind of shady between the tall rows of buildings on either side, so I didn't need to use an ND filter and I could just get away with choosing a high-numbered f-stop to keep the shutter open long enough to create some motion blur. I did not "pan" with the train as it was moving—I aimed directly down the track with my camera on the tripod. It took quite a few tries to get the timing right (those trains move fast).

POST-PROCESSING: The buildings were leaning backward more than I'd like, so first, I applied a Lightroom lens profile, and then, in the Transform panel, I clicked Upright Auto to make them more upright (see page 225). To give it a vintage look, I applied the Vintage 04 creative profile (see page 223), increased the Amount slider to 200, and then I dragged the WB Temp slider a bit toward yellow. I bumped the Contrast all the way up, added a dark vignette around the outside edges, lots of Texture and Clarity, and I increased the Highlights a bit to blow out the sky to white for effect. I added extra contrast using the Tone Curve panel (see page 212) by choosing Strong Contrast from the Point Curve pop-up menu, and finally, I added sharpening.

The Recipe for Getting This Type of Shot

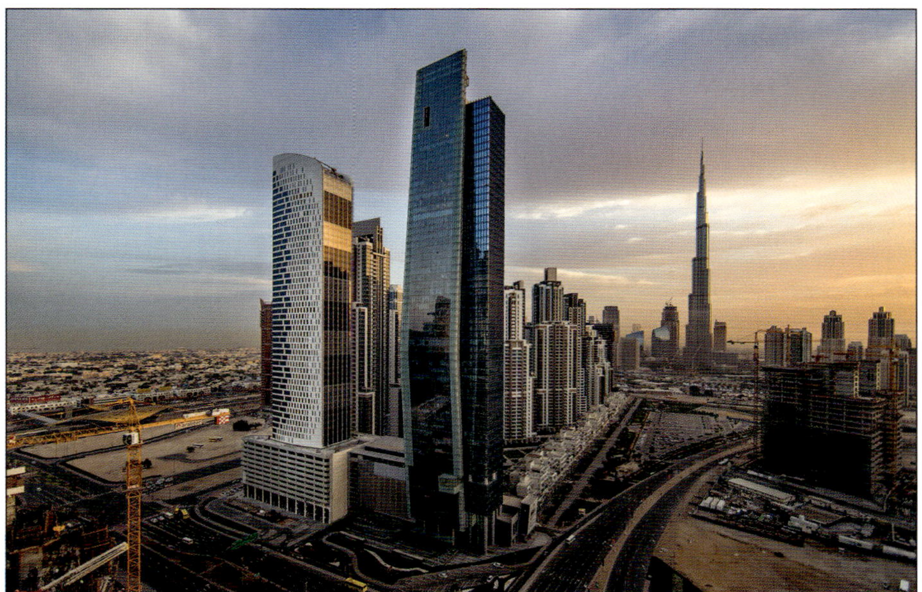

Characteristics of this type of shot: Sweeping cityscape from a high point of view with soft light and color in the sky.

Location: The Oberoi Hotel, Dubai, United Arab Emirates

GEAR: Taken on a full-frame body, hand-held, with a 14mm prime lens.

SETTINGS: Shot in low light, my aperture was f/3.5, ISO 800 (to get a high enough shutter speed for a sharp shot), and shutter speed was 1/800 of a second (I could've lowered my ISO and used a slower shutter speed—that's explained below).

KEY TECHNIQUE: Here, it's access. I was staying at the Oberoi Hotel (picked by the folks who organized the event), and as soon as I had its info, I started looking for where I could shoot from. I found that they had a rooftop bar and Google Earth showed it would have a great view of the world's tallest building: Burj Khalifa (seen in the back right above). I sent a note to the hotel's concierge before I arrived, letting them know I was a photographer and asking if there was any way I could shoot from the rooftop bar at dawn. They were happy to oblige, and they had a security guard meet me who unlocked the door and gave us the run of the place. For this shot, I was standing on a bar stool to get up high enough to get my camera over the safety glass surrounding the bar. So, I had to hold my camera out away from my body (less stability) to take the shot, so I knew there would be some movement (not including me shaking from my intense fear of heights), hence the high ISO.

POST-PROCESSING: As usual, I added a lot of Contrast and bumped up Lightroom's Dehaze slider to remove some of the haze in the scene (see page 212). I also used the Brush tool to brighten the two backlit buildings on the left. I added Texture and Clarity to bring out detail, and of course, I finished off by adding sharpening.

The Recipe for Getting This Type of Shot

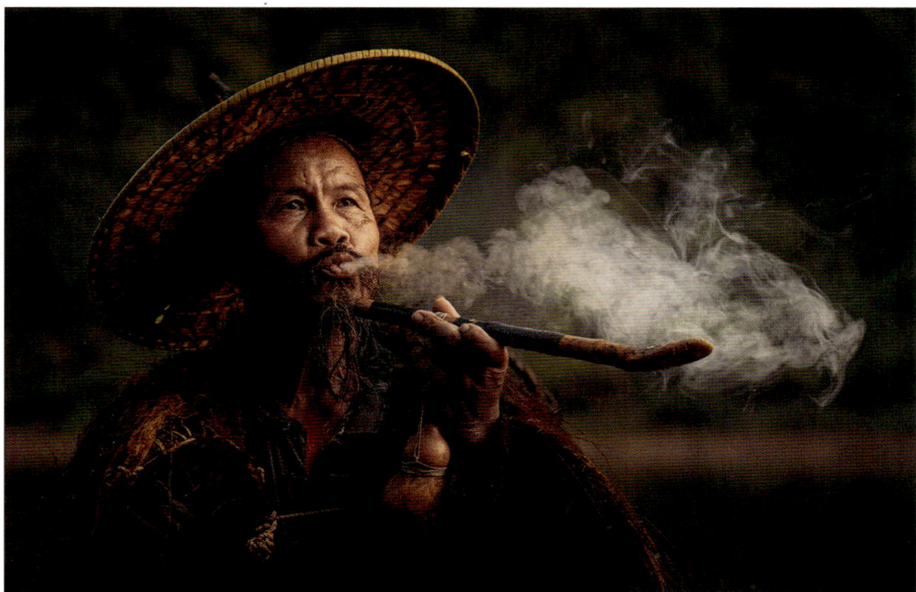

Characteristics of this type of shot: A posed environmental portrait with a simplified scene and an out-of-focus background behind the subject.

Location: Li River, China

GEAR: Taken on a full-frame mirrorless body, hand-held, with a 24–240mm lens.

SETTINGS: Shot at an aperture of f/6.3 with –1.3 Exposure Compensation, ISO 400, and with a shutter speed of 1/200 of a second. It was shot at 140mm.

KEY TECHNIQUE: Remember when I talked about hiring a model (on page 191)? That's what I did here. This gentleman was a fisherman for most of his life, but after the river was fished to the point there were no fish left, he and his family retired and now he models for photographers. We contacted a fixer (see page 6) based in China to arrange for the model to be available for a dawn shoot where we could pose and position him (so the natural early morning light was giving him kind of a dramatic Rembrandt-style lighting), giving all the instructions to our fixer to translate for us. The light is soft and flattering because these shots were taken right after dawn and not in direct sunlight, as the sun hadn't cleared the mountains around us.

POST-PROCESSING: Besides adding Contrast (like always), the biggest thing I did here was to warm up the white balance, dragging Lightroom's Temp slider a bit toward yellow. I also added Texture and a bit of Clarity to give the smoke more detail, but I added the Clarity using the Brush tool, just painting over the smoke itself, because applying it to the entire image would apply the Clarity to the out-of-focus background, which usually looks kind of weird (Clarity looks kind of artificial when applied to blurry backgrounds, so I avoid it). I also darkened the edges all the way around the image to focus more attention on our subject (see page 226).

The Recipe for Getting This Type of Shot

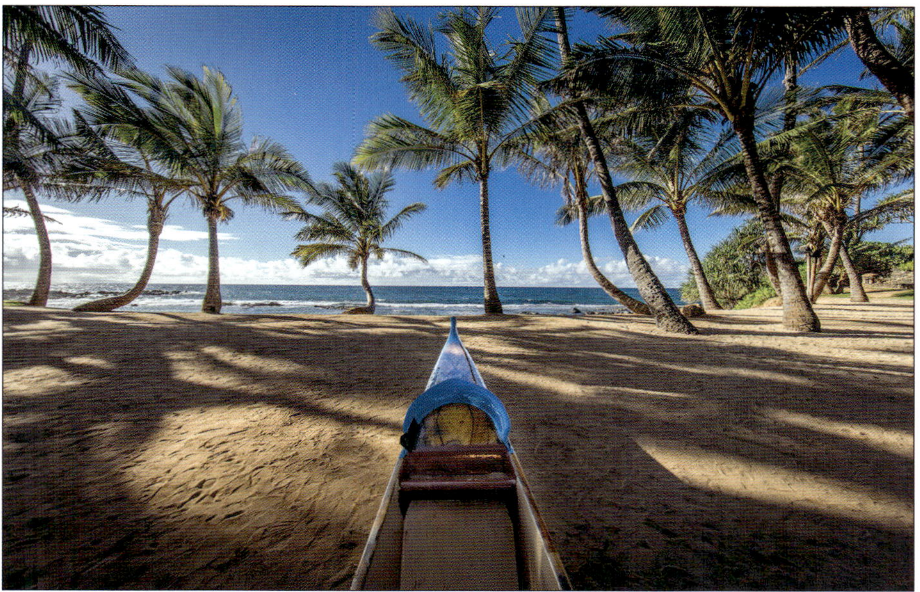

Characteristics of this type of shot: A wide, tropical, vacation-style shot taken on a bright, sunny, blue sky day.

Location: Mama's Fish House, Maui, Hawaii

GEAR: Taken on a full-frame body, hand-held, with an 11–24mm f/4 wide-angle lens (the widest lens I own) at 11mm.

SETTINGS: Shot with the aperture set at f/7.1, the ISO at 100, and a shutter speed of 1/250 of a second. The long, soft shadows let you know this shot was taken later in the day, around an hour or so before sunset.

KEY TECHNIQUE: It's the composition, but essentially two parts of it. The first is the compositional choice of using an ultra-wide-angle lens to capture so much of the scene in front of me, giving it a wide-open feel. The second part is using the front part of this outrigger on the beach as the foreground element, leading the viewer into the scene. Also, despite the many palm trees, it's a very simple, clean scene. It's essentially just the front of the boat, the palms, the beach, and the ocean. Not a bunch of junk on the ground, or creeping in from the sides, or lying on the beach.

POST-PROCESSING: Just adding Contrast (as always), and using Photoshop's Healing Brush tool to remove any distracting scratches and junk inside the outrigger itself. I added some Texture and a little bit of Clarity to make the end of the outrigger look a little shiny. To make the sky bluer, I used the Lightroom technique on page 217. And, I added sharpening to finish off the image.

The Recipe for Getting This Type of Shot

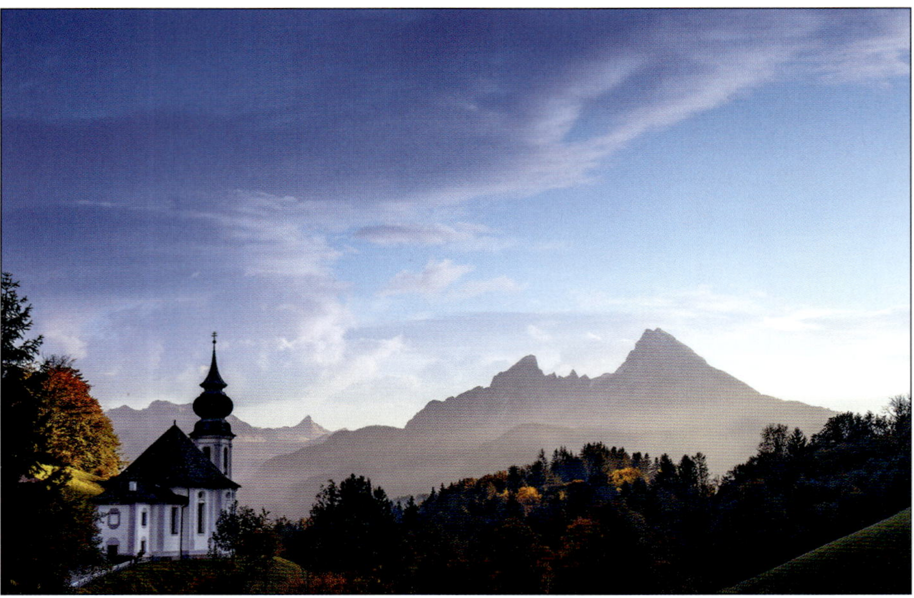

Characteristics of this type of shot: A landscape-style travel shot with soft light and our subject in the shadows and offset from the center.

Location: The pilgrimage church Maria Gern, near Berchtesgaden, Germany

GEAR: Taken on a full-frame body, hand-held, using a 24–105mm lens.

SETTINGS: I zoomed out to 43mm to get a wide view. I didn't want to go out fully wide because it would make the church too small in the frame. Shot in aperture priority mode at f/9, ISO 400, and a shutter speed of 1/1600 of a second.

KEY TECHNIQUE: First, it's a great location—a tiny, picturesque church in a beautiful mountain scene. The key technique is the composition, and by a putting the church over to one side, it still remains the subject of the shot, but it doesn't take over the scene. It's almost a negative space type of composition because your eye is drawn directly to the church, despite its small size in the frame. The church and trees in the foreground work to help lead the viewer into the image, as well.

POST-PROCESSING: There's a lot of haze in this shot, but that haze also helps to give the image depth, so taking it all away won't make the image stronger, just more shallow. So, while I added a little of Lightroom's Dehaze slider (see page 212), I only added a little. I also added Contrast, Texture, and a hint of Clarity, along with some sharpening to finish off the image.

The Recipe for Getting This Type of Shot

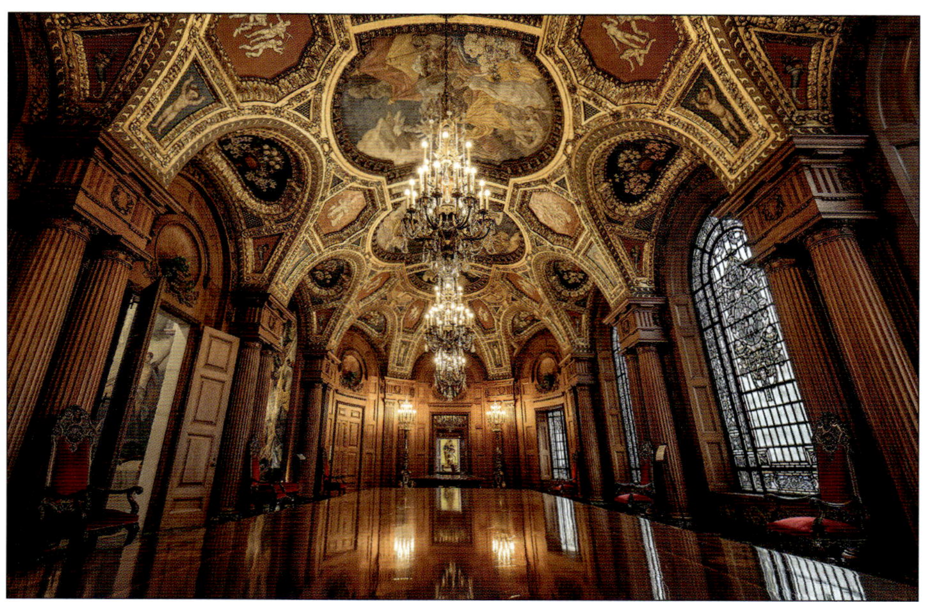

Characteristics of this type of shot: A Gothic-looking interior shot with an epic feel and lots of warm tones.

Location: Elks National Memorial and Headquarters, Chicago, Illinois

GEAR: Taken on a full-frame mirrorless body, with a 16–35mm lens at 16mm, and mounted on a Platypod Ultra.

SETTINGS: Shot at f/11, ISO 100, and a shutter speed of 1.6 seconds, using Exposure Bracketing (see page 117), which takes three shots (combined into one shot in post): one normal exposure, one two stops lighter, and one two stops darker.

KEY TECHNIQUE: The epic feel comes from a recipe I use often in my travel photography, which is to use a super-wide-angle lens, down low, and tilted upward, so it includes the ceiling. It gives the image an epic, larger-than-life type of feel (this is a fairly small room, but it looks much larger thanks to that technique). To get that mirror-like reflection, I put my camera directly on the end of the table, mounted on a Platypod Ultra, tilted up a bit. When you get really close to a floor or table like this, you pick up a ton of reflections. This table doesn't look nearly as reflective when you're standing there (it's a nicely polished wood dining table, but it's not a mirror), but when you get the lens that close to the table, it becomes incredibly reflective.

POST-PROCESSING: Start by combining the three images into a single HDR image (see page 229), which helps capture all the detail of the interior without blowing out the stained glass windows. One thing taking an HDR image like this allows you to do is open up the shadows a ton (using the Shadows slider), without introducing a bunch of noise. I also added Contrast and a lot of Texture, and the nice shine comes from adding Clarity. Of course, like always, I finished it off by adding sharpening.

The Recipe for Getting This Type of Shot

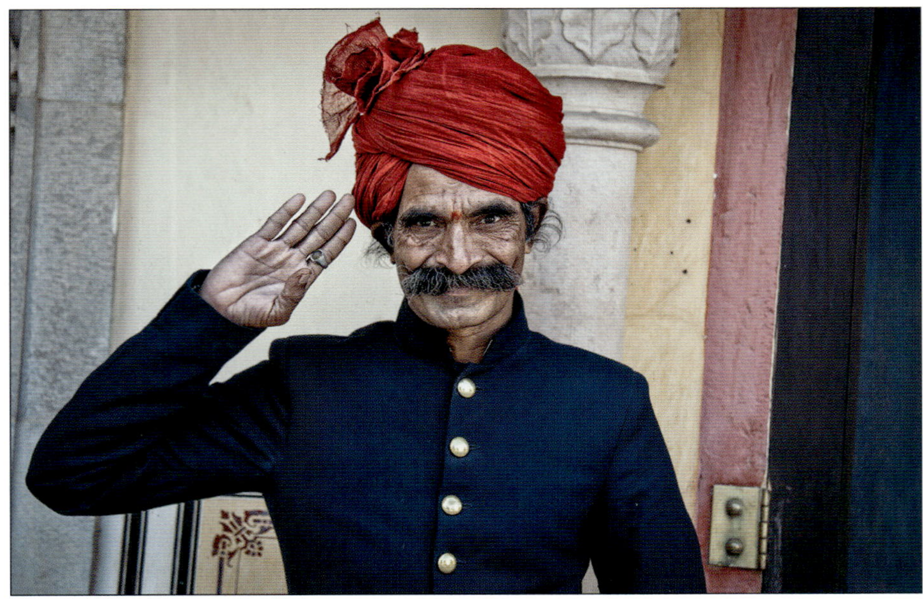

Characteristics of this type of shot: A location portrait with a great pose on a simple background.

Location: Jaipur, India

GEAR: Taken on a full-frame body, hand-held, with a 28–300mm f/3.5-5.6 lens.

SETTINGS: Shot while on a tour of the city, I zoomed in to 100mm and set my aperture to f/5.6 to get the background just a little bit soft behind him. ISO was 200 and shutter speed was 1/160 of a second (the shutter speed was slower like this because he's not in direct sun).

KEY TECHNIQUE: I was on a walking tour, heading inside a building, where this gentleman was dressed in this costume outside in the courtyard and would pose for photographers for a fee. If he saw you had a serious camera, he would call out to you, so I went over and took a few shots. Before I go over and accept an offer like this (it was around $1 to get him to pose here), I look around the immediate area for a contrasting background, so when I engage them, I first ask if it's okay if they move over to that background. They're always happy to oblige, and they're very patient. They're professionals at posing, and they're usually very friendly and chatty.

POST-PROCESSING: I did the standard things in Lightroom—adding Contrast and stuff—but when I see someone whose face has a lot of texture and character, I add more Clarity than usual. It brings out every nook and cranny and it can look really great, plus it accentuates all the detail in the image. Adding a lot of Clarity can make the image look darker, so you usually have to increase the Exposure slider a bit to brighten the image back up. Lots of sharpening added, too (see page 227).

The Recipe for Getting This Type of Shot

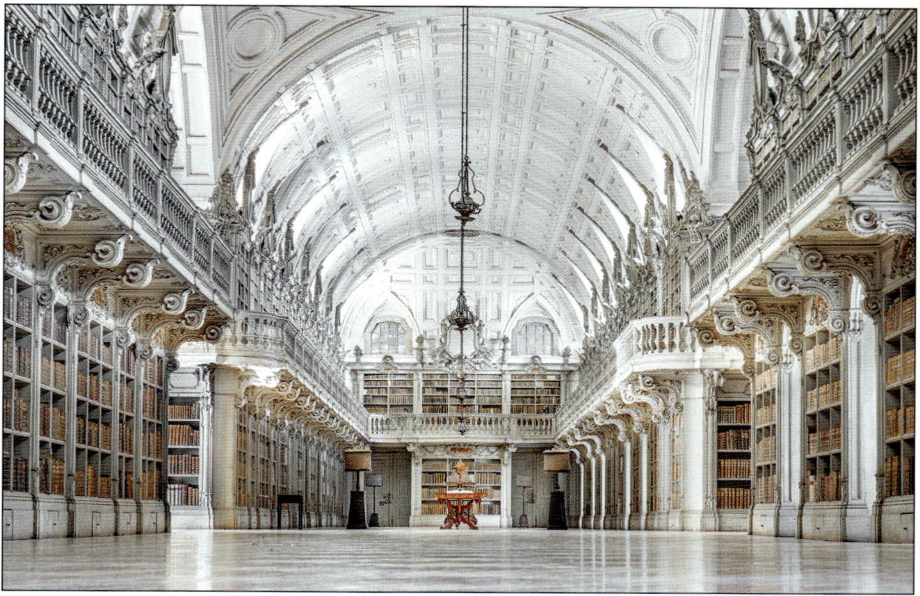

Characteristics of this type of shot: A bright interior shot taken on a public tour.

Location: Mafra National Palace Library, Mafra, Portugal

GEAR: Taken on a full-frame body, with a 70–200mm lens at 70mm, and mounted on a Platypod Ultra.

SETTINGS: Shot at f/4, ISO 400, a shutter speed of 1/8 of a second, and with Exposure Bracketing turned on (see page 117) because of the range of brightness in the room, from the very bright ceiling to parts of the hallway that were in shadows.

KEY TECHNIQUE: The key technique here was making the interior look as big and epic as it was by using that combination of getting down really low and using a super-wide-angle lens (see page 188). This was taken on the public tour and they had a little gallery area at the far end of this hall, but you were not allowed to actually enter the hall (they had ropes and stanchion in place and two security guards). So, when I got a chance, I made my way right up to the ropes and set my camera on the floor with the self-timer turned on.

POST-PROCESSING: First, in Lightroom, I combined the bracketed shots into a single HDR image (see page 229). After that, the challenge here was getting the color right and the light balanced. The Auto white balance setting on my camera made the white library look kind of yellowish, but the parts that were in the shade had a blue tint. So, I dragged the Temp slider toward blue until the interior looked white again, and then I switched to the Brush tool and painted with a yellowish white balance over those blue areas to make them look white. I also used the Brush tool, with the Exposure set to 0.50 to help brighten some of the areas in the shadows. Then, I added a little Contrast, Texture, and sharpening.

The Recipe for Getting This Type of Shot

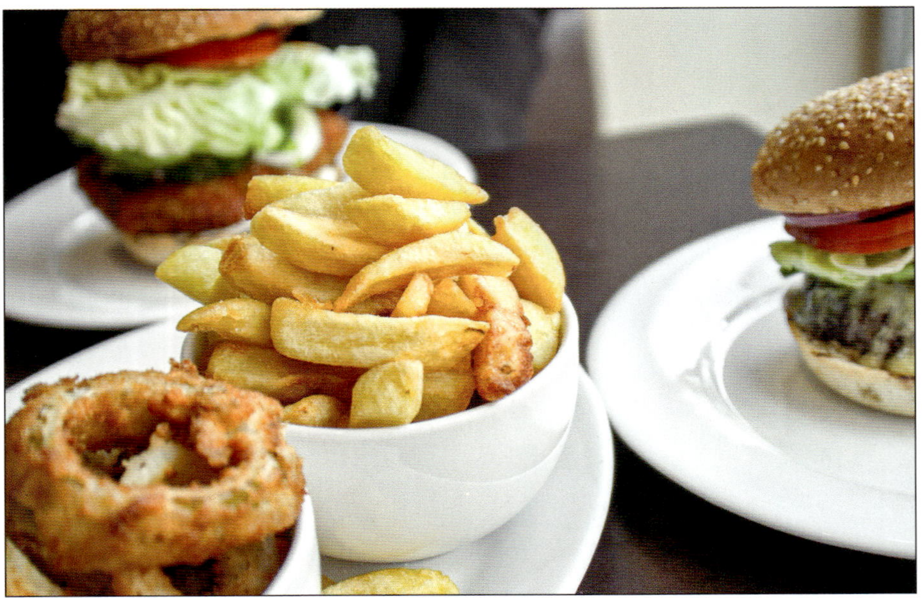

Characteristics of this type of shot: A nice, tight food shot of some super-yummy burgers, fries, and onion rings.

Location: Gourmet Burger Kitchen (GBK), Oxford, England

GEAR: Taken on a full-frame body, hand-held, with a 28–300mm lens.

SETTINGS: This was shot at 28mm. I like to get back farther and zoom in more, but there was a table too close to me to do that. Aperture was f/3.5, with ISO 800, and shutter speed at 1/1000 of a second (I didn't need that fast a shutter speed, so I didn't really need that high an ISO, but I think I was temporarily affected by the size and juiciness of the burgers. That's my out).

KEY TECHNIQUES: There are two things: (1) making sure you ask to either sit outdoors, or in this case, right next to the window, so your lighting is great, and (2) not showing the full plate of food and instead, getting in tight. Use your lowest possible f-stop, stand back a bit from the table, and zoom in really tight, which puts the background out of focus (and part of the foreground, as well). You'll often see food shots like this where you get in really tight, and then tilt the camera to the right or left a bit to make it dynamic (though I didn't do that here, but it's a popular choice).

POST-PROCESSING: Not really much to do to this image, just the standard stuff in Lightroom—adding Contrast and sharpening—but you have to be careful, especially shooting indoors, that your plates don't get a blue tint. Mine had a tinge of blue, so I dragged the Temp slider to the right, toward yellow, until the blue tint went away and the plates looked white again (see page 207).

The Recipe for Getting This Type of Shot

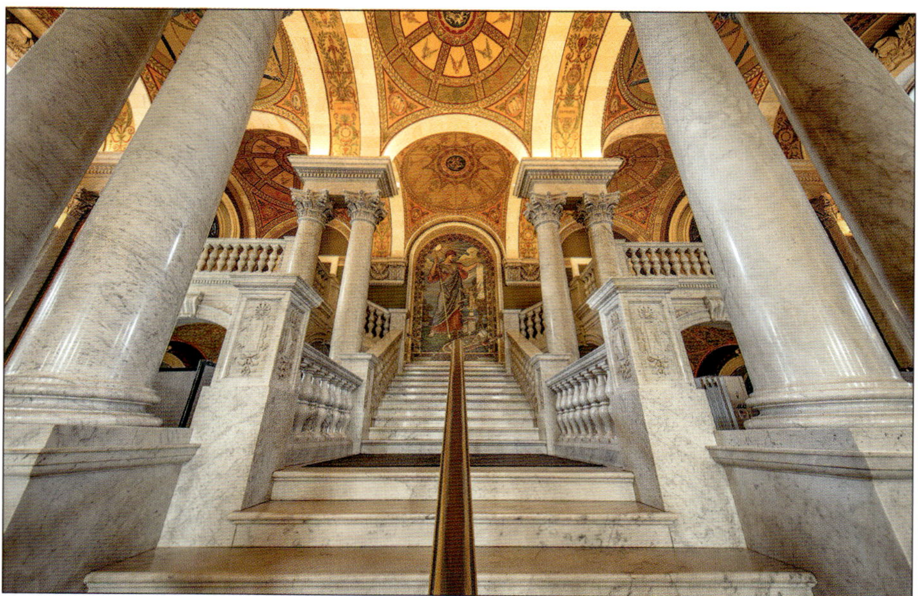

Characteristics of this type of shot: A classic interior shot with a wide floor-to-ceiling view with lots of detail and texture.

Location: The lobby of the Library of Congress, Washington, DC

GEAR: Taken on a full-frame body, with an 11–24mm f/4 lens at 13mm, mounted on a travel tripod, using a cable release to take the shot to minimize any camera shake.

SETTINGS: Shot at an aperture of f/11, ISO 100, and a shutter speed of 1/2 a second, with Exposure Bracketing turned on (though I'm not sure it was really necessary).

KEY TECHNIQUES: Two things: (1) It's the symmetry. We love symmetry in photos (see page 110), and I was careful to line my camera up with the bottom of the railing to make sure it was truly centered (in shots where the symmetry is pretty much the subject, you have to nail being in the center of the image). And, (2) the super-wide-angle lens and lower angle lets you see all the way up to the beautiful detail in the ceiling, so you have the feeling of really being there.

POST-PROCESSING: After combining the bracketed exposures into a single shot in Lightroom (see page 229), I added a lot of Contrast, dragged the Shadows slider almost all the way to the right to open them up (you can do that with HDR images, without seeing a bunch of noise—it's part of the magic of shooting with Exposure Bracketing, and then making an HDR image), then I added a lot of Texture, and added some Clarity to make everything a bit shiny. The white balance isn't exactly accurate or those columns would be gray. Instead, I thought it looked better a little warmer, so I dragged the Temp slider a little bit toward yellow. Just a bit. And, of course, I sharpened the living daylights out of it.

The Recipe for Getting This Type of Shot

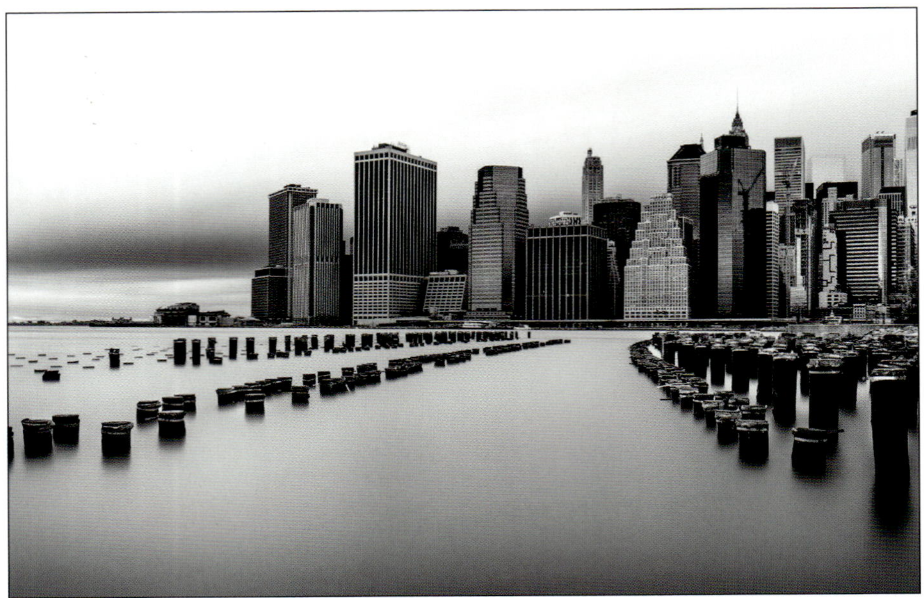

Characteristics of this type of shot: A cityscape with soft, silky water and leading lines drawing you into the photo.

Location: Brooklyn Bridge Park, Pier 1 Palisade, Brooklyn, New York

GEAR: Taken on a full-frame body, with a 16–35mm lens zoomed in to 35mm, and mounted on a Platypod Ultra, sitting on the rocks using the Ultra's spiked legs (out of frame). I added a 10-stop ND filter in front of my lens to darken the scene, so I could get a really long exposure (see page 115).

SETTINGS: I'm trying to keep my exposure long and my depth of field very deep, so I set my aperture at f/16. My ISO was set to 100 and my shutter speed was 151 seconds (2.5 minutes).

KEY TECHNIQUES: The location is a big factor, and I chose it because of the pylons, which I could use as both a foreground object and leading lines, leading the eye into the image. Another key technique is the very long exposure, which took the choppy, uninteresting water you'd normally see and replaced it with that smooth, smoky, silky water you see here, courtesy of the 10-stop ND filter. A last key technique is placing the camera down low on the rocks, right at the water's edge. That low angle really makes a big difference.

POST-PROCESSING: In Lightroom, the first thing I did was to convert the image to black and white using one of the built-in B&W creative profiles (there are 17 to choose from. See page 224). After that, I added even more Contrast than usual and lots of Texture, and of course, Clarity to help make the buildings shiny, and I finished off with lots of sharpening.

The Recipe for Getting This Type of Shot

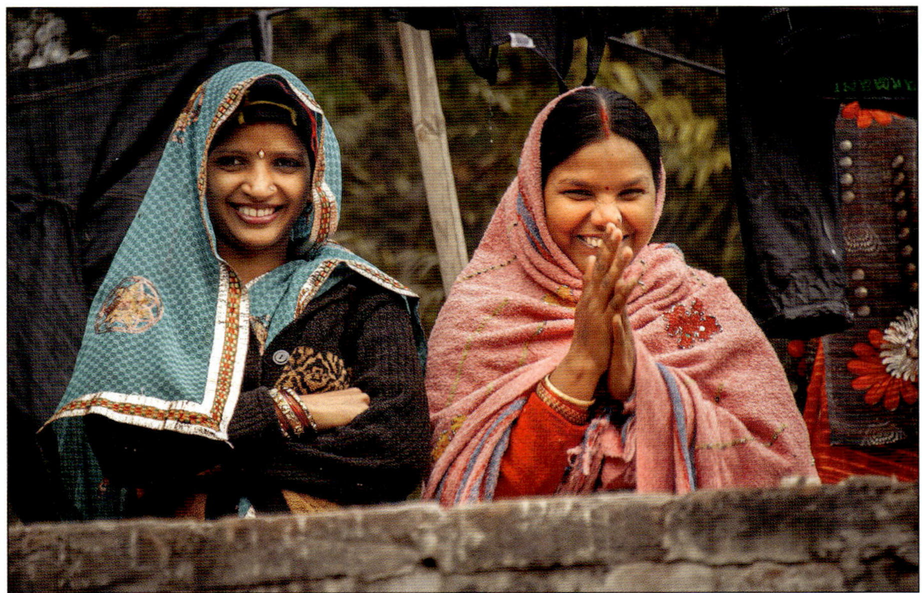

Characteristics of this type of shot: A candid portrait taken while on a walking tour where the environment is key to the shot, so you zoom out wider than normal for a portrait to include it.

Location: Agra, Uttar Pradesh, India

GEAR: Taken on a full-frame body, hand-held, with a 28–300mm lens at 300mm.

SETTINGS: Shot at f/5.6, ISO 200, and a shutter speed of 1/125 of a second.

KEY TECHNIQUE: In addition to the environment, hands-down, it was giving them a friendly smile and tacitly asking (by holding up my camera while smiling), "Is it okay if I take your photo?" They giggled and nodded and I got this shot. I just got this one frame as we were walking by with our small tour. They were on top of a small roof doing the day's laundry, so I couldn't do the sharing part, but I thanked them and they waved and giggled some more, and it was really a cute moment. For more on this (the full smile, shoot, and share technique), see page 76.

POST-PROCESSING: I don't add as much Contrast to portraits as I would to other travel shots because it makes the subject's skin tone look too saturated and unnatural. I added a tiny bit of Texture, but skipped the Clarity (it looks great on older men with craggy skin, but it's not very flattering in portraits of women or children). I also used Lightroom's Brush tool to darken the trees behind them to help them stand out, and I darkened the edges all the way around the image by adding a post-crop vignette (see page 226). Of course, I finished off the shot with some sharpening, but not too much for an image of a softer nature like this.

The Recipe for Getting This Type of Shot

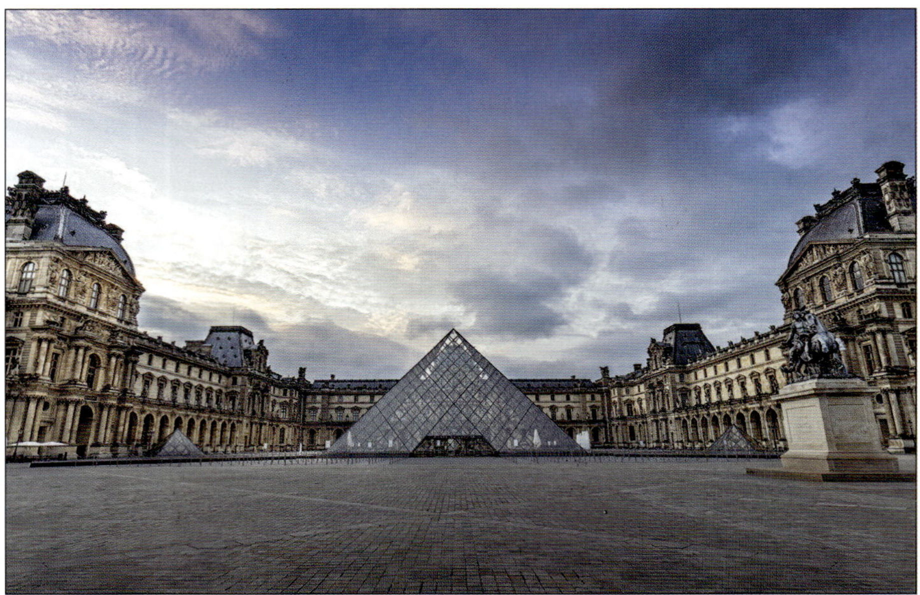

Characteristics of this type of shot: A wide shot of a classic attraction, but taken without the distraction of tourists.

Location: The Louvre Museum, Paris, France

GEAR: Taken on a full-frame mirrorless body, with a 16–35mm lens at 16mm, and mounted on a travel tripod.

SETTINGS: Shot at an aperture of f/11 (my go-to aperture for keeping as much in focus as possible), ISO 100, and shutter speed at 1/125 of a second.

KEY TECHNIQUE: Hands-down, the key technique here is getting a tourist-free shot, and to do that I got up before dawn and got in place ready to shoot. Getting up that early pretty much ensures you'll be there all by yourself. This was taken shortly after sunrise and right before the sun got up so high that the light turned harsh (you can see the sunlight just starting to hit the right side of the Louvre). Compositionally, I set my horizon line low since there was a pretty nice sky and I wanted to show more of it (see page 98). I used a super-wide-angle lens at 16mm to capture almost the full side-to-side view of the Louvre from this angle. I could have walked back farther to get the towers on either end fully in the shot, but it would add some grass to my foreground, so I decided to stick with the clean look of the cobblestones.

POST-PROCESSING: The sky didn't look as deep and rich in the original image, so I did a trick in Lightroom I use often, which is to use the Exposure slider to darken the entire image until the sky looks really nice, and then I drag the Shadows slider nearly all the way to the right to open up the shadows on the building. Works like a charm. Then, I added lots of Contrast, Texture, and Clarity and finished up with, of course, lots of sharpening.

The Recipe for Getting This Type of Shot

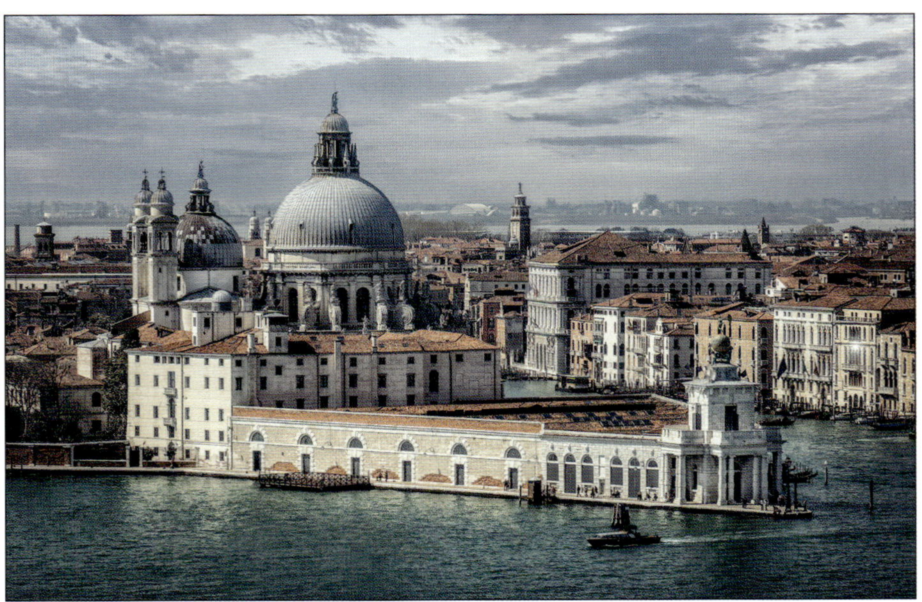

Characteristics of this type of shot: A cityscape shot, but framed with a single building as the focus of the shot.

Location: The top of San Giorgio Maggiore campanile (bell tower), Venice, Italy

GEAR: Taken on a full-frame body, hand-held, with a 70–200mm f/2.8 lens at 150mm.

SETTINGS: Shot at f/2.8, ISO 100, and shutter speed at 1/3200 of a second.

KEY TECHNIQUES: There are two: (1) The high vantage point here is what really makes the shot. This is shot from the top of a bell tower on a tiny island just across from Venice's Piazza San Marco. It's much less crowded (with hardly any line at all, versus the main bell tower at San Marco), and I love the view from here. That high angle gives you a less-common view of the Punta della Dogana museum (in front), with the beautiful soaring dome of the Basilica di Santa Maria della Salute right behind it, making it look like it's all one building. The other technique (2) is using a long zoom lens, which gives a compression to the scene that makes everything look closer together. You don't get that compression with wide-angle lenses, so while it looks like a wide-angle shot, it's actually taken at 150mm.

POST-PROCESSING: The standard Lightroom stuff, but I used the technique to darken the sky I explained on the previous page. Besides adding a lot of Contrast, and a lot of Texture and Clarity, I jumped over to Photoshop to use the Healing Brush tool to remove a bunch of pylons in the foreground of the shot in the water right in front of the building. It was a little messy, and removing them simplified the shot and made it stronger. Then, of course, I sharpened the heck out of it.

Index

J

JPEG images
    memory cards for, 63
    shooting RAW vs., 55, 205

K

kids, photos of, 146

L

landscape photos, 38, 240
leading lines, 101, 235, 246
Lens Corrections panel, 225
lenses
    choosing for travel, 50–51
    cleaning cloth for, 73
    fixing problems caused by, 225
    wide-angle, 95, 119, 130, 188
    zooming in with, 90
level shooting, 99
light
    beautiful, 24, 41
    blue hour, 155
    dramatic, 31, 79
    low, 91, 139, 195
    window, 81
Light, Gesture, and Color (Maisel), 163
Lightroom Classic
    Auto corrections, 206
    Blacks slider, 208, 211
    Brush tool, 211, 212, 216, 221, 222
    Clarity slider, 204, 212, 213
    Contrast slider, 212, 218
    creative profiles, 223–224
    Dehaze slider, 212
    Detail panel, 227
    Exposure slider, 208, 215, 218, 221
    group sharing, 175
    Highlights slider, 210, 218
    HSL/Color panel, 217
    Lens Corrections panel, 225
    Linear Gradient mask, 215–216
    Map feature, 193
    multi-photo layouts, 152
    photo book feature, 172
    Photo Merge options, 228–229
    Post-Crop Vignetting effect, 226
    RAW profiles, 205
    resetting sliders in, 222
    Select Sky mask, 218, 219
    Shadows slider, 209

Slideshow feature, 179
    Temp slider, 207, 215
    Texture slider, 204, 213
    Vibrance slider, 220
    white balance presets, 207
    Whites slider, 208, 218
    See also post-processing
Linear Gradient mask, 215–216
Locardi, Elia, 156
location scouting, 10
long exposures, 115, 187, 235
long lenses, 78, 249
"looks" added to images, 223
low perspective, 95, 183, 188, 246
low-light situations
    indoor portraits in, 91
    phone camera used in, 139
    trick for shooting in, 195
Luminar plug-in, 214

M

macro photos, 143
magazine assignments, 125
magnifying glass button, 49
Maisel, Jay, 108, 163
manual shooting mode, 116, 120
Map feature, 193
markets, photos of, 159
Matisse, Henri, 29
McNally, Joe, 33, 79
memory cards, 59, 63
menus, photos of, 159
messy scenes, 162
Milky Way photos, 119
models, hiring, 191, 238
motion, showing, 35, 123, 236
movie research, 17
MPIX.com photo lab, 171
multi-photo layouts, 152

N

ND Filter Timer app, 115
NDTimer app, 115
negative space, 107, 240
neutral density (ND) filters, 71, 115, 187
nighttime photos, 120

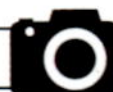

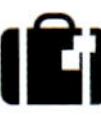
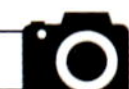

ON1 Professional Plugin Bundle

For Photoshop and Lightroom.

Save 30%

with promo code: **KELBY30**

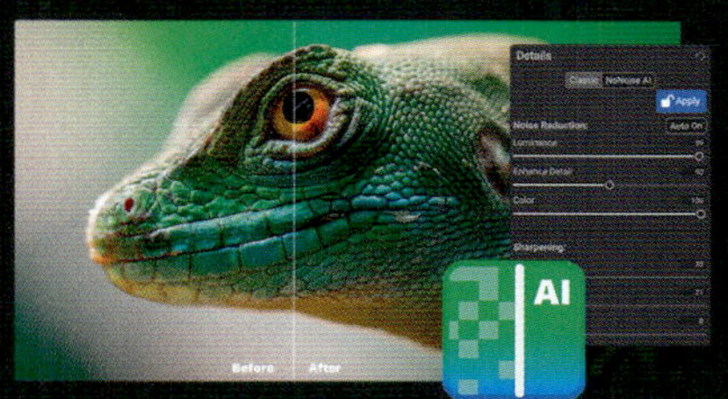

ON1 NoNoise AI

The New Standard in Noise
Reduction Software

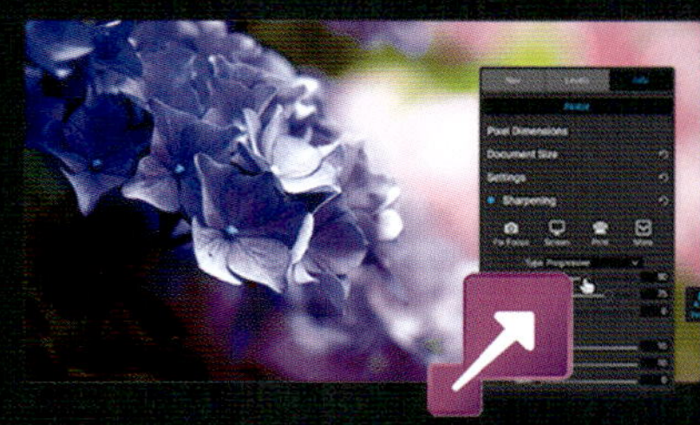

ON1 Resize

The Industry Standard in
Image Enlargements

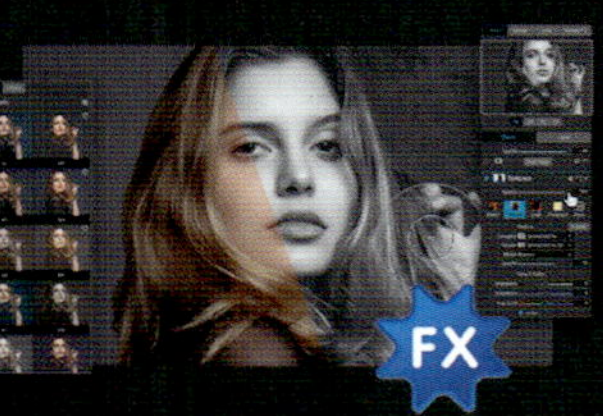

ON1 Effects

Your Photos, Your Style

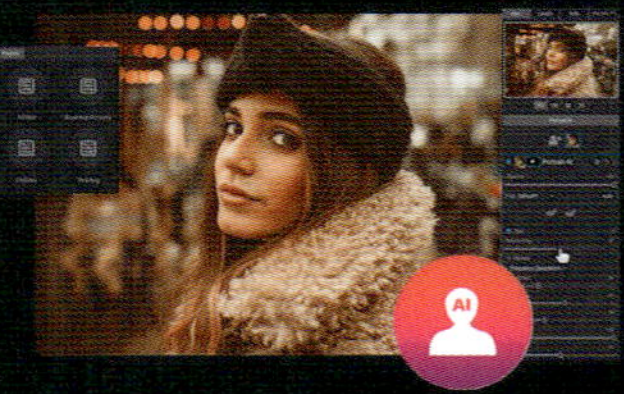

ON1 Portrait AI

Simply Better Portrait Editing

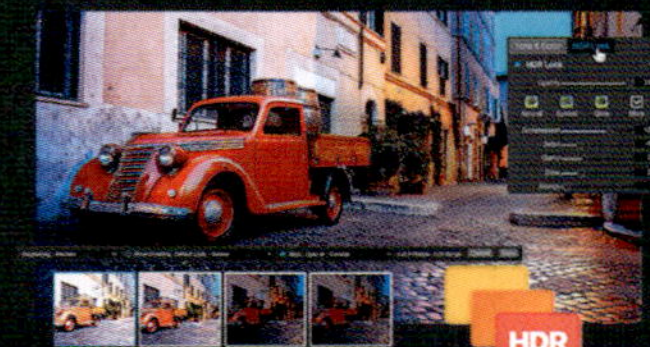

ON1 HDR

Flawless HDR Photos

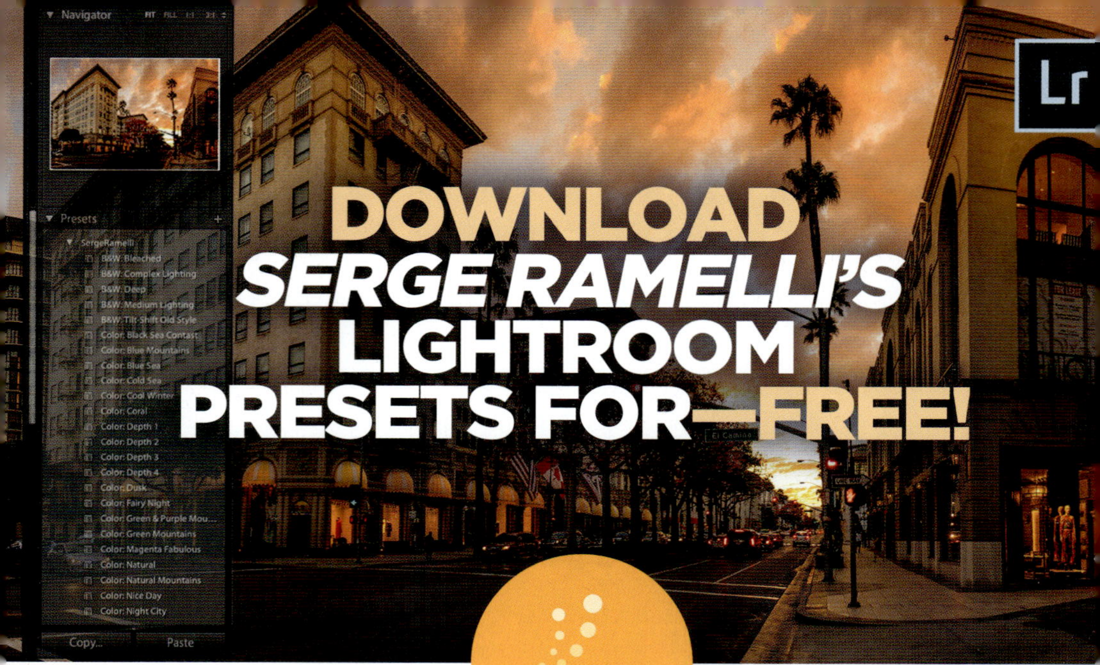

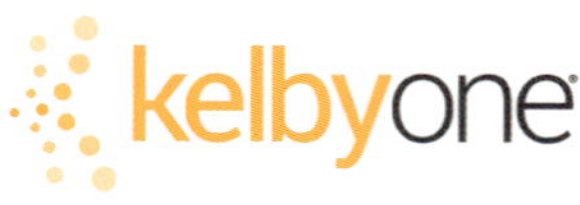

DOWNLOAD SERGE RAMELLI'S LIGHTROOM PRESETS FOR—FREE!

Take Your Travel Images to the Next Level—With Easy Post Processing

At KelbyOne our goal is to provide you with the knowledge and tools to create the type of images you've always dreamed of. This is why we like to occasionally provide free presets, brushes, eBooks and more. Transform your travel photos in Lightroom with 70 powerful presets created by travel and landscape photographer Serge Ramelli. Serge has provided everything—from B&W to Pastels and Warm Skies to Gloomy Nights— to easily boost your images from good to amazing.

visit **kel.by/lspresets** to redeem.

kelbyone